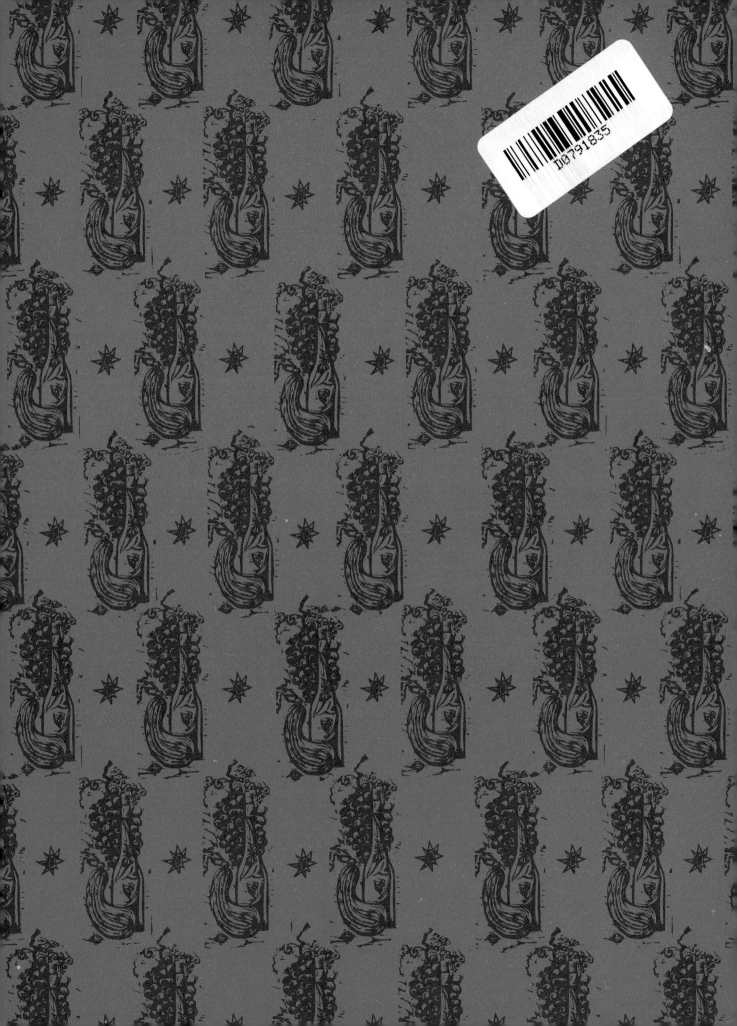

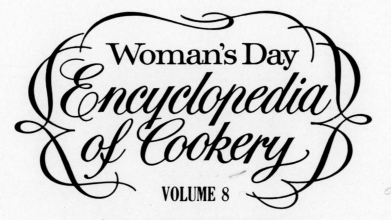

Woman's Day
Encyclopedia of Cookery

VOLUME 8

in 12 volumes—over 2,000 pages—
with more than 1,500 illustrations in color,
1,000 entries and 8,500 recipes
1,200 menus, 50 specialty cook books
and a host of delightful features by distinguished food writers.

Prepared and edited by the Editors of Woman's Day
Editor: EILEEN TIGHE
Managing Editor: EVELYN GRANT   *Food Editor:* GLENNA MCGINNIS
Art Consultant: HAROLD SITTERLE   *Photographic Editor:* BEN CALVO
Associates: OLIVIA RISBERG, CHARLOTTE SCRIPTURE,
CAROLYN STORM, JOHANNA BAFARO

SPECIAL PROJECT STAFF
Editor: NIKA STANDEN HAZELTON   *Art Director:* LEONARD A. ROMAGNA
Associates: L. GERALDINE MARSTELLER, HELEN FEINGOLD,
SUSAN J. KNOX, INEZ M. KRECH

FAWCETT PUBLICATIONS, INC.   NEW YORK

Printed in U.S.A. by
FAWCETT-HAYNES PRINTING CORPORATION
Rockville, Maryland

Table of Contents

VOLUME 8

MOISTEN TO PECAN

Definitions and 745 Recipes
How to buy, store, prepare, cook, and serve •
Nutritive Food Values • Caloric Values

To help you plan more varied meals
with the recipes in this volume

Foreword

To the best of our knowledge, no work of this magnitude ever has been undertaken by any author, editor, or publisher in America. The editors of Woman's Day, with a special staff of experts, present to you this Encyclopedia of Cookery, a comprehensive and colorful library on all culinary matters. The twelve-volume encyclopedia contains in its 2,000 pages over 8,500 recipes from all over the world, 1,500 food illustrations in color, 1,200 menus, 50 special cook books and over 1,000 food definitions. In addition, there are full details about all foods, their nutritive and caloric values, how to buy, serve, prepare, and cook them. There is a history of food and cooking, articles on nutrition, diet, entertaining, menu planning, herbs and spices. Every topic of culinary interest is covered. Five years of intensive work have gone into its preparation, backed by twenty-five years of food and cookery experience in the publication of Woman's Day.

We think you will find this Encyclopedia of Cookery the most complete and authoritative work ever published on the subject. It is a library for everyone who cares about good food and the fine art of preparing it.

The Editors

VOLUME 8

MOISTEN, MOIST—In culinary usage moisten means to add a small amount of liquid to an ingredient or combination of ingredients, as when milk is added to flour and other dry ingredients in the making of biscuits, cakes, etc. Only enough liquid is added to make the ingredients slightly wet, or moist. The term is really used to describe the absence of dryness, rather than wetness.

MOLASSES—The thick brown syrup that is separated from raw sugar during the various stages of refinement.

The sugar cane is cut close to the ground because the lowest ends are the richest in sugar. The stalks are torn into small pieces and passed through three sets of rollers which extract a dark-grayish, sweet juice. The juice is boiled down to a thick syrupy mass which includes crystals of sugar. This heavy syrup is then put into containers with holes through which the liquid drips, leaving the crystallized raw sugar behind. The liquid is molasses.

The best grade of molasses is obtained by crude milling processes, as the syrup contains more sugar at this point. If the syrup is boiled more than once, the first boiling produces a darker, thicker, less-sweet product which is used in cakes and candies. Blackstrap molasses, a cattle food and industrial product as well as a popular health food, is the result of a third boiling.

The word "molasses" comes from the Portuguese *melaco* derived from the Latin root *mel,* which means "honey," and *aceus,* which means "resembling."

To Americans the word "molasses" means both the syrup that is separated from the raw sugar in the first stages of production and the syrup that is taken from the raw sugar while it is being refined. The English call this second product "treacle."

Sorghum molasses is the syrup from the stalk of a group of grains which look much like corn. This syrup is a pure product from which no sugar is extracted. It has the consistency, color, and taste of molasses.

Molasses syrup was probably first eaten by the Chinese and the Indians. Its American history began when Columbus introduced it to the West Indies. It soon became an important crop and was called the life blood of Colonial trade. It was the prime sweetener in America until after the Civil War although homegrown maple sugar and syrup, honey, and sorghum were used regionally.

Molasses was considered so necessary a part of life that the founders of the colony of Georgia promised: "To each person sent upon the charity for his maintenance in the Colony for one year he will have . . . 44 Gallons of Strong Beer, 64 Quarts of Molasses for brewing of beer." The "Mothers, Wives, Sisters, or Children of such Men" got no beer, but did receive the same 64 quarts of molasses.

Molasses was used to make doughnuts in New England; it formed the base under the crumb topping of the Pennsylvania Dutch shoofly pie; it was eagerly eaten by Maine children for Sunday night supper poured over buttered bread; it sweetened "mustgodown," an old Maine concoction of crusts of rye and Indian corn bread soaked with molasses and topped with cream. Baked beans, corn breads, and puddings of all sorts, countless cookies and cakes were all made with molasses. It was poured over pancakes, biscuits, and hot breads. Only molasses gives the old-time flavor to countless dishes cooked by our forefathers.

Molasses was more than a food; it was used also for its medicinal properties. In earlier days it was a spring tonic; a mixture of sulphur and molasses was a must for every household, to purify the blood and revive the system after a winter's starchy diet.

Availability and Purchasing Guide—Available bottled, light and dark. Light molasses has a more delicate flavor than the dark and is often used as a table syrup. It can also be used for general cooking purposes. Dark molasses has a tangy flavor and is particularly good for making foods in which many spices are

1 — Taffy Sundae Sauce
2 — Molasses-Peach Meringues
3 — Barbecued Lima Beans
4 — Molasses Barbecued Spareribs
5 — Molasses Layer Cake
6 — Molasses Cookies
7 — Molasses Spiced Fruit

present, i.e.: Indian pudding and ginger-bread. Blackstrap molasses is available in health-food stores.

Storage
☐ Kitchen shelf, unopened: 1 year
☐ Refrigerator shelf, opened: 1 to 2 months

Nutritive Food Values—A fair source of iron and calcium.
☐ Light, 3½ ounces = 252 calories
☐ Dark, 3½ ounces = 232 calories
☐ Blackstrap, 3½ ounces = 213 calories

MOLASSES BARBECUED SPARERIBS

Allow 1 pound spareribs per serving. Cut into serving pieces. Sprinkle lightly with salt and put in shallow baking pan. Bake in preheated moderate oven (350°F.) for 1¼ hours, or until very tender. Pour off all the fat. Brush generously with Molasses Barbecue Sauce, and bake for about 30 minutes longer, basting and turning several times.

Molasses Barbecue Sauce
1 cup molasses
1 cup prepared mustard
1 cup cider vinegar

Mix molasses and mustard well. Stir in vinegar. Makes 3 cups.

QUICK BARBECUED BAKED BEANS
2 tablespoons molasses
2 tablespoons prepared mustard
Juice of ½ lemon
1 teaspoon Worcestershire
4 cups (two 1-pound cans) baked beans
1 pound frankfurters (optional)

Combine molasses, mustard, lemon juice, and Worcestershire; heat. Add beans and simmer for about 10 minutes. Or put in casserole, top with frankfurters, and bake in preheated moderate oven (350°F.) for about 30 minutes. Makes 4 to 6 servings.

BARBECUED LIMA BEANS

Mix ¼ cup molasses, 1 tablespoon prepared mustard, 1 tablespoon vinegar, ½ cup ketchup, dash each of Worcestershire and hot pepper sauce. Heat in skillet. Add 2 packages frozen Fordhook Lima beans, cooked, and simmer for a few minutes. Makes 6 servings.

MOLASSES-OAT WAFFLES
3 cups milk
¾ cup molasses
3 cups quick-cooking rolled oats
3 eggs
½ cup cooking oil
¾ cup unsifted all-purpose flour
3½ teaspoons baking powder
¾ teaspoon baking soda
1 teaspoon salt
Molasses-Honey-Butter Sauce

Heat milk and molasses; pour over oats. Let cool. Add beaten eggs, oil, and sifted dry ingredients. Bake in hot waffle iron. Serve with Molasses-Honey-Butter Sauce. Makes about 7 medium waffles.

Molasses-Honey-Butter Sauce
Combine ½ cup molasses with 1 cup each of honey and corn syrup, ¼ cup butter or margarine, and a pinch of salt; heat.

MOLASSES GINGERBREAD
½ cup soft butter or margarine
¾ cup sugar
1 egg
1 cup molasses
2½ cups sifted all-purpose flour
1½ teaspoons baking soda
½ teaspoon salt
1 teaspoon ground cinnamon
½ teaspoon each of ground cloves and ginger
1 cup hot water

Cream butter and sugar until light. Beat in egg and molasses. Add sifted dry ingredients and beat until smooth. Blend in hot water. Pour into greased pan (13 x 9 x 2 inches), and bake in preheated moderate oven (325°F.) for about 35 minutes. Serve warm with butter, if desired.

MOLASSES SPICED FRUIT
1¾ cups (one 1-pound can) cling peach halves
1¾ cups (one 1-pound can) pear halves
1¾ cups (one 1-pound can) whole apricots
1¾ cups (one 1-pound can) sliced pineapple
2 teaspoons whole cloves
1 cinnamon stick
½ cup molasses
⅓ cup vinegar

Drain syrup from fruits. To syrup, add 1 teaspoon cloves and the cinnamon. Stud fruit with remaining cloves. Bring syrup to boil and boil until reduced to 2 cups. Stir in molasses and vinegar. Heat. Add fruit and heat gently. Serve hot or cold with meat or poultry. Keeps well if stored in the refrigerator. Makes 10 to 12 servings.

TOP-STOVE INDIAN PUDDING
2 cups milk
2 tablespoons yellow cornmeal
¼ cup molasses
2 tablespoons sugar
¾ teaspoon ground ginger
¼ teaspoon salt
2 eggs

Scald milk in top part of double boiler. Add cornmeal slowly, stirring constantly. Cook for 20 minutes, stirring occasionally. Add molasses, sugar, ginger, and salt. Pour over slightly beaten eggs; return to double boiler and cook for 2 or 3 minutes longer. Serve warm with cream or vanilla ice cream if desired. Makes 4 servings.

MOLASSES FIG PUDDING
⅓ cup cornmeal
1 cup undiluted evaporated milk
1 cup water
½ teaspoon salt
2 tablespoons butter or margarine
¾ cup molasses
½ teaspoon ground ginger
¼ teaspoon ground cinnamon
¾ cup chopped figs

1 egg, beaten until foamy

Cook cornmeal, milk, water, and salt in top part of double boiler for 1 hour. Stir occasionally to prevent lumping. Add remaining ingredients. Pour into a buttered baking dish. Bake in preheated moderate oven (350°F.) for 20 minutes. Serve hot with cream. Makes 4 servings.

MOLASSES-PEACH MERINGUES
7 to 12 peach halves (one 1-pound, 13-ounce can), drained
⅓ cup molasses
1 tablespoon butter
½ cup heavy cream
2 egg whites
¼ cup sugar

Put peach halves in shallow baking dish. Cover with molasses and dot with butter. Bake in preheated hot oven (425°F.) for 10 minutes. Pour cream around peaches. Beat egg whites until stiff but not dry. Gradually add sugar and beat until very stiff. Pile some meringue on top of each peach half and brown in hot oven (400°F.) for about 5 minutes. Serve warm. Makes 7 to 8 servings.

MOLASSES CHIFFON PIE
9-inch pie shell, baked
1 envelope unflavored gelatin
½ cup sugar
⅛ teaspoon salt
3 eggs, separated
1 cup milk
⅓ cup molasses
1 tablespoon dark rum or 1½ teaspoons rum flavoring
1 cup heavy cream, whipped
Slivered nuts

Chill pie shell. In top part of double boiler mix gelatin, 2 tablespoons sugar, and the salt. Beat together egg yolks and milk; add to gelatin mixture with molasses. Cook over boiling water, stirring, until mixture is slightly thickened. Remove from heat and stir in rum. Chill until mixture begins to set. Beat egg whites until stiff but not dry. Gradually add 6 tablespoons sugar and beat until very stiff. Fold in gelatin mixture; then fold in whipped cream. Pile lightly in pie shell. Chill. Decorate with slivered nuts. Makes 6 servings.

MOLASSES LAYER CAKE
¾ cup shortening
⅔ cup sugar
3 eggs
¾ cup molasses
2¾ cups sifted all-purpose flour
1 teaspoon baking soda
1 teaspoon ground cinnamon
¾ teaspoon salt
1 cup milk
Fluffy Molasses Frosting

Cream shortening well; add sugar gradually, beating until light and fluffy. Add eggs, one at a time, beating thoroughly after each addition. Add molasses and mix well. Sift in dry ingredients alternately with milk, beating until smooth. Pour into 2 round 9-inch layer-cake pans lined on bottom with wax paper. Bake in preheated moderate oven (350°F.) for 35 to 40 minutes. Cool. Spread Fluffy Molasses Frosting between layers and on top and sides of cake.

Fluffy Molasses Frosting

2 egg whites
¼ cup water
1 cup sugar
2 tablespoons molasses
⅛ teaspoon salt
½ teaspoon vanilla extract

Combine egg whites, water, sugar, molasses, and salt in top part of double boiler. Beat over boiling water with rotary or electric beater until frosting stands in peaks, 5 to 7 minutes. Remove from heat, add vanilla, and beat to cool slightly.

MOLASSES COOKIES

½ cup shortening
1 cup sugar
½ cup water
1 cup molasses
3½ cups unsifted all-purpose flour
½ teaspoon salt
1 teaspoon baking soda
1½ teaspoons ground ginger
½ teaspoon ground cloves
¼ teaspoon ground allspice
Seeded raisins and sugar

Cream shortening and sugar until light and fluffy. Combine water and molasses. Sift flour with remaining ingredients except last 2. Add alternately to first mixture with water and molasses, blending well after each addition. Chill overnight. Roll out a small amount of dough at a time to ⅛- to ¼-inch thickness. Cut with 3-inch cookie cutter. Put on greased cookie sheets. Top each cookie with a raisin and sprinkle with sugar. Bake in preheated moderate oven (350°F.) for 10 to 12 minutes. Makes about 3 dozen.

TAFFY SUNDAE SAUCE

¾ cup butter or margarine
¾ cup sugar
¾ cup molasses
¾ cup diluted evaporated milk
1½ teaspoons vanilla extract
1 cup pecans

Melt butter; add sugar and molasses. Bring to rolling boil; reduce heat and boil for 2 minutes, stirring constantly. Remove from heat and cool slightly. Stir in remaining ingredients. Serve hot over waffles, or hot or cold over ice cream. Makes about 2½ cups.

HOT MOLASSES CIDER

6 whole cloves
2 lemon slices
4 cups apple cider or apple juice
¼ cup molasses
1 cinnamon stick
Juice of 1 lemon

Insert cloves in lemon slices. Add cider, molasses, and cinnamon. Bring to boil and simmer for 10 minutes. Add lemon juice. Makes 4 to 6 servings.

MOLD, MOULD—A utensil in which a jelly, pudding, or other preparation is shaped. The dish made in such a utensil is also referred to as a mold. Examples are gelatin desserts and salads, frozen puddings and ice creams, and pâtés. As a verb, "to mold" means to shape a substance into a certain form. For example, cookies may be shaped in cookie molds or with the hands, butter is shaped in a wooden butter press.

Mold is also the common name for several varieties of minute, threadlike fungi which reproduce themselves by spores (seed dust). They grow on almost anything that is moist or damp and secluded from direct light rays, but they flourish best on foods such as bread, cheese, and fruits which, because they are soft, permit the threads to strike down into them. Dampness, warmth, and seclusion being the principal incentives to their growth, the best preventives are dryness, low temperature, and good air circulation. Molds especially favor acid foods, hence their preference for many fruits and the fact that even pickles put in strong vinegar will mold if exposed to the air. Relatively dry foods such as flour and crackers kept in a dry temperature stay free from molds but any moisture in the air will make them more vulnerable. Special varieties of mold are used in the ripening of a number of famous cheeses such as Roquefort, Blue, and Stilton to which they give their typical character. Molds are not otherwise employed in food manufacture.

There is also a kind of green mold (*Penicillium notatum*) from which a strongly antibacterial, relatively nontoxic acid substance known as penicillin is extracted.

MOLLUSK—One of a large phylum, *Mollusca*, containing most of the animals popularly called shellfish, except the crustaceans. Edible mollusks include snails, mussels, clams, oysters, and cuttlefish (squid). All of these shellfish have a soft unsegmented body protected by a calcareous shell.

MONOSODIUM GLUTAMATE—A natural product derived from glutamic acid, one of the twenty-two amino acids which are the building blocks of all protein. It is also known as MSG. It is used as an intensifier of the natural flavors of foods that are not fruits or sweet foods.

It comes to us from the Orient where it was originally produced from seaweed and where it is an integral part of Chinese and Japanese cookery. MSG is now prepared from cereal gluten, especially wheat gluten, and from desugared beet-sugar molasses. Japan is the largest producer. The United States also produces some. It is possible to obtain a product that is over ninety-nine and nine-tenths per cent pure. MSG is used in food processing, in institutions, and in the home.

The mode of action of MSG is still disputed; some consider it a flavoring agent, others, a flavor intensifier. It is used commercially in canned and dried soups, fowl and fish products, and some meat and vegetable products.

In the home it is used in stews, meat, poultry, soup, and vegetables such as spinach and Lima beans. It is sold plain or seasoned in various ways.

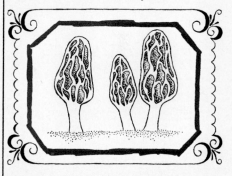

MOREL by *Lucy Kavaler*—An aged peasant woman walking in the woods happened to meet the devil. The sight of her good, wise, wrinkled, and pitted face roused him to such a pitch of fury that he seized her, tore her into little pieces, and scattered them on the ground. The final triumph was hers, however, because wherever a piece fell, a morel sprang up. This old folk legend is one of the first attempts to explain the contradiction between the incomparable flavor and pitted appearance of the morel.

Although the morel is unquestionably a mushroom, it does not belong to the same, *Basidiomycetes,* class of fungi. Instead, it is a member of the somewhat more primitive *Ascomycetes,* along with another fungus prized by gourmets, the truffle. Morel fanciers welcome the differentiation as proof of what they know instinctively: the morel is like no other mushroom in the world.

When gourmets trade reminiscences about the best foods they have eaten, conversation almost invariably turns to the morel. And yet most Americans have never savored the tiniest morsel. A luxury restaurant in New York City recently invited a group of private-school seniors to a meal designed to teach them how to order the perfect dinner. Morels were on that ideal menu, but in a *croustade.* Although these mushrooms are at their best simply sautéed in butter, restaurants seek ways of stretching their scant and costly supplies. One chef confesses with mingled pride and horror that he has paid as much as ten dollars a pound for morels. The problem is that of inducing a hunter to part with any, and no one has succeeded in growing morels commercially.

Some years ago a law had to be passed in Germany forbidding inhabitants of rural areas from burning the woods around their villages. The regulation proved hard to enforce, because the citizens had discovered that morels grow particularly well in devastated wooded areas.

Considering all this, it would be only natural to assume that the morel is extremely rare. Natural, perhaps, but incorrect. Morels, members of the genus *Morchella,* are common to the entire United States and much of Europe as well. They may be growing in your backyard, in the city park, vacant lots, on hillsides, and, most often, on the outskirts of woods (even those that have not been burned out). The morel is easy to distinguish because of its spongy cap, ridged with irregular pits. The shape is quite like a miniature Christmas tree, standing on a stem that is no more than one-third of the total height. For all its renown, it is a little mushroom, a mere two to six inches high, although an occasional "giant," a few inches taller, is found. The color ranges from a gentle pleasing tan to a rich brown. The entire mushroom, cap as well as stem, is hollow and rather brittle. The season, however, is so short, a fleeting fortnight in any given location, that it is as easy to miss morels as to see them. And finding them one year does not guarantee future success, because morels seldom appear in the same place two years running.

During the brief season, occurring in February in the south and May in the north, the hidden mycelium insures the survival of the species by producing two or three good-size crops of spore-bearing morels, one after the other. Some hunters go on a morel binge and attempt to satisfy a year's hunger, while others prepare for the famine ahead by drying the surplus. When reconstituted later, the original flavor returns.

Further evidence of the eminence of the morel can be found in so unlikely a place as the post office. Plants have been depicted on thousands of stamps for many years, but it was not until 1958 that mushrooms made their initial postal appearance. In the first mushroom series issued by Rumania, the one-leu (eight-cent) stamp bears the magnificent picture of a morel.

MORNAY—The name of a white or béchamel sauce to which cheese, an essential ingredient, has been added. A Mornay sauce may also contain eggs for further enrichment.

The name is also used to describe a method of preparing delicate foods, such as fish, eggs, or chicken, with Mornay Sauce.

MORNAY SAUCE

    3 tablespoons butter or margarine
    3 tablespoons all-purpose flour
    ½ teaspoon salt
    ⅛ teaspoon white pepper
    ¾ cup chicken bouillon
    ¾ cup light cream
    ½ onion
    ½ cup grated Parmesan cheese
    ½ cup Swiss cheese

Melt butter. Blend in flour and seasonings. Gradually stir in bouillon and cream. Add onion in one piece. Cook over low heat, stirring constantly, until smooth and thick. Continue to cook, stirring, for 5 minutes. Remove onion. Add cheeses and stir until melted. Makes 1½ to 2 cups.

SCALLOPS MORNAY

    1 pound sea scallops
    8 tablespoons butter or margarine
    1 tablespoon fresh lemon juice
      Salt and pepper
    3 tablespoons all-purpose flour
    1 cup light cream
    2 tablespoons grated Parmesan cheese

Wash and dry scallops. If very large, cut into several pieces. Melt 3 tablespoons butter. Add lemon juice and scallops. Cover and cook for 2 or 3 minutes. Season with salt and pepper to taste. Melt 3 tablespoons butter and blend in flour. Gradually add the cream and cook, stirring constantly, until smooth and thickened. Stir in scallops and cheese. Add more salt and pepper, if necessary. Pour into shallow baking dish (1 quart) and dot with remaining butter. Bake in preheated moderate oven (350°F.) for about 15 minutes. Makes 4 servings.

CHICKEN MORNAY

    6 tablespoons butter or margarine
    6 tablespoons all-purpose flour
    3 cups milk
    6 stuffed olives, sliced
    ½ cup diced pimiento
    ¼ cup sherry
    3 cups diced cooked chicken
      Salt and pepper
    8 ounces wide noodles, cooked and
      drained
    1 cup grated Parmesan or hard
      Gruyère cheese

Melt butter and blend in flour. Gradually add milk and cook, stirring constantly, until smooth and thickened. Add olives, pimiento, sherry, and chicken. Season with salt and pepper to taste. Line a shallow baking dish (2 quart) with the noodles. Cover with the chicken mix-

ture. Sprinkle with the cheese. Bake in preheated hot oven (400°F.) for 15 to 20 minutes. Makes 6 servings.

MORNING-GLORY or TRUMPET CAKE—This is one of the prettiest and most unusual cakes ever made. Baked spongecake is cut into quarters and rolled into cones, the shape of ice-cream cones. These are dipped into colored sugar and put together to look like a bouquet of morning glory or trumpet vine. The cake originated in Pennsylvania Dutch country, where it was used for social gatherings, weddings, and firemen's outings. (It is also called fireman's cake). The serving was easy since each guest can help himself to a cone and eat it out-of-hand.

MORNING-GLORY CAKE

    9 eggs, at room temperature
    2 cups granulated sugar
    ¼ cup water
    2 cups sifted all-purpose flour
    2 teaspoons baking powder
    ½ teaspoon salt
    1 teaspoon vanilla extract
    1 cup confectioners' sugar
      Red sugar

Beat eggs with wire whisk, rotary beater, or in electric mixer until frothy. Add granulated sugar, 1 tablespoon at a time, and continue beating for 15 minutes. Beat in 2 tablespoons water. Fold in sifted dry ingredients; add vanilla. Blend confectioners' sugar and remaining water; set aside for frosting. Line two or three 9-inch layer-cake pans on bottom with wax paper. With large mixing spoon put 3 spoonfuls of batter in each pan, smoothing evenly. Bake in preheated moderate oven (350°F.) for 8 minutes, or until very lightly browned. Loosen edges and turn out on board; carefully peel off paper. Cut each layer into quarters. Working quickly, roll each quarter into a cone, with top of layer on outside. Dip open end of each cone into frosting, then into red sugar. Arrange circle of cones on 12-inch cake plate with points toward center. Repeat until all of batter is used, making the circumference of each layer of cones smaller than the last. Use halves of broken or unattractive cones to fill hollow spots in the center.

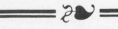

MORTADELLA—Italian-style sausage composed of very finely chopped cured pork and beef with added cubes of back fat. It is delicately spiced, smoked at high temperatures, and air-dried. German-style mortadella is a high grade, finely chopped bologna with cubes of fatty pork and pistachio nuts added.

The original mortadella came from Italy and the only meat it contained was pork. The medieval town of Bologna, which is considered by many Italy's capital of good eating, excels in mortadella and other Italian sausages. From Bologna comes the slang name by which mortadella and similar mildly seasoned sausage meats are known in America, "baloney."

Mortadella is available wherever cold cuts are sold.

MOUSSAKA—Also spelled "musaka" and "mousaka," this is a casserole dish found throughout the Near East. Its origin is credited to Greece. The classic version is made with meat and eggplant in layers, but there are an infinite number of variations in the ingredients.

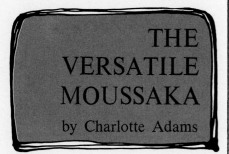

THE VERSATILE MOUSSAKA
by Charlotte Adams

There is a great Greek dish which has some unvarying characteristics but greatly varying ingredients, and also has the happy faculty of lending itself to further variation by venturesome cooks. The Greeks have a word for it, moussaka, but they tell us with firmness that this word is not translatable.

The best known moussaka is made from chopped meat and eggplant. But again, throughout Greece and a good part of the Near East, which has adopted moussaka with enthusiasm, there are many variations on this basic theme. In Greece we have eaten moussaka made with artichokes, with zucchini, and with potatoes. Invariably the dish is topped with a béchamel sauce and sprinkled with cheese, sometimes with bread crumbs added.

Ordinarily moussaka is baked in one dish, which is the way we present our recipes. In the finest restaurants of Athens it is considered very elegant to arrange it in individual shallow baking dishes and sometimes you may like to serve it this way.

Each of these moussakas is a complete main course in itself. However, there isn't one of the variations which wouldn't combine well with a fresh green salad. And if you wish to keep the meal truly Greek, why not serve their own delicious salad with it?

EGGPLANT MOUSSAKA

1 medium eggplant
Fat for frying
1 pound beef chuck, ground
1 teaspoon olive oil
Salt and pepper
1 recipe Béchamel Sauce (see page 1190)
½ cup freshly grated Parmesan cheese

Slice eggplant, without peeling, about ½ inch thick. Fry in fat or oil over brisk heat until lightly browned on both sides. Meantime, cook beef in the olive oil until it loses its red color, stirring often with a fork to keep it broken up. Season to taste with salt and pepper. Place a layer of eggplant slices in the bottom of a shallow 1½-quart baking dish. Put meat on top of them. Add another layer of eggplant slices. Pour Béchamel over and sprinkle cheese on top. Bake in preheated hot oven (400°F.) for 15 to 20 minutes, or until top is golden-brown and crisp. Makes 4 servings.

BEEF-ASPARAGUS MOUSSAKA

1 average bunch of asparagus or 2 packages (10 ounces each) frozen asparagus spears
Salt and pepper to taste
1 teaspoon fresh lemon juice
1 pound beef chuck, ground
1 tablespoon olive oil
Freshly grated horseradish to taste
1 recipe Béchamel Sauce (see page 1190)
½ cup fine bread crumbs
Butter for dotting

Cut fresh asparagus into even lengths which will fit into your baking dish. Cook in boiling salted water until tender. Drain well. (Or cook frozen spears according to package directions.) Lay in the bottom of a shallow 1½-quart baking dish. Season with salt and pepper and sprinkle lemon juice over. Cook beef in olive oil until it loses its red color, stirring frequently so that the meat will remain broken up. Season with salt and pepper and freshly grated horseradish to taste. Spread over asparagus. Pour Béchamel over all. Sprinkle bread crumbs on top. Dot with butter. Bake in preheated hot oven (400°F.) for 15 to 20 minutes, or until crumbs are nicely brown. Makes 4 servings.

FRIED-TOMATO MOUSSAKA

4 medium tomatoes
All-purpose flour
Bacon fat
Salt and pepper
1 tablespoon sugar
1 pound beef chuck, ground
1 teaspoon dried basil
1 tablespoon olive oil
1 recipe Béchamel Sauce (see page 1190)
½ cup grated Parmesan cheese

Wash tomatoes and cut, unpeeled, into ½-inch slices. Dip into flour and fry in bacon fat until nicely brown on both sides. Season to taste with salt and pepper. Place half of slices on bottom of shallow 1½-quart baking dish, and sprinkle half of sugar over them. Meantime, cook beef mixed with basil in olive oil, stirring frequently with a fork to keep the meat broken up, until it loses its red color. Spread meat over tomato slices and top with remaining tomato. Sprinkle with remaining sugar. Pour Béchamel over all. Sprinkle grated cheese on top. Bake in preheated hot oven (400°F.) for 15 to 20 minutes, or until top is crisp and brown. Makes 4 servings.

Note: This dish is also delicious made with fried green tomatoes. Dip them into cornmeal instead of flour, and sprinkle with brown sugar instead of white.

BEEF-MUSHROOM MOUSSAKA

12 large mushrooms
3 tablespoons butter or margarine
Salt and pepper
1 tablespoon minced parsley
¼ cup dry red wine
1 pound beef chuck, ground
2 tablespoons minced chives
½ teaspoon chili powder
1 recipe Béchamel Sauce (see page 1190)
½ cup grated Parmesan cheese

Stem mushrooms and peel them if necessary. Sauté in 2 tablespoons butter for 5 minutes. Place in the bottom of shallow 1½-quart baking dish, season with salt and pepper, and sprinkle with minced parsley. Pour in wine. Meantime, cook beef in 1 tablespoon butter, stirring frequently with a fork to keep it broken up, until it loses its red color. Season to taste with salt and pepper; mix in chives and chili powder thoroughly. Spread over mushrooms. Cover with Béchamel and sprinkle with grated Parmesan. Bake in preheated hot oven (400°F.) for 15 to 20 minutes, or until golden-brown. Makes 4 servings.

LENTIL MOUSSAKA

2 cups quick-cooking lentils
1 teaspoon salt
1 onion, stuck with 2 cloves
1 bay leaf
Bouquet of parsley
6 skinless frankfurters, ground
1 teaspoon prepared mustard
1 tablespoon olive oil
1 recipe Béchamel Sauce (see page 1190)
½ cup grated Parmesan cheese

Cook lentils in salted water to cover with onion, bay leaf, and parsley for 25 to 30 minutes, or until tender. Remove onion, bay leaf, and parsley, and drain, reserving ¼ cup of the cooking liquid. Place lentils in bottom of shallow 2-quart baking dish and add reserved liquid. Mean-

Béchamel Sauce   **Chicken-Corn Moussaka**

Eggplant Moussaka   Greek Salad

time, heat the ground frankfurters with the mustard in the olive oil, stirring frequently to keep meat broken up. Do not brown. Spread over lentils. Pour Béchamel over. Sprinkle with grated cheese. Bake in preheated hot oven (400°F.) for 15 to 20 minutes, or until nicely brown on top. Makes 4 servings.

LAMB-CARROT MOUSSAKA
- 10 medium carrots
- ½ cup chopped fresh mint
- 1 tablespoon sugar
- ½ cup hot milk (about)
  Salt and pepper
- 1 pound lean lamb, ground
- 1 tablespoon minced onion
- 1 tablespoon minced green pepper
- 2 tablespoons butter or margarine
- 1 recipe Béchamel Sauce (see page 1190)
- ½ cup fine bread crumbs
  Butter for dotting

Scrape carrots, cut up coarsely, and cook in boiling salted water until tender. Drain and place in a blender with mint, sugar, and milk and whirl until puréed. Or put through a food mill. The resulting purée should be moist and fluffy, but not runny, so add more milk if necessary. Season to taste with salt and pepper and place in the bottom of a shallow 2-quart baking dish. Meantime, cook lamb, onion, and green pepper in the butter, stirring frequently with a fork to keep meat broken up, until it loses its red color. Season to taste with salt and pepper and spread over carrot purée. Cover with Béchamel. Sprinkle bread crumbs on top and dot with butter. Bake in preheated hot oven (400°F.) for 15 to 20 minutes, or until crumbs are golden-brown. Makes 4 servings.

LAMB-VEGETABLE MOUSSAKA
- 2 packages (10 ounces each) frozen mixed vegetables
- 1 tablespoon butter
- 2 tablespoons light cream
  Salt and pepper
- 1 pound lean lamb, ground
- 4 stuffed olives, chopped fine
- 1 tablespoon olive oil
- 1 recipe Béchamel Sauce (see page 1190)
- ½ cup grated Gruyère cheese

Cook vegetables according to package directions. Drain well, add butter and light cream, and mix. Season to taste with salt and pepper. Place in the bottom of a shallow 1½-quart baking dish. Meantime, cook lamb and chopped olives in the olive oil until lamb loses its red color, stirring frequently with a fork to keep it broken up. Season to taste with salt and pepper. Spread over vegetables. Cover with Béchamel. Sprinkle grated cheese over all and bake in preheated hot oven (400°F.) for 15 to 20 minutes, or until cheese is delicately brown. Makes 4 servings.

PORK MOUSSAKA WITH BRUSSELS SPROUTS

2 packages (10 ounces each) frozen Brussels sprouts
3 large onions, minced
¼ cup butter or margarine
⅓ cup water
Salt and pepper
2 cups ground cooked pork
¼ teaspoon ground sage
1 cup medium cream sauce
½ cup prepared poultry stuffing
Butter for dotting

Cook Brussels sprouts according to package directions. Drain well. Meantime, cook minced onions in 3 tablespoons butter over low heat until soft, adding more butter if necessary. Do not brown. Add water, cover, and cook at a simmer until water has evaporated, 20 to 30 minutes. Season to taste with salt and pepper. Mix onions with Brussels sprouts and place in the bottom of a shallow 1½-quart baking dish. Warm the pork in 1 tablespoon butter, mix in the sage well, and add salt and pepper to taste. Spread over Brussels sprouts, cover with cream sauce, and sprinkle on poultry stuffing. Dot with butter. Bake in preheated hot oven (400°F.) for 15 to 20 minutes, or until crumbs are brown. Makes 4 servings.

CHICKEN MOUSSAKA WITH PEAS

2 packages (10 ounces each) frozen peas
1 egg, well beaten
¼ cup butter or margarine
Salt and pepper
2 cups ground cooked chicken
Ground nutmeg to taste
1 recipe Béchamel Sauce (at right)
½ cup grated Gruyère cheese

Cook peas according to package directions. Drain, reserving about 1 cup of cooking liquid. Put peas through food mill or whirl (with reserved liquid) in a blender. The purée should be soft and fluffy but not runny, so add reserved liquid gradually to achieve the right consistency. Beat in egg, half of butter, and salt and pepper to taste. Put into the bottom of a shallow 1½-quart baking dish. Meantime, warm ground chicken in remaining butter. Season with salt and pepper to taste and blend in ground nutmeg thoroughly. Spread over the purée of peas. Cover with Béchamel and sprinkle with grated cheese. Bake in preheated hot oven (400°F.) for 15 to 20 minutes, or until golden-brown. Makes 4 servings.

CHICKEN-CORN MOUSSAKA

2 packages (10 ounces each) frozen corn kernels
5 tablespoons butter or margarine
2 teaspoons paprika
½ cup heavy cream
Salt and pepper
2 cups ground cooked chicken
1 recipe Béchamel Sauce (at right)
½ cup grated Gruyère cheese

Cook corn according to package directions. Drain well. Sauté for 5 minutes in ¼ cup of the butter, stirring constantly. Add 1 teaspoon paprika and the cream. Season to taste with salt and pepper, and place in the bottom of shallow 1½-quart baking dish. Warm the ground chicken in 1 tablespoon butter, being careful not to let it brown. Mix in 1 teaspoon paprika well, and spread chicken over corn. Pour Béchamel over all, and top with grated cheese. Bake in preheated hot oven (400°F.) for 15 to 20 minutes, or until top is golden and crisp. Makes 4 servings.

BÉCHAMEL SAUCE

2 tablespoons butter or margarine
2 tablespoons flour
1 tablespoon finely chopped onion
1 cup chicken bouillon
2 tablespoons heavy cream
Salt and pepper

Melt butter. Combine flour with it smoothly. Stir in onion. Add bouillon slowly, stirring constantly, until thickened. Add cream, season to taste, and simmer very gently for about 15 minutes. Strain, if desired. Makes about 1 cup.

GREEK SALAD

1 small head lettuce
1 cucumber
2 ripe tomatoes
1 cup cubed Greek feta cheese
12 Greek black olives
1 medium onion, sliced thin
½ cup julienne beets
6 anchovy fillets, cut up
1 tablespoon capers
½ cup olive oil
Vinegar to taste
1 teaspoon powdered mustard
Salt to taste

In a large wooden bowl put lettuce torn coarsely, cucumber sliced thin, tomatoes cubed, cheese, olives, onion, beets, anchovy fillets, and capers. Mix oil, vinegar, and mustard with salt to taste and pour over salad. Toss gently so as not to break up cheese cubes. Makes 4 to 6 servings.

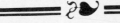

MOUSSE—A French word which, literally translated, means "froth." In culinary language, it is used for a rich dish that is spongy or frothy: in other words, light. Mousses can be either savory or sweet, hot or cold.

Savory mousses may be made from fish, meat, vegetables, or cheese, and lightened with beaten egg white or gelatin. When hot they are set in a dish of water and either steamed or baked in the oven.

Cold mousses, usually dessert mousses, are also made frothy, although very often whipped cream is added for further fluffiness and lightness.

The classic cold mousse is chilled, but not frozen. However, nowadays mousses frozen in a freezer or in the refrigerator tray are accepted as members of the family.

A mousse is an elegant dish excellent to serve when entertaining since it can be assembled and, in many cases, even fully prepared beforehand.

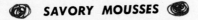

SAVORY MOUSSES

HOT FISH MOUSSE

1¼ pounds fresh or frozen salmon steaks or other fish
¾ teaspoon salt
¼ teaspoon pepper
1 teaspoon Worcestershire
1 teaspoon onion juice
3 egg whites
1 cup heavy cream, beaten

Steam salmon steaks in water to cover until fish flakes; drain. Force fish through food chopper, using fine blade. Add seasonings and mix well. Add unbeaten egg whites, one at a time, blending thoroughly after each addition. Fold in cream. Pour into well-buttered 1-quart casserole. Place in pan of hot water. Bake in preheated moderate oven (375° F.) for 40 minutes, or until firm. Serve with cucumber sauce, or lemon or parsley butter. Makes 4 servings.

HAM MOUSSE

1 cup chicken bouillon
1 cup milk
1 envelope unflavored gelatin
2 egg yolks
½ teaspoon salt
1 teaspoon powdered mustard
Dash of hot pepper sauce
1½ cups ground cooked ham
½ teaspoon onion juice
1 teaspoon vinegar
Few sprigs of parsley, minced
¼ cup mayonnaise
⅓ cup heavy cream, whipped
Watercress

Put bouillon and milk in top part of double boiler. Sprinkle gelatin on the liquids. Beat in egg yolks, salt, mustard, and hot pepper sauce. Put over simmering water, stirring constantly, until mixture thickens slightly and coats a metal spoon. Remove from heat and cool. Fold in remaining ingredients except watercress. Pour into 1-quart mold and chill until firm. Unmold and serve garnished with watercress. Makes 4 to 6 servings.

CHICKEN MOUSSE

1 envelope unflavored gelatin
2 tablespoons cold water
¾ teaspoon salt
⅛ teaspoon cayenne
3 egg yolks, slightly beaten
1 cup hot chicken bouillon
1 green onion, minced
¼ cup mayonnaise
⅓ cup heavy cream, whipped
Salad greens

Soften gelatin in the cold water. In top part of double boiler, mix seasonings and egg yolks. Stir in bouillon and cook over boiling water, stirring constantly, until smooth and thickened. Add gelatin and stir until dissolved. Cool. Fold in remaining ingredients except greens. Pour into mold (1 quart), and chill until firm. Unmold on salad greens. Makes 4 servings.

 **SWEET MOUSSES**

CHOCOLATE MOUSSE

1 package (6 ounces) semisweet chocolate pieces
2 eggs, separated
⅓ cup water
¼ cup firmly packed light brown sugar
1 teaspoon vanilla extract

Melt chocolate over hot water. Beat egg yolks and water lightly. Gradually add chocolate, beating rapidly. Beat egg whites until stiff but not dry. Gradually add sugar, beating until glossy. Fold in chocolate mixture and vanilla. Pile lightly into small sherbet glasses and chill. Makes 4 to 6 servings.

CREAM-CHEESE MOUSSE

1 envelope unflavored gelatin
1 cup pineapple juice
1½ cups sugar
1 cup orange juice
Juice of 1 lemon
12 ounces soft cream cheese
½ teaspoon almond extract
¼ teaspoon salt
½ cup toasted slivered blanched almonds
1 cup heavy cream, whipped

Turn refrigerator control to coldest setting. Sprinkle gelatin on pineapple juice in saucepan. Add sugar; heat, stirring, until gelatin and sugar are dissolved. Cool. Add orange and lemon juice. Blend cheese with next 3 ingredients. Stir in first mixture; fold in cream; pour into freezing trays and freeze until firm. Makes 8 servings.

FRUIT CREAM MOUSSE

1 cup each of grape and apple juices
¼ cup lime juice
10 tablespoons very fine granulated sugar
1 cup heavy cream
½ teaspoon vanilla extract
½ cup chopped nuts

Turn refrigerator control to coldest setting. Mix fruit juices and ½ cup sugar. Pour into refrigerator tray and freeze until firm. Whip cream and fold in 2 tablespoons sugar, the vanilla, and half of nuts. Spread over frozen fruit juices in tray. Freeze until firm. Serve garnished with remaining nuts. Makes 6 servings.

LEMON MOUSSE

2 tablespoons cornstarch
¼ teaspoon salt
1 cup sugar
1 cup milk
3 egg yolks, slightly beaten
⅓ cup fresh lemon juice
Grated rind of 1 lemon

2 cups heavy cream, whipped

Turn refrigerator control to coldest setting. In top part of small double boiler mix cornstarch, salt, and sugar. Add milk. Cook over boiling water for about 15 minutes, stirring frequently. Pour slowly over egg yolks, stirring constantly. Mix well and return to double boiler; cook for 1 minute, stirring. Add lemon juice and rind, and chill. Fold in cream. Pour into refrigerator trays and freeze until firm. Makes 8 servings.

CRANBERRY MOUSSE

1 package (3 ounces) soft cream cheese
¼ cup sugar
⅛ teaspoon salt
1 cup heavy cream, whipped
2 cups (one 1-pound can) whole-berry cranberry sauce

Turn refrigerator control to coldest setting. Beat cream cheese until fluffy. Stir in sugar and salt and fold into cream. Add cranberry sauce and mix lightly. Pour into refrigerator tray and freeze until firm. Makes 6 servings.

BLUEBERRY MOUSSE

4 cups cultivated blueberries, washed
2 cups water
2 cups sugar
Juice of ½ lemon
2 cups heavy cream

Cook blueberries in water for 15 minutes to extract all juice. Strain. Add sugar and lemon juice to blueberry liquid. Return to heat and cook for 5 minutes. Remove from heat and cool. Divide mixture between 2 ice trays and put into freezer. In 1 hour, stir with spoon. Repeat at intervals until mixture begins to set. When whole tray has partially frozen, whip cream very stiff and stir some into frozen mixture in each tray. Return to freezer; stir occasionally while mousse is hardening to be sure cream does not separate. Let freeze overnight. Serve in sherbet or parfait glasses. Makes 8 to 10 servings.

CANTALOUPE MOUSSE

1 envelope unflavored gelatin
¼ cup cold water
3 cups puréed ripe cantaloupe (1½ medium melons)
½ cup sugar
1 cup heavy cream, whipped

Turn temperature control of refrigerator to coldest setting. Soften gelatin in cold water. Cook puréed cantaloupe and sugar until mixture is heated. Stir in gelatin. Stir until gelatin is dissolved. Chill until slightly thickened. Fold in heavy cream. Freeze until firm in 2 freezing trays. Makes 8 to 10 servings.

CHOCOLATE-MINT MOUSSE

6 ounces (1 small package) semisweet chocolate pieces
½ ounce (½ square) unsweetened

chocolate
3 tablespoons hot water
¼ cup butter
4 eggs, separated
1 cup heavy cream
⅓ cup sugar
Pastel mints, broken into bits

Add chocolate to hot water; stir until blended. Add butter; remove from heat. Beat egg yolks; gradually add to hot chocolate mixture. Cool. Whip half of cream and add sugar. Beat egg whites until stiff but not dry. Fold cream and egg whites into chocolate mixture. Put into twelve 4-ounce cups with lids and freeze until firm. Whip remaining ½ cup cream. Put 12 spoonfuls of whipped cream on a cookie sheet. Freeze until firm. Remove from cookie sheet with a spatula and put frozen cream in a plastic bag or container. At serving time, top mousse with whipped cream and bits of broken mints. Makes 12 servings.

MOUSSELINE—A culinary term applied to a variety of preparations made light and airy by the addition of whipped cream or beaten egg white. These dishes include *gâteau mousseline,* a spongecake concoction; *pommes mousseline,* mashed potatoes with cream; and mousse-type mixtures of fish, meat, or poultry, made from gelatin. A mousseline sauce is made with part cream and part hollandaise.

HAM MOUSSELINE

1 envelope unflavored gelatin
⅓ cup cold water
2 egg yolks
¾ teaspoon salt
Dash of cayenne
1 teaspoon powdered mustard
1 can condensed consommé
1 cup ground cooked ham
1 slice of onion, minced
¼ cup mayonnaise
¼ cup heavy cream, whipped
Lettuce

Soften gelatin in the cold water. Mix egg yolks, salt, cayenne, and mustard in top part of double boiler. Beat until thick and lemon-colored. Add consommé and cook, stirring, over boiling water until mixture thickens enough to coat a metal spoon. Add gelatin and stir until dissolved. Cool. Add ham, onion, mayonnaise, and cream. Pour into 1-quart mold and chill until firm. Unmold on bed of lettuce. Makes 4 servings.

POMMES MOUSSELINE

6 medium potatoes
Salt
Butter or margarine
1 to 1½ cups light cream, scalded
Pepper
½ cup soft bread crumbs

Peel potatoes, cut into large pieces, and cook in small amount of boiling salted water until tender. Drain and mash. Put potatoes into top part of double boiler and add ¼ cup butter. Beat in cream to desired consistency. Season with salt and pepper to taste. Heat well over boiling water. Just before serving, top with the crumbs, browned in 2 tablespoons butter. Makes 4 to 6 servings.

MOUSSELINE SAUCE

- 3 egg yolks
- ¼ teaspoon salt
- Dash of cayenne
- 1 tablespoon fresh lemon juice
- ½ cup melted butter
- 3 tablespoons hot water
- ⅓ cup heavy cream, whipped

In top part of double boiler, beat egg-yolks with wooden spoon. Add salt, cayenne, and lemon juice. Stir in butter. Then stir in hot water. Put over hot, not boiling, water and cook, stirring constantly, for 4 or 5 minutes, or until mixture thickens. Fold in cream and heat gently, stirring. Serve on poached fish. Makes about 1¼ cups.

GÂTEAU MOUSSELINE

- 1⅓ cups sifted cake flour
- ½ teaspoon baking powder
- ½ teaspoon salt
- 1½ cups sugar
- 6 eggs, separated
- 1 teaspoon cream of tartar
- ¼ cup water
- 1 teaspoon each vanilla and lemon extracts
- Cream Filling
- Glaze

Sift flour, baking powder, salt, and 1 cup of the sugar into small mixing bowl. In large mixing bowl, combine egg whites and the cream of tartar; beat until soft mounds begin to form. Gradually add remaining sugar, sprinkling 2 tablespoons at a time over whites and beating until very stiff peaks are formed. Do not underbeat. Combine egg yolks, water, and flavorings. Add to sifted dry ingredients and beat ½ minute, or just enough to blend. Then fold egg-yolk mixture into beaten egg whites until blended. Pour into 3 layer-cake pans (9 inch) lined on the bottom with wax paper. Bake in preheated moderate oven (350°F.) for 30 minutes, or until done. Turn out on racks, peel off paper, and cool cakes. Put layers together with Cream Filling and spread top with Glaze. Chill until ready to serve.

Cream Filling

In saucepan mix ½ cup sugar, ⅛ teaspoon salt, and 1 tablespoon cornstarch. Stir in ¾ cup milk and cook, stirring constantly, until smooth and thickened. Stir small amount of mixture into 2 egg yolks, slightly beaten. Stir egg-yolk mixture into mixture remaining in saucepan and cook gently, stirring, for 2 or 3 minutes longer. Cool; then chill. Fold in ½ cup heavy cream, whipped.

Glaze

Mix 1 cup sifted confectioners' sugar with enough plum brandy or other liqueur to make a rather thin frosting.

MOZZARELLA—A soft white cheese of Italian origin, shaped traditionally in ovals the size of a fist. Mozzarella has a mild flavor. It is eaten fresh and it is used in cooking.

The original Mozzarella came from the country around Naples and was made from buffalo's milk, since buffaloes are used as draft animals in the region. However, even in Italy, most Mozzarella is now made from cow's milk, but the buffalo variety is superior in taste. It is made in an unusual way: the milk curd is pulled in scalding hot water and kneaded; formerly by hand and now by machine.

Mozzarella has always been much used in Italian cookery and is an essential ingredient of eggplant parmigiana and of pizza.

MUFFIN—A small round bread which can be leavened with baking powder, baking soda, or yeast. Muffins made without yeast, as quick breads, are typical of native American cookery.

When leavened with baking powder or baking soda, the muffin is mixed by sifting all the dry ingredients together with any nuts or fruits folded in and all the liquid ingredients added at one time. The batter should be mixed only until the dry ingredients are moistened. The batter, which looks lumpy and rough, is then spooned into well-greased special pans called muffin pans which come in a variety of sizes. The most general size is two-inch rounds with six or twelve cups in the pan. The muffins are baked at a high temperature for a short length of time and are generally served hot with some kind of spread.

Raised muffins are prepared like yeast rolls and are rich in eggs and butter. Dough is first allowed to rise in bowl, then beaten well and put in greased muffin pans to rise again before baking. Raised muffins have muffinlike texture but are finer-grained.

English muffins are one type of muffin leavened with yeast. The dough is prepared as is any yeast dough and cut into three-inch rounds. The rounds are baked on a preheated lightly greased griddle on the top of the range. The muffin is cooked until golden-brown on both sides.

BLUEBERRY MUFFINS

- 5 tablespoons sugar
- 1½ cups blueberries, washed and dried
- 3 cups sifted all-purpose flour
- 1½ teaspoons salt
- 4½ teaspoons baking powder
- 2 eggs
- 1½ cups milk
- ½ cup melted shortening

Sprinkle 2 tablespoons sugar on blueberries. Into large mixing bowl sift flour, salt, baking powder, and remaining sugar. Beat eggs well; add milk and shortening. Add at once to dry ingredients. Stir quickly and lightly until just mixed. Mixture will be lumpy. Gently fold blueberries into batter. Fill well-greased muffin pans two-thirds full. Bake in preheated hot oven (425°F.) for 25 to 30 minutes. Remove from pan. Makes about 16 muffins.

SAVORY CORN MUFFINS

- 1 cup sifted all-purpose flour
- ¾ teaspoon salt
- ¼ teaspoon baking soda
- 2 teaspoons baking powder
- 1 cup yellow cornmeal
- 1 tablespoon sugar
- 1 cup buttermilk or sour milk
- 1 small onion, grated
- ½ teaspoon poultry seasoning
- ¼ cup melted pork drippings
- ¼ cup fried-out pieces of pork fat

Sift dry ingredients; stir in buttermilk, onion, poultry seasoning, drippings, and fat. Turn into well-greased muffin pans and bake in preheated hot oven (400° F.) for about 30 minutes. Makes 8 muffins.

SWEET-POTATO MUFFINS

- 1¾ cups sifted all-purpose flour
- 1 teaspoon salt
- 3 teaspoons baking powder
- 1 tablespoon brown sugar
- ½ cup coarsely chopped walnuts
- 2 eggs, beaten
- ¾ cup milk
- 1¼ cups mashed cooked sweet potatoes
- ¼ cup melted butter
- Ground cinnamon
- Granulated sugar

Sift first 3 ingredients into bowl. Add brown sugar and nuts; mix well. Combine next 4 ingredients and mix well. Add to first mixture, stirring just enough to moisten dry ingredients. Fill greased 2¼-inch muffin cups two thirds full of batter. Bake in preheated hot oven (425° F.) for about 25 minutes. Sprinkle tops with mixture of cinnamon and granulated sugar. Makes 12 muffins.

RICE MUFFINS

- 1½ cups sifted all-purpose flour
- 2 teaspoons baking powder
- ½ teaspoon salt
- 2 tablespoons sugar
- 3 tablespoons soft shortening
- 1 cup cold cooked rice
- 1 egg, beaten
- 1 cup milk

Sift dry ingredients. Cut in shortening with 2 knives or pastry blender. Add rice, egg, and milk; mix only enough to moisten dry ingredients. Half fill 2¾-

inch muffin pans. Bake in preheated hot oven (425°F.) for 25 minutes. Makes 12 muffins.

APPLE-CORN MUFFINS

⅔ cup yellow cornmeal
2 tablespoons sugar
1 teaspoon salt
1 cup milk, scalded
1 egg, beaten
1 cup sifted all-purpose flour
2 teaspoons baking powder
2 cups thinly sliced peeled eating
  apples

Mix cornmeal, sugar, and salt. Add milk and egg and blend well. Sift together flour and baking powder. Stir into first mixture, then fold in apples. Bake in greased 2¾-inch muffin pans in preheated moderate oven (350°F.) for 25 to 30 minutes. Makes 12 muffins.

EGGLESS MUFFINS

Sift together 2 cups sifted all-purpose flour, 3 teaspoons baking powder, ¾ teaspoon salt, and 1 tablespoon sugar. Add 1¼ cups cold water; mix just enough to dampen flour. Fill hot greased muffin tins two thirds full and bake in preheated hot oven (400°F.) for 30 minutes, or until lightly browned. Makes 8 large muffins.

RAISED MUFFINS

¼ cup water*
1 package active dry yeast or 1
  cake compressed yeast
½ cup boiling water
¼ cup sugar
3 tablespoons butter or margarine
1½ teaspoons salt
½ cup undiluted evaporated milk
2 eggs, beaten
3½ cups sifted all-purpose flour

*Use very warm water (105°F. to 115°F.) for dry yeast; use lukewarm (80°F. to 90°F.) for compressed. Sprinkle dry yeast or crumble cake into water. Let stand for a few minutes; then stir until dissolved. Pour boiling water over sugar, butter, and salt. Add milk, yeast, eggs, and about half of flour. Beat very well. Beat in remaining flour. Cover and let rise until doubled, about 1½ hours. Beat well and fill 18 greased 2¾-inch muffin cups two thirds full. Let rise until doubled, about 1 hour. Bake in preheated moderate oven (375°F.) for about 25 minutes. Makes 18 muffins.

ENGLISH MUFFINS

1 package active dry yeast or 1
  cake yeast
1½ cups lukewarm water*
2 tablespoons sugar
4 cups sifted all-purpose flour
½ cup nonfat dry-milk crystals
1 egg, slightly beaten
3 tablespoons soft butter or margarine
1½ teaspoons salt
  White cornmeal

Sprinkle dry yeast or crumble cake yeast into ½ cup warm water. *Use very warm

water (105°F. to 115°F.) for dry yeast; use lukewarm water (80°F. to 90°F.) for compressed. Let stand for a few minutes, then stir until dissolved. In a large bowl stir together remaining 1 cup warm water, sugar, 2 cups of the flour, and the nonfat milk. Add yeast mixture and beat well. Add egg, butter, salt, and 1 cup flour. Stir until dough clears the bowl. Spread remaining flour on board, turn out dough and knead for about 10 minutes, adding a little more flour if necessary. Put in greased bowl, cover and let rise until doubled in bulk. Turn out on floured board and pat out gently to almost the desired thickness. *Do not knead.* Sprinkle well with cornmeal and roll to ¼-inch thickness. Cut carefully with sharp 3-inch to 4-inch cutter. Put on sheets of wax paper sprinkled with cornmeal. Cover and let rise until doubled in bulk. Bake on ungreased griddle with temperature a little lower than that used for pancakes. Allow 7 to 8 minutes for browning each side. Makes about 16 large muffins.

MULBERRY—A tree of the genus *Morus,* and its edible berrylike fruit. Mulberries are native to the mild-climate areas of Europe, Asia, and America. Although not raised commercially in the United States, they are found growing wild from Massachusetts to Nebraska, and south to the Gulf States. There are three principal varieties: black, red, and white. The leaves of the white mulberry, *Morus alba,* are used in silkworm cultivation.

Mulberries resemble blackberries in shape and structure, ranging in color from white through red to black. The fruit is soft and bland in taste and can be eaten raw. Cooked, it is used in making desserts, preserves, and wine.

Caloric Value

☐ 3½ ounces, raw = 62 calories

MULBERRY JELLY

3 pounds ripe mulberries
½ cup strained fresh lemon juice
7 cups sugar
1 bottle liquid pectin

Put mulberries in saucepan and crush. Heat gently until juice starts to flow, then simmer, covered, for 15 minutes. Put in jelly cloth or bag, and squeeze out juice. Measure 3 cups into a very large saucepan. Add lemon juice and sugar, and mix well. Put over high heat and bring to boil, stirring constantly. At once stir in pectin. Then bring to a *full rolling boil and boil hard for 1 minute,* stirring constantly. Remove from heat, skim off foam with metal spoon, and pour quickly

into hot sterilized jars. Seal. Makes about eight ½-pint jars.

MULL—To make a hot drink of wine, cider, beer, and sometimes fruit juices by beating and flavoring with sugar, spices, eggs, etc.

MULLED WINE

1 quart Madeira, sherry, or Tokay
¼ teaspoon grated nutmeg
4 eggs
¼ cup brandy
  Sugar

In top part of double boiler over direct heat, bring wine and nutmeg almost to the boiling point. Beat eggs until light and stir in brandy. Pour heated wine onto egg mixture. Add sugar to taste. Put back in double boiler and cook over hot water for 2 minutes, beating constantly with rotary beater. Serve hot in small cups. Makes 10 servings.

MULLED CIDER

Bring just to the boiling point: 4 cups apple cider, 6 whole cloves, and a cinnamon stick. Remove spices and serve hot. Makes 4 cups.

HOLIDAY MULLED CIDER

½ teaspoon whole cloves
  Two 2-inch pieces cinnamon
2 quarts water
⅔ cup loose tea or 30 tea bags
¼ cup sugar
2 quarts apple cider or apple juice
½ cup fresh lemon juice
4 red apples
8 whole cloves
¼ cup red cinnamon hearts
  Thin Sugar Syrup

Add cloves and cinnamon stick to water. Bring to a boil. Add tea. Cover and brew for about 4 minutes. Stir and strain. Add sugar and stir. Add apple cider and lemon juice. Peel and core apples, but leave whole. Stick 2 cloves into each apple. Add cinnamon hearts to Thin Sugar Syrup. Poach apples in Thin Sugar Syrup. Pour mulled cider into serving bowl and add apples. Serve hot. Makes 4 quarts.

Thin Sugar Syrup

Combine 1 cup sugar and 2 cups water. Bring to a boil. Simmer, covered, for 3 minutes. Syrup is now ready for poaching. Makes about 2½ cups syrup.

MULLED GRAPE JUICE

2 cups unsweetened grape juice
1 cup water
1 cup sugar
1 cinnamon stick
6 whole cloves
  Juice of 1 lemon

Mix juice, water, and sugar in saucepan. Tie spices in a small cheesecloth bag and add to liquid. Bring to a boil. Stir and allow to stand over very low heat for 10 minutes. Remove spice bag and add lemon juice. Bring again just to a boil. Serve hot. Makes 4 servings.

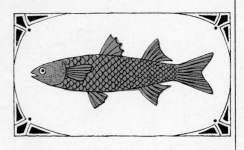

MULLET—The name is used to describe several families of important food fish widely distributed throughout the world. The best known are the gray mullets of the family *Muglidae* which include the genera known as striped and white mullets; and the red mullets, including striped red mullet, surmullet, and goatfish, of the family *Mullidae. Mullus barbatus,* found in the Mediterranean and considered a great delicacy since ancient times, is a very small variety averaging about six inches in length. In the Mississippi Valley several suckers of still a third fish family, *Catostomidae,* are called mullets. Mullets are found in almost all temperate and warm waters. They are of moderate size, from a half to five pounds in weight. Their flesh is tender, white, and firm-textured with a sweet, delicate taste. The flesh contains a clear yellow oil with a mild nutlike flavor.

Availability and Purchasing Guide— Available all year. They are most generally marketed in the South Atlantic and Gulf States, but are occasionally to be found elsewhere. They are sold whole, drawn, dressed, and filleted; fresh or frozen, salted and smoked.

Storage—Fresh fish is very perishable. Wrap in moisture-proof paper or place in a tightly covered container in the coldest part of the refrigerator.

Keep frozen fish solidly frozen until ready to use. Once thawed, use immediately. Do not refreeze.

Wrap smoked fish tightly and refrigerate.

☐ Fresh, refrigerator shelf, raw: 1 or 2 days

☐ Fresh, refrigerator shelf, cooked: 3 or 4 days

☐ Smoked, refrigerator shelf: 1 to 2 weeks

☐ Fresh, raw; and smoked, refrigerator frozen-food compartment, prepared for freezing: 2 to 3 weeks

☐ Fresh, refrigerator frozen-food compartment, cooked, prepared for freezing: 3 to 4 weeks

☐ Frozen, refrigerator frozen-food compartment: 2 months

☐ Fresh, prepared for freezing, raw or cooked; smoked; or frozen, freezer: 1 year

Caloric Value

☐ Striped mullet, 3½ ounces, raw = 146 calories

Basic Preparation—Wash fish in cold salted water. Do not allow fish to remain in water as it may lose flavor and nutrients. Frozen fish should be thawed in the refrigerator; allow about 8 hours for 1 pound of fish.

Mullets are best cooked by dry-heat methods: small mullets can be broiled or panfried; larger fish are good baked.

☐ **To Freeze**—Freeze as soon as possible. Clean and dress. Wash thoroughly in running cold water. Dip into a solution of 4 cups water to 1 tablespoon ascorbic acid for 20 seconds. Wrap in moisture-vapor-proof wrapping, excluding all air from package. Seal.

BROILED MULLET
2 whole mullets, about 2 pounds each
All-purpose flour
Melted butter or cooking oil
Salt and pepper
Lemon wedges

Grease broiler rack. Dust fish with flour and brush with butter. Put on rack and broil about 6 inches from unit for 3 to 5 minutes on one side. Turn and brush with butter. Broil for 5 to 8 minutes. Season with salt and pepper to taste, and serve with lemon wedges. Makes 4 servings.

BAKED MULLET
1 mullet, about 4 pounds
1 small onion, sliced
Butter or margarine
½ cup chopped parsley
Dried thyme, salt, and pepper

Clean and split fish. Put in greased shallow baking dish. Brown onion lightly in 1 tablespoon of butter. Arrange onion on fish and sprinkle with ¼ cup parsley. Season to taste with thyme, salt, and pepper. Dot with butter and bake in preheated hot oven (425°F.) for 20 minutes, or until fish flakes easily with a fork. Serve with melted butter to which remaining parsley has been added. Makes 4 to 6 servings.

MULLIGATAWNY—An Indian soup whose name means "pepper water." It may be a thin clear soup or a thick one, made with meat or chicken, usually the latter, and it has a curry flavor. Mulligatawny is highly seasoned with salt, pepper, lemon juice, and clove in addition to the curry powder. Rice, eggs, and cream are optional ingredients.

MULLIGATAWNY
1 frying chicken, about 3 pounds, cut up
3 medium onions
1 celery stalk, diced
3 carrots, sliced
6 cups water
1 garlic clove, minced
¼ cup butter or margarine
⅓ cup all-purpose flour
2 tablespoons curry powder
Dash each of ground cloves and cayenne
Salt and pepper
Juice of 1 lemon
Hot cooked rice
Parsley

Wash chicken and put in large kettle. Add 2 onions, quartered, the celery, carrots, and water. Bring to boil, cover, and simmer for 30 minutes. Cook remaining onion, chopped, and the garlic in the butter until golden. Blend in flour and curry powder. Add 1 cup broth from chicken and cook until thickened, stirring constantly. Add to chicken and simmer for 30 minutes longer. Add cloves, cayenne, salt and pepper to taste, and the lemon juice. Serve with rice and a garnish of parsley. Makes about 1½ quarts, or 4 servings.

MUSCAT, MUSCATEL—Muscat is the name of several varieties of grapes of the species *vinifera,* cultivated especially for making raisins and wine. The muscat is a white or black grape with a sweet and musty flavor. It is grown in many parts of the world, including Italy, France, and the San Joaquin Valley in California.

Muscatel, the wine made from the muscat grape, is a sweet dessert wine which can vary in color from golden or russet-amber to light red. It is a sweet, rich, and fruity wine with the typical aroma and flavor of the grape.

ITALIAN MUSCATELS
Butter (about ½ cup)
1 cup unblanched almonds
1 cup sugar
2 tablespoons dried grated orange peel
1½ cups sifted all-purpose flour
1½ teaspoons baking powder
1½ teaspoons each of ground cinnamon and allspice
½ cup muscatel
Frosting
Colored sugar

Melt ½ teaspoon butter in skillet; add almonds and brown over low heat. Cool. Chop. Cream ½ cup butter; gradually beat in sugar; add orange peel and almonds. Sift flour with baking powder and spices; add alternately with wine to butter mixture. Chill for 1 hour. Turn out on sugared board; pat or roll gently to ⅓-inch thickness. Cut with 1½-inch scalloped cookie cutter, put on greased cookie sheets. Bake in preheated moderate oven (350°F.) for 12 to 15 minutes. While hot, frost and sprinkle with colored sugar. Makes 8 dozen cookies.

Frosting

Add 1 teaspoon fresh lemon juice to 2 unbeaten egg whites; stir in confectioners' sugar until of spreading consistency.

MUSHROOM by Lucy Kavaler—A

lump of jelly in a fallen log, a row of glaring yellow shelves down the trunk of an oak, a sphere resembling an abandoned white basketball, all of these are mushrooms. Some mushrooms nourish us, some sicken, some produce drunkenness, some induce visions, and some kill. Who can describe a mushroom? It can

look like a button, an ear, a bird's nest with eggs in it, a trumpet, cone, bear's head, saddle, or clump of coral. There are thousands of varieties, 3,000 in this hemisphere alone, ranging in color from the tan of the little mushroom of the field to crimson, yellow, blue, green, white, black, or a combination of two or three of these. The cap can be smooth, or pitted, tufted, dotted, warted, convoluted, or spongy.

Whatever the appearance, what we see is but the fruit of the plant, containing the spores or seeds. Beneath the soil or within the rotting log lies a tangled mass of threads, the mycelium or body, taking in food and growing. Mushrooms are fungi, members of the enormous and

varied group of living things which are responsible for decay. They belong to the *Basidiomycetes* class, together with such far less attractive organisms as smuts and rusts. Like most other fungi, mushrooms lack chlorophyll, which means that, unlike green plants, they cannot manufacture their own food but must obtain nourishment from others, living or dead.

When the mycelium is mature enough to reproduce, a sudden rain or a damp night provides the needed stimulus and the fruit springs up with a force sufficient to crack rocks or sidewalks. Millions of spores fall from the underside of the cap in a matter of hours. Some varieties appear only fleetingly above the earth; the little mushroom that rose so proudly at

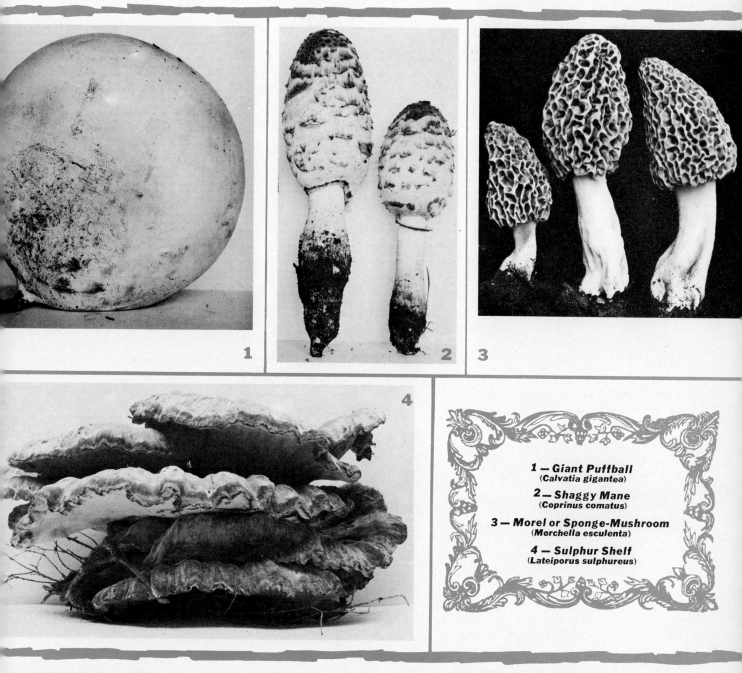

1 — **Giant Puffball**
(Calvatia gigantea)

2 — **Shaggy Mane**
(Coprinus comatus)

3 — **Morel or Sponge-Mushroom**
(Morchella esculenta)

4 — **Sulphur Shelf**
(Lateiporus sulphureus)

dawn may be gone by noon. But the plant is not dead; it lives on unseen to bring up its fruit another season.

Requiring neither sunlight nor warmth, mushrooms can be grown in the basement at home rather easily. Commercially, more than 165 million pounds are raised in special houses or in caves. While the French farm more than twenty varieties, the American industry, centering in Kennett Square, Pennsylvania, cultivates a single variety, *Agaricus campestris.* This is the one sold in food stores, and the average American has never tasted any other. Those who would vary the mushroom diet pick wild ones whose flavor defies categorization. It can be bland or peppery, nutty or sweet, resemble veal cutlet, breast of chicken, steak, sweetbreads, kidneys, or oysters. The aroma runs the gamut from delightful to a stink like rotten fish.

In the dark hours before dawn a group of newspaper reporters and printers clamber onto a chartered bus and journey to fields and woods to gather mushrooms. They must be on their regular jobs by seven A.M., but not one would forego his prework labor. The city where this occurs is Prague, Czechoslovakia, but the wild enthusiasm is as typical of mushroom hunters in Chicago, Paris, Tokyo, or New York.

Although about fifty of the species growing wild in America are edible, experts urge the amateur to concentrate on those few that are easy to identify. These have been dubbed "The Foolproof Four" by one of the country's great mushroom experts, Clyde M. Christensen. First is the peerless *morel.* Then comes the *shaggymane,* never served in restaurants, even in Europe, because it has just a few hours of perfection before the cap dissolves into an unsavory inky fluid. Resembling white shako hats with brownish tufts sticking out, most shaggymanes are no longer than a child's hand, although a few reach heights of twenty inches. The incomparable flavor is best brought out by steaming for five minutes and then adding a touch of cream or melted butter. The *sulphur shelf* grows in rows of yellow or orange shelves on trees and logs and does not look like something to eat, but its taste is similar to white meat of chicken when fried, stewed, or chopped in croquettes. The *puffball's* name describes it well, as no stem can be seen. It is white, firm, and fleshy and can be of golfball dimensions or, like the one discovered in Minnesota a few years ago, measure two feet in height and weigh forty-five pounds. The imaginative cook can prepare puffball steaks, breaded cutlets, or creamed purée of puffball.

The lure of other species is so strong that many hunters ignore the danger, although danger there is. A single mouthful of certain mushrooms belonging to the *Amanita* family can bring on one of the most agonizing illnesses known to man. Death claims about half of those stricken. Yet the *Amanita* is so delicious that, just before being shaken by the first seizure, one woman asked the cook for the recipe. Most poisonous mushrooms are not so virulent, bringing stomach upsets rather than death. None of the old wives' tales is reliable: nonedible mushrooms, popularly known as toadstools, will not necessarily tarnish silver, turn dark in salt water, or milky in vinegar. As poisonous and edible varieties often look alike, even experts can be fooled. In the wet summer of 1963, one of the best mushroom seasons in recent French history, forty-five experienced mushroom pickers died of poisoning and a far greater number were sickened.

Not all poisonous mushrooms are unpleasant in their effects. One *Amanita* causes intoxication, and not too long ago an Englishman arrested for drunken driving insisted that mushroom, not whisky, was at fault. Others of the *Psilocybe* species, found most often in Mexico and South America, induce a visionary state and have been revered as sacred by Indian tribes for generations. A chemical substance, psilocybin, isolated from them has become the newest of the mind drugs to tantalize psychiatrists and sensation seekers.

The incredible properties and seemingly miraculous birth of mushrooms caused primitive peoples to view them as supernatural. Still today, the more we learn about them, the more we are seized by their strange fascination.

Availability — Mushrooms of *Agaricus campestris,* the species cultivated commercially, are available all year round, but are especially plentiful and at their best during the fall and winter. Fresh mushrooms are sold in bulk. They are also available canned, packed in water with or without butter added, as whole mushrooms, caps, slices, and chopped mushrooms. Mushrooms are available frozen. Dried whole mushrooms, slices, caps, and stems are available.

Purchasing Guide — Fresh mushrooms should be white, with firm caps and beige-colored stems. The fluted formation between cap and stem should be light brown in color. Size of caps ranges between ¾ inch and 3 inches.

Storage — Lay fresh mushrooms on a shallow tray or rack and cover them with a large soft paper towel moistened with water and wrung about half dry. Place the mushrooms in the refrigerator in a way that will allow air to circulate around them; do not put them at the bottom or against anything.

☐ Fresh, refrigerator shelf, raw and covered loosely: 1 week

☐ Fresh, cooked; and canned, opened, refrigerator shelf: 4 to 5 days

☐ Fresh, refrigerator frozen-food compartment, prepared for freezing: 2 to 3 months

☐ Fresh, prepared for freezing; and frozen, freezer: 1 year

☐ Dried or canned, kitchen shelf: 1 year

Caloric Values (for *Agaricus campestris*)

☐ Fresh, 3½ ounces, raw = 28 calories

☐ Canned, 3½ ounces, solids and liquid = 17 calories

Basic Preparation — Before removing stems, wipe mushrooms with damp cloth; or, if necessary, rinse quickly in cold water and wipe dry. Do not ever soak in pan of water. It is not necessary to peel mushrooms. Cut crosswise into slices; or cut into slices, cutting from round side down through the stems; or remove stems and use caps, saving stems for future use. Prepare only as many at a time as you plan to cook. Mushrooms should not stand in the air very long after being prepared. To prevent mushrooms from darkening during cooking, use lemon juice.

☐ **To Sauté Fresh Mushrooms** — Heat a large-surfaced heavy skillet or griddle. Add enough butter to coat surface generously. Keep adding as needed. When very hot but not dark brown, arrange mushrooms, sliced or whole, all over the surface. Test for heat. They should begin to sizzle immediately. Watch carefully. As soon as the edges begin to brown, turn them. Lightly brown on other side. This takes about 4 minutes. Lift out onto soft paper towels. Dust ever so lightly with salt and sometimes a small pinch of ground ginger.

☐ **To Sauté Caps for Cocktails** — Sauté quickly in butter, round side down, for about 3 minutes. Turn and sauté for about 4 minutes longer. The larger mushroom caps may require approximately 10 minutes. Serve hot.

☐ **To Sauté Canned Mushrooms** — Sauté canned mushrooms before adding them to almost all foods. The flavor is pointed up and far more distinctive. Drain liquid from caps, slices, or chopped mushrooms. Turn into sieve to drain. Save liquid for future use in soups, sauces, and casseroles. When drained, place on soft paper towels. If necessary, shift to fresh paper. They will not be perfectly dry, but excess moisture will be absorbed. Now follow the directions given for fresh mushrooms.

When substituting canned mushrooms for cooked fresh ones, contents of one 6-ounce can = 1 pound fresh mushrooms, cooked.

☐ **To Freeze**—Use firm mushrooms and process as soon as possible. They bruise and deteriorate rapidly. Wash and remove base of stem. Freeze small mushrooms whole. Cut large ones in four or more pieces. To prevent browning, add 1 teaspoon citric acid, 1 tablespoon lemon juice, or ½ teaspoon ascorbic acid to every quart of water used in scalding. Scald medium or small whole mushrooms for 4 minutes; cut pieces, 3 minutes. Chill, drain, and package. If mushrooms are very mild in flavor, steam them instead of scalding. Before steaming, put them in water containing 1½ teaspoons citric acid or 1 teaspoon lemon juice to 1 pint water for 5 minutes. Steam whole mushrooms not larger than 1 inch across for 5 minutes; small or quartered, 3½ minutes; and sliced, 3 minutes. Chill at once in cold water, drain, package, and freeze. Or cut washed mushrooms in slices ¼ inch thick and sauté in butter for 2 minutes. Cool quickly, and pack. Pour excess butter over packed mushrooms. Package in meal-size amounts.

☐ **To Dry Fresh Mushrooms**—Do not peel. Mushrooms should be dried quickly. Spread on a board or paper and put in a sunny place on a hot dry day or in a very slow oven with the oven door open until thoroughly dried. Store tightly covered.

☐ **To Prepare Dried Mushrooms**—Wash in lukewarm water, and then let stand in almost boiling water: 30 minutes for whole mushrooms, 20 minutes for slices. Pat dry, and chop or mince. Use as a condiment in soups and sauces.

Mushroom Cook Book

APPETIZERS, RELISHES, AND SOUPS

MUSHROOM CANAPÉS
Drain 1 can (4 ounces) mushroom caps. Marinate overnight in ½ cup tarragon French dressing. Add dash of hot pepper sauce. Roll rich pie pastry to ⅛-inch thickness and cut into thirty-six 2-inch squares. Put a well-drained mushroom in center of each, rounded side up. Fold corners to center. Bake in preheated very hot oven (450°F.) for 12 to 15 minutes.

MUSHROOM COCKTAIL
Wipe fresh mushrooms, about the size of a quarter, with a damp cloth and remove stems. Make mushroom stock by cooking stems in just enough boiling salted water to cover, simmering until liquid is reduced by half. Strain, reserving stock. (Use stems for other dishes.) Grate small amount of onion into stock. Add mushroom caps and simmer in mushroom stock for 10 minutes, or until mushrooms are firm but tender. Drain mushroom caps and chill. Stock may be used to flavor other dishes. Place small footed glasses on small plates. Arrange crisp lettuce leaves around base of each glass; place chilled mushrooms on lettuce. Half-fill glasses with ketchup seasoned with Worcestershire, salt, pepper, and a dash of hot pepper sauce or cayenne. Dip mushrooms into sauce.

MUSHROOM LIVER PÂTÉ
½ pound mushrooms, sliced
1 tablespoon butter or margarine
1 pound liverwurst
1 tablespoon chopped green onions
1 teaspoon soy sauce
1 cup dairy sour cream
¼ cup brandy
Dash of cayenne
1 teaspoon sharp prepared mustard
Parsley
Melba rounds

Sauté mushrooms in butter. Have liverwurst at room temperature; mash; blend with mushrooms and rest of ingredients except last 2. Pile in dish, garnish with parsley, and chill. Serve with Melba rounds. Makes about 4 cups.

PICKLED MUSHROOMS
2 tablespoons salt
4 cups water
1 pound small fresh mushrooms, trimmed but not peeled
1 small onion, chopped
1 garlic clove, chopped
½ cup chopped parsley
1 bay leaf
⅛ teaspoon pepper
¾ teaspoon dried thyme
2 cups dry white wine
2 cups white vinegar
½ cup olive oil
3 tablespoons fresh lemon juice

Add salt to water. Wash mushrooms in this and drain. Combine all remaining ingredients and bring to a boil. Add mushrooms; boil up once. Lower heat and simmer mushrooms, covered, for 10 minutes, or until just tender. Cool and chill for at least 2 hours in own juice. Drain before serving. Makes 4 to 6 servings.

INSALATA DI FUNGHI CRUDI
(Italian Raw-Mushroom Salad)
½ pound fresh mushrooms
¼ teaspoon salt
¼ teaspoon pepper
½ teaspoon dried oregano
3 tablespoons fresh lemon juice
½ cup olive oil

Cut stem ends from mushrooms and reserve for other use. Wash mushrooms, dry with paper towel, and slice evenly. Combine remaining ingredients. Add mushrooms, and toss. Let stand at room temperature for about 2 hours. Makes 3 cups.

Note: You can make it ahead and store it, covered, in the refrigerator.

RUSSIAN PIROSHKI
1 box (13¾ ounces) hot-roll mix
1 pound fresh mushrooms
2 tablespoons butter
2 tablespoons minced fresh parsley
3 green onions with tops, minced
½ teaspoon salt
¼ teaspoon pepper
2 tablespoons all-purpose flour
⅓ cup dairy sour cream
2 hard-cooked eggs, shelled and chopped
1 to 2 egg yolks

Prepare roll mix according to directions. Let rise. In the meantime stem and wash the mushrooms. Wipe dry with paper towel and slice the caps thinly. If fairly large, chop each slice into halves. Sauté in butter for 3 minutes. Add parsley, onions, salt, and pepper. Sauté for 1 minute more. Mix in flour; when smooth, remove from heat. Add sour cream and chopped eggs. Stir well and let cool. Punch down the dough and put on a floured board. Knead several times. Pinch off a small piece of dough about the size of a walnut. Roll back and forth between the palms of the hands to make smooth. Flatten into an oval ⅛ inch thick. Place 1 teaspoon of the mushroom filling in the center. Bring up the edges of the dough to the center, around the filling, and pinch securely together. Turn over and place on a buttered cookie sheet. Repeat for each one.

Cover with a cloth and let rise in a warm place until almost doubled in size and very light. Mix the egg yolk with a little water and brush the rolls with it. Bake in preheated hot oven (450°F.) for 15 minutes. Reduce heat to moderate (350°F.) and cook for 10 minutes longer. Serve warm. Or cool and place in plastic bags in the freezer. When ready to use, brush with melted butter or margarine and warm in preheated moderate oven (350°F.) for 20 minutes. Makes about 40.

CREAM-OF-MUSHROOM SOUP

1 pound fresh mushrooms
1 medium onion, minced
¼ cup butter or margarine
2 tablespoons all-purpose flour
6 cups milk
1 bay leaf
4 parsley sprigs
1 whole clove
Salt and pepper
Dash each of cayenne and mace
½ cup heavy cream
2 egg yolks

Wash and trim mushrooms. Chop coarsely, then force through food chopper. In top part of double boiler over direct heat, cook mushrooms and onion in the butter. Blend in flour. Scald milk with bay leaf, parsley, and clove. Strain into first mixture. Put over boiling water and cook, stirring constantly, until thickened. Force mixture through a sieve and put back in double boiler. Season with salt and pepper; add cayenne and mace. Stir in cream beaten with egg yolks and heat well, stirring. Makes 4 to 6 servings.

SWISS MUSHROOM CONSOMMÉ

½ pound mushrooms, finely chopped
6 cups hot consommé
1 cup dry sherry
Pepper

Simmer mushrooms in consommé until just tender. Just before serving, stir in sherry and add pepper to taste. Makes 6 servings.

MAIN DISHES

FRICASSEE OF MUSHROOMS AND OYSTERS, OR OYSTERS AND CLAMS

2 tablespoons butter or margarine
2 tablespoons finely chopped onion
2 tablespoons sliced celery
3 tablespoons all-purpose flour
½ cup chicken bouillon and ½ cup oyster liquid or 1 cup of either
Salt and pepper to taste
1 cup broiled fresh mushroom caps
½ cup hot heavy cream
2 cups oysters or 1 cup oysters and 1 cup clams
½ teaspoon Worcestershire
1 tablespoon sliced pimiento

Melt butter; cook onion and celery in it until soft. Add flour; blend. Add bouillon. Season with salt and pepper. Add mushrooms and cream, and cook for a moment. Simmer oysters in their liquid only until edges curl; drain; reheat in sauce. Add Worcestershire and pimiento. Makes 4 servings.

MUSHROOMS WITH CRABMEAT

16 large mushroom caps
⅓ cup melted butter or margarine
1½ cups crabmeat, flaked

2 eggs
3 tablespoons mayonnaise
¼ cup minced green onions
2 teaspoons fresh lemon juice
½ cup soft bread crumbs
2 tablespoons butter

Dip washed mushroom caps into melted butter. Place them, cap side down, in a buttered baking dish. Combine crabmeat, eggs, mayonnaise, green onions, lemon juice, and half of bread crumbs. Fill mushroom caps with mixture. Sprinkle with remaining bread crumbs and dot with butter. Bake in preheated moderate oven (375°F.) for 15 minutes. Makes 4 servings as a main-dish casserole or, as an appetizer, it will make 8 servings.

CRUSTED MUSHROOMS AND OYSTERS

Make 8 to 10 small biscuit-shape rolls, using packaged yeast-roll mix. Set rolls 2 inches apart in pan. Bake in preheated moderate oven (375°F.) for about 15 minutes, or until a good crust is formed. When cold, cut slice from top; remove soft crumbs. Brush outside of "shell" with egg white and dip into finely chopped parsley or watercress. Fill with oysters and mushrooms prepared as follows: Wash, drain, and pick over 2 cups (1 pint) oysters. Heat in saucepan until gills curl. Heat one 4-ounce can of mushrooms in their own juice, or cook same amount of fresh mushrooms, which have been wiped with a damp cloth, in a little cream until tender.

Melt 3 tablespoons butter or margarine, blend in 3 tablespoons all-purpose flour, and add 2½ cups light cream. Season with scant teaspoon salt, ¼ teaspoon white pepper, ¼ teaspoon paprika, and 2 tablespoons sliced pimiento. Add oysters and mushrooms; heat piping hot. Fill rolls with mixture. Garnish each plate with celery curls and olives. A salad of oranges, grapefruit, Malaga and Tokay grapes is delicious with this. Makes 4 servings.

MUSHROOMS WITH BAKED CRAB IN SHELLS

6 tablespoons butter or margarine
3 tablespoons all-purpose flour
2 cups milk or light cream
½ teaspoon salt
1 teaspoon fresh lemon juice
Grated rind of 1 lemon
Dash of hot pepper sauce
1 tablespoon minced pimiento
1 tablespoon minced scallions or 2 teaspoons minced onion
1 pound fresh mushrooms, sliced
1 pound fresh crabmeat or 2 cans (6½ ounces each) crabmeat
Bread crumbs and butter

Melt ¼ cup of the butter and stir in flour. Cook, stirring constantly, until golden. Gradually add milk. Cook, stirring constantly, until sauce is thickened and smooth. Add salt, lemon juice, lemon rind, hot pepper sauce, pimiento, and

scallions. Cook mushrooms in remaining butter until golden. Add to sauce. Pile crabmeat into buttered baking shells. Top with mushroom sauce. Sprinkle with bread crumbs and dot with butter. Bake in preheated moderate oven (350°F.) for 15 minutes, or until golden-brown. Makes 6 servings.

LOBSTER AND MUSHROOMS PARMESAN

2 tablespoons butter or margarine
2 tablespoons all-purpose flour
¼ teaspoon powdered mustard
½ cup water
1 can condensed cream-of-mushroom soup
2 cans (6 ounces each) lobster
¼ cup grated Parmesan cheese
Paprika

Melt butter and blend in flour and mustard. Add water and soup. Cook, stirring, until thickened. Remove membranes from lobster and add to sauce. Fill 4 shells or individual baking dishes with mixture. Sprinkle with cheese and paprika. Broil slowly until golden brown. Makes 4 servings.

COD WITH MUSHROOM-AND-WINE SAUCE

2 cans (3 ounces each) sliced mushrooms
¼ cup butter or margarine
2 pounds partially thawed frozen cod fillets
Salt and pepper
All-purpose flour
½ cup white wine

Drain mushrooms, reserving liquid. Cook mushrooms in skillet in 2 tablespoons butter until brown; remove from skillet. Cut fish into 8 pieces; roll in seasoned flour and fry in skillet with remaining butter until brown on both sides. Remove fish to heated platter. Put mushrooms back in skillet; add mushroom liquid and wine. Heat; pour over fish. Makes 4 to 6 servings.

BAKED FISH FILLETS IN MUSHROOM-CHEESE SAUCE

1 pound frozen fish fillets
Salt
1 can (10½ ounces) cream-of-mushroom soup
1 cup grated sharp Cheddar cheese
¼ cup sherry
⅛ teaspoon pepper
Paprika

Cut fish into serving pieces and arrange in shallow baking dish. Sprinkle lightly with salt. Mix remaining ingredients except paprika. Spread on fish. Sprinkle with paprika. Bake in preheated moderate oven (375°F.) for about 25 minutes. Makes 3 servings.

LIVER AND MUSHROOMS

1 pound cooked chicken or lamb liver (broiled, fried, or braised) cut into pieces
1 cup broiled fresh mushrooms
1 cup brown sauce (gravy from cooking the liver is good, thickened and well seasoned)

Pickled Mushrooms

Champignons Farcis

Neapolitan Pork Chops with Mushrooms

2 tablespoons fresh orange juice
1 teaspoon fresh lemon juice

Combine ingredients. Heat thoroughly. Serve with baked potatoes or on toast. Makes 3 to 4 servings.

Note: Calf's or beef liver—especially young beef—is excellent; even pork liver may be used.

CHINESE BEEF WITH MUSHROOMS
2 tablespoons minced onion or 4 green onions, sliced
3 tablespoons cooking oil
1½ pounds lean beef, cut into ¼-inch slivers
2 tablespoons soy sauce
2 cans (4 ounces each) sliced mushrooms, drained, or ½ pound fresh mushrooms, sliced thin

Sauté onion in hot oil until soft. Add beef. Sauté for 3 minutes, stirring constantly. Push meat to one side of skillet; stir in soy sauce. Add mushrooms and sauté in pan juices until tender. Mix with meat. Cook, covered, over moderate heat for 3 minutes longer. Makes 4 servings.

NEAPOLITAN PORK CHOPS WITH MUSHROOMS
3 tablespoons olive oil
1 garlic clove, minced
6 pork chops, trimmed of excess fat
Salt and pepper to taste
2 tablespoons tomato paste
½ cup dry white wine
1 pound mushrooms, sliced

Heat olive oil in heavy skillet and brown garlic and pork chops in it on all sides. Pour off excess fat. Season chops with salt and pepper. Add tomato paste, wine, and mushrooms. Simmer, covered, for 40 minutes to 1 hour, depending on thickness of chops. Stir occasionally and add a little water if necessary. Makes 4 to 6 servings.

MUSHROOM-STUFFED PORK CHOPS
½ pound mushrooms
½ medium green pepper
1 medium onion
2 tablespoons butter or margarine
½ teaspoon salt
⅛ teaspoon pepper
6 double center-cut loin pork chops (about 3 pounds)
Salt and pepper

Chop mushrooms, green pepper, and onion. Sauté in butter in skillet for 5 minutes, or until lightly browned. Add salt and pepper. Make a slit in pork chops almost to the bone. Sprinkle inside and out with salt and pepper. Fill chops with mushroom mixture. Put in flat baking dish or roasting pan and add ½ cup water. Bake, uncovered, in preheated moderate oven (350°F.) for 1½ hours, or until done. Serve garnished with parsley. Makes 6 servings.

ORIENTAL PORK WITH MUSHROOMS
1 pound boned lean pork
3 tablespoons margarine
Salt and pepper to taste

1 onion, chopped
2 or 3 celery stalks, sliced
1 pound fresh mushrooms, sliced
Pinch each of ground ginger and nutmeg
2 tablespoons each of sherry and soy sauce
Hot cooked rice

Cut pork into thin strips. Brown in margarine. Season with salt and pepper. Add onion, celery, mushrooms, ginger, and nutmeg. Simmer, covered, for 20 minutes. Add sherry and soy sauce. Cover; simmer for 10 minutes. Serve on hot cooked rice. Makes 4 servings.

BROILED MUSHROOMS WITH BACON
Wipe large fresh mushrooms with damp cloth and remove stems. Put 1 drop of onion juice in each cap and wrap in ½ slice of bacon, fastening with toothpick. Put bacon-wrapped mushrooms on rack and broil until mushrooms are tender and bacon is crisp. Turn twice during broiling. Serve on buttered toast.

HOLLYHOCK-HOUSE MUSHROOMS AND CHICKEN, BARRISTER STYLE
¼ cup butter or margarine
1 tablespoon cornstarch
2 tablespoons flour
1½ cups chicken bouillon
1 cup light cream
½ cup heavy cream
Salt and pepper to taste
2 cups cold boiled chicken, cut into generous blocks or diced
1 cup broiled fresh mushrooms
½ cup sliced pimientos
1 truffle (optional)
¼ cup thinly sliced celery, cooked for 10 minutes
2 egg yolks, slightly beaten

Melt butter in saucepan. Mix cornstarch and flour; add to butter; stir until blended. Add chicken bouillon and cream. Add seasonings and heat to boiling point, stirring constantly. Add chicken, mushrooms, pimientos, a shredded truffle if desired, and celery. Heat to boiling. Remove from heat; add egg yolks, stirring constantly. Makes 4 to 6 servings.

EGGS RIALTO
½ pound fresh mushrooms
¼ cup butter or margarine
6 eggs
¼ cup heavy cream
Salt and pepper to taste
1 teaspoon Worcestershire
1 tablespoon chopped parsley
3 tablespoons grated Parmesan cheese
1 tablespoon sherry
Toast

Trim mushrooms and slice. Melt butter and sauté mushrooms in it until golden-brown. Beat eggs with heavy cream, salt and pepper, and Worcestershire. Stir in parsley, cheese, and sherry. Pour egg mixture over mushrooms. Scramble lightly. Serve spooned over toast. Makes 3 or 4 servings.

MUSHROOM-BARLEY CASSEROLE
½ cup minced onion
5 tablespoons butter or margarine
1 cup uncooked medium pearl barley
3 cups boiling chicken or beef consommé
½ pound mushrooms, sliced
1 teaspoon salt
¼ teaspoon freshly ground pepper
Garlic salt to taste

Sauté onion in 3 tablespoons of butter until soft, but not brown. Stir in barley; cook over medium heat for 3 to 5 minutes, or until barley begins to brown. Stir constantly. Add boiling consommé very slowly (barley will sizzle). Cook, covered, over lowest possible heat until barley has absorbed the liquid and is tender, 45 minutes to 1 hour, depending on the quality of the barley. Fifteen minutes before barley is cooked, sauté mushrooms in remaining butter until barely tender. Season with salt, pepper, and garlic salt; add to barley. Cook until barley is done. Makes 4 to 6 servings.

MUSHROOM SANDWICHES
Cook ½ pound mushrooms, chopped, in 1 tablespoon butter. Blend in 1 tablespoon flour, add ⅓ cup milk or bouillon, and cook until thickened. Add ½ teaspoon Worcestershire, dash of cayenne, and salt to taste. Spread on buttered bread or toast. Makes 4 sandwiches.

BAKED MUSHROOMS IN CREAM
For each dozen large fresh mushrooms:
12 drops onion juice
½ teaspoon salt
¼ teaspoon pepper
1 tablespoon butter
½ cup light cream
Toast, or hamburger patties

Wipe mushrooms with damp cloth; remove stems, reserving for soup or sauce. Put 1 drop of onion juice in each cap; arrange mushrooms, cap side down, in glass baking dish. Add seasonings. Dot with butter; pour cream over. Cover and cook in preheated hot oven (400°F.) for 15 minutes, or until mushrooms are tender. Serve on buttered toast or over broiled hamburger.

GREEN BEAN, CASHEW, AND MUSHROOM CASSEROLE
1 pound green beans, cut into 1-inch pieces
¼ cup chopped cashew nuts
¼ cup butter or margarine
½ pound mushrooms, sliced
3 tablespoons flour
1 teaspoon seasoned salt
¼ teaspoon salt
¼ teaspoon white pepper
1½ cups milk
1 tablespoon instant minced onion
3 tablespoons grated Parmesan cheese

Cook beans in 1 inch of boiling salted water; drain. Sauté nuts in butter for 5 minutes; remove nuts. Add mushrooms to butter and cook until lightly browned. Blend in flour and seasonings. Add milk and cook, stirring, until thickened. Add beans, half of nuts, and the onion. Mix well and pour into shallow casserole. Sprinkle with remaining nuts and the cheese. Bake in preheated moderate oven (350°F.) for about 20 minutes. Makes 6 servings.

MAIN-DISH ACCOMPANIMENTS

SAUTÉED MUSHROOMS
2 pounds mushrooms, caps only
¼ cup butter or margarine
½ teaspoon salt
¼ teaspoon pepper
Juice of 1 lemon

Place mushrooms evenly, cap side down, in skillet with hot butter. Season with salt and pepper. Cook until brown. Turn mushrooms and cook until liquid has evaporated and only butter remains in skillet. Stir lemon juice into mushrooms. Serve immediately, pouring the butter in the skillet over mushrooms. Makes 4 to 6 servings.

Note: For a luncheon dish, serve on hot toast.

CHAMPIGNONS FARCIS
(Stuffed Mushrooms, French Style)
Allow 2 large mushrooms per serving. The following filling will stuff 12 mushrooms. Remove mushroom stems and chop. Cook 3 slices bacon until crisp; remove bacon and pour off fat, leaving about 2 tablespoons. Add mushroom stems, 1 onion, chopped fine, and ¼ cup chopped green pepper. Cook until tender. Add 1 cup soft stale bread crumbs, crumbled bacon, 2 tablespoons chopped parsley, ½ teaspoon seasoned salt, a little chicken stock to moisten, and season with salt and pepper. Stuff mushroom caps. Place in shallow baking pan with small amount of water (water should be about ¼ inch deep). Bake in preheated slow oven (325°F.) for about 25 minutes.

STUFFED MUSHROOMS, ITALIAN STYLE
16 large fresh mushrooms
6 ounces sweet Italian sausage
1 garlic clove, minced
3 tablespoons olive oil
2 tablespoons minced parsley
¼ cup grated Parmesan cheese
¼ cup water

Wash mushrooms. Remove stems and chop fine. Remove casing from sausage and put meat in skillet with chopped stems, garlic, and 1 tablespoon oil. Cook, breaking up meat with fork, until lightly browned. Add 1 tablespoon oil, the parsley, and cheese. Fill mushroom cavities with the mixture, rounding up tops, and put in shallow baking pan. Put remaining oil and the water in bottom of pan. Bake in preheated moderate oven (350°F.)

for about 20 minutes. Makes 4 servings.

MUSHROOMS, POLISH STYLE
¾ pound mushrooms, thinly sliced
1 tablespoon fresh lemon juice
1 tablespoon minced onion
¼ cup butter or margarine
¼ teaspoon salt
⅛ teaspoon pepper
1 tablespoon flour
2 tablespoons grated Parmesan cheese
1 cup heavy cream
2 egg yolks, slightly beaten
2 tablespoons soft bread crumbs

Sprinkle mushrooms with lemon juice. Simmer, tightly covered, with onion and 3 tablespoons of the butter. Season with salt and pepper; stir in flour and cheese. Cook for about 3 minutes. Place in buttered individual baking dishes. Beat together cream and egg yolks. Pour over mushrooms. Sprinkle with bread crumbs and dot with remaining butter. Bake in preheated moderate oven (375°F.) for about 15 minutes. Makes 6 servings.

MUSHROOMS STEWED IN WINE
2 pounds mushrooms, thinly sliced
⅓ cup olive oil
2 tablespoons chopped chives or 1 tablespoon minced onion
2 teaspoons fennel seeds
⅓ cup chopped parsley
1 teaspoon salt
¼ teaspoon white pepper
¾ cup dry white wine

Sauté mushrooms in hot olive oil with chives, fennel seeds, and parsley for 5 minutes. Season with salt and pepper. Add wine. Cook, covered, over low heat for 5 minutes. Makes 4 to 6 servings.

MUSHROOMS STUFFED WITH PURÉE OF GREEN PEAS
2 packages (10 ounces each) frozen green peas
½ teaspoon crumbled dried basil or thyme
¼ cup minced onion
½ cup plus 1 tablespoon melted butter or margarine
½ teaspoon salt
¼ teaspoon pepper
12 large mushroom caps
½ cup grated Swiss cheese

Cook peas according to package directions, adding basil. Drain; purée in electric blender or force through a fine sieve. Sauté onion in 1 tablespoon butter until soft. Combine peas and onion and season with salt and pepper. Dip mushroom caps into ½ cup melted butter and place, cap side down, in buttered baking dish. Add remaining melted butter to peas and onion mixture. Stuff mushroom caps. Sprinkle with grated cheese and bake in preheated hot oven (400°F.) for 10 to 15 minutes, or until cheese is bubbly. Makes 4 to 6 servings.

MUSHROOM POTATO PIE
3 cups rich mashed potatoes
1½ cups sliced mushrooms
¼ cup minced onion

2 tablespoons butter or margarine
1 teaspoon fresh lemon juice
¼ teaspoon salt
⅛ teaspoon pepper
½ cup dairy sour cream

Place half of mashed potatoes in a layer in a well-buttered 9-inch pie pan. Sauté mushrooms and onion in hot butter. Stir in lemon juice, salt, and pepper. Top potatoes with mushrooms and sour cream. Cover with remaining potatoes. Bake in preheated moderate oven (350°F.) for about 35 minutes. To serve, cut into wedges. Makes 6 servings.

POTATOES AND MUSHROOMS WITH CHEESE
4 to 5 medium potatoes, peeled and thinly sliced
¼ teaspoon each of salt and pepper
1 garlic clove, thinly sliced
½ cup butter or margarine
1½ pounds mushrooms
1 cup grated Swiss cheese
Small bunch of parsley, chopped
1 small onion, chopped fine
2 cups heavy cream

Season potatoes with salt and pepper. Rub a baking dish with garlic and butter it well. Put in alternately a layer of potatoes and a layer of mushrooms until all are used, ending with a layer of potatoes. Sprinkle over each layer some of the cheese, parsley, and onion. Cover top layer of potatoes with cream. Sprinkle on another layer of cheese and some lumps of butter. Bake in preheated moderate oven (375°F.) for 45 minutes, or until potatoes are done (test with knife). Makes 6 to 8 servings.

MUSHROOMS NEWBURG
1 pound fresh mushrooms
3 tablespoons butter or margarine
2 tablespoons sliced celery
1 tablespoon onion juice
⅛ teaspoon paprika
1 tablespoon flour
1 cup hot medium cream
1 tablespoon fresh orange juice
1 tablespoon grated orange rind
1 tablespoon white grape juice or sherry
Salt, pepper, cayenne, ground nutmeg

Wipe mushrooms with damp cloth; remove stems. Melt butter in pan; add mushrooms, celery, onion juice, and paprika. Cover; simmer until mushrooms are tender. Stir in flour. Add cream; cook for a moment more. Add orange juice, rind, and grape juice. Season to taste with salt, pepper, cayenne, and nutmeg. Serve in individual dishes, on toast, or in croustades. Makes 4 servings.

SCALLOPED MUSHROOMS AND TOMATOES
½ pound fresh mushrooms
¾ cup melted butter or margarine
6 tomatoes or 2¼ cups (one 1-pound, 4-ounce can) tomatoes, drained
3 tablespoons all-purpose flour
1 cup tomato juice
1 tablespoon minced onion or 2

Stuffed Mussels

tablespoons minced chives
½ cup each of cracker crumbs and
  bread crumbs

Wipe mushrooms with damp cloth; cut each mushroom into halves. Cook for 10 minutes in 3 tablespoons butter. Slice tomatoes. Arrange alternate layers of tomatoes and mushrooms in glass baking dish. In a saucepan blend 3 tablespoons butter and the flour; add tomato juice. When thick, add onion. Pour over mixture in baking dish. Mix crumbs and toss in remaining butter. Cover mixture with crumbs and bake until crumbs are golden-brown. Makes 4 servings.

CREAMED SPINACH AND MUSHROOMS

  2 pounds spinach
  2 tablespoons butter or margarine
  ¼ pound mushrooms, sliced
  1 tablespoon flour
    Dash of ground nutmeg
    Salt and pepper
  ¼ cup milk or light cream

Wash spinach and cook, without adding water, until tender; drain. Chop. Melt butter; add mushrooms and cook until tender, about 4 minutes. Blend in flour, nutmeg, and salt and pepper to taste. Add milk and cook until thickened, stirring. Add spinach and heat well. Makes 4 to 6 servings.

MUSKELLUNGE or MUSKY—A freshwater fish of the pike family which is found in the Great Lakes, Lake Champlain, the upper Mississippi, the lakes of Canada, and the St. Lawrence River. The fish is greenish brown in color, spotted with black. In weight it can vary from seven to forty pounds and on occasion can reach sixty to eighty pounds. Muskies are great game fish, and sportsmen admire them for their fighting agility. They are not generally available in fish markets.

The flesh of the musky is lean, white, firm, and delicious. It can be broiled, baked, or panfried.

Caloric Value

☐ 3½ ounces, raw = 109 calories

MUSKELLUNGE WITH CRABMEAT AND LOBSTER DRESSING

    One 15-pound muskellunge
  3 cups soft bread crumbs
  ¾ cup chopped parsley
  ½ cup diced green pepper
  1 pimiento, diced
  ¾ cup chopped green onions
    One 6-ounce can lobster
    One 6-ounce can crabmeat
  1 teaspoon salt
    Freshly ground pepper
  ⅛ teaspoon cayenne
  1 teaspoon grated lemon rind
  2 eggs, well beaten
  ½ cup melted butter or margarine
  ½ cup dry white wine
    Garnishes: maraschino cherries, raw
      carrot, watercress, lemon wedges
    Butter Sauce

Wash and clean muskellunge. Leave on head and tail, but remove the eyes. Combine next 12 ingredients and stuff fish. If no large pan is available, shape a pan big enough out of double-thickness heavy-duty foil and place on a cookie sheet. Bake in preheated moderate oven (350° F.) for 1½ hours; baste every 10 minutes with a mixture of melted butter and wine. Place fish on a heated serving platter; place cherries in eye sockets and a carrot in the mouth. Garnish platter with crisp watercress and lemon wedges. Serve with Butter Sauce. Makes 20 servings.

Butter Sauce
In a double boiler melt 1½ cups butter or margarine; add 1½ cups finely minced parsley.

MUSSEL—A bivalve mollusk, world-wide in distribution, which includes both salt-water and fresh-water varieties. It is the salt-water mussel, found in great profusion on both the Atlantic and Pacific coasts, which is generally eaten.

Mussels cling by a dark, hairy beard to rocks, wharves, and mud. It is best to pick them at low tide because the fresh, live ones are exposed at that time. When a mussel is pulled from its home, there should be some jerking and resistance and some of the beard should be visible as a sign that the mussel is still alive.

The shell of a mussel is so thin that there is considerably more food in a pound of them than in the same amount of oysters or clams. They can be eaten raw but are tougher than oysters and clams and are more palatable when cooked. Their meat is yellow with a sweet and delicate flavor. Mussels may be steamed, fried, creamed, stuffed, curried, or used in sauces, soups, and salads.

Occasionally, on the West Coast only and not oftener than every few years, there is a poisonous organism which affects mussels and clams. It is called the "red tide" because it turns the shellfish bright red. They should not be eaten during this period, and the invasion is usually well publicized in the newspapers. It lasts for a period of several months. Fish or other shellfish are not affected.

Availability and Purchasing Guide—Available year round, sold alive in the shells, which should be tightly closed. Mussel meats are also available canned.

Storage—Plan to use mussels as soon as possible after purchase. They are very perishable.
- [ ] Refrigerator shelf: 1 to 2 days

Nutritive Food Values—High in protein, no fat, fair amounts of calcium and iron.
- [ ] Fresh, 3½ ounces, shelled and raw = about 80 calories

- [ ] Canned, 3½ ounces, drained = 114 calories

Basic Preparation—Scrub mussels well and rinse in water several times to remove sand and grit. Remove beard.
- [ ] **To Steam**—Place cleaned mussels in a kettle with ½ cup boiling water. Cover and steam for about 5 minutes, or until shells open. Remove top half of shells and serve with melted butter and fresh lemon juice.

STUFFED MUSSELS
- 16 large mussels
- 2 medium onions, minced
- ¼ cup olive oil
- ½ cup uncooked rice
- 1 cup hot water
- 2 tablespoons pine nuts
- 2 tablespoons dried currants or finely chopped seedless raisins
- 1 tablespoon chopped parsley
- ½ teaspoon salt
- ¼ teaspoon pepper
- Fresh lemon juice

Scrape mussel shells thoroughly and wash. Pry shells open without separating. Remove black part of the mussel and the beard. Rinse well. Soak mussels in cold water while making the stuffing. Cook onions in hot olive oil until soft and golden. Stir in rice and mix well. Cook over medium heat for 3 minutes, or until rice is yellow and opaque. Add hot water, pine nuts, currants, parsley, salt, and pepper. Cover tightly and cook for 15 minutes, or until rice is tender and liquid is absorbed. Cool. Stuff each mussel with some rice mixture. Tie shut with string. Place mussels in layers in deep saucepan. Cover with boiling water. Put a plate that fits into the saucepan directly over mussels to keep them down. If necessary, weight plate with can or other heavy object. Cook over lowest possible heat for 20 minutes. Drain, but do not disturb mussels until cooled. Remove strings. Chill, and serve with lemon juice. Makes 3 or 4 servings as an appetizer.
Note: This may also be used as a stuffing for peppers, squash, tomatoes, or chicken.

MUSSELS MARINIÈRE
- 6 tablespoons butter or margarine
- 1 garlic clove, minced
- 1 medium onion, chopped
- 1 bay leaf
- 40 fresh mussels, scrubbed and debearded
- Salt and pepper to taste
- ¾ cup dry white wine
- ¼ cup all-purpose flour
- ½ cup heavy cream
- 2 egg yolks
- ¼ cup chopped parsley

Heat 3 tablespoons butter in deep kettle. Cook garlic and onion in it for 2 minutes. Add bay leaf and mussels and sprinkle with salt and pepper. Add wine. Simmer, covered, over low heat for about 10 minutes, or until shells open. Remove mus-

sels. Remove and discard top shells, but leave mussels in bottom shells. Put mussels in soup plates. Strain liquid in saucepan and bring to a boil. Knead remaining butter with flour. Make into pellets the size of a filbert. Stir pellets into liquid and cook, stirring constantly, until sauce is thickened and smooth. Beat heavy cream with egg yolks. Remove sauce from heat and stir in egg mixture. Return to heat. Heat through without boiling. Pour sauce over mussels. Sprinkle with parsley. Serve with a separate plate for discarded mussel shells. Makes 4 to 6 servings.

BELGIAN MUSSELS MARINIÈRE
- 10 quarts mussels, in the shell
- 3 celery stalks, diced
- 2 medium onions, sliced
- ¼ cup chopped parsley
- 1 garlic clove
- 1 large lemon, sliced
- ⅔ cup water

Scrub mussels. Wash in lukewarm water, changing water 3 times. Put celery, onions, parsley, garlic, lemon, and water in a deep kettle. Cook, covered, for 10 minutes, or until vegetables are tender. Add mussels. Cover kettle and steam for 15 minutes, or until all mussels are open. Shake kettle occasionally to prevent sticking. Discard all unopened mussels. Serve in the broth with a side dish of French-fried potatoes. Makes 4 to 6 servings.

CURRIED MUSSELS
- 4 dozen mussels in shells
- 1 teaspoon salt
- ¼ cup butter or margarine
- 1 onion, minced
- Few parsley sprigs, chopped
- 1 celery stalk, finely diced
- ½ cup dry sauterne
- ⅛ teaspoon powdered thyme
- 1 teaspoon curry powder
- ¼ cup dairy sour cream
- Toast triangles

Scrub mussels well and rinse under running water. (If time permits, soak mussels for 2 hours in large kettle filled with water. Discard any mussels that float.) Put 1 inch of water in large kettle. Add salt and mussels, cover, and steam for 3 minutes, or until shells begin to open. Remove and drain, reserving broth. Take mussels from shells and remove beards. Strain broth through sieve. Melt butter; add onion, parsley, and celery. Cook for 2 or 3 minutes, and add wine and thyme. Blend curry powder with ¼ cup broth. Add to mixture in skillet and simmer for 5 minutes. Add mussels, and heat. Stir in sour cream and serve hot on toast triangles. Makes 4 servings.

MUSSEL SALAD
Prepare mussels as in Curried Mussels above. Chill. Marinate for 1 to 2 hours in well-seasoned French dressing. Serve on shredded lettuce with mayonnaise, watercress, capers, and a sprinkling of paprika.

MUSTARD—Any of several herbs cultivated for its pungent seeds and/or leaves.
The seeds are used to make the various
forms of mustard seasonings, the leaves
are used as a vegetable and known as
mustard greens. The mustard plant belongs to the large *Brassica* group, a family which includes many well known
vegetables: broccoli, Brussels sprouts,
Chinese cabbage, collards, kale, kohlrabi,
red cabbage, rutabaga, and turnips.

The word "mustard" is derived from
the old French *mostarde* or *moustard,*
which meant a condiment made from
mustard seed and must, the juice of
grapes or other fruit before and during
fermentation. The French acquired the
art of making mustard from the Romans
who invaded Gaul in the 1st century B.C.
The Romans and Greeks used mustard in
cooking much as we do today.

Mustard has had a long culinary history, and a medical one as well. Pliny the
Elder, the 1st-century A.D. Roman writer,
reported it to be effective in curing hys-
terical females, those who swoon from
epilepsy or lethargy, and persons who
suffer "all deep-seated pains in any part
of the body." The later Middle Ages
prized mustard as a cold cure. Even today
mustard leaves, mustard baths, mustard
poultices, and mustard tisanes are often
used to relieve chest congestion and
break up colds.

One of the most enthusiastic supporters
of the use of mustard was John Evelyn, a
17th-century Englishman who wrote a
treatise on "Sallets (salads)." He claimed
that mustard, both the leaf and seed, "is
of incomparable effect to quicken and
revive the Spirits; strengthening the Memory, expelling heaviness, preventing the
Vertiginous Palsie." In short, so "necessary an Ingredient to all cold and raw

Salleting, that it is very rarely, if at all,
to be left out."

MUSTARD GREENS

The mustard plant species most commonly used for mustard greens is *Brassica
juncea,* known as Leaf, Indian, or Chinese
mustard. The leaves are of many sizes
and shapes. Some well known varieties
include Elephant Ear, with large plain
leaves, and Fordhook Fancy and Southern Curled, curly-leafed varieties. The
leaves, which have a peppery flavor, are
boiled as a potherb or used raw, chopped
and added to green salads.

Availability and Purchasing Guide—
Peak months are December through February, at which time mustard greens are
widely available. In some areas they are
available year round. Look for fresh,
young, crisp leaves with a good green
color.

Mustard greens are also available frozen
and, in limited quantities, canned.

Storage—Wash and trim. Cover or wrap
in moisture-proof paper and store in refrigerator.

☐ Fresh, refrigerator shelf: 3 to 8 days
☐ Refrigerator frozen-food compartment, prepared for freezing: 2 to 3
   months
☐ Freezer, prepared for freezing: 1 year

Nutritive Food Values—Excellent source
of vitamin A, thiamine, riboflavin, and
ascorbic acid.

☐ 3½ ounces, raw = 31 calories
☐ 3½ ounces, cooked and drained =
   23 calories

Basic Preparation—Cut off roots; remove
imperfect leaves. Wash well by lifting in
and out of water about 3 times. Cook,
covered, in small amount of boiling salted
water. A piece of salt pork or bacon may
be added during cooking. Cook until
tender, for 15 to 30 minutes. Drain; cut
coarsely with scissors. Season with salt
and pepper. If pork or bacon has not
been used, add butter.

☐ **To Freeze**—Wash thoroughly and trim,
removing tough stems and leaves. Blanch
in boiling water for 2 minutes. Chill in
cold water for 5 minutes. Drain and pack
into containers, leaving ½-inch headspace. Cover.

MUSTARD SEED

Most of the mustard seed used for making the various mustard seasonings come
from *Brassica nigra,* the black mustard
plant, and *B. hirta* or *alba,* the white
mustard plant. Black mustard is a tall
annual (up to four feet) with yellowish-
green smooth leaves and bright-yellow
flowers. White mustard is a smaller annual, growing to about eighteen inches,
with tender edible green leaves. The seeds
of the black mustard are smaller and

sharper than those of the white mustard.

Whole seeds are used for pickles and
pickling, in boiling fish and vegetables,
and as a garnish for salads. The powdered mustard is used in preparing meats,
gravies, sauces, creamed fish and vegetables, in cheese and egg dishes, potato
salad, and molasses cookies. Prepared
mustard (powdered mustard to which
vinegar, water, and perhaps other seasonings have been added) is widely used in
cooking and as a table condiment.

Availability and Purchasing Guide—Two
types of mustard seeds are available:
white or yellow seeds and a dark-brown
seed, also called Oriental mustard. Yellow and brown powdered mustard is
available. (The prepared mustard served
in Chinese restaurants is powdered brown
mustard mixed with water.)

A large variety of prepared mustards
are available: the hot, or more highly
seasoned, mustards include those called
Bahamian, Dusseldorf, English, and German; the milder types include the Creole
or Louisiana and most other standard
American types. Dijon mustard, which
originated in Dijon, France, is generally
a mild mustard, but is occasionally prepared in a highly seasoned form, in which
case it is labeled as "extra strong." Also
available are prepared mustards with
horseradish added and herb mustard
sauces.

SPICED MUSTARD GREENS

   2 pounds fresh mustard greens
   ¼ pound salt pork
   ½ cup boiling water
   ½ teaspoon mixed pickling spices
   1 teaspoon sugar
1¾ teaspoons salt
   ¼ teaspoon pepper
   1 tablespoon chopped onion

Wash mustard greens in water 4 or 5
times and slice coarsely. Set aside. Cut
pork into slices ⅛ inch thick. Fry until
about half done in a very large saucepan. Add hot water and greens. Cover
and cook for 35 minutes, or until mustard greens are tender. Tie spices in a
cheesecloth bag and add along with
sugar, salt, pepper, and onion 10 minutes before cooking time is up. Remove
spice bag and serve greens hot with a
small piece of salt pork on each serving.
Makes 6 to 8 servings.

FRESH MUSTARD GREENS
WITH BACON

   2 pounds fresh mustard greens
   ½ cup boiling water
   ½ teaspoon salt
   3 tablespoons bacon fat
   3 strips of crisp bacon, crumbled

Cut off coarse stems of mustard greens,
wash and cut into 2- to 3-inch lengths.
Place in saucepan with water, salt, and
bacon fat. Cover and cook only until
tender, about 30 minutes. Cooking time

depends upon the age of the greens. Remove from heat and toss lightly with crumbled crisp bacon. Serve hot. Makes 6 servings.

MUSTARD SPREAD

1 cup sugar
½ cup all-purpose flour
3 tablespoons powdered mustard
1 tablespoon ground turmeric
2 cups cider vinegar

In top part of double boiler mix dry ingredients; add vinegar and cook over boiling water until thick. Pour into hot sterilized jars; seal. Makes two ½-pint jars.
Note: Serve on hot or cold meats.

MUSTARD BUTTER

Cream ½ cup softened butter. Stir in 1 teaspoon or more prepared mustard or ¼ to ½ teaspoon powdered mustard.
Note: Use for sandwiches, fish, meat, and vegetables.

MUSTARD MAYONNAISE

Stir 2 teaspoons prepared mustard into 1 cup mayonnaise.
Note: Use for sandwiches, fish, seafood, vegetables, and salads.

MUSTARD CREAM SAUCE

Add 2 or more teaspoons prepared mustard to 1 cup white sauce.
Note: Use for fish, seafood, meats, and vegetables.

MUSTARD SAUCE WITH WHIPPED CREAM

1 cooked egg yolk
1 raw egg yolk
2 teaspoons prepared mustard
2 tablespoons white vinegar
Salt and pepper
1 cup heavy cream, whipped

Combine cooked egg yolk, raw egg yolk, mustard, vinegar, and salt and pepper to taste. Blend thoroughly. Fold into whipped cream. Serve immediately. Makes about 2 cups.

Note: Use for fish, seafood, meats, and vegetables.

MUTTON by James A. Beard—Good

mutton is a delight. Unfortunately millions of people have been deprived of the opportunity of enjoying it because the market has been overrun with something only resembling mutton that tastes like no meat known to man and smells even worse. True mutton, such as the best Canadian or the Southdown mutton of England, and a small amount to be found in the United States, is carefully fed mature sheep that has been treated extraordinarily well and, after slaughtering, has been carefully prepared for the market: hung long enough to give it tenderness and excellent flavor. Although good mutton often acquires quite heavy fat, a reliable butcher will always trim it well.

The most traditional and certainly the most famous cut is the great English mutton chop. This, correctly speaking, is a thick chop, two to two-and-a-half inches thick, cut across the double loin. It is often boned and rolled around a kidney. This chop is broiled or roast-broiled to a pink rareness, or to the taste of the eater. Other chops are cut from the loin, sometimes three inches or more thick. A certain restaurant in New York that serves a perfect chop skewers it together and roast-broils it to taste. Salt and pepper are all that is needed.

Leg of mutton, if well hung, is superb when roasted quite rare and served piping hot on very hot plates. Good accompaniments are mashed turnips or rutabagas, crisp browned potatoes, and *ratatouille*. All these complement the flavor and texture of the meat and create a remarkably satisfying blend.

One drinks beer or ale with a good mutton chop or else a fine red wine of the more robust type: a Hermitage from the Rhone Valley or a Barbera from Italy or California. With a roast of mutton, again a fine Hermitage or perhaps a Pomerol, with its earthy quality, from the Bordeaux district would provide the proper balance.

Mutton is oftentimes poached in a court bouillon. When prepared in this fashion it should be done rare and can be served with a rather pungent sauce, a Béarnaise, for instance, or a Provençal sauce made with anchovies, black olives, and garlic.

In France, a famous dish is haricot of mutton, which is braised meat cooked with potatoes and onions until there is a delicious, tender union of flavors and textures. The English have adapted this dish as well, although less successfully.

Mutton, in short, is a great experience. Sidney Smith once immortalized it thus:

Gently stir and blow the fire,
Lay the mutton down to roast;
Dress it quickly, I desire
In the drippings put a toast.
That I hunger may remove—
Mutton is the meat I love.

Availability—Imported from Canada in small quantities and available by special order from specialty butchers.

BROILED MUTTON CHOPS

Have chops very thick and cook exactly as you would steak. Do not overcook if you want them juicy and tender. A 1½-inch chop will cook medium rare in 10 to 15 minutes.

MUTTON STEAK

Have steaks cut 1½ inches thick. Grill, basting with a mixture of garlic butter and red wine, for 8 minutes per side for rare.

HARICOT DE MOUTON
(Mutton Stew)

4 pounds boned shoulder or breast of mutton
2 tablespoons meat drippings
1 teaspoon sugar
Salt and pepper
¼ cup all-purpose flour
6 cups boiling water
1 garlic clove
2 tablespoons tomato paste
2 parsley sprigs
1 thyme sprig
½ bay leaf
2 pounds potatoes (6 medium)
10 small white onions

Cut meat into 1½-inch cubes. Heat drippings and sauté meat cubes with sugar in ovenproof skillet with top or Dutch oven until they are brown on all sides. Season with salt and pepper. Stir in flour. Stir until flour is well browned. Gradually stir in boiling water. Add remaining ingredients except potatoes and onions. Bring to a boil, cover, and simmer for 1 hour. Meantime, peel potatoes and cut into quarters. Place with peeled onions in skillet or Dutch oven. Cover. Bake in preheated moderate oven (350°F.) or simmer on surface for 1 hour longer. Makes 6 to 8 servings.

KARJALANPAISTI
(Karelian Hot Pot)

½ pound boneless lean pork
1 pound boneless beef
1 pound boneless mutton
Water
1 teaspoon salt

Cut meat into fairly small cubes. Put into a casserole or earthenware pot and pour on just enough water to cover. Add salt. Put into preheated hot oven (400°F.) for 30 minutes. Reduce heat to very slow (250°F.) and continue cooking for 5 to 6 hours. This dish is always served from the pot in which it was cooked, with boiled potatoes. Makes 6 servings.

JAMAICAN CURRIED MUTTON

2 pounds boneless mutton
1 teaspoon salt
1 teaspoon pepper
1 onion, minced
3 teaspoons curry powder
2 tablespoons cooking oil
1½ cups water
2 medium potatoes, peeled and diced
Hot cooked rice
Chutney

Wipe meat with a damp paper towel and cut into 1-inch pieces. Season with the salt and pepper, and rub in onion and curry powder. Let stand for 1 hour. Heat oil, add meat, and brown on all sides. Add the water, cover, bring to boil, and simmer until meat is tender, about 1 hour. Add potato and cook, covered, until very soft and mixture is slightly thickened. Serve on hot rice, accompanied by chutney. Makes 6 servings.
Note: Lamb can be substituted for the mutton.

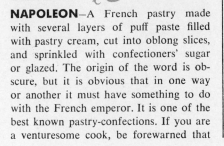

NAPKIN—A fabric or paper square used at the table for wiping lips or fingers. The word napkin came into English from the French, which was derived from the Latin word *mappa*. This word also gave birth to the modern words "map," "napery," and "apron."

The Romans used napkins at their banquets and the custom spread from Rome to Britain and France during the conquests of those two countries. Medieval English directions for eating instruct: "Drye thy mouthe aye wele and fynde (fine). When thou shall drynke (either ale or wyne)."

In the early days of the American colonies only the rich could afford to have fine linen napkins shipped from England and so the colonial housewife often made her own napkins from homespun. This rough material would stand up well under hard usage. But because all washing had to be done by hand, it was necessary not to be too lavish with the presentation of clean napkins.

Napkin rings for many years were common. Each member of the family had a ring, often with his initials on it, which he slipped around his rolled napkin. The same napkin would be used from meal to meal, saving much laundry. Nowadays, although cloth napkins and napkin rings are still in use, paper napkins make it possible for everyone to have a fresh napkin at each meal.

Modern custom dictates that the napkins be folded and placed upon the table with the silver. They should be removed from the table and placed in the lap. Sometimes, for very intricate eating of extra juicy foods like lobster, they are tied around the neck, like a baby's bib.

NAPOLEON—A French pastry made with several layers of puff paste filled with pastry cream, cut into oblong slices, and sprinkled with confectioners' sugar or glazed. The origin of the word is obscure, but it is obvious that in one way or another it must have something to do with the French emperor. It is one of the best known pastry-confections. If you are a venturesome cook, be forewarned that its taste depends on the freshness and lightness of the puff paste and the goodness of the butter that goes into its making. If you have no talent for baking, be of good cheer. Many fine pastry cooks believe that Napoleons are best bought in a bakery or pastry shop.

NAPOLEONS

Prepare Puff Paste (page 1304) and roll ⅛ inch thick. Cut into strips 3 inches wide and 14 inches long. Put on cookie sheets covered with 2 layers of unglazed brown paper; prick with fork. Cover with another cookie sheet to keep flat. Bake in preheated very hot oven (450° F.) for 5 minutes. Reduce heat to moderate (350°F.) and bake for 15 minutes longer. Remove top cookie sheet and bake for 15 minutes longer, or until pastry is dry and brown. When cold, trim off edges. Make 2 piles of 3 strips each, putting well-chilled Vanilla Cream Filling (page 1309) between layers.

EASY NAPOLEONS

1 package (3¼ ounces) vanilla pudding and pie filling mix

1 cup milk
½ package pastry mix, prepared as label directs
½ cup prepared dessert topping mix
¾ cup confectioners' sugar
  Water
1 square (1 ounce) semisweet chocolate

Mix pudding and milk in saucepan. Cook and stir over medium heat until mixture comes to a full boil. Cover surface with wax paper and chill. Meanwhile, roll pastry into a rectangle 14 x 10 inches. Cut 3 equal lengthwise strips, each about 14 x 3¼ inches. Put strips on baking sheet. Prick well with a fork. Bake in preheated hot oven (425°F.) for 12 minutes, or until golden-brown. Beat chilled pudding until light and fluffy and fold in prepared topping. Spread 2 of the pastry strips with pudding mixture. Stack one on top of the other. Mix confectioners' sugar and 1½ tablespoons water. Spread on third strip. Melt chocolate over hot water. Gradually blend in 1 to 1½ teaspoons water until mixture is thin enough to pour. Drizzle from a spoon in lengthwise lines over top, about ½ inch apart. To give a rippled effect, run edge of a knife across lines of chocolate. Put on top of stacked layers. Chill for 2 hours. With quick strokes of a sharp knife, cut into six 2-inch pieces. Makes 6 servings.

NASTURTIUM—An herb noted for its fragrance and beauty in the garden and fragrance and flavor in the kitchen. The word is a combination of the Latin *nasus*, "nose" and *torquere*, "to twist," the nose-twister, since its odor makes the nostrils quiver and twist. This herb came originally from the Peruvian Andes. There are two types: one which grows very tall and the other a low-growing, more abundantly flowering type, *Tropaeolum minus*. Since the flowers of the latter type are so eye-appealing, the many culinary uses for its foliage, seeds, flowers, buds, and pods are almost lost sight of. Everything but the root is edible. The young tender stems and leaves are good in salads, the chopped young leaves are delicious in sandwiches, the blossoms in fruit salads, and minced blossoms can be blended into creamed butter or cheese for use as a spread. The unripe and still green seeds have a peppery taste and can be used as a substitute for capers. A single seed in a cup of tea is delicious.

PICKLED NASTURTIUM SEEDS

6 tablespoons salt
  Water
2 cups (about) small, ripe green nasturtium seeds
3 cups white vinegar
2 bay leaves
1 large whole mace
12 white peppercorns

¼ cup sugar
1 dried hot chili

Dissolve salt in 4 cups water. Soak nasturtium seeds in the mixture for 2 days. Drain and rinse with cold water. Cover with fresh cold water and let stand for 1 day. Drain very well and pack into hot sterilized jars. Boil remaining ingredients together for 10 minutes. Pour over seeds. Cool slightly and seal. Let stand for 3 months before using. These resemble capers and can be substituted for them. Makes about three ½-pint jars.

NEAPOLITAN, À LA NAPOLITAINE

—The word is English, the phrase is French, and the literal meaning is "in the manner of Naples," the Italian city. However, the term has several culinary usages. Its simplest usage is to describe dishes coming from, or popular in, Naples, such as the Neapolitan Antipasto Salad traditionally served there at Christmas time. It consists of cauliflower, anchovies, Italian olives, olive oil, wine vinegar, and slices of eel or shrimp.

In American usage, the word is most often applied to a dish prepared with tomatoes in some form, such as pork chops, Neapolitan; spaghetti, Neapolitan; etc.

Still another usage, most commonly in French cookery, is to describe an ice cream or other dessert, salad, cookie, or other dish which is made in three contrasting layers. The usual ice cream combination is chocolate, vanilla, and strawberry and is popular commercially.

PORK CHOPS AND SPAGHETTI, NEAPOLITAN

1 can (28 ounces) Italian tomatoes
1 can (6 ounces) tomato paste
2 garlic cloves, minced
2 teaspoons salt
¼ teaspoon pepper
½ teaspoon oregano
½ teaspoon sweet basil
¼ teaspoon sage
1 bay leaf
2 cups water
4 lean pork chops, about 1½ pounds
8 ounces fine spaghetti

Put all ingredients except chops and spaghetti in large saucepan. Bring to boil and simmer, uncovered, for 1 hour, stirring occasionally. Trim meat from chops, leaving it in large pieces. Brown on all sides in skillet. Add meat and drippings to sauce, and simmer for 1 hour longer. Cook and drain spaghetti. Put on hot platter and cover with pork and sauce. Makes 4 servings.

NEAPOLITANS

Dark Dough:

1 cup soft butter or margarine
1½ cups firmly packed dark brown sugar

2 eggs
3 cups sifted all-purpose flour
¼ teaspoon salt
1 teaspoon baking soda
½ teaspoon cinnamon
½ teaspoon cloves
1 cup finely chopped nuts
6 ounces (1 package) semisweet chocolate pieces, finely chopped

Light Dough:

½ cup soft butter or margarine
¾ cup granulated sugar
1 egg
1 teaspoon vanilla extract
½ teaspoon almond extract
2 cups sifted all-purpose flour
½ teaspoon salt
¼ teaspoon baking soda
2 tablespoons water
¾ cup finely chopped raisins
12 chopped candied cherries

■ To make dark dough: Cream butter; add sugar and eggs; beat until light. Add sifted dry ingredients, nuts, chocolate; mix well.

■ To make light dough: Cream butter; add sugar, egg, and flavorings; beat until light. Add sifted dry ingredients and remaining ingredients; mix well.

■ To combine: Pack half of dark dough into wax-paper-lined loaf pan (9 x 5 x 3 inches). Add light dough, and pack firmly. Pack in remaining dark dough and chill for at least 24 hours. Turn out; cut into thirds lengthwise. Cut crosswise into ¼-inch slices. Bake in preheated hot oven (400°F.) for about 10 minutes. Makes about 8 dozen.

NEAPOLITAN ICE CREAM

2 cups milk
3 eggs, beaten
¾ cup sugar
⅛ teaspoon salt
1 cup heavy cream, whipped
1 tablespoon vanilla extract
  Orange Ice

Turn refrigerator control to coldest setting. Heat milk in top part of double boiler over boiling water. Mix eggs, sugar, and salt. Gradually stir in hot milk. Return to double boiler and cook over simmering water, stirring constantly, until mixture thickens and coats a metal spoon. Remove from heat and cool. Fold in cream and vanilla. Pour into 2-quart loaf pan (9 x 5 x 3 inches) and freeze until firm. Press Orange Ice firmly and evenly on top of vanilla layer and freeze until firm. To unmold, set pan on tray or serving plate and wrap in a hot cloth until dessert slides out. Cut into slices. Makes 8 servings.

Orange Ice

1 cup sugar
2 cups water
1 cup fresh orange juice
2 tablespoons fresh lemon juice
  Grated rind of 1 orange

Boil sugar and water together for 5 minutes; cool. Add fruit juices and grated rind. Strain and put in refrigerator tray. Freeze until firm.

Near Eastern Cookery

by William Clifford

*Renowned for a subtle use of herbs and spices,
the Near East offers a superb variety of dishes from
delicately seasoned lamb, spicy pilafs,
to exotic fruits and honeyed pastries.*

The lands surrounding the eastern end of the Mediterranean are full of history, religion, poetry, and good food. Olives and dates, lamb and rice, yogurt and syrupy pastries, these all evoke the Near East as surely as Scheherazade, the Crusades, and the Suez Canal. Olive oil means more to the ordinary Arab than the oil that comes from the wells of Arabia and Iran.

Religion has been a strong force in the Near East since Biblical times. Today most of the people are Moslem. Christian minorities live in Egypt, Lebanon, and Turkey; Jews in Israel. Not all Moslems are Arabs, however (Turks and Persians, for example); and not all peoples who speak Arabic belong to the Near East.

In recent centuries the Ottoman (Turkish) Empire ruled the whole area; when it came to an end with the First World War, there was hardly any important dish that belonged to only one country. Fortunately the Turks are outstanding gourmets, as a visit to Istanbul's restaurants, markets, delicatessens, candy shops, and homes readily confirms. They greatly influenced Greek cooking but borrowed from Greece the popular eggplant casserole, *moussaka,* now enjoyed as far east as Iran. It was in Iran that Turks learned the cultivation of rice and passed it on to the Arabs.

Influence was often reciprocal, both within the area and between it and Europe. The Near East gave the apricot to Europe in Roman times, but Europe paid its debt with the orange. Arabs took the date palm wherever they traveled, across North Africa or east to the Indies.

Recent European immigration to Israel has brought a new wave of influence, and today in that country you may find Russian and Viennese cooking side by side with Arabic. Because the last suits the climate and resources, and because it is healthy and good, it is gaining favor in Israel as the years go by.

The total use to which the Arabs put the date palm and its fruit shows the imagination and frugality needed for survival in the desert. Besides the dates themselves, the heart of the date palm is a recognized delicacy, like the heart of the coconut palm. The tree's sap is fermented to make a popular drink, and Arabs distill perfume from its flowers. Domestic animals eat the date pits. The wood supplies the lumber for parts of a simple house and makes excellent cooking fuel. Fronds are the raw material for lattice walls, animal pens, fences, packing cases (dates are transported in date-frond baskets or crates), weapons, and decorations. People eat the fruit at every meal and between meals, both fresh and dried, stuffed with nuts or dried fruits such as apricots, rolled in sugar. Stuffed dates are also cooked in thick sugar syrup.

In Egypt people begin the day with a hearty breakfast of beans, eggs, and cheese, as well as dates and other fruits, coffee or tea. Lunch is similar, and toward the end of the afternoon Egyptians like to spend a social hour and have a snack at a coffeehouse. This is such an important meeting place that Egyptian businessmen sometimes have the name of their regular coffeehouse engraved on their cards. The main meal comes at night, when the accumulated heat of the day has begun to dissipate. In other less torrid lands ordinary country people eat their principal meal at noon, having a lighter evening repast of salad, cheese, olives, and any of the tidbits and dips that make up *meza*, the Arab feast of appetizers.

M uch European influence is evident in the food and whole style of living of such great modern cities as Beirut and Cairo. But you realize you are not far from the traditional nomadic life of the desert when you catch sight of an oil-rich sheikh in town for a spree or a business conference. And the *suqs*, the large covered bazaars of the cities, are still closely tied to the land. Here in great shaded oases, places of refuge from the glaring sun and the jumble of traffic, city and country people mingle to look over all the foodstuffs, clothing, household necessities, and crafts that the nation produces or imports. Here too are flower

and jewel merchants, knife sharpeners and cloth dyers, bathhouses, and restaurants and stalls with prepared food. At major intersections of the mazelike paths there are a few large shops, but mainly the *suqs* are filled with little stalls run by a single man or small family.

People come here partly for the social experience and partly to shop, especially for food. And what an exciting way of shopping it is—something like a supermarket, but many times the size and with lots of personal attention. First of all your nose is tantalized by the aromas of coffee, incense, perfume, oils, herbs, and spices. Then your eyes fall on mounds of brilliantly colored fresh vegetables, eggplants of all sizes (this is the potato of the whole Near East, so cheap and easy is it to grow), giant leeks, many kinds of squash, greens, and all the familiar legumes. You buy dried peas and beans at separate stalls, and stop at others for rice and noodles, yogurt and cheese, eggs, honey in round combs the size of a dinner plate, olives and pickles, spices and herbs including the ever-popular garlic.

Dried fruits and nuts have their own purveyors. So do the pastries and candies, the nut-filled *Baklava* and *Kadayif* (see recipes), the Turkish delight, marzipan, fudge, and glazed fruit. Cool fresh fruits are esteemed by these desert peoples for their uniquely refreshing qualities, melons particularly, figs, pomegranates, oranges, grapes, mangoes in Egypt—whatever the region and season provide.

At the butchers' shops you discover that the favorite meats are lamb and goat. Specialists deal in liver, kidneys, brains, tails, and feet. People also enjoy chickens and turkeys, ducks and geese. There are a few who eat game birds, giant hares, and venison, but many Moslems avoid wild birds as they do pork. Everyone knows that a bird may harbor the soul of his own recently departed grandmother, who is still capable of choking him in the act of eating her out of house and home.

In coastal areas where fish is plentiful, part of the bazaar is bright as a rainbow with their colors. The fish stalls are gay with festoons of lemons and banks of leafy parsley. The eastern Mediterranean countries enjoy all varieties of salt-water and fresh-water fish, shellfish, and roe. Turkey's caviar from the Black Sea is second only to Iran's great sturgeon roe from the Caspian. Smoked swordfish is very popular in Turkey.

Errand boys are everywhere in the *suqs*, and the hardest-working of them are the ones carrying trays piled high with dishes cooked in the great ovens of the bakers. These dishes are sent by

housewives who have no oven at home and who are preparing a special feast, perhaps for a holiday, a family celebration, or the arrival of a guest. The world is full of proverbial hospitality, but Near Eastern hospitality must be at least first among equals.

Even the humblest Near Eastern host gives all possible comfort and food to a guest, regardless of the hardship. Modern psychology has caught up with the old Arabic proverb which says, bluntly, "the food equals the affection." An abundant table must be set at all times, and guests are coaxed to eat and eat until they can eat no more. The proverb is a two-edged sword, however, and the guest is *obliged* to eat a lot in order to show proper regard for his host. It is only common courtesy for him to loosen his belt a notch halfway through dinner, to prove that he is trying.

F ew visitors actually see the traditional banquet where a sheep's head is displayed before a desert sheikh, who offers the eye to the honored guest and consigns the right foreleg to the current favorite in his entourage. A more common feast features a whole lamb or kid roasted on a spit, served on a giant copper tray with mounds of rice or wheat pilaf, garnished with several roasted chickens and hard-cooked eggs, accompanied by Arab bread to scoop up the food. A very important sheikh might multiply all the quantities several times, displaying on a single enormous tray several sheep or a whole young camel plus chickens and turkeys, vegetables, grape leaves, and bread, all on a mountain of pilaf. When he and his court have finished, the lesser members of the family and tribe gather around the tray to feast on the generous remains.

Pilaf is the festive national dish of the whole Near East. Whether it is called *pilav* or *pilau* or *pilaw* or *pello*, it is the same basic dish, usually made from unpolished long-grain rice, enriched with fat and sometimes vegetables and bits of meat, spiced and seasoned (see recipes). Besides rice it can be made from bulgur, coarse cracked wheat, although wheat goes more commonly into bread. In some areas people eat more bread than either rice or cracked wheat; Iran, for example, probably has the highest per capita consumption of bread of any country in the world. In most of the Near East bread is made flat and round (in Iran it is flat and long, like a small surfboard), lightly leavened, without milk or shortening. It is slightly chewy and comes with a pocket in the middle, handy for making sandwiches. Wheat turns up again in the processed semolina called *Couscous* (see recipes), which may be made into anything from a porridge to a pilaf or a sweet dessert.

Common Near Eastern cooking fats are olive and sesame oil, butter and *samneh* or ghee (clarified butter from goat, sheep, or camel milk), and mutton fat. A good rule is to use animal fat when the dish is to be eaten hot, oil when it is likely to be eaten cold. Many cooked dishes, especially vegetables, are better cold than hot.

The most popular spice is probably cinnamon, the most popular herb undoubtedly garlic. This "blessed herb" of the lily family is said to stimulate the circulation of the blood and even to be good for rubbing into open wounds. The many other herbs that grow wild in the Near East are put to good use, although now and then an enthusiastic cook will go too far in the mixture of ingredients and seasonings, as in the Aristophanes comedy where an overly complicated dish causes the women to rebel against its preparation. It was composed of fish and mussels, poultry and various wild birds, rabbits and brains, two sauces, wine, honey, and herbs. More to the modern taste is a *Shish Kebab* (see recipes), delicately seasoned with lemon juice and marjoram.

————◆————

The Moslem faith forbids wine, and many people in the Near East do not drink. But some ignore the prohibition, while others reason that the distillation of alcohol, as opposed to its fermentation, was not invented until after the pronouncement, and it is only wine that is banned. Arak (*raki* in Turkey), an anise-flavored grape brandy, is popular throughout the area; Egyptians call it lion's milk; Turks, the dew of heaven. Iran makes vodka and brandy similar to Italian *grappa*. Turkey, Lebanon, Israel, and Egypt make table wines. Country people ferment date-palm juice, rice, barley. Popular nonalcoholic drinks include such fruit juices as lemon, orange, apricot, and pomegranate, carbonated drinks (especially ginger ale), anisette, thin yogurt (safer and less perishable than milk), tea, and many herb teas. Experts can prepare glasses of striped tea, like a pousse-café, with clear syrup at the bottom, a green layer of lemon leaf or dried lime-flower tea, and a reddish-brown layer from tea leaves on top.

It is coffee that unquestionably has pride of place as a drink. Arab or Turkish coffee is made from the highest-quality beans (the famous Mocha beans come from Yemen, in southern Arabia),

roasted over a charcoal fire, and ground just before use, either in a stone mortar or a cylindrical brass grinder. You ask for your coffee sweet, medium, or without sugar, and water with the requested sweetening is first brought to a boil in a small open pot. Then the finely ground coffee is added, stirred well, and allowed to boil up until foamy. The pot is removed from the fire until the foam goes down, then returned and boiled up twice more. Drops of cold water are sprinkled on it as it is removed and the brew is poured quickly into small serving cups, grounds and all. As soon as the grounds have settled, the coffee is sipped from the top, very hot. It is never stirred.

Coffee is always brewed to order in small quantities. It is served ceremoniously to the oldest person first. Usually the happier the occasion, the more sugar is used. Saudi Arabians add cardamom seeds or cinnamon to the pot while brewing; others may add orange-flower water. Some who can afford it sip coffee every hour of the day. It is expensive, and its service is therefore a compliment to the guest. Much business is settled over coffee.

Nomadic traditions account for many features of Near Eastern life. In much of the area cookery is like folklore, never written down but passed on verbally and by demonstration from one generation to another. Lamb is favored over beef because pasturage is poor and nomads can herd sheep. It is natural, too, for people on the move to cook their meat on a spit, over an open campfire. If Mesopotamia (in modern times called Iraq) was the cradle of civilization, it may well have been these nomads who first put meat on a stick and held it over coals to begin the art of civilized cooking.

APPETIZERS

Meza in Arabic, *mezeler* in Turkish, this is the Near Eastern assortment of appetizers designed to accompany the drinking of arak. It can be as simple as a handful of olives or as elaborate as appetite and bankroll allow—fifty dishes or more. It serves as an afternoon or evening snack or comes at the beginning of a formal dinner.

CAVIAR
The finest fresh caviar from Iran is eaten well chilled with thin-sliced bread and sweet butter. Teheran gourmets do not add onion, egg, or even lemon juice. Favorite drinks with it are well-chilled

vodka, straight, and dry champagne.

ROE SALAD
¼ pound red caviar, or any available pressed roe
2 slices of white bread, trimmed, soaked in water, and drained
½ garlic clove, mashed
6 tablespoons fresh lemon juice
1 cup olive oil

Use a large mortar or a bowl with wooden spoon, or use blender. Mash and pound caviar with bread and garlic until smooth. Gradually add lemon juice and oil, beating constantly until mixture is a light purée. If it is too thick or becomes dry from standing, it can be thinned with a few drops of water. Like many *meza* dishes this is dipped or scooped up with pieces of bread torn from the round flat Arab loaf. Makes 4 or more hors-d'oeuvre servings.

BRAIN SALAD
2 pounds lamb brains
1 teaspoon salt
3 tablespoons fresh lemon juice
2 tablespoons minced onion
Lettuce leaves
Sliced tomatoes

Remove membrane and veins, and soak brains in cold water for 30 minutes. Boil in water to cover with the salt for 30 minutes, or until tender. Drain and allow to cool. Slice thin, sprinkle with lemon juice and onion, and arrange on lettuce with tomato slices. Makes 8 or more hors-d'oeuvre servings.

STUFFED GRAPE LEAVES, I
1 pound fresh grape leaves or 1 jar (12 ounces)
¾ pound lamb, ground
1 cup uncooked rice
½ teaspoon ground cinnamon
Salt and pepper
½ cup water
Lamb bones
2 tomatoes, sliced
2 garlic cloves, sliced
2 cups lamb broth or chicken bouillon

Wash and blanch fresh grape leaves, or rinse bottled ones. Combine meat, rice, cinnamon, and salt and pepper to taste with the water. Place 1 teaspoon of the mixture in center of each leaf and roll up, beginning with bottom where stem has been removed, then folding in sides, and ending with top point. Roll tightly enough so that leaves hold together, but allow for swelling of rice. Place bones on bottom of casserole, cover with tomatoes and garlic, and arrange rolls on top, close together, in as many layers as necessary. Press down firmly, add broth, and cook, covered, for 1 hour. Makes 10 or more hors-d'oeuvre servings.

Note: Serve this hot with a sauce of fresh lemon juice, minced garlic, and mint simmered in the pot for the last few minutes with the grape leaves, or cold with a squeeze of lemon.

Bareh Pello

Caviar

STUFFED GRAPE LEAVES, II

Grape leaves may also be stuffed with cooked as well as uncooked rice and without meat.

- 2 onions, chopped
- ½ cup olive oil
- 2 cups cooked rice
  Salt and pepper
- 1 pound grape leaves
- 1 cup tomato juice
- ¼ cup fresh lemon juice

Fry onions in 2 tablespoons of the olive oil. Add rice, remaining oil, and salt and pepper to taste. Place 1 teaspoon of the mixture on each leaf and roll up as described in preceding recipe, but as tightly as possible. Line bottom of casserole with grape leaves and arrange stuffed leaves in layers. Add tomato and lemon juice

and simmer, covered, for 30 minutes. Serve hot or cold. Makes 10 or more hors-d'oeuvre servings.

EGGPLANT WITH SESAME

- 1 large eggplant
- 3 tablespoons sesame paste (tahini)*
  Juice of 2 medium lemons
- 1 garlic clove, crushed
  Salt
  Olive oil
  Parsley and/or pomegranate seeds

Broil eggplant over coals until skin is charred and pulp soft, or roast in oven: the former gives a desired smoky taste. Peel and mash pulp until smooth. Add 1 tablespoon water to sesame and stir. Add lemon juice, garlic, and salt to taste, and combine with eggplant. Chill thor-

oughly and spread on flat plate. Make slight depression in center and fill with oil. Decorate with parsley or fresh pomegranate seeds, or both. Makes 4 or more servings.

*Sesame paste is available in food stores specializing in Near Eastern products and in health-food stores.

MASHED CHICK-PEAS WITH SESAME

- 2½ cups (one 20-ounce can) chick-peas
- 1 garlic clove, crushed
- 4 tablespoons sesame paste (tahini)
- ¼ cup fresh lemon juice
  Salt
  Olive oil
  Parsley

Rinse chick-peas under cold water and put a dozen aside. Mash remaining chick-peas in bowl and add garlic, sesame paste,

pepper to taste, and mix thoroughly. May be served with lettuce, cabbage, or grape leaves to use as scoops rather than bread. Makes 6 servings.

PICKLED TURNIPS

10 small white turnips
 2 beets
 2 cups water
 1 cup vinegar
 2 teaspoons salt
 6 garlic cloves

Wash and peel turnips and beets. Cut turnips as though to make ¼-inch slices but leave attached at one end of each turnip. Soak in water overnight. Wash, and place in jar or jars with all other ingredients for at least 3 days. These lightly pickled rose-colored turnips are very popular as *meza*. Other popular pickles include cucumber, dill, and almost any vegetable.

Of the many other dishes appropriate for *meza*, it may be sufficient to mention black olives, often dressed with oil and garlic, asparagus and artichokes in oil or vinaigrette, smoked fish, and small stuffed tomatoes, peppers, onions, and eggplant. Here is a recipe for stuffed tomatoes that works equally well with the others.

STUFFED TOMATOES

 8 tomatoes
 1 medium onion, chopped
 2 tablespoons butter
 ½ pound lamb, ground
 ½ cup cooked rice
 1 teaspoon chopped mint
 1 teaspoon chopped dill
    Salt and pepper

Slice tops off tomatoes and remove pulp and seeds. Sauté onion in butter, add lamb, and cook for 5 minutes. Add rice, mint, dill, and salt and pepper to taste. Fill tomatoes with mixture and replace tops. Place in casserole with ¼ cup water, cover, and simmer or bake in preheated slow oven (325°F.) for 30 minutes. Serve hot or cold. Makes 8 servings.

YOGURT

ARAB CHEESE

This cousin to cottage cheese is made by adding salt to yogurt and putting it in a cheesecloth bag to hang and drip dry overnight. It is usually eaten with olive oil, bread, and olives, at any time of the day, but especially at breakfast.

TURQUOISE YOGURT

The name is a French word that means simply "Turkish" and an English word that means green-blue in color. With a pinch of imagination the combination of seasonings gives this appearance.

 2 medium cucumbers, peeled, seeded, and diced
    Salt

and lemon juice, stirring until mixture is a smooth purée. If too thick, add a little water. Season with salt to taste. Chill, and serve on flat plate with oil in center, garnished with parsley and whole chickpeas. If Arab bread is unavailable, this and other *meza* may be eaten with any bread, toast, or sesame-seed crackers. Makes 4 or more servings.

BEAN SALAD

 ½ pound dried white beans
 3 tablespoons olive oil
 2 tablespoons fresh lemon juice
 1 medium onion, minced
 ¼ cup chopped parsley
    Salt and pepper
    Tomatoes
    Black olives

Soak beans and boil until soft; drain and chill. Mix with oil and lemon juice, onion and parsley, and salt and pepper to taste. Serve garnished with tomatoes and olives. Makes 6 servings.

MINT AND PARSLEY SALAD

 1   cup fine bulgur (cracked wheat)
 1   cup minced onions
 1½ cups chopped parsley
 ½   cup chopped mint
 1   cup chopped tomatoes
 1   cup fresh lemon juice
 ¾   cup olive oil
     Salt and pepper

Soak bulgur in water for 1 hour; drain and press out moisture. Mix with onions and knead to bring out onion juice. Add all other ingredients, including salt and

1 garlic clove, minced
2 tablespoons fresh lemon juice
2 cups yogurt
1 teaspoon chopped dill
2 tablespoons olive oil
1 tablespoon chopped mint

Sprinkle cucumbers with salt, let stand for 15 minutes, and pour off liquid. Mash garlic in bowl with lemon juice; add yogurt, dill, and cucumbers; mix well, and chill. Sprinkle with olive oil and mint. May be served as an appetizer or accompaniment to pilaf, as a cold soup, or as a hot soup (heated but not boiled). Makes 4 or more servings.

MEAT, FISH, AND CHEESE

IRANIAN SHISH KEBAB
3 pounds lamb, well trimmed, cut into large cubes
1 cup yogurt
1 medium onion, grated
Pepper
Salt
Powdered sumac*

Place lamb in yogurt with onion and pepper to taste; marinate overnight or for 24 hours in refrigerator. Thread on skewers and cook over hot charcoal for about 15 minutes, turning frequently. Season with salt to taste and sprinkle with powdered sumac. A separate skewer of tomatoes may be cooked for a shorter time and served with the meat. Makes 4 to 6 servings.
*Powdered sumac is available in food stores specializing in Near Eastern products.

TURKISH SHISH KEBAB
1 tablespoon fresh lemon juice
1 tablespoon olive oil
6 peppercorns, crushed
1 teaspoon dried sweet marjoram
2 pounds lean lamb, cubed
Salt to taste

Mix lemon juice, oil, peppercorns, and marjoram. Rub over meat and let stand for at least 15 minutes. Thread on skewers and broil over charcoal until done, turning frequently. Season with salt. Serve with rice or Bulgur Pilaf (page 1215). Makes 4 servings.

ARAB SHISH KEBAB
2 pounds baby lamb, cubed
2 teaspoons salt
½ teaspoon peppercorns, crushed
12 small onions, peeled and halved

Rub meat with salt and pepper and let stand for 15 minutes or longer. Thread on skewers, alternating cubes of meat with onion halves. Broil over hot charcoal, turning frequently. Slip off skewer into Arab bread and eat as sandwich, with salad accompaniment. Makes 4 servings.

KIBBEH (Meat Loaf)
The Lebanese national dish, a pounded lamb mixture called kibbeh, *is served in a dozen different ways. Here are three of the most popular, beginning with the Near Eastern equivalent of steak tartare.*

2 pounds loin lamb, well trimmed and cubed
2 medium onions, minced
1 teaspoon salt
¼ teaspoon pepper
2 cups bulgur (cracked wheat)

Pound meat, onions, salt, and pepper until very smooth. Rinse bulgur in running water, press to remove moisture, and knead into meat. Continue pounding with mallet or pestle, dipped occasionally into cold water, until *kibbeh* is moist and smooth, about 1 hour. Spread on plate, sprinkle with olive oil, add salt to taste, and eat raw with bread and scallions. Makes 6 to 8 servings.
Note: Preparation can be simplified by having butcher grind meat. Or put meat through grinder using finest blade, first alone, then with onions, then with cracked wheat. Grind all ingredients together 2 or 3 more times, adding a little ice water for smoothness.

KIBBEH BI SANIEH (Stuffed Meat Loaf)
½ pound lamb, ground
1 medium onion, chopped
½ cup pine nuts
1 teaspoon salt
½ teaspoon pepper
¼ teaspoon ground cinnamon
Raw kibbeh prepared as in recipe above
½ cup melted butter

Sauté meat in ungreased skillet for 5 minutes. Add all other ingredients except *kibbeh* and butter and cook for another 5 minutes. Spread half of raw *kibbeh* evenly in bottom of buttered baking pan, add ground meat mixture, and cover with remaining raw *kibbeh*. Using knife dipped into cold water, cut into diamonds or squares through to bottom and around edges. Pour melted butter over meat and bake in preheated moderate oven (350°F.) until well browned, about 30 minutes. Makes 8 servings.

KIBBEH BI LABAN (Meatballs in Yogurt)
Raw kibbeh and meat stuffing prepared as in preceding recipe
4 cups yogurt
1 cup cooked rice
1 teaspoon salt
2 garlic cloves, crushed
Dried mint

Shape *kibbeh* into patties, place a spoonful of stuffing between each two of them, and press edges together. Heat yogurt with rice, salt, and garlic. Place patties in yogurt sauce and simmer until done. If sauce tends to dry, add water. Serve

with mint rubbed between palms of hands and sprinkled as powder on meat. Makes 8 servings.

STUFFED ROAST KID
This dish, typical of a Saudi Arabian family feast, may be made with either kid or baby lamb, dressed by the butcher for roasting.

1 kid or baby lamb (about 12 pounds)
½ cup minced onion
1 tablespoon salt
1 teaspoon pepper
2 tablespoons ground coriander
4 cups cooked rice
2 cups sliced onions
1 cup raisins
1 cup almonds, chopped
2 cups pistachio nuts
1 cup butter

Rub animal inside and out with minced onion, salt, pepper, and coriander. Combine all other ingredients except butter; stuff and sew up animal. Roast on spit over charcoal or in pan in preheated slow oven (325°F.), basting frequently with butter. Makes 8 or more servings.

STUFFED ROAST CHICKEN
1 roasting chicken (3½ to 4 pounds)
1 cup cooked rice
1 chicken liver, chopped
2 tablespoons butter or olive oil
¼ cup raisins
½ cup pine nuts
Salt and pepper
Juice of 2 large lemons

Wash and dry chicken. Combine remaining ingredients except lemon juice. Stuff chicken with mixture and sew up vent. Rub with lemon juice and roast, uncovered, in preheated slow oven (300°F.) for 2 hours, basting every 30 minutes with lemon and pan juices. Makes 4 to 6 servings.

CHERKES TAVUGU (Circassian Chicken)
This is the famous chicken with walnuts, and there must be as many ways of making it as there are Turks. The chicken can be boiled, arranged in quarters on boiled rice, and covered with a sauce of pounded nuts (almonds and hazelnuts as well as walnuts), onion, red pepper, butter, and chicken bouillon. Or it can be shredded after boiling, combined with pounded walnuts, bread crumbs, egg, shallots, paprika, and bouillon, shaped into cutlets, and fried in butter. More commonly it is a cold dish, and here one of the refinements is to serve ground or shredded dark meat of chicken on slices of white meat. Another is to sprinkle the dish with walnut oil colored with paprika.

1 roasting chicken (3½ to 4 pounds)
2 cups shelled walnuts
1 tablespoon paprika
3 slices of white bread
2 cups chicken bouillon

Boil or simmer chicken with usual seasonings until tender; shred or cut into small bites. Cool. Grind walnuts twice with paprika and press in cheesecloth to extract red oil. Soak trimmed bread in chicken bouillon, squeeze, and combine with ground nuts. Grind 3 more times, slowly adding bouillon to make a thin paste or sauce. Mix chicken with half of paste, and chill. Spread remaining paste on top and sprinkle with walnut-paprika oil. Makes 6 servings.

CHELLO KEBAB

So many Iranians like *Chello Kebab* that there are restaurants specializing in this meal, one popular version of which is nothing more than a yogurt-marinated *shish kebab* (see *Iranian Shish Kebab,* page 1214) served with a rather plain but special pilaf, or in Iranian, *Pello.*

PELLO (Iranian Pilaf)

    2 cups uncooked rice
    1 medium potato, peeled and sliced
       thin
    1 medium onion, peeled and sliced
       thin
    6 tablespoons butter
       Salt and pepper
    ½ teaspoon ground saffron

Cook rice in boiling salted water until half done, 10 to 15 minutes, and drain. Place potato and onion in butter, melted in the bottom of a casserole with a tight lid, and sauté briefly. Do not stir but keep in a flat layer. Pile rice on top, adding salt and pepper to taste, and saffron soaked in ¼ cup cold water. Cook gently for 30 minutes or more. The bottom layer should not burn, but it should get crusty and deep orange in color. Place casserole in water for a few minutes to help loosen crust, and turn out with crust on top of mound of rice. Makes 6 or more servings.

BAREH PELLO

A fancier dish than the preceding Pello, *this is typical of the pilaf that has won the affection of the whole Near East.*

    ½ pound lamb, cut into small cubes
       or diced
    2 onions, chopped
    2 tablespoons butter
    ¼ cup raisins
    ¼ cup pine nuts
    2 garlic cloves, minced
    2 tomatoes, peeled and chopped
       (optional)
    1 cinnamon stick
    6 cloves
       Salt and pepper to taste
    1 cup uncooked rice
    3 cups bouillon

Sauté meat and onions in butter for 5 minutes. Add all other ingredients except rice and bouillon, and sauté until well mixed. Add rice and bouillon, cover, and cook over high heat for 5 minutes after

mixture comes to a boil; then cook over medium heat until rice is done. Makes 4 servings.

KILICH SHISH
(Turkish Swordfish on Skewers)

    2 pounds swordfish, cut into 1- to
       1½-inch cubes
    ½ cup olive oil
    ½ cup fresh lemon juice
    12 bay leaves
    2 medium tomatoes, cut into small
       wedges
    1 lemon, cut into thin half-moons
    ¼ cup chopped parsley
       Salt and pepper

Marinate fish for 2 hours or more in ¼ cup oil, ¼ cup lemon juice, and the bay leaves. Thread fish on skewers, alternating cubes with tomato wedges, lemon slices, and bay leaves. Grill on charcoal for 8 to 10 minutes, turning frequently. Serve with sauce made of ¼ cup oil, ¼ cup lemon juice, the parsley, and salt and pepper to taste. Makes 4 servings.

BÖREK (Filled Pastry)

If you like to make puff pastry or can buy it, you should try this Turkish specialty. Börek *can be made large or small, filled with spinach or cheese, or both, or with mushrooms, chicken, or meat. Do not use* phyllo *pastry (like strudel dough), which is for Baklava (see page 1216).*

    ½ pound puff pastry
    ½ pound soft cheese such as cream,
       cottage, or ricotta
    ¼ cup minced parsley
    1 egg, beaten
    2 tablespoons milk
    2 tablespoons butter, melted

Roll out dough and cut into rounds. Mix cheese, parsley, and egg together, adding 1 tablespoon of milk if too dry. Put 1 spoonful of mixture on each pastry round, double over, and seal edges with milk. Place on greased baking sheet, brush with melted butter, and bake in preheated moderate oven (350°F.) for 30 minutes, or until lightly browned. May also be deep fried. Makes 4 servings.

VEGETABLES, CEREALS, AND PASTAS

RICE WITH NOODLES

Rice pilafs may also be slightly sweetened, not for dessert, but to serve with meat; or they may be made with a few vegetables but no meat, or made using any dried peas and beans or noodles in combination with the rice. Here is a recipe for the last.

    2 cups uncooked rice
    ½ cup fine noodles
    ¾ cup butter
    2 teaspoons salt

Soak rice in hot water for 30 minutes;

drain. Fry noodles in butter until lightly browned, add rice and salt, and stir to coat rice well with butter. Add 3 cups water and cook over high heat until water is nearly absorbed. Add more water if necessary. Leave pan covered over lowest heat possible until rice is dry. Makes 6 or more servings.

BULGUR PILAF

A specialty of Syria and Lebanon, bulgur is not only combined with meat (see Kibbeh, *page 1214) and salad (see* Mint and Parsley Salad, *page 1213), but it is also made into a pilaf just like rice.*

    ½ cup butter
    2 cups coarse bulgur (cracked wheat)
    1 medium onion, chopped
    4 cups bouillon
       Salt and pepper

Melt butter in casserole and sauté bulgur briefly. Add onion, which has been separately sautéed until soft. Heat bouillon and add with salt and pepper to taste. Cover and bake in preheated moderate oven (350°F.) for 30 minutes. Stir with fork and bake for 15 minutes longer. Makes 6 servings.

COUSCOUS

Made from durum or other hard wheat, processed by rolling and steaming, this grain is the national dish of Morocco and Algeria. Egyptians and Saudi Arabians like it made into a mushy stew with meat and vegetables. The Lebanese, like the Moroccans, make it into a pilaf.

    1 package (500 grams, about 18
       ounces) couscous*
    5 cups bouillon
    6 tablespoons butter or oil
    1 teaspoon salt

Place dry *couscous* in casserole and stir in hot bouillon a little at a time. Add butter and salt, stirring until well mixed over medium heat. Cover and reduce heat to simmer. Cook for 20 minutes. Makes 6 or more servings.

*Couscous is available in food stores specializing in Near Eastern products.

COUCOU SABZI
(Iranian Spinach and Parsley Pie)

Totally unrelated to Couscous, *this belongs in any gourmet's collection of egg dishes. The recipe here is that of Mrs. Mahbubeh Stave.*

    1 pound spinach, chopped
    2 cups chopped parsley
    1 large leek or 4 scallions, chopped
       (both green and white parts)
    6 eggs, lightly beaten
       Salt and pepper
    2 tablespoons butter
       Seasoned yogurt

Wilt vegetables by heating for a couple of minutes in covered kettle. Cool and combine with eggs and salt and pepper to taste. Heat 1 tablespoon butter in heavy skillet. Pour in eggs, cover, and cook over low heat until top is no longer runny. Turn out of pan onto plate, bottom side up. Add remaining butter to skillet and slide pie back in. Cover and cook until well done. Serve hot or cold with seasoned yogurt. Makes 6 servings.

STUFFED GREEN PEPPERS

- 4 large green peppers
- 1 pound lamb, ground
- 1 large onion, chopped
- 1 teaspoon chopped dill
- 1 teaspoon chopped mint
- 4 garlic cloves, crushed
- ¼ cup uncooked rice
- 1 tablespoon tomato paste
  Salt and pepper
- 2 tablespoons olive oil
  Water

Choose peppers that will stand upright if possible. Cut off tops carefully and remove seeds and membranes. Combine all other ingredients except oil and water, and stuff. Arrange peppers in casserole with oil and ½ cup water. Any leftover stuffing may be made into meatballs and placed between the peppers. Bake in preheated moderate oven (350°F.) for 1 hour, adding more water if needed. This same stuffing may be used for large zucchini, whole eggplant, and other vegetables. Makes 4 servings.

Note: The seasonings may be varied, especially by the addition of 1 teaspoon ground coriander, ½ teaspoon ground cuminseed, and ¼ teaspoon cayenne for an Indian overtone.

DESSERTS

BAKLAVA (Filled Pastry)

This confection can be bought by mail or carried home ready-made from any Near Eastern grocery or restaurant. If you want to make it yourself, you should still buy the thin sheets of phyllo *pastry from the baker or grocer who specializes in it. Even Near Eastern women recognize that it is so hard to make they leave it to a few professionals.*

- 2 pounds phyllo pastry sheets
- 2 cups sweet butter, melted
- 1½ pounds walnuts or pistachios, finely chopped
- 4 cups sugar
- 1 teaspoon fresh lemon juice
  Orange-flower water or rosewater (optional)

Butter a baking tray of adequate size for the sheets of dough and with sides at least 2 inches high. Pile up 4 sheets of dough and brush liberally with butter. Repeat, buttering every fourth sheet, until the pile is 1 inch high. Spread evenly with nuts. Again pile up sheets of dough for another inch, buttering every fourth one and using up all of the butter. Cut diagonally to make diamond shapes about

1 inch wide. Bake in preheated very slow oven (250°F.) for 2½ hours. While hot from oven, pour on syrup made of 2 cups water and 4 cups sugar cooked until thick, then sprinkled with lemon juice. An additional sprinkling of orange-flower water is optional. Cool before serving. Makes 20 or more servings.

KADAYIF
(Shredded-Wheat Dessert)

- 4 large shredded-wheat biscuits
- 1 tablespoon ground cinnamon
- 1 cup white corn syrup
- 1 cup chopped walnuts
- 2 cups heavy cream, whipped

Crush biscuits to shreds, sprinkle with cinnamon, and toast in oven. When brown, cover with syrup and let stand overnight. Mix in nuts and divide mixture into individual servings on plates or bowls. Add whipped cream. Makes 6 servings.

STEWED RAISINS

- ¼ cup sugar
- 1 cup raisins
- 2 tablespoons pine nuts
- 1 tablespoon orange-flower water
- 1 teaspoon fresh lemon juice

Dissolve sugar in 2 cups water, add raisins, and bring to boil. Remove from heat and let stand overnight. Add nuts, orange-flower water, and lemon juice. Serve cold. Makes 6 servings.

MAAMOUL (Farina Cakes)

- 2½ cups cooked farina
- ½ cup butter, softened
- 1 cup milk
  All-purpose flour
- 2 cups chopped almonds or pistachios
- 1 cup sugar
- 2 tablespoons rosewater
  Confectioners' sugar

Mix farina in bowl with ¼ cup softened butter. Cover with milk and refrigerate overnight. Stir several times. When ready to bake, add remaining butter and enough flour to make dough hold its shape. Mix nuts, sugar, and rosewater. Make small cones out of farina dough, fill with nut mixture, and bake in preheated moderate oven (350°F.) for about 15 minutes, until golden-brown. Sprinkle with confectioners' sugar while hot. Makes 12 or more servings.

EISH EL SERAYA (Palace Bread)

- ½ cup butter
- ½ cup sugar
- ½ pound honey
- 6 slices of white bread, trimmed and crumbled
- 1 cup heavy cream, whipped

Combine butter, sugar, and honey, and cook gently until thick. Add bread crumbs and stir well. Pour onto greased plate and cut into diamond shapes when cold. Serve with whipped cream. Makes 4 or more servings.

NECTAR—The word, which is of Greek origin, has two meanings. First, according to the poets of ancient Greece, nectar was the drink of the gods who lived on Mount Olympus. It was poured by Hebe, goddess of youth, and brought immortality to the drinkers. The poet Homer describes nectar as resembling red wine. Whatever the exact content of the mythological nectar, the word is now used to describe any delicious inspiring beverage.

The second meaning of the word nectar is a botanical one: a sweet liquid secreted by a plant. Bees feed on plant nectar. The composition of the nectars of the different plants varies, but it is mostly water, with sugar and grape sugar and minute quantities of other carbohydrates. The plant nectar best known to children is that of the honeysuckle flower; most of us remember biting off the end of the flower and sucking a sweet drop of juice.

NECTARINE—A delicate variety of peach, smaller in size, roundish, and with a smooth skin that ranges in color from orange-yellow to red, sometimes mixed with green. The flesh is very juicy and may be red, yellow, or white in color. The fruit contains a pit.

Nectarines taste best eaten or used raw; in cooking, they lose their delicacy of flavor and firmness of flesh.

Availability—Available during summer and early fall with peak season in June to July. California produces most of the crop.

Purchasing Guide—Select fresh, plump, firm but not hard fruit with good color. A slight softening along the seam is a guide for ripeness. Immature fruit is green and will shrivel rather than ripen. Nectarines are usually sold by the pound or by the dozen.

Nutritive Food Values—Fair source of vitamins A and C.

☐ 3½ ounces, raw = 64 calories

NESSELRODE or A LA NESSELRODE—A name used for a number of food preparations in the elegant French manner, including a game soup, a rich barley and rice soup thickened with eggs and cream, a cold dish of thrushes stuffed with *foie gras* and truffles, and above all the best known of the Nesselrode preparations, a dessert pudding.

The classic Nesselrode was a mixture of custard enriched with heavy cream, chestnut purée or pieces, candied orange peel, crystallized cherries, raisins, and currants, and flavored with Maraschino liqueur. Modern versions may contain gelatin and other flavorings. Nesselrode is considered one of the most elegant of all desserts.

The Nesselrode mixture can be molded, frozen, or used to fill a baked pie shell. Also made, at home and commercially, are Nesselrode sauces which contain candied fruits and peels, chestnuts, and flavoring in a heavy sugar syrup. The sauces are used on ice creams and puddings.

The dishes à la Nesselrode were invented, it is said, by Monsieur Mouy, the French chef of Count Karl Robert Nesselrode (1780-1862), and named after his master. Count Nesselrode was a Russian statesman who played a decisive role in the forming of the Holy Alliance. He was a man of enormous power and he also had a penchant for handsome, lavish living, in keeping with his position and the times.

CLASSIC NESSELRODE PUDDING

    8 egg yolks
    ½ cup sugar
    ¼ teaspoon salt
  3½ cups milk or light cream
    2 teaspoons vanilla extract
    1 cup sweetened chestnut purée
    ½ cup diced candied orange peel
    ½ cup whole candied cherries
    ½ cup each of dried currants and

Classic Nesselrode Pudding

raisins
½ cup Malaga wine
2 cups heavy cream, whipped
⅓ cup Maraschino liqueur
Glacéed chestnuts

Beat egg yolks and stir in sugar and salt. Scald milk and stir hot milk gradually into egg yolks. Cook in top part of double boiler over hot water. Cook, stirring, until mixture thickens and coats a spoon. Add vanilla. Cool and then chill. Gradually beat custard into chestnut purée. Add orange peel, cherries, currants, and raisins to Malaga. Let stand until fruit is well soaked. Drain fruit and stir into custard. Whip cream and gradually beat in Maraschino. Fold whipped cream into custard. Pour mixture into a 3-quart mold.* Cover with foil. Freeze until half frozen. Remove cover and stir to distribute fruit. Cover again and freeze until firm. Unmold by dipping mold for a few seconds into lukewarm water. Surround with glacéed chestnuts. Makes 10 to 12 servings.

*The classic recipe is poured into a charlotte mold with a lid which is hermetically sealed by filling opening with butter.

JELLIED NESSELRODE PUDDING
2 envelopes unflavored gelatin
¼ cup water
2 cups milk
⅔ cup sugar
¼ teaspoon salt
4 eggs, separated
1 teaspoon vanilla extract
2 teaspoons rum extract
¼ cup each of chopped almonds, raisins, and dates
2 tablespoons diced citron
½ cup chopped candied cherries

Soak gelatin in water for 5 minutes. Place milk in top part of double boiler and scald. Add soaked gelatin, ⅓ cup sugar, and salt. Stir until dissolved. Beat egg yolks and beat in some of the milk mixture. Stir this into the remaining milk mixture and cook, stirring constantly, over boiling water until thickened. Let stand until cold. Chill until slightly thickened. Beat egg whites until foamy; gradually beat in ⅓ cup sugar. Continue beating until stiff. Fold in gelatin mixture, flavorings, and fruits. Turn into 1½-quart mold. Chill until firm. Unmold. Garnish with whipped cream, a maraschino cherry, and pieces of citron, if desired. Makes 6 to 8 servings.

SNOW PUDDING WITH NESSELRODE SAUCE
2 envelopes unflavored gelatin
1 cup water
1¼ cups sugar
⅛ teaspoon salt
1¼ cups boiling water
2 teaspoons grated lemon rind
½ cup fresh lemon juice
4 egg whites, stiffly beaten
Nesselrode Sauce

Sprinkle gelatin over water. Add sugar, salt, and boiling water. Stir until completely dissolved. Add lemon rind and lemon juice. Blend thoroughly. Set in pan of ice water and chill until mixture starts setting and is the consistency of unbeaten egg whites. Stir occasionally. Add egg whites slowly to lemon mixture. Beat until mixture begins to hold its shape. Pour into 1½-quart mold. Chill for several hours or until firm. Unmold and serve with Sauce. Makes 8 to 10 servings.

Nesselrode Sauce
½ cup sugar
½ cup white corn syrup
½ cup orange juice
½ cup water
¼ cup halved red maraschino cherries
¼ cup halved green maraschino cherries
½ cup slivered blanched almonds
½ cup candied pineapple pieces
2 teaspoons rum or sherry extract

Combine sugar, corn syrup, orange juice, and water. Bring to a boil and simmer for 5 minutes. Add remaining ingredients and blend well. Chill before serving. Makes about 2 cups.

NESSELRODE PIE
1 envelope unflavored gelatin
¾ cup sugar
¼ teaspoon salt
1 cup milk
4 eggs, separated
2 tablespoons brandy or rum
3 tablespoons chopped seedless raisins
¼ cup diced mixed candied fruit
1 baked 9-inch pastry shell or a crumb crust
Sweetened whipped cream
Shaved semisweet chocolate

In top part of small double boiler mix gelatin, ¼ cup sugar, and the salt. Stir in milk. Add egg yolks and beat slightly to blend. Put over simmering water and cook, stirring constantly, until thickened and mixture coats a metal spoon. Remove from heat and add brandy. Chill until thickened but not firm. Beat egg whites until foamy. Gradually add remaining sugar, beating until stiff, but not dry. Fold this meringue, raisins, and diced fruit into gelatin mixture. Pile lightly into pastry shell and chill until firm. Spread with whipped cream and decorate with a ring of shaved chocolate.

NEWBURG
NEWBURG—The word describes a combination of heavy cream, thickened with egg yolks and flavored with wine, usually Madeira or sherry, but sometimes brandy. It is generally made into a sauce, Newburg sauce, in which seafood is served.

Lobster Newburg is considered one of the world's richest dishes. Delmonico's, a New York restaurant at one time famed for its *haute cuisine,* is credited with first serving it. The story about its introduction concerns a valued patron named Ben Wenberg who showed the chef of Delmonico's how lobster was cooked in South America. The happy chef named the creation Lobster Wenburg but later, when Mr. Wenberg was banished for indecorous behavior in the elegant dining room, the dish was renamed Lobster Newburg.

The original recipe for Lobster Newburg follows. This recipe is taken from a "complete treatise of analytical and practical studies on the culinary art" edited by Charles Ranhofer, Chef of Delmonico's from 1862 to 1894.

Cook six lobsters each weighing about two pounds in boiling salted water for twenty-five minutes. Twelve pounds of live lobster when cooked yields from two to two-and-a-half pounds of meat and three to four ounces of lobster coral. When cold detach the bodies from the tails and cut the latter into slices, put them into a *sautoir,* each piece lying flat, and add clarified hot butter; season with salt and fry lightly on both sides without coloring; moisten to their height with good raw cream; reduce quickly to half and then add two or three spoonfuls of Madeira wine; boil the liquid once more only, then remove and thicken with a thickening of egg-yolks and raw cream. Cook without boiling, incorporating a little cayenne and butter; warm it up again without boiling, tossing the lobster lightly, then arrange the pieces in a vegetable dish and pour the sauce over.

Availability—Newburg sauce is available canned, as is shrimp and lobster Newburg. Lobster Newburg is also sold frozen.

SHRIMPS NEWBURG
2 pounds raw shrimps
½ cup butter
¼ cup brandy
2 cups heavy cream
6 egg yolks, well beaten
Salt and paprika

Shell and devein shrimps. Wash and drain thoroughly. Melt butter in a chafing dish and sauté shrimps until flesh becomes opaque and shrimps are pink, about 10 minutes. Pour brandy over shrimps and ignite. In another saucepan heat heavy cream just to boiling point. Beat some cream into egg yolks. Add egg mixture to remaining cream and cook over low heat, stirring constantly, until sauce thickens. Add salt and paprika to taste. Pour sauce over shrimps. Serve immediately. Makes 6 servings.

NEW ENGLAND: Character and Cookery

by Louise Dickinson Rich

New England, tucked away in the northeast corner of the nation, is the smallest regional division of the United States; yet it contains more variety than any other area of its size in the country, possibly in the world. All of the six states except Vermont have access to the sea. In the south the sandy beaches of Connecticut and Rhode Island are lapped by the warm waters of Long Island Sound. To the east stretches the open ocean, sending in great rollers to crash against the long and lonely outer shore of Cape Cod, to wash clean the eighteen miles of New Hampshire's pebble beaches, and to batter with a tremendous icy surf the towering granite ledges of the coast of Maine. Offshore lie hundreds of islands, some of them—Nantucket, Vinalhaven, Mt. Desert —large enough to support whole villages; and some so small that only gulls, terns, and colonies of seals can find sustenance on them.

Interior New England is as various as the shoreline. To the west, in New Hampshire and Vermont, rise the forested ridges of the Green and White Mountains and the suave contours of Massachusetts' Berkshire Hills. The mountainsides are steep and wild; but in the sheltered valleys are villages and little farms, their sparse fields ringed with walls of the stones man-handled from the grudging acres. Between the mountains and the sea is a rolling plain where the towns are surrounded by open meadows, orchards, and occasional groves of trees. Here are the cities, too, and the great industrial areas. Throughout New England there are thousands of lakes and ponds, warm and shallow in the three southern states, incredibly deep and cold in the mountains.

There are moors and heaths and swamps in New England, and natural caves and underground streams, and even a small desert; and the whole region is drained by rivers with names like music —the Connecticut, the Androscoggin, the Merrimack, the Penobscot, and the noisy Narraguagus. None of these things is the largest or the smallest, the longest or the deepest, or the most important in the world. They are only of the proper size to be taken to the heart. Almost nothing in New England is of superlative degree except the beauty; that and the weather.

Forecasters of the United States Weather Bureau consider assignment to New England the equivalent of banishment to the salt mines of Siberia. A record of professional competence is impossible to maintain where the weather is unpredictable from day to day, almost from hour to hour. Storms unaccountably change their paths as they approach New England. Canadian cold fronts move erratically south. Mile-high banks of fog from the Fog Factory—the point offshore where the warm Gulf Stream and the cold Labrador Current converge— march in from the sea, reducing visibility to a circle of wet blueberry bushes. Blizzards howl down from the north, plunge the mercury to twenty below zero, and pile driven snow into twelve-foot drifts; or a heat wave rolls in from the Midwest and for days and nights on end the thermometer registers over ninety. Hurricanes scream destructively up from Hatteras, leveling stands of pine, blowing roofs off barns, disrupting the power lines, and completely immobilizing factories and shipyards.

Then, as if in penance, suddenly the weather becomes absolutely perfect. The sky is high and blue, the air has a diamond sparkle, the breeze is soft and caressing, the sunshine is as blandly warm as new milk, and the shadow as freshly cool as the underside of a young leaf. Days like those are among the things that bind New Englanders to New England.

For life in New England even now is not always easy, and in the past has been extremely difficult and dangerous. The first settlers were the Plymouth Pilgrims, who landed on the shores of Massachusetts Bay in December of 1620. It was the worst possible time of year to arrive unprepared in a wilderness. There was no shelter, no crops to harvest, and no one to turn to for aid anywhere in the whole hemisphere. The supplies with which the tiny *Mayflower* had set out had dwindled to almost nothing during the long voyage. The town-bred men of the party were not skilled in hunting or fishing, and the native fruits and berries were long past their season. The bitter cold and knife-edged blizzards were shocking and terrible to people accustomed only to England's comparatively mild winters. Before spring came, over half the company was dead of cold, exposure, starvation, and disease.

Yet the Pilgrims would not give up. When the *Mayflower* set sail for England, not one went with her. Sustained by their belief in the God in whose Name they had left their homes and all that was familiar, they persisted. They learned quickly from the friendly Indians of the vicinity: learned about corn and squash and pumpkins, those Indian staples; learned about netting codfish and dipping alewives during the spring run up the brooks, and salting and drying them against the winter; about clams and oysters and lobsters; about using herring to fertilize the corn hills; and what greens and berries were edible; and how to make spruce tea to ward off scurvy; and how to tap the maple trees and boil the sap down for sweetening. Before winter closed in again, their colony stood firm on its feet.

It was then, in the brilliance of a New England autumn, that they set aside the feast day that has come down to us as Thanksgiving. Then they established the precedence of turkey-on-Thanksgiving for all Americans; but they had already set a tradition for New England cookery. Every New Englander gets a hankering every now and then for a good old salt-codfish dinner; and no New England housewife is ever without plenty of cornmeal on hand for Indian pudding and hasty pudding, for anadama bread and johnnycake (once journey-cake because it served well for snacks on journeys), and for dredging fresh fish before frying.

After the Pilgrims had proved that it really was possible to live in New England, others followed their lead. These had no easier time. In addition to man's ancient and implacable foes—the wind and the weather, the vagaries of the climate, and the difficulties of wresting a living from starved, stony, and tip-tilted fields—they had to fight enemies of their own making. Their thoughtless and rather stupid treatment of the native Indians soon turned the tribes against all Englishmen. The French, who were beginning to colonize Canada, took pains to promote cordial relationships with their red brothers. Consequently, when war broke out between England and France, the Indians had no difficulty in choosing sides in what are now known as the French and Indian Wars.

This series of conflicts amounted to an eighty-five-year span of guerrilla warfare broken by short and uneasy truces.

During that period no English settler on his remote farm along the Maine coast or up the Connecticut Valley slept soundly. Always the inner ear listened for the bark of the watchdog or the owl hoot that signaled attack by a marauding war party drifting silently through the forest from the north to burn, kill, scalp, plunder, and abduct. Whole villages were destroyed overnight, and countless isolated cabins; and no one knows how many men were put to death or how many women and children carried away into lifelong captivity.

Still the stubborn New Englanders held on, burying their dead, licking their wounds, and doggedly rebuilding on the ruins of the past. They survived the Revolution, in which they acted as a buffer between the rest of the thirteen colonies and British-held Canada; and the War of 1812, which demolished their promising merchant marine. They survived epidemics that wiped out families of ten or twelve in a few days; and early frosts that destroyed a whole summer's work in a single night; and the seasons when the herring and mackerel inexplicably disappeared; and the years when there was no summer at all—or too much summer, so that wells went dry and crops burned. They tightened their belts and braced their feet and made-over, made-do, or did without. They learned to laugh and joke in adversity—bitter laughter, often, and grim joking—as a weapon against despair.

And so was evolved the Yankee type, remarkably distinct and coherent throughout the entire region. By and large, New Englanders are independent, self-reliant and self-respecting, full of initiative, inventive, both bold and cautious, contrary, industrious and frugal, all frequently to the point of eccentricity. They are wry humorists, too, although their humor is unapparent to many. They are the result of a process of selection by their environment. The harsh climate, inhospitable land, and turbulent history killed the weak and drove the soft away to easier-living places. Those that remained were the tough ones, the stubborn ones, the ones who never knew when they were licked. Their descendants to this day are exactly like them—defensive because through history they have been on the defense against a variety of perils from all quarters; closemouthed and tightfisted because from generation to generation they have had to be in order to survive. They are hard for outsiders to understand and often even harder to like; but nobody can withhold respect from them.

The character of the New Englander and the conditions under which he lived, and in many places still lives, combined to develop a typical school of cookery. This is distinguished by heartiness, thriftiness, and inventiveness.

Heartiness, when applied to food in New England, means filling, nourishing, sustaining; a meal that sticks to the ribs through the long hard hours that it takes to haul a gang of a hundred lobster traps off Maine's treacherous coast, to put up a cord of firewood in the wintry woods of Vermont, to track a wounded deer all day through blowdown and swamp. Because return from any of these enterprises and others like them could not be set definitely, these hearty meals had to be good keep-warms and warm-ups, dishes that would not be ruined by hours in the warming oven or by being returned to the stove. New England cooks leaned heavily on solid stews and chowders, on baked beans, boiled dinners, and pot roasts, which are actually improved by standing and blending.

Thriftiness is, of course, economy; and no one is as ingenious in its practice as a New England housewife. Her rule of thumb is never to buy anything that you can get for nothing, never use an ingredient for which you can find a cheaper substitute, and never throw any food away. Put leftover meat and vegetables into hash or kettle-soup, and serve last night's stray piece of pie for breakfast.

Even today in the country women take their baskets in the spring and gather greens—dandelions, young dock, and marsh marigolds, and the peppery goose grass and tender fiddleheads. In the words of their great-great-grandmothers, who never heard of vitamins, they tell their families that these things have "virtue," that they will purify the blood. Later in the season they pick "pie timber"—wild strawberries, raspberries, blackberries, cranberries, gooseberries, and the versatile blueberries, good in muffins, griddle cakes, and gingerbread. They substitute molasses for sugar whenever possible—in baked beans, oatmeal bread, and doughnuts, and on hot cereal; and tried-out salt pork or chicken fat for butter in cream sauces. The flavor resulting is delicate and subtle. When fish and meat are expensive, they make huge kettles of corn chowder, of parsnip stew, and they are old hands at watercress and sorrel soups. They are sparing of everything, never using a spoonful when a pinch will do; of everything, that is, except time and effort.

For a characteristic of many of the older traditional New England dishes is that they need long and carefully supervised cooking. In the days of their origins, women stayed at home, where a wood fire burned day and night in the iron range or fireplace. Baking beans or Indian pudding all day long used no more fuel than was normal, nor did simmering a stew for hours. Since she was there anyhow, it was no great inconvenience for the housewife to give the kettle an occasional stir or to add a little water to the pot once in a while. She did not have to worry about running up the utility bill or being late for the Garden Club meeting.

All New England cookery is not of this homespun variety. Even before the Revolution many New Englanders had begun to amass fortunes based on the fishing, lumbering, and fur-trading industries. The products, sold largely abroad, required transportation; so shipbuilding became a major occupation. The sailing vessels that came off the ways from Massachusetts' Fore River to the Long Reach above Bath, Maine, were the finest the world has ever seen. They reached the peak of their perfection in the famous clipper ships of the China trade, which have been called the most beautiful objects ever turned out by American craftsmen. Captained by Yankees and manned by Yankee crews, these lovely ships girdled the globe, bringing home strange foreign cargoes—ginger and the spices of the Orient, lemons and mangoes, litchi nuts and kumquats, and rare wines and liqueurs—to add a touch of the exotic to the plain New England fare; bringing home, too, men who had eaten strange things in strange places and broadened their tastes.

Very often the captain of a vessel took along with him on a two-years' voyage his wife and family. These women were typical New Englanders, curious, intelligent, and experimental. In ports at the far corners of the earth they were entertained, as befitted captains' ladies, by merchant princes and high dignitaries, and served the best delicacies each had to offer. Back home again in their snug New England kitchens, they tried out new recipes, adapting them with versatility and ingenuity to Yankee taste and the limitations of the local foodstuffs. Their efforts added sophistication and elegance to the fare of a region that was basically provincial, giving it scope and variety.

The cookery of New England takes us back to the days when we were new on this continent and on through the years of our growth and coming of age as a free country. To partake of it is to share the past with those who went before us to make our own estate possible, whether they lived out their lives in lonely frontier clearings or crossed the seven seas in tall ships with shining sails. It is a part of our national heritage.

NEW ENGLAND COOK BOOK

Stews and chowders, seafood and fish,
baked beans, Yankee pot roast, boiled dinners,
muffins, griddle cakes, berries and pies. These are
the traditional hearty dishes of New England.

SOUPS

OLD-FASHIONED NEW ENGLAND FISH CHOWDER

¼ cup (2 ounces) diced salt pork
¾ cup sliced onions
2 cups diced peeled raw potatoes
2 cups hot water
1½ pounds haddock, cod, or ocean-perch fillets
Salt and pepper
2 cups light cream
Butter

Render salt pork in a skillet until it is nicely browned. Add onions and sauté them gently. Add potatoes and hot water and cook for a few minutes, or until potatoes are only partly done. Then add fish fillets and cook until they are easily flaked with a fork. Season to taste with salt and pepper and add the cream. Let all heat through and serve in bowls, topping each serving with a generous pat of butter. Makes about 2 quarts.

CLAM CHOWDER

¼ pound salt pork, diced
1 cup finely chopped onions
2 pounds potatoes, finely diced
Clam liquor
4 cups shucked clams, chopped
Milk
Salt and pepper

Render salt pork in a skillet; take out crisp pieces. Add onions and cook over low heat until done but not brown. Pour this mixture over potatoes; add clam juice and simmer until potatoes are nearly done.

Add clams and bring to a boil. This basic mixture can be stored in the refrigerator or frozen. Before using the chowder, dilute it with an equal quantity of milk. Heat to the boiling point, but do not boil it. Season to taste with salt and pepper. Sprinkle with salt pork. Makes about 2½ quarts.

SEAFOOD STEW

4 slices salt pork, diced
¼ cup butter or margarine
½ teaspoon each salt, celery salt, and paprika
2 teaspoons Worcestershire
2 cups bottled clam broth
1 pound cod or haddock, skinned, boned, and cut in pieces
½ pound shelled shrimps, cooked and cleaned
½ pound cooked lobster meat
3 cups milk
1 cup medium cream

Cook salt pork until crisp and browned. Drain off fat and reserve pork. Put butter, seasonings, and clam broth in kettle and bring to boil. Add fish and seafood and simmer, covered, until tender. Add reserved pork and remaining ingredients, and heat. Makes 4 servings.

SEAFOOD

OYSTER OR CLAM SCALLOP

Butter a deep pie plate. Put a layer of cracker crumbs on bottom. Dot with butter. Add a layer of oysters or clams and season with salt, pepper, paprika, and a little sautéed onion. Add another layer of crumbs, then a layer of oysters or clams, and top with crumbs. Dot with butter. Barely cover with light cream. Bake in preheated moderate oven (350° F.) for about 30 minutes.

CLAM PIE

Grind enough raw deep-sea clams to fill pastry-lined pan. Sprinkle with cracker crumbs and salt and pepper; add lump of butter and a little clam juice. Cover with pastry and bake in preheated moderate oven (350°F.) for 30 minutes.

OYSTER AND SHRIMP PIE

¼ cup butter or margarine
¼ cup all-purpose flour
½ teaspoon each of celery salt and onion salt
¼ teaspoon white pepper
2 cups milk
½ pint (1 cup) raw oysters
1½ cups cooked shrimps
2 tablespoons chopped parsley or chives
Pastry for 2-crust 9-inch pie, unbaked

Melt butter and blend in flour and seasonings. Gradually stir in milk. Cook over medium heat, stirring, until thickened. Add oysters, shrimps, and parsley. Pour into pastry-lined pie dish, top with pastry, and seal edges. Slit top to allow escape of steam. Bake in preheated very hot oven (450°F.) for 10 minutes; reduce heat to moderate (350°F.) and bake for about 20 minutes. Makes 6 to 8 servings.

OYSTERS BAKED IN SHELLS

Select large oysters. Scrub shells well in running cold water. Arrange in baking pan with rounded side down. Bake in preheated very hot oven (450°F.) until shells open. Pry off top shells and serve oysters at once on the half shell. Pass bowl of clarified butter to which fresh lemon juice and grated horseradish have been added. For appetizer allow 6 oysters per serving. For main dish allow 12.

CREAMED CODFISH AND BAKED POTATOES

1 pound raw salt codfish
6 medium potatoes
⅛ pound fat salt pork
2 cups light cream
2½ tablespoons all-purpose flour
1 egg yolk
2 hard-cooked eggs
Pepper to taste

Cover fish with cold water. Bring to boil and drain. Repeat until excessive saltiness has been eliminated. Simmer in fresh water until tender. Drain. Bake well-scrubbed potatoes in preheated hot oven (450°F.) for 45 to 60 minutes, until potatoes are tender. Place thinly sliced salt pork on rack in baking pan and set in oven with potatoes. Watch closely; when pork is crisp and brown, remove from oven. Heat cream in top part of double boiler over boiling water; add flour mixed to smooth paste with cold water; stir until thickened. Mix in beaten egg yolk just before removing from heat. Add codfish, separated into medium-size pieces, and sliced hard-cooked eggs. Pour into shallow dish or deep platter. Sprinkle with pepper and crumbled salt pork. Serve with hot baked potatoes. Makes 6 servings.

SUNDAY-MORNING FISH BALLS

1 cup raw salt codfish
2 cups sliced potatoes
1 teaspoon butter
¼ teaspoon salt
⅛ teaspoon pepper
1 egg, beaten
Fat for deep frying

Cover fish with cold water and let stand for about 1 hour; drain. Place fish on top of potatoes in a kettle; cover with boiling water and cook until potatoes are soft. Drain well; mash fish and potatoes; then beat with fork until mixture is very light. Blend in remaining ingredients except fat. Drop by tablespoonfuls into hot fat (375°F. on a frying thermometer) 2 inches deep and fry until golden-brown, about 1 minute. Drain on unglazed paper. Serve at once. Makes 2 dozen.

BAKED SEAFOOD HEARTHSIDE

½ cup butter or margarine
¾ cup all-purpose flour
3 cups light cream
Salt and pepper
Dash each of ground nutmeg and thyme
1 cup dry white wine
6 medium fillets of sole
1 cup each of cooked scallops, shrimps, and lobster meat
Grated Parmesan cheese
Fine dry bread crumbs
Butter

In top part of double boiler over boiling water melt butter. Blend in flour. Gradually stir in cream and cook over low heat, stirring constantly, until thickened. Then cook for about 10 minutes longer, stirring occasionally. Season with salt and pepper, nutmeg and thyme. Stir in wine. Roll up sole fillets and put in well-buttered 3-quart casserole. Add scallops, shrimps, and lobster. Pour sauce over fish. Sprinkle with grated Parmesan cheese and fine dry bread crumbs. Dot generously with butter. Set in pan of hot water and bake in preheated moderate oven (350°F.) for 45 minutes. Brown under broiler if necessary. Makes 6 servings. Rice and a green salad go very well with this.

Seafood Stew   Old-Time Spiced Bread Pudding

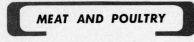

MEAT AND POULTRY

BOILED DINNER, NEW ENGLAND STYLE

3 pounds corned-beef brisket
1 medium onion
1 bay leaf
1 garlic clove
5 peppercorns
4 whole beets
4 potatoes
5 or 6 small carrots
5 or 6 small onions
1 tablespoon caraway seeds
1 head cabbage, coarsely shredded

Wash corned beef; put in kettle and cover with boiling water. Add medium onion, bay leaf, garlic, and peppercorns. Cover and simmer for 3½ hours, or until meat is tender. Meanwhile, cook beets separately and slip off skins. Add potatoes, carrots, and small onions to meat during last 35 minutes of cooking. Add caraway seeds and small amount of broth to cabbage. Cook for 10 to 12 minutes, or until tender. Put cabbage on center of platter, cover with sliced meat, and arrange other vegetables around. Leftover meat can be served cold or chopped with vegetables for hash. Makes 4 servings.

Note: Dilute broth with water to use in making bean or pea soup.

YANKEE POT ROAST

4 pounds bottom round, chuck, or rump of beef
Fat
4 medium onions, minced
2 medium white turnips, diced
4 carrots, diced
2 cups diced celery
Few sprigs of parsley
2 teaspoons salt
¼ teaspoon pepper
1 cup water
½ cup tomato juice
4 medium potatoes, quartered
All-purpose flour

Brown meat slowly on all sides in small amount of fat in heavy kettle. Pour off fat. Put meat on small rack in kettle. Add remaining ingredients except potatoes and flour. Cover and simmer for 4 hours, or until meat is tender, turning occasionally. One hour before meat is done, put potatoes on top of meat. When done, remove meat to a hot platter and surround with potatoes and vegetable mixture. Add enough water to liquid left in kettle to make desired amount of gravy. Thicken with flour blended with a little cold water. Makes 4 servings, with meat left over.

MEAT AND VEGETABLE HASH

3 cups coarsely chopped cooked meat
2 large baking potatoes, peeled and diced
2 onions, chopped
1 green pepper, chopped
2 celery stalks, minced

1 teaspoon powdered mustard
1 teaspoon salt
1 teaspoon garlic salt
¼ teaspoon ground savory
1½ cups meat broth or leftover gravy mixed with water

Meat and vegetables may be forced through food chopper, using coarse blade. Combine all ingredients. Pack into well-greased shallow baking pan. Bake, covered, in preheated moderate oven (375° F.) for 45 minutes. Uncover and brown under broiler. Serve with ketchup or chili sauce. Makes 6 servings.

BROILED HONEYCOMB TRIPE WITH MUSTARD SAUCE

Cut tender fresh honeycomb tripe in 6- x 4-inch pieces. Select "pocket" tripe for this. Season with salt and pepper and sprinkle with flour. Dip in olive oil and sprinkle generously with fine, dry bread crumbs. Broil slowly over charcoal or under broiler until well browned and done. Serve with Mustard Sauce.

Mustard Sauce

Melt 1 tablespoon butter in saucepan, and add 1 tablespoon minced onion. Add 2 tablespoons vinegar and simmer for 2 minutes. Blend 2 teaspoons powdered mustard with a little water. Mix with 1 can beef gravy. Add to first mixture and cook for 5 minutes. Strain and serve. Makes about 1¼ cups.

BREAKFAST PORK AND APPLE PIE

6 large tart cooking apples, peeled, cored, and thinly sliced
1 cup soft maple sugar
¼ teaspoon pepper
1 teaspoon ground cinnamon
Dash of ground ginger
Pastry for 2-crust, 9-inch pie, unbaked
½ pound salt pork, diced

Mix apples with sugar and spices. Line 9-inch pie pan with pastry. Arrange apples in pastry and sprinkle with salt pork. Top with remaining pastry, seal edges, and cut vents. Bake in preheated hot oven (450°F.) for 10 minutes. Reduce heat to moderate (325°F.) and bake for 1¼ hours longer. Makes 6 to 8 servings.

CHICKEN BAKED IN CREAM

Cut 2 frying chickens into quarters. Season each piece with salt and poultry seasoning. Dredge generously with all-purpose flour. Arrange pieces close together in 3-quart casserole. Dot generously with butter. Cover and bake in preheated moderate oven (350°F.) for 1 hour. Pour 2 cups heavy cream over all. Cover and continue baking for 30 minutes longer. Sprinkle with paprika and ⅔ cup chopped raw celery. Makes 8 servings.

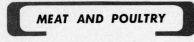

VEGETABLES AND SALADS

BACON-CORN FRITTERS

Mix 1½ cups drained canned whole-kernel corn; 2 eggs, beaten; ¼ cup all-purpose flour; 1 teaspoon baking powder; ½ teaspoon salt; and dash of pepper. Add 2 slices of bacon cooked and crumbled. Drop by tablespoonfuls into hot bacon fat in skillet. Cook until browned on both sides and done. Serve with butter, and with syrup, if desired. Makes 4 servings.

BOILED WHITE BEANS

1 quart dried pea or yelloweye beans, washed and drained
2 quarts water
1 cup meat broth
½ cup maple syrup
2 onions, chopped
1 tablespoon salt
1 teaspoon white pepper
4 beef marrow bones
¼ pound salt pork, sliced

Soak beans in water overnight. Next morning simmer until tender, adding more water if necessary. Add broth, maple syrup, onions, and seasonings. Put marrow bones in bottom of bean pot. Add beans. Put salt-pork slices on top, cover, and bake in preheated very slow oven (250°F.) for 4 to 6 hours, adding more broth if necessary. Makes 8 to 10 servings.

BAKED PUMPKIN

1 small pumpkin (about 3 pounds)
Melted butter or margarine
Salt and pepper to taste

Scrub pumpkin and cut into serving pieces. Scrape out seeds and stringy portion. Brush with melted butter and sprinkle with salt and pepper. Arrange, cut side down, in greased baking pan. Add a small amount of water. Bake in preheated hot oven (400°F.) for 30 minutes. Turn, brush again with butter, and sprinkle with salt and pepper. Bake for 30 minutes longer, or until tender, brushing occasionally with butter. With fork, mash in shell; serve. Makes 4 servings.

PARSNIP CAKES

2 cups mashed cooked parsnips
1 tablespoon melted butter or cooking oil
1 tablespoon all-purpose flour
1 teaspoon salt
Dash of pepper
1 egg
Cracker crumbs
Butter for frying

Mix parsnips with next 5 ingredients. Shape into flat cakes. Dip into crumbs, covering completely. Put in refrigerator to chill. Fry until brown in hot butter. Makes 4 to 6 servings.

GLAZED PARSNIPS

2 pounds parsnips
¼ cup butter or margarine

Salt to taste
½ cup maple syrup

Wash parsnips and cook in boiling water until tender. Cool, scrape, halve, and remove cores. Melt butter in skillet; add parsnips and sprinkle lightly with salt. Add maple syrup. Cook until slightly browned and glazed, turning once. Makes 6 to 8 servings.

JELLIED CRANBERRY SALADS

1½ cups fresh cranberries, rinsed and drained
½ orange
1 cup sugar
1 package (3 ounces) lemon-flavored gelatin
    Water
½ cup diced celery
½ cup chopped walnuts

Force cranberries and orange through food chopper. Add sugar and let stand, stirring occasionally, until sugar dissolves. Dissolve gelatin in ½ cup boiling water. Drain fruits and measure juice. Add enough water to juice to make 1½ cups liquid. Add liquid to gelatin and stir in fruits. Add celery and walnuts. Pour mixture into custard cups. Chill until firm. To serve, unmold in lettuce cups and serve with mayonnaise mixed with equal measure of sweetened whipped cream. Makes 4 to 6 servings.

CUCUMBER JELLY SALAD

1 package (3 ounces) lemon-flavored gelatin
    Hot water
½ teaspoon each of celery salt and onion salt
1 teaspoon prepared horseradish
2 tablespoons white vinegar
2 to 3 cucumbers
    Chopped mint or parsley

Dissolve gelatin in 1 cup hot water. Add seasonings and vinegar. Chill until mixture begins to set. In the meantime peel cucumbers and cut into halves lengthwise. Discard seeds. Force cucumbers through grinder or shred fine; 2 large cucumbers make about 1 cup shredded. When gelatin is partially set, stir in cucumbers and some chopped mint. Pour into shallow dish or 8-inch square pan and chill until set. To serve, cut into cubes and arrange on greens. Makes 6 servings.

DOUBLE-BOILER SALAD DRESSING

⅔ cup cider vinegar
3 eggs, beaten
1 teaspoon white pepper
2 teaspoons salt
1 teaspoon powdered mustard
¼ cup butter or margarine
1 cup milk

Heat vinegar to scalding in top part of double boiler. Combine eggs and seasonings. Stir in a little hot vinegar. Turn egg mixture into remaining vinegar. Add butter and heat over hot water, stirring constantly, until custard coats spoon. Cool. Add milk, pour into covered jar, and chill. A spoonful of sugar may be added if desired. Makes about 1½ cups.

BREADS

INDIAN MEAL RAISED BREAD

1½ cups milk
2 packages active dry yeast or 2 cakes compressed yeast
½ cup lukewarm water*
½ cup dark molasses
1 tablespoon salt
6 to 6½ cups sifted all-purpose flour
¾ cup yellow cornmeal
1 tablespoon melted lard

Scald milk; cool to lukewarm. Sprinkle or crumble yeast into water. *Use very warm water (105°F. to 115°F.) for dry yeast; use lukewarm (80°F. to 90°F.) for compressed. Let stand for a few minutes, then stir until dissolved. Add dissolved yeast to milk with molasses, salt, and 3 cups flour. Beat thoroughly. Cover and let stand in warm place until full of bubbles. Beat thoroughly again; add cornmeal, lard, and more flour, enough to make a stiff dough. Turn out on a lightly floured board and knead until smooth, about 10 minutes. Form into ball and place in greased bowl. Brush with a little melted fat, cover, and let rise until doubled in bulk. Punch down; divide into halves; form into 2 loaves. Place in greased loaf pans (9 x 5 x 3 inches). Cover and let rise in warm place until doubled in bulk. Bake in preheated hot oven (425°F.) for 15 minutes; then reduce heat to moderate (375°F.) and bake for 30 minutes longer. Makes 2 loaves.

ANADAMA BREAD

2 cups milk
½ cup yellow cornmeal
2 teaspoons salt
⅓ cup molasses
3 tablespoons butter or margarine
2 packages active dry yeast or 2 cakes compressed yeast
⅓ cup lukewarm water*
5 cups sifted all-purpose flour

Combine milk, cornmeal, and salt in top part of double boiler. Cook over boiling water for at least 5 minutes, stirring constantly. Add molasses and butter and cool to lukewarm. Pour into mixing bowl. Sprinkle or crumble yeast into water. *Use very warm water (105°F. to 115°F.) for dry yeast; use lukewarm (80°F. to 90°F.) for compressed. Let stand for a few minutes, then stir until dissolved. Add dissolved yeast to cornmeal mixture. Add 2 cups flour. Beat thoroughly. Add remaining flour and beat thoroughly. Turn out onto board, adding more flour if necessary, and knead for 10 minutes. Put in greased bowl and let rise until doubled in bulk. Knead and shape into 2 loaves; put loaves in greased loaf pans (9 x 5 x 3 inches). Let rise until doubled. Bake in preheated moderate oven (375°F.) for 50 minutes. Makes 2 loaves.

CUSTARD CORN BREAD

1 cup yellow cornmeal
½ cup all-purpose flour
1 teaspoon cream of tartar
½ teaspoon baking soda
½ teaspoon salt
4 to 5 tablespoons sugar
1½ cups milk
1 egg, well beaten

Combine all ingredients in the order mentioned. Mix well. Pour mixture into well-greased 8-inch square pan. Bake in preheated hot oven (400°F.) for 30 to 35 minutes. Cut into squares and serve warm with butter.

BLUEBERRY BREAKFAST CAKE

⅓ cup shortening
1 cup sugar
1 egg
½ teaspoon salt
¼ teaspoon baking soda
1 teaspoon baking powder
½ teaspoon each of ground cinnamon and ground nutmeg
2½ cups sifted all-purpose flour
1 cup buttermilk
1 cup fresh blueberries, rinsed and drained

Cream shortening and gradually beat in sugar. Beat in egg. Sift dry ingredients together and add alternately with buttermilk to first mixture. Fold in blueberries. Pour batter into greased 9-inch square pan. Bake in preheated moderate oven (375°F.) for 35 to 40 minutes. Serve hot with butter.

MOLASSES JOHNNYCAKE

1 cup sifted all-purpose flour
4 teaspoons baking powder
1 teaspoon salt
1 cup yellow cornmeal
1 egg, beaten
¼ cup molasses
1 cup milk
¼ cup shortening, melted

Sift flour with baking powder and salt. Mix in cornmeal. Combine egg, molasses, and milk; stir into dry mixture. Blend in melted shortening. Pour into greased 8-inch square pan. Bake in preheated hot oven (400°F.) for 25 minutes. Makes one 8-inch square cake.

BUTTERNUT-BANANA BREAD

½ cup butter or margarine
¾ cup sugar
3 eggs
2½ cups sifted all-purpose flour
½ teaspoon salt
¾ teaspoon baking soda
1 teaspoon baking powder
3 bananas, mashed
½ cup chopped butternuts

Cream butter until light and fluffy. Gradually beat in sugar. Add eggs, one at a time, and beat thoroughly. Add dry ingredients which have been sifted together, bananas, and nuts. Mix until just blended. Do not overmix or bread will be tough. Pour into greased loaf pan (9 x 5 x 3 inches). Bake in preheated moderate oven

Oysters Baked in Shells

Boston Cream Pie

Boiled Dinner, New England Style

(350°F.) for 35 minutes, or longer if needed. Test for doneness with toothpick. Bake a day before cutting. Makes 1 loaf.

FRIED TOADS

2 cups rye meal
1 cup yellow cornmeal
1 cup sour milk or buttermilk
1 egg, well beaten
1 teaspoon baking soda
⅔ cup dark molasses
½ teaspoon salt
Fat or lard for deep frying

Combine all ingredients except fat and blend well. Add a little extra sour milk if mixture is too thick. Drop by tea-spoonfuls into hot deep fat (380°F. on a frying thermometer) and fry for about 30 minutes. Serve at once. Makes about 4½ dozen toads.

Note: This is the New England version of Hush Puppies.

DUMFUNNIES

2 tablespoons sugar
1 egg, beaten
½ teaspoon salt
2 tablespoons melted butter
3 cups sifted all-purpose flour (about)
1 teaspoon baking soda
1 cup buttermilk
Fat for deep frying
Maple syrup

Beat sugar into egg; add salt and butter. Sift 2 cups flour with soda and add to first mixture alternately with buttermilk, a small amount at a time. Add more flour, enough to make dough stiff enough to knead. Turn out on floured board and knead well. Place in greased bowl; cover with cloth and let stand for 2½ hours. Turn dough out on floured board. Cut off strips about 1½ inches wide and twist into rings. Fry in deep hot fat (350°F. on a frying thermometer) until golden-brown on one side; turn and brown on other side. Drain on unglazed paper. Serve warm with warm maple syrup. Makes 3 dozen.

HASTY PUDDING

4 cups water
1 teaspoon salt
1 cup yellow cornmeal

Bring water and salt to boil over direct heat in top part of double boiler; sprinkle in cornmeal, stirring constantly. Cook over boiling water for 30 minutes, stirring occasionally. Sweeten to taste with maple syrup, honey, molasses, or sugar; serve in deep bowls with milk or cream. Makes 8 servings.

DESSERTS

INDIAN PUDDING

Originally, Indian pudding was baked in the warm ashes of an old brick oven for many hours longer than the three speci-fied here; but this adapted recipe gives a result as close to the original as a modern stove can do.

4 cups milk
¼ cup yellow cornmeal
⅔ cup dark molasses
⅓ cup sugar
¼ cup butter or margarine
¾ teaspoon ground cinnamon
⅜ teaspoon ground ginger

In top part of double boiler scald 3 cups milk. Mix cornmeal with another ¼ cup milk and stir it into the hot milk. Cook the mixture, stirring occasionally, for 15 minutes over simmering water; then add molasses, sugar, and butter. Season this batter with cinnamon and ginger; cook it for another 5 minutes; then pour it into a well-buttered baking dish. Pour on ¾ cup cold milk (do not stir in!) and bake pudding in preheated slow oven (300°F.) for 3 hours. Let stand to "whey" for 30 minutes. Serve warm, with vanilla ice cream, if desired. Makes 4 to 6 servings.

DATE-GRAHAM PUDDING

½ cup sugar
½ cup graham (whole-wheat) flour
1 teaspoon salt
½ cup cold water
2 cups boiling water
¾ cup diced pitted dates
Whipped cream

In top part of double boiler mix first 4 ingredients. Gradually stir in the boiling water and cook over direct heat for 10 minutes, stirring constantly. Add dates. Put over simmering water, cover, and cook for 1¼ hours, stirring occasionally. Cool; then chill. Serve with whipped cream. Makes 4 servings.

STEAMED CHOCOLATE PUDDING

½ cup soft butter or margarine
½ cup sugar
1 egg, beaten
1 teaspoon vanilla extract
1 cup sifted all-purpose flour
2 teaspoons baking powder
½ teaspoon salt
⅓ cup milk
2 ounces (2 squares) unsweetened chocolate, melted
Hard sauce

Cream butter and sugar until light and fluffy. Add egg and vanilla. Beat until blended. Add sifted dry ingredients alter-nately with milk, beating until smooth. Stir in chocolate. Put in greased pudding mold (1 quart), cover tightly, and put on rack in kettle. Add boiling water to come halfway up sides of mold. Cover kettle and steam pudding for about 1 hour. Turn out of mold and serve warm with hard sauce. Makes 4 to 6 servings.

GRAPE-NUTS PUFF PUDDING

¼ cup butter or margarine
1 teaspoon grated lemon rind
1 cup sugar
2 eggs, separated
3 tablespoons fresh lemon juice
2 tablespoons all-purpose flour

¼ cup grape-nuts
1 cup milk

Cream butter and lemon rind. Gradually add sugar, beating until blended. Beat in egg yolks. Then add lemon juice, flour, grape-nuts, and milk. Mix well and fold in stiffly beaten egg whites. Put in greased casserole (1 quart) and set in pan of hot water. Bake in preheated slow oven (325°F.) for 1 hour and 15 minutes. Serve warm or cold, with whipped cream, if desired. Makes 4 servings.

BAKED APPLE TAPIOCA

3 cups sliced tart apples
2 tablespoons butter or margarine
¼ teaspoon cinnamon
⅓ cup quick-cooking tapioca
1 cup firmly packed light brown sugar
½ teaspoon salt
2½ cups water
2 tablespoons fresh lemon juice
Cream

Arrange apples in greased casserole (1½ quart). Dot with the butter and sprinkle with the cinnamon. Mix remaining in-gredients except cream in saucepan. Cook and stir over medium heat until mixture comes to a boil. Pour over apples. Cover and bake in preheated moderate oven (375°F.) for 25 minutes, or until apples are tender. Remove from oven and stir. Serve warm with cream. Makes 6 serv-ings.

OLD-TIME SPICED BREAD PUDDING

6 slices of bread buttered generously with about ¼ cup butter
1 cup firmly packed dark brown sugar
½ teaspoon each of ground allspice and cinnamon
¼ teaspoon salt
2 eggs
2½ cups milk, scalded
Cherry Jam

Dice buttered bread into 1½-quart shal-low pudding pan. Sprinkle with sugar mixed with spices. Beat salt and eggs slightly. Gradually beat in milk and pour over bread. Bake in preheated moderate oven (325°F.) until set, about 30 min-utes. Top with cherry jam. Makes 6 servings.

COUNTRY FRITTERS

2½ cups sifted all-purpose flour
1 teaspoon baking powder
½ teaspoon salt
2 eggs, beaten
1½ cups milk
Lard for deep frying

Combine first 5 ingredients. Drop by tablespoonfuls into deep hot lard (375° F. on a frying thermometer) and fry until brown, for 3 or 4 minutes. Serve warm with maple syrup or stewed fruit. Makes 6 to 8 servings.

APPLE SLUMP

6 large Rhode Island greening apples
2 cups water
1 cup sugar

1½ cups sifted all-purpose flour
¼ teaspoon salt
2 teaspoons baking powder
¼ cup butter or margarine
½ cup milk

Peel and core apples and slice into large skillet. Add water and sugar, cover, and cook over medium heat until apples are almost tender. Make biscuit dough with remaining ingredients. Pat out into round the size of skillet. Place dough on top of apples, cover, and simmer for about 20 minutes, or until dough is cooked. To serve, turn bottom side up on chop plate. Pass cinnamon sugar and heavy cream. Makes 4 to 6 servings.

LEMON SLUMP
Grated rind and juice of 2 lemons
2 cups sugar
2 cups water
2 cups sifted all-purpose flour
1 teaspoon each of cream of tartar and baking soda
¼ teaspoon salt
1 cup milk (about)

Mix lemon rind and juice with sugar and water. Bring to a boil, lower heat, and simmer. Sift flour with cream of tartar, baking soda, and salt. Stir in enough milk to make a dough that will drop from the end of a spoon. Drop dough by tablespoons into simmering sauce. Simmer for 10 minutes, then cover and simmer for 10 minutes longer. Serve dumplings plain, with sauce, or with whipped cream. Makes 6 to 8 servings.

MRS. PARSON'S RECEIPT FOR CREAM
1 cup milk
1 egg yolk, well beaten, or 1 whole egg, well beaten
1 teaspoon vanilla extract
¼ cup sugar
Dash of salt

Combine ingredients in top part of a double boiler and cook over hot water until mixture becomes thick and creamy. Pour into serving dishes and chill. Serve topped with sweetened whipped cream. Makes 2 servings.

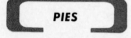

PIES

SQUASH PIE
2 cups mashed cooked Hubbard squash
¾ cup firmly packed brown sugar
¾ teaspoon cinnamon
½ teaspoon each of ground mace and nutmeg
¼ teaspoon ground ginger
½ teaspoon salt
3 tablespoons butter or margarine, melted
1 tablespoon molasses
2 eggs, slightly beaten
2 cups milk, scalded
Pastry for 1-crust 9-inch pie, unbaked

Combine all ingredients except pastry and mix well. Turn into a 9-inch pie pan lined with pastry rolled ⅛ inch thick.

Bake in preheated hot oven (450°F.) for 20 minutes. Reduce heat to moderate (350°F.) and bake for 30 minutes longer, or until firm in center.

APPLE-RAISIN-NUT PIE
Pastry for 9-inch lattice pie, unbaked
5 cups cored peeled and sliced cooking apples (8 to 10)
1 cup raisins
½ cup chopped nuts
1 cup firmly packed dark brown sugar
2 teaspoons ground cinnamon
Dash each of ground cloves and nutmeg

Roll out half of pastry and line 9-inch pie pan. Mix remaining ingredients and fill lined pan. Roll out rest of pastry, cut into ½-inch strips, and arrange on top in lattice fashion. Moisten edges with water, and seal. Bake in preheated hot oven (425°F.) for 10 minutes. Reduce heat to moderate (375°F.) and bake for 30 to 35 minutes. Makes 6 to 8 servings.

CHERRY DEEP-DISH PIES
2 cans (1 pound each) water-packed pitted red sour cherries
¼ cup quick-cooking tapioca
⅔ cup sugar
⅛ teaspoon each of salt and ground cinnamon
Pastry (1½ cups flour recipe), unbaked

Drain cherries, reserving ⅔ cup juice. Mix juice with tapioca, sugar, salt, and ground cinnamon. Add cherries. Pour mixture into 4 individual baking dishes. Top with strips of pastry, lattice fashion. Bake in preheated hot oven (400° F.) for 35 to 40 minutes. Serve warm, plain or with heavy cream or ice cream.

■ **One-Dish Variation**—May be made into 1 large pie. Pour cherry mixture into 8-inch square baking dish. Cover completely with a rectangle of pastry. Bake in preheated hot oven (425°F.) for about 30 minutes, or until crust is browned and juice begins to bubble through slits in crust.

CAKES AND COOKIES

RIBBON CAKE
1 cup butter or margarine
2 cups sugar
4 egg yolks, beaten
1 cup milk
3½ cups sifted all-purpose flour
3½ teaspoons baking powder
½ teaspoon salt
4 egg whites, stiffly beaten
½ cup raisins, chopped
1 cup dried currants
1 pound citron, diced
2 tablespoons molasses
2 teaspoons brandy
1 teaspoon ground cinnamon
Red jelly
Vanilla Frosting

Cream butter and sugar and add egg yolks. Stir in milk. Sift flour with bak-ing powder and salt and gradually add to first mixture, mixing well after each addition. Fold in egg whites. Divide batter into thirds. Grease three 9-inch square pans. Pour two thirds of batter into two pans. Add rest of ingredients except jelly and frosting to remaining batter; mix well and turn into third pan. Bake in preheated moderate oven (375°F.). White layers will take 30 to 35 minutes; fruit layer 45 to 50 minutes. Turn out on cake racks to cool.

Place one white layer on a large plate; spread with red jelly. Set fruit layer over this and spread with red jelly. Top with remaining white layer. Trim sides, if necessary, to make straight edges. Frost top and sides with Vanilla Frosting. Makes one 9-inch square cake.

Vanilla Frosting
1 tablespoon butter
¼ cup hot milk
3 cups sifted confectioners' sugar
1 teaspoon vanilla extract

Melt butter in milk; add sugar and vanilla. Mix well and spread on cake.

BOSTON CREAM PIE
½ cup butter or margarine
2½ cups sifted cake flour
3 teaspoons baking powder
½ teaspoon salt
1½ cups granulated sugar
¾ cup plus 2 tablespoons milk
1 teaspoon vanilla extract
2 eggs
Cream Filling
Confectioners' sugar

Stir butter just to soften. Sift in flour, baking powder, salt, and granulated sugar. Add ¾ cup milk and the vanilla. Mix until dry ingredients are dampened. Then beat for 2 minutes at low speed of electric mixer or 300 vigorous strokes by hand. Add eggs and remaining milk. Beat for 1 minute longer in mixer or 150 strokes by hand. Pour into 2 layer-cake pans (9 inches), lined on the bottom with paper. Bake in preheated moderate oven (375°F.) for 20 to 25 minutes. Turn out on cake racks, and peel off paper. Cool, and put together with Cream Filling. Sprinkle top with confectioners' sugar. Makes 8 servings.

Cream Filling
½ cup sugar
2½ tablespoons cornstarch
⅛ teaspoon salt
1½ cups milk
2 egg yolks, beaten
1 teaspoon vanilla extract

In heavy saucepan mix sugar, cornstarch, and salt. Add ½ cup milk, and stir until smooth. Add remaining milk, and cook over low heat, stirring constantly, until smooth and thickened. Stir mixture into egg yolks. Put back in saucepan, and cook for 2 minutes longer, stirring constantly. Cool, and add vanilla.

ANTHELIAS' SOUR-MILK GINGERBREAD CUPCAKES

½ cup dark molasses
1 teaspoon baking soda
½ teaspoon salt
1 tablespoon ground ginger
½ cup sugar
1 tablespoon butter, softened
1 cup sour milk or buttermilk
2¼ cups sifted all-purpose flour

Mix molasses with ½ teaspoon baking soda. Add salt, ginger, sugar, butter, and sour milk. Beat well. Gradually beat in flour sifted with remaining baking soda. Spoon mixture into greased muffin pans. Bake in preheated hot oven (400°F.) for 20 to 25 minutes. Makes 12 cupcakes.

OLD-FASHIONED HERMITS

½ cup sugar
⅓ cup shortening
1 egg
3 cups sifted all-purpose flour
½ teaspoon salt
1 teaspoon ground cinnamon
½ teaspoon ground nutmeg
¼ teaspoon ground cloves
½ cup dark molasses
½ cup buttermilk
1 cup seedless raisins

Cream together sugar and shortening. Beat in egg. Sift dry ingredients and add alternately with molasses and buttermilk which have been mixed together. Stir in raisins. Drop by teaspoons onto greased cookie sheet. Bake in preheated moderate oven (350°F.) for 8 to 10 minutes, or until lightly browned. Cool on a rack. Makes about 6 dozen cookies.

BUTTERMILK SNICKERDOODLES

½ cup shortening
1 cup sugar
2 eggs, well beaten
2½ cups sifted all-purpose flour
1 teaspoon baking powder
½ teaspoon each of baking soda and salt
1 teaspoon ground cinnamon
½ teaspoon each of ground allspice and cloves
¾ cup buttermilk
⅓ cup each seeded raisins and dried currants
½ cup chopped nuts

Cream shortening and sugar. Add eggs. Mix and sift dry ingredients and add alternately with buttermilk. Stir in fruits and nuts. Pour into greased and floured 2½-inch muffin pans, filling two thirds full. Bake in preheated moderate oven (375°F.) for about 25 minutes. Makes 24.

PRESERVES

PRESERVED PUMPKIN CHIPS

1 small pumpkin (about 3 pounds)
6 cups sugar
Grated rind and juice of 3 lemons
⅛ teaspoon salt

Pare pumpkin and remove seeds and

Breakfast Pork and Apple Pie

---

stringy portion. Cut pumpkin into ½-inch squares about ⅛ inch thick. Mix with sugar, grated lemon rind, and salt; let stand overnight. Cook slowly until pumpkin becomes transparent and syrup thickens, stirring occasionally to prevent sticking. Add lemon juice; cook for 10 minutes longer. Pour into hot sterilized jars; seal. Serve as relish with meat, or for dessert with cream cheese and crackers. Makes about 3 pints.

CHOWCHOW
- 18 large tomatoes, peeled and chopped fine
- 1 small head of green cabbage, chopped
- 2 green peppers, seeded and chopped
- 1 red pepper, seeded and chopped
- 1 cup cider vinegar
- 1 cup sugar
- 2 teaspoons ground cinnamon
- 1 teaspoon each of ground allspice and ground cloves
- 6 tablespoons salt
- 1 large onion, peeled and chopped

Combine all ingredients. Cover tightly and simmer until vegetables are tender, at least for several hours. Spoon into hot sterilized jars; seal. Makes 8 pints.

CANDY

MRS. BENSON'S RECEIPT FOR FUDGE
- 4 cups sugar
- ¼ teaspoon salt
- ½ cup butter or margarine
- 1 cup milk
- 4 ounces (4 squares) unsweetened chocolate
- 2 teaspoons vanilla extract

Combine all ingredients except vanilla in a saucepan. When mixture comes to a boil, let it boil hard for about 9 minutes. Cool fudge to lukewarm. Add vanilla. Beat until creamy. Pour mixture into a 9-inch square pan. Chill until firm. Cut into squares. Makes 2½ pounds.

POPCORN BALLS
- ⅔ cup maple syrup
- 2 teaspoons butter
- ⅓ cup sugar
- ¼ teaspoon salt
- 2 quarts popped corn

Cook syrup, butter, sugar, and salt together, stirring constantly, until candy thermometer reaches 275°F., or until syrup separates into hard threads when dropped into cold water. Pour over corn in large dish. Mix well. Let cool slightly. When cool enough to handle, butter hands and shape into balls. Wrap each ball individually in wax paper. Makes about 2 dozen balls, depending on size.

GRANDMOTHER'S MINT WAFERS
- 2 cups sugar
- 1 cup water
- 6 drops of oil of peppermint or spearmint
- Red or green coloring (optional)

Combine sugar and water in small saucepan. Bring to boil and cook until mixture becomes cloudy, stirring briskly. Remove from heat and add flavoring and coloring if desired. Drop quickly by teaspoonfuls onto wax paper. Makes about 1 pound.

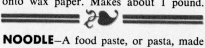

NOODLE—A food paste, or pasta, made of flour, water, and egg yolks. (It is the addition of the egg solids that makes the difference between noodles and spaghetti or macaroni.) Noodles are a favorite of countries as dissimilar as China and Italy, and they may be prepared in a great variety of ways. Widely available commercially, in many countries they are still made at home, too.

Availability and Purchasing Guide—Commercially made noodles are sold packaged in fine, medium, and wide widths. Some are cut into squares, some are shaped into bows, and some of the fine noodles are shaped into noodle "nests." Also available are noodles enriched with thiamine, riboflavin, iron, and niacin; and spinach, or green, noodles, noodles to which about three per cent of spinach solids have been added.

Noodles are available canned in many combinations, such as goulash with noodles; chicken with noodles; and turkey, beef, and chicken noodle soups. There are dry soup mixes containing noodles and a packaged chicken noodle dinner.

Storage—Store uncooked noodles in a cool dry place.
- ☐ Kitchen shelf: 3 to 6 months
- ☐ Refrigerator shelf, cooked and covered: 4 to 5 days
- ☐ Refrigerator frozen-food compartment, prepared for freezing: 3 to 4 weeks
- ☐ Freezer, prepared for freezing: 1 year

Nutritive Food Values—Primarily a source of carbohydrates.
- ☐ Noodles, 3½ ounces, cooked = 125 calories

Basic Preparation—Plan to serve noodles as soon as they are cooked. Cook them in plenty of boiling salted water. Keep water boiling rapidly to prevent noodles from sticking together. To lasagna noodles add 2 tablespoons oil to the cooking water to keep them from sticking. The ideal consistency for noodles is *al dente,* still chewy. All noodles should be drained immediately after cooking, and rinsed in hot water, or separated with a fork to prevent sticking.

BASIC NOODLE DOUGH
- 1½ cups sifted all-purpose flour (about)
- ½ teaspoon salt
- 2 eggs

Sift flour and salt into bowl. Make a little well in center and drop in slightly beaten eggs. Work with fingers until mixture becomes a very stiff paste; if it is too moist, more flour must be added. Divide dough into halves and roll into two balls. Put floured tablecloth or pastry cloth on wooden board or marble, wooden, or enamel kitchen table. Place dough on cloth and with floured rolling pin roll very thin. You will have to turn dough often, rolling it first on one side, then on the other, flouring cloth and rolling pin occasionally. It takes a strong right arm to get this dough thin enough. Roll up dough tightly into a long roll and, with sharp knife, cut into crosswise slices about ¼ inch thick. Separate slices. Dry for 1 hour, more or less, but do not let all the moisture evaporate or dough will crumble. Store in a jar. Makes about 8 ounces.
- ■ To Make Tagliatelli—Roll up dough as above and, with sharp knife, cut into very thin crosswise slices about ⅛ inch thick. Proceed as directed above.
- ■ To Make Cannelloni—Roll dough very thin and cut into 6-inch squares; use at once, or store.
- ■ To Make Lasagna—Roll dough very thin and cut into 3-inch strips; use at once, or store.

FLORENTINE CANNELLONI
Use Basic Noodle Dough (above), or buy broad (2½- to 3-inch) noodles. Drop a few at a time into a large kettle of salted water. Cook for 5 to 7 minutes, or until chewy but not raw. Drain. Spread each piece with 1 tablespoon or so of Filling. Roll up like little muffs. Place side by side, one layer deep, in casserole or individual baking dishes. Pour Cheese Sauce over cannelloni. Sprinkle with more grated Parmesan cheese. Set in cold broiler; turn up heat to medium. Broil until mixture is heated through, top is brown, and cheese is melted. Serve at once, very hot. Makes 6 servings.

Filling
- ½ pound mushrooms
- 1 small garlic clove
- 3 tablespoons olive oil
- 1 cup ground cooked chicken
- 1 hard-cooked egg, sieved
- ⅛ teaspoon each of ground thyme and rosemary
- Cream to hold mixture together (1 to 2 tablespoons)

Grind mushrooms and garlic together in food chopper, and brown lightly in hot oil. Add all other ingredients, and mix. Cool slightly.

Cheese Sauce
- 2 tablespoons butter or margarine
- 2 tablespoons all-purpose flour

1 cup chicken bouillon
½ cup light cream
Salt and pepper
½ cup grated Parmesan cheese

Melt butter in skillet. Add flour and stir to form smooth paste. Add bouillon and cream, stirring slowly all the while. Add salt and pepper to taste. Cook until you have a medium-thick sauce. Add cheese.

CABBAGE-NOODLE POTPOURRI

2 eggs
2 cups sifted all-purpose flour
1½ teaspoons salt
2 tablespoons water
½ pound bacon
1 onion, chopped
1 head cabbage (about 2 pounds)
⅛ teaspoon pepper
½ teaspoon paprika

Beat eggs; add flour, ½ teaspoon salt, and enough water to make a very stiff noodle dough. Knead on floured board until smooth. Roll out into very thin sheet. Let each side dry for 30 minutes. Cut into 1-inch squares. Dice bacon; fry until crisp; remove bacon. Cook onion in fat until browned. Add coarsely shredded cabbage, pepper, paprika, and remaining salt. Cover and cook for 20 to 30 minutes, or until tender. Cook noodles in boiling salted water until tender. Drain. Mix cabbage, noodles, and bacon. Makes 4 servings.

SHRIMP NOODLE SKILLET

2 tablespoons butter or margarine
½ cup chopped green pepper
1 garlic clove, crushed
⅛ teaspoon pepper
4 cups clam juice
About 4 cups (8 ounces) fine noodles
1 can (6 ounces) mushrooms
¼ cup canned pimientos, chopped
2 cans (5 ounces each) shrimps, drained

Melt butter in 10-inch skillet. Add green pepper and garlic and cook over low heat for 5 minutes. Add pepper and clam juice and heat to boiling point. Gradually add noodles so that mixture continues to boil. Cook, uncovered, for 5 minutes, stirring occasionally. Add undrained mushrooms, pimientos, and shrimps. Cook for 5 minutes longer, stirring occasionally, or until thoroughly heated. Makes 4 to 6 servings.

RUMANIAN NOODLES

1 pound fine noodles
1 pound fresh pork, ground
1 slice of bread, soaked in milk and squeezed dry
1 leek, minced
2 teaspoons fennel seeds
¼ cup chopped parsley
1 teaspoon salt
½ teaspoon pepper
4 eggs
⅔ cup light cream
½ cup grated cheese
¼ cup butter or margarine

Cook noodles only three-quarters tender. Combine pork, bread, leek, fennel seeds,

parsley, and salt and pepper. In large shallow baking dish place alternate layers of noodles and meat mixture, ending with noodles. Beat eggs with cream and cheese. Pour over noodles. Dot with butter. Bake in preheated moderate oven (350°F.) for 40 minutes, or until pork is done. Makes 4 to 6 servings.

CHOP-SUEY SKILLET

6 tablespoons butter or margarine
½ pound pork, cut into 1-inch strips
2 medium-size onions, sliced
2 medium-size green peppers, cut into strips
4 cups chicken bouillon
2 cups (one 1-pound can) chop-suey vegetables
½ cup (one 4-ounce can) pimientos, drained and sliced
1¼ teaspoons salt
¼ teaspoon pepper
About 4 cups (8 ounces) fine noodles
1 medium-size tomato, sliced
¼ cup chopped parsley

Melt ¼ cup of the butter in 10-inch skillet. Add pork and cook over medium heat, stirring occasionally, until pork is browned on all sides. Add onions and green pepper, and cook for 5 minutes. Add bouillon, undrained chop-suey vegetables, pimientos, salt, pepper, and remaining butter. Heat to boiling point. Gradually add noodles so that mixture continues to boil. Cook, uncovered, over low heat, stirring frequently, until noodles are tender. Garnish with tomato slices and parsley. Makes 4 servings.

PARTY NOODLE SUPREME

½ cup butter or margarine
⅓ cup all-purpose flour
2½ cups hot chicken bouillon
¾ cup light cream
⅓ cup white wine
2 teaspoons salt
½ teaspoon white pepper
6 or 8 large mushrooms
1 cup cooked ham, cut into strips
8 ounces medium noodles
2 cups diced cooked chicken
½ cup grated Parmesan cheese

Heat half of butter. Blend in flour. Gradually add bouillon, stirring constantly. Add cream and cook, stirring, until sauce is smooth and thickened. Add wine and salt and pepper and remove from heat, but keep hot. Slice mushroom stems. Heat remaining butter; in it, sauté sliced mushrooms, whole mushroom caps, and ham. Remove caps and reserve. Cook and drain noodles. Combine noodles and chicken with sauce and sliced mushrooms and ham. Turn into 6 or 8 individual baking dishes. Top each with a mushroom cap and some grated cheese. Bake in preheated hot oven (400°F.) for 20 minutes. Makes 6 to 8 servings.

HAM AND NOODLE RABBIT

3 tablespoons all-purpose flour
1 teaspoon salt
2 teaspoons powdered mustard

⅛ teaspoon hot pepper sauce
1 pound Cheddar cheese, shredded
3 tablespoons butter or margarine
12 ounces (1 can or bottle) beer or ale
2 cups diced cooked ham
8 ounces medium noodles, cooked

Mix together flour, salt, mustard, hot pepper sauce, and cheese. Melt butter. Stir in cheese mixture and cook over low heat until smooth, stirring constantly. Add beer and continue stirring over low heat until thoroughly blended. Add ham and noodles and mix well. Heat if necessary. Makes 4 to 6 servings.

Tongue and Noodle Rabbit

For ham in above recipe, substitute 2 cups diced cooked smoked tongue.

THE POOR PARSON'S NOODLE DISH

3 tablespoons bacon fat
2 onions, minced
½ cup minced green pepper
1 or 2 cans (4 ounces each) sliced mushrooms, drained
4 cups ground cooked meat
3 cups beef bouillon
3 tablespoons all-purpose flour
¼ cup water
Dash of hot pepper sauce
1 teaspoon salt
½ teaspoon pepper
½ teaspoon crumbled dried thyme, basil, or other favorite herb
8 ounces medium noodles, cooked

Melt bacon fat and cook onions and green pepper in it until soft. Push to one side and add mushrooms. Sauté for 5 minutes, covered. Add meat and cook for 5 minutes more. Add bouillon. When boiling, thicken with the flour mixed with water into a smooth paste. Stir in seasonings. Simmer for 15 minutes, stirring occasionally. Add noodles, and heat. Makes 6 servings.

MEATBALL-NOODLE SKILLET

1 egg
1 pound ground beef
½ cup fine dry bread crumbs
⅓ cup chopped parsley
1 medium onion, chopped
1 tablespoon grated lemon rind
2 teaspoons salt
½ teaspoon pepper
⅛ teaspoon ground nutmeg
¼ cup olive or salad oil
2 tablespoons butter or margarine
3½ cups (one 1-pound, 12-ounce can) tomatoes
Water
1 teaspoon crumbled dried oregano
2 bay leaves
About 4 cups (8 ounces) medium noodles

To make meatballs, mix together egg, beef, bread crumbs, parsley, onion, lemon rind, 1 teaspoon salt, ¼ teaspoon pepper, and the nutmeg. Shape into 1½-inch balls.

Heat oil and butter in 10-inch skillet. Add meatballs and cook over medium heat until browned on all sides, stirring occasionally. Cover and cook over low heat for 15 minutes. Drain tomatoes into separate pan; reserve tomatoes. To tomato liquid add enough water to make 4 cups. Add oregano, bay leaves, and remaining salt and pepper; pour on meatballs in skillet. Heat mixture to boiling point. Gradually add noodles so that mixture continues to boil. Cook, uncovered, over low heat, stirring frequently, for 12 to 15 minutes, or until noodles are almost tender. Add reserved tomatoes and cook for 5 minutes longer. Makes 4 to 6 servings.

NOODLES WITH EGGS AND BACON
12 bacon strips, diced
1 pound medium noodles, freshly cooked, drained, and rinsed
¾ cup butter or margarine
4 egg yolks
  Salt and freshly ground pepper
  Grated Parmesan cheese

Fry bacon until crisp. Remove crisp pieces and drain fat from skillet, leaving about 2 tablespoons. Toss drained and rinsed hot noodles with butter until well blended. Pour noodles into skillet with crisp bacon pieces. Add egg yolks and salt and pepper to taste. Cook over medium heat for ½ minute to just set eggs. Top with freshly grated Parmesan cheese. Makes 4 to 6 servings.

BUTTERED NOODLES WITH CASHEW NUTS
Cook ½ pound wide noodles according to directions on package. Drain. Season. Pour over ½ cup split cashew nuts browned in ½ cup butter. Makes 4 servings.

NOODLES POLONAISE
4 cups (8 ounces) wide noodles
¼ cup butter or margarine
½ cup fine dry bread crumbs
1 hard-cooked egg, chopped
1 tablespoon chopped chives or parsley
½ teaspoon salt

Cook noodles; drain. Melt butter in skillet and brown crumbs in it. Add chopped egg, chives, and salt; mix well. Add noodles and toss to coat. Heat through, stirring. Makes 4 to 6 servings.

HUNGARIAN NOODLE AND CHEESE CASSEROLE
3 cups (6 ounces) wide noodles
1 cup cottage cheese
1 cup dairy sour cream
1 garlic clove, minced
3 tablespoons minced onion
1 pimiento, chopped
  Dash of hot pepper sauce
¾ teaspoon steak sauce
¼ teaspoon salt
½ cup grated mild Cheddar, Gouda, or Edam cheese

Cook and drain noodles. Combine with all other ingredients except grated cheese. Turn into buttered 1½-quart casserole. Sprinkle with cheese. Bake in preheated moderate oven (350°F.) for 30 minutes. Makes 4 servings.

TWO-CHEESE NOODLES
4 ounces wide noodles
1 cup dairy sour cream

1 egg, beaten
½ teaspoon curry powder
1 cup creamed cottage cheese
½ teaspoon salt
⅓ cup seedless raisins
2 tablespoons butter or margarine, melted
¾ cup soft bread crumbs
2 tablespoons grated Parmesan cheese

Cook noodles in boiling salted water; drain. Mix remaining ingredients except last 3. Toss with noodles. Put in shallow broilerproof casserole. Mix butter and crumbs; sprinkle on noodle mixture with grated cheese. Bake in preheated moderate oven (350°F.) for 20 minutes. Place under broiler for a few minutes to brown top. Makes 4 servings.

AUSTRIAN HAM AND NOODLE DISH
½ pound wide noodles, broken
1 pound cooked ham, diced
1 cup light cream
2 eggs, beaten
¾ teaspoon salt
½ teaspoon pepper
½ cup grated Parmesan or Swiss cheese
2 tablespoons melted butter or margarine

Cook and drain noodles. Combine with ham. Place in buttered shallow baking dish. Beat cream and eggs together. Add salt (if the ham is not salty) and pepper. Pour over ham and noodles. Sprinkle with cheese and butter. Bake in preheated moderate oven (350°F.) for 45 minutes. Makes 4 to 6 servings.

PORK-CHOP AND NOODLE SKILLET
¼ cup butter or margarine
4 pork loin chops, 1 inch thick
2 teaspoons salt
½ teaspoon ground nutmeg
4 cups apple juice
  About 4 cups (8 ounces) wide noodles
4 canned spiced crabapples
  Parsley sprigs

Melt butter in 10-inch skillet. Sprinkle pork chops with 1 teaspoon salt. Arrange pork chops in skillet and cook over medium heat until browned on both sides, 15 to 20 minutes. Add nutmeg and ½ cup apple juice. Cover and cook over low heat for 45 minutes, turning pork chops occasionally. Remove pork chops. Add remaining apple juice and remaining salt. Heat to boiling point. Add noodles gradually so that mixture continues to boil; cook over medium heat, stirring frequently, for about 20 minutes, or until noodles are tender. Add pork chops and heat to serving temperature. Garnish with crabapples and parsley. Makes 4 servings.

GREEN NOODLES WITH BASIL
1 pound green noodles
1 or 2 garlic cloves, minced
1 cup soft butter or margarine
1 teaspoon salt
1 teaspoon pepper
3 tablespoons shredded fresh basil leaves or 2 teaspoons crumbled dried basil
1 cup grated Parmesan or Swiss cheese

Cook noodles. Drain; return to kettle.

Add remaining ingredients and toss well. Makes 4 to 6 servings.
Note: Use fresh basil if you can; it makes a big difference.

HUNGARIAN ALMOND POPPY-SEED NOODLES
Cook ½ cup slivered blanched almonds in ¼ cup melted butter until golden. Add 2 tablespoons poppy seeds and 1 tablespoon paprika. Cook for 3 minutes, stirring constantly. Toss with hot cooked noodles (8-ounce package). Makes 4 to 6 servings.

FETTUCINE ALFREDO
1 pound noodles
½ cup fresh sweet butter, cut into pieces
2 cups freshly grated Parmesan cheese
½ teaspoon pepper

Cook noodles. Drain. Place in hot deep serving dish. Add butter, cheese, and pepper and toss thoroughly but quickly. Cheese and butter should melt into a creamy sauce that coats the noodles. Makes 6 servings.

THREE-TONE BUFFET NOODLES
Cook 8 ounces medium plain noodles according to package directions and dress with ¼ cup butter or margarine. Keep hot. Do the same with 8 ounces green noodles of the same size. Cook another 8 ounces medium plain noodles and dress with about 1 cup heated plain tomato sauce. Toss thoroughly and drain off excess sauce, if any. Noodles must be dry. Arrange noodles on heated platter in three groups: green noodles first, white ones in the middle, and red ones last. Serve plenty of grated Parmesan cheese separately. Makes 6 to 8 servings.

PRUNE-NOODLE PUDDING
6 ounces (3 cups) wide noodles
  Salt
3 eggs, separated
¾ cup sugar
1 cup milk
8 ounces (1¼ cups) dried prunes, pitted, soaked until soft, and chopped
¼ cup chopped nuts
2 teaspoons fresh lemon juice
1 teaspoon vanilla extract

Cook noodles in boiling salted water until tender; drain. In top part of small double boiler beat egg yolks and 1 egg white with ½ cup of the sugar until blended. Add milk and cook over simmering water, stirring constantly, until mixture is slightly thickened and coats a metal spoon. Add noodles, prunes, nuts, lemon juice, and vanilla. Put in buttered 1½-quart casserole. Beat remaining egg whites with a dash of salt until foamy. Gradually add remaining sugar, beating until stiff. Pile lightly onto mixture in casserole. Bake in preheated slow oven (325°F.) for 15 minutes, or until lightly browned. Serve warm or cold. Makes 6 servings.

NORWEGIAN COOKERY

by Nika Hazelton

Norway is a fishing country and
the cold waters of the northern sea
provide the cod, haddock, herring, salmon
and trout, unexcelled in quality, that
form the basis of the national cuisine

The scenery of Norway, from one end to the other, is beautiful beyond belief. The sea surrounds the mountains embracing them with the long arms of the fjords, and the mountains are part of the sea, dotting it with islands that make the heart long to go back to them. But it is the friendliness, the openhearted hospitality of the Norwegian people, that win the visitor at first meeting. Like Americans, Norwegians will take the stranger into their homes, and make him feel welcome immediately.

Norway is a fishing country, and the excellence of the fish and the way it is cooked cannot be praised sufficiently. The cold waters of the northern sea, lakes, and streams give a firmness of texture and a sweetness of flavor beyond compare to cod, haddock, herring, plaice, salmon, and trout; fish that constitute the greater part of the Norwegian diet. In the fish markets, which to the stranger's surprise are odorless, fish is bought within hours of its catching, or freshly killed, for all of Norway's towns are close to the fish-rich waters. It is a heartwarming sight to see a Norwegian housewife choosing the daily fish for her family. The fish is cooked with equal care, and since its quality is so superior, the Norwegians cook it plainly. First it is soaked in cold water and then it is briefly boiled or sautéed and served with a butter or herb sauce. The fish is cooked in servings, so that the second helping will come to the table as freshly cooked as the first. The livers, which do not taste like fish oil, and the tongues are eaten sautéed. Cod is the most highly prized fish. Herring is a standby in the daily diet, as in all of Scandinavia, and served in a multitude of ways, fresh, pickled, and preserved, the latter as a topping for the open-face sandwiches eaten for lunch or snacks.

A special Norwegian favorite is *fiske-pudding,* fish ground extremely fine, mixed with cream, sometimes with butter, and steamed. This mousse is served hot, with butter sauce, or sliced and sautéed, or cold as a sandwich topping. Norwegians also favor shrimps and crayfish.

The meats which Norway produces and eats in quantity are lamb and mutton. Whether it is the sweetness of the mountain pastures, or the tasty grass of the salt-water farms on which they feed, their meat is delicious.

Game birds of every kind, including the Arctic ptarmigan, and venison play a great part in Norway's diet. Much of Norway's terrain is vast forest; only 2.7 per cent of the country's 119,240 square miles are farming land, the rest being naked rock or deep forests. The products of the majestic, wonderfully silent Norwegian woods are cooked with great deli-

cacy, often with wine and with sour cream. Reindeer meat is one of the products of the forest cooked this way; the taste resembles that of beef, with just a touch of sweetness. Compotes of lingonberries, prunes, or apples are standard game accompaniments.

As for vegetables, potatoes and cabbage reign supreme, closely followed by carrots, turnips, and green vegetables in season.

Norwegians love fruit. Norwegian apples are excellent, and so are the berries of the north, lingonberries, blueberries, strawberries, and Arctic cloudberries, called *multer,* which look like yellow blackberries and taste both tart and sweet. Cooked and served with cream, they are festive fare, the Christmas dessert.

Like all Scandinavians, the Norwegians make very good pancakes, called *lefse,* and waffles which, surprisingly, they eat cold. The dark and rye Norwegian breads, including the flatbreads, are simply marvelous and the backbone of the diet.

Norwegian food has a certain family resemblance to other Scandinavian food. But it is less rich than the Danish and it relies far more on fish, game, and smoked meats than the Swedish, and the baking is also on a less lavish scale than that of Sweden, although fully as good.

APPETIZERS AND SOUPS

ISBJØRNØYE (Polar Bear's Eye)
- 12 flat anchovy fillets, chopped
- 2 medium potatoes, cooked, peeled, and chopped
- 6 onion slices, chopped
- 1 large beet, cooked, peeled, and chopped
- 6 raw egg yolks

On each of 6 plates make a circle of anchovies, potatoes, onions, and beets. Carefully place a raw egg yolk in the center of the circle. Chill and serve with flatbread and butter. Makes 6 servings.

KJØTTSALAT (Meat Salad)
Hearty salads of meat, chicken, game, or fish are popular on the Norwegian appetizer table and for cold suppers.

- 1 cup julienne strips of cooked beef, veal, or lamb
- 1 cup julienne strips of baked or boiled ham
- 1 tablespoon minced onion
- 6 tablespoons salad oil

- 2 tablespoons cider vinegar
- ½ teaspoon pepper
- 1 teaspoon minced parsley
- ¼ cup heavy cream or dairy sour cream
- 1 hard-cooked egg, sliced
- 1 boiled or pickled beet, sliced

Mix cut meats with onion. Beat together oil, vinegar, pepper, and parsley. Stir cream into dressing. Mix with meats, combining lightly. Garnish with sliced egg and beet. If served on appetizer table, where small servings are spooned onto guests' plates, this amount makes 6 servings. Or if served as a main-dish salad, makes 2 or 3 servings.

SPINATSUPPE (Spinach Soup)
- 2 pounds fresh spinach or 2 packages (10 ounces each) frozen chopped spinach
- 6 cups hot beef bouillon
- 3 tablespoons butter or margarine
- 2 tablespoons all-purpose flour
- 1 teaspoon salt
- ¼ teaspoon pepper
- ⅛ teaspoon ground nutmeg
- 2 hard-cooked eggs, sliced

Trim and wash fresh spinach thoroughly. Chop coarsely. Or thaw frozen spinach. Cook spinach in hot bouillon for 10 minutes. Drain, reserving liquid. Keep spinach hot. Melt butter and stir in flour. Add reserved liquid, stirring it in gradually. Cook over low heat, stirring occasionally, until slightly thickened. Simmer for 5 minutes. Add spinach, salt, pepper, and nutmeg, blending mixture thoroughly. Simmer, covered, for 5 minutes longer. Serve garnished with slices of hard-cooked egg. Makes 4 to 6 servings.
Note: In some homes a poached egg is placed in each plate.

KIRSEBÆRSUPPE (Cold Cherry Soup)
- 2½ pounds ripe cherries
- 2½ cups sugar
- 2½ quarts water
- 1-inch piece of cinnamon stick
- Juice of ½ lemon
- Grated rind of ½ lemon
- 2 cups sherry

Wash and stem cherries. Remove pits but do not discard them. Combine cherries, sugar, and water in large enamel or agate kettle and heat to boiling. Simmer for a few minutes. With slotted spoon, put cherries into large bowl. Put cherry pits in a small heavy plastic bag. Wrap bag with a towel and crush pits by hitting them with a hammer. Add crushed cherry pits to hot cherry juice with cinnamon stick and lemon juice and rind. Stir and let boil for 3 or 4 minutes. Remove from heat, strain, and pour over cherries. Chill. Just before serving add sherry. Makes 8

or more soup servings, 12 or more large beverage servings.

Note: Should be served very cold, in chilled glasses or bowls. Plain cookies or wafers go with this traditional favorite.

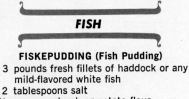

FISH

FISKEPUDDING (Fish Pudding)
- 3 pounds fresh fillets of haddock or any mild-flavored white fish
- 2 tablespoons salt
- ¼ cup cornstarch or potato flour
- ⅛ teaspoon ground nutmeg
- 2 cups light cream
- 2 cups milk
- Shrimp or Lobster Sauce

Rinse fillets; drain. Cut into small pieces and sprinkle with salt. Put fish through food chopper using finest blade. Mix ground fish with cornstarch and nutmeg. Put through chopper 4 more times. (A blender may be used instead of food chopper but the milk and cream must be blended with the fish.) Gradually beat in all the cream and milk. Mixture should be just thick enough to shape into balls which will hold their shape. Spoon two thirds of mixture into buttered 1½-quart baking dish. Cover tightly with foil. Set in shallow pan of hot water. Bake in preheated moderate oven (350° F.) for 40 to 60 minutes. Shape remaining fish mixture into balls about 1½ inches in diameter. Cook in lightly salted simmering water for 20 minutes. Drain; set aside and keep warm. To serve, turn mold out on warmed platter and garnish with cooked fish balls. Serve with hot Shrimp or Lobster Sauce. Makes about 12 servings.

Rekesaus (Shrimp Sauce)
- 1 pound shrimps
- 6 tablespoons butter or margarine
- ¼ cup all-purpose flour
- 3 cups milk or 1½ cups milk and 1½ cups fish stock
- 1 tablespoon dairy sour cream
- ½ teaspoon salt
- ½ teaspoon sugar
- 2 tablespoons sherry

Cook shrimps, clean, and cut into pieces. Melt half of butter in a large saucepan. Stir in flour and mix well. Add milk gradually, stirring constantly. Add remaining butter, sour cream, salt, and sugar. Mix and cook over low heat, stirring constantly, until smooth and thickened. Add shrimps and cook for 1 minute longer. Add sherry; remove from heat. Serve hot with Fish Pudding. Makes 2 cups.

Hummersaus (Lobster Sauce)
Substitute 2 cups cut-up cooked lobster meat for shrimps in above recipe.

Note: Leftover sauce (either shrimp or lobster) may be reheated in double boiler over hot water. Add 1 teaspoon sherry and use for a fish dish next day.

AVKOKT TORSK (Boiled Cod)
Rinse a 3- to 4-pound cod inside and out. The cod may be cooked whole or cut into slices. For sliced cod, cut off head and reserve. Cut fish into 1½-inch slices. Place whole fish or slices in deep bowl. Cover with ice cubes and set under running water to firm flesh. Drain and pat dry.

If using sliced cod, boil water in large kettle adding 2 tablespoons salt for each quart. Put fish slices and head into boiling water. Let water come to a boil, then simmer for 1 to 3 minutes. Do not overcook.

If using whole fish, wrap it in a long piece of cheesecloth, leaving long ends for handles. Place fish in cold water barely to cover, leaving ends outside of pan. To each quart of water added, add 2 tablespoons salt. Bring to a boil, lower heat, and simmer for 6 to 8 minutes a pound, depending on size of fish. Grasp ends of cloth and lift out fish. Drain well.

Peel tiny new potatoes and cook in vegetable steamer over boiling water. To serve, place cod and steamed potatoes on hot platter. Serve with drawn or Creamed Butter, chopped hard-cooked egg, grated fresh horseradish, and chopped parsley. Makes 4 to 6 servings.

Creamed Butter
- ¾ cup butter or margarine
- ½ teaspoon salt
- ⅛ teaspoon ground white pepper
- 1 to 2 teaspoons fresh lemon juice

Cream butter in a warm bowl until it has the consistency of mayonnaise. Stir in remaining ingredients, blending well. Makes about ¾ cup.

RØKET KOLJE (Smoked Haddock)
- 2 pounds smoked haddock
- 1 tablespoon salt
- 6 cups water
- 4 large carrots, cooked and diced
- ¼ cup chopped parsley
- 1 cup butter or margarine, softened
- 2 hard-cooked eggs, shelled and chopped

Skin haddock and cut into 4 serving pieces. Cook haddock in salt and water for 10 minutes. Drain. Serve with carrots and parsley. Cream butter until light and

fluffy. Gradually beat in chopped eggs and blend well. Spoon egg-butter sauce over each portion of hot fish. Makes 4 servings.

HAUGESUNDSK SPEDESILD (Haugesund Pickled Herrings)
- 2 large pickled herrings
- 3 tablespoons cider vinegar
- 3 tablespoons salad oil
- 1 teaspoon pepper
- 3 tablespoons sugar
- 1 small onion, minced
- 1 cup coarsely chopped pickled beets
- Minced parsley

Rinse herrings and soak for 12 hours. Cut into strips ½ x 1 inch. Arrange pieces to resemble the fish before it was cut. Mix vinegar, oil, pepper, and sugar. Pour mixture over herring and let stand for several hours. Serve garnished with onion, beets, and minced parsley. Makes 4 servings.

Note: Serve with boiled potatoes and thick dairy sour cream.

KOKT ØRRETT (Boiled Trout)
- 4 small whole trout
- 1 cup cider vinegar
- Water
- 1 tablespoon salt
- ½ cup butter or margarine, softened
- ½ cup chopped parsley
- Lemon wedges

Wash trout. Put trout in a shallow pan and add vinegar and enough water just to cover fish. Add salt. When water just starts to boil, remove from heat and let stand covered, for 15 to 20 minutes. Drain and carefully lift fish to a platter. Cream butter until light and fluffy and blend in parsley. Serve parsley butter with fish and garnish platter with lemon wedges. Makes 4 servings.

FISKEGRATENG (Fish au Gratin)
- 2 cups skinned boned cooked fish
- ¼ cup butter or margarine
- ¼ cup all-purpose flour
- 3 cups milk
- 1 teaspoon salt
- ¼ teaspoon pepper
- 4 eggs, separated
- 2 tablespoons sherry
- Dry bread crumbs

Break fish into bite-size pieces. Melt butter and stir in flour. Gradually stir in milk, salt, and pepper. Cook over low heat, stirring constantly, until smooth and thickened. Gradually beat hot sauce into beaten egg yolks. Add sherry and flaked fish. Beat egg whites until stiff but not dry. Fold egg whites into fish mixture. Grease 1½-quart casserole and sprinkle with fine bread crumbs. Pour

fish mixture into casserole. Bake in pre-heated moderate oven (375°F.) for 45 minutes. Makes 4 servings.

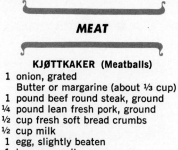

MEAT

KJØTTKAKER (Meatballs)

1 onion, grated
  Butter or margarine (about ⅓ cup)
1 pound beef round steak, ground
¼ pound lean fresh pork, ground
½ cup fresh soft bread crumbs
½ cup milk
1 egg, slightly beaten
1 teaspoon salt
¼ teaspoon ground nutmeg
  Dash of ground allspice
3 tablespoons all-purpose flour
1½ cups beef bouillon or water

Cook onion in 2 tablespoons melted butter for 2 or 3 minutes. Combine with meats, bread crumbs, milk, egg, and seasonings. Mix well and shape into firm balls about 1 inch in diameter. Brown a few at a time, shaking pan to prevent sticking. Allow meatballs to brown all over. Remove from pan. Stir in flour and gradually stir in bouillon. Cook over low heat until thickened, stirring constantly. Makes 4 servings.

PYTT I PANNE (Hash and Eggs)

3 cups chopped cooked meat
6 medium potatoes, cooked, peeled, and chopped
1 cup beef gravy
1 teaspoon salt
¼ teaspoon pepper
6 eggs

Mix meat with potatoes, gravy, salt, and pepper. Heat until mixture simmers. Carefully drop eggs over the meat and cook, covered, until eggs are firm. Makes 6 servings.

JULESKINKE (Christmas Ham)

1 fresh ham (9 to 10 pounds)
1 cup plus 1 tablespoon sugar
3 tablespoons fine salt
2 tablespoons saltpeter
4 cups light beer
4 cups dark beer
1½ pounds coarse salt

Rub fresh ham with a mixture of 1 tablespoon sugar, the fine salt, and 1 tablespoon saltpeter. Let stand for 24 hours. Combine 1 cup sugar, remaining saltpeter, beer, and coarse salt. Bring to boil and pour mixture over ham in a crock or enamelware kettle. Let stand, covered, in a cold place for 3 weeks. Make sure brine covers ham entirely. If necessary, make additional brine. Turn meat in brine every day. Reserve brine.

Blomkål I Rekesaus   Kjøttsalat

Isbjørnøye

Fiskepudding med Hummersaus

Hang ham to dry in an airy place. Smoke.* When ready, simmer for 4 hours in boiling unsalted water. Cool in reserved brine. Remove rind with sharp knife. Serve ham hot or cold with fresh vegetables. Leave ham in brine to keep juicy. Makes 12 to 14 servings.

* To smoke ham: Hang scrubbed and well-dried meat in smokehouse. Build a small fire of green hardwood such as hickory, oak, pecan, or apple. Do not use resinous woods. Keep temperature between 80°F. and 90°F. Open ventilators the first day. On second day, close ventilators and smoke until ham has the desired color. A thin haze of smoke will smoke meat best.

FÅRIKÅL (Lamb and Cabbage)
    4 pounds boneless lamb, cut into 2-inch cubes
    1 medium head green cabbage, cut into 1-inch wedges
    1 celeriac, peeled and diced, or 1 cup diced celery
 1½ teaspoons salt
    ⅓ cup all-purpose flour
      Boiling bouillon or water
    2 tablespoons peppercorns tied in cheesecloth bag
    ½ cup dairy sour cream

Trim excess fat from lamb. In a heavy saucepan place a layer of meat, fatty side down. Top with cabbage and sprinkle with some of celeriac, salt, and flour. Repeat until you have at least 3 layers of meat and vegetables. Add bouillon to cover lamb and cabbage halfway. Add peppercorns. Cover tightly and bring to a boil. Lower heat and simmer for 1½ to 2½ hours, or until meat is tender. Add more bouillon to keep mixture from sticking. Remove peppercorns. Stir sour cream into mixture and reheat, but do not boil. Serve with boiled potatoes and pickled beets. Makes 4 to 6 servings.

LAMMEKJØTT I SURSAUS (Lamb Shanks with Sour-Cream Sauce)
    6 lamb shanks
      Salt and pepper
    3 tablespoons butter or margarine
    1 large onion, chopped
 1½ cups dry white wine
    ½ cup beef bouillon
    2 tablespoons all-purpose flour
    3 tablespoons water
    3 tablespoons chopped fresh dill
    1 cup dairy sour cream

Trim excess fat from lamb shanks. Wash and pat dry. Rub meat with salt and pepper. Heat butter in skillet and brown lamb shanks on all sides. Transfer shanks to a deep kettle. Add onion to pan drippings and sauté until tender. Pour onion with drippings over shanks. Add wine and bouillon. Simmer covered, for about 1½ hours, or until tender. Remove shanks to a hot platter. Strain stock and return to kettle. Mix flour and water to a smooth paste and stir into stock. Cook over low heat until smooth and thickened, stirring constantly. Stir in dill and sour cream. Return lamb shanks to sauce and reheat but do not boil. Serve with steamed potatoes sprinkled with chopped fresh dill and a cucumber salad. Makes 6 servings.

PUSS PASS (Lamb Stew)
    2 pounds boneless lamb, cubed
    8 large potatoes, peeled and diced
    8 carrots, scraped and sliced
    ½ head green cabbage, cored and shredded
    1 teaspoon peppercorns
    2 teaspoons salt
    1 tablespoon all-purpose flour
    1 cup water

Put meat and vegetables in layers in a large heavy saucepan. Add peppercorns, salt, and flour. Pour water over the top. Cover and simmer for 2 to 3 hours. Makes 8 servings.

REINSDYRSTEIK (Saddle of Reindeer)
    4-pound saddle of reindeer or venison
   10 tablespoons butter or margarine
    1 tablespoon salt
    1 teaspoon pepper
    2 cups boiling water
    1 tablespoon all-purpose flour
    1 cup dairy sour cream
    ⅓ cup diced Muenster cheese

Wash meat and dry. Spread meat with ½ cup butter and sprinkle with salt and pepper. Put meat in shallow roasting pan in preheated very hot oven (450°F.) for 15 minutes, or until meat is lightly browned. Reduce heat to moderate (350° F.), add water, and continue cooking for 2½ to 3 hours, or until meat is tender. Baste meat frequently during cooking. Put meat on a platter. Melt 1 tablespoon butter and stir in flour. Gradually stir in pan drippings. Cook over low heat, stirring constantly, until smooth and thickened. Stir in sour cream and Muenster cheese. Continue cooking until cheese melts. Add 1 more tablespoon butter and remove gravy from heat, stirring until butter melts. Serve gravy with meat. Makes 8 servings.

VEGETABLES AND SALADS

SURKÅL (Cabbage with Caraway)
    1 small head green cabbage, cored and shredded

    2 tablespoons all-purpose flour
    1 teaspoon salt
    1 tablespoon caraway seeds
    2 tablespoons butter or margarine
 1¼ cups diluted consommé
    2 tablespoons vinegar
    1 tablespoon sugar

Put shredded cabbage in large saucepan. Sprinkle cabbage with flour, salt, and caraway seeds. Heat butter with consommé and pour hot mixture over cabbage. Cover and simmer for 1½ hours, or until cabbage is tender. Stir in vinegar and sugar. Serve immediately. Makes 4 to 6 servings, depending on size of cabbage.

BLOMKÅL I REKESAUS (Hot Cauliflower with Shrimps)
    1 large cauliflower
    2 cups milk
    ½ medium onion, minced
    2 sprigs of fresh dill
    ¼ cup butter or margarine
    ¼ cup all-purpose flour
    1 teaspoon salt
    ¼ teaspoon ground white pepper
    2 cups cooked and shelled shrimps, chopped
    ¾ cup heavy cream, whipped
   12 whole shrimps, cooked and shelled
    2 tablespoons minced fresh dill

Trim cauliflower, wash thoroughly, and cook whole in boiling salted water. Meanwhile make sauce. Combine milk, onion, and dill. Bring to a boil. Strain milk and keep hot. Melt butter and stir in flour. Cook mixture over low heat for 3 minutes. Do not brown. Stir hot milk gradually into mixture and cook over low heat, stirring constantly, until smooth and thickened. Cook for 2 minutes longer. Season with salt and pepper. Add chopped shrimps and cook over very low heat until heated through. Fold whipped cream into sauce. Place hot cauliflower on serving dish and pour sauce over it. Decorate with whole shrimps and minced dill. Makes 4 to 6 servings.

NEDLAGTE RØDBETER (Pickled Beets)
    3 pounds medium-size beets
      Water
    2 teaspoons caraway seeds
    4 cups cider vinegar
    ¾ cup sugar

Wash beets. Do not peel. Add water to cover and cook at a simmer until beets are tender. Do not prick beets too often or they will "bleed." Drain and cool. Peel beets and cut into very thin slices. Place slices in sterilized jars and sprinkle caraway seeds over the top. Combine vinegar and sugar and bring to boil. Pour hot mixture over the beets. Seal and

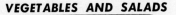

cool. Store for at least 2 weeks before using. Makes about 3 pints.

SOMMERSALAT (Summer Salad)

1 head Boston lettuce
2 large potatoes, cooked, peeled, and sliced
2 hard-cooked eggs, shelled and chopped
1 cup cooked green peas
¼ cup salad oil
2 tablespoons vinegar
2 tablespoons prepared mustard
1 teaspoon salt
1 teaspoon sugar
2 large tomatoes, sliced

Trim lettuce and separate leaves. Wash and drain thoroughly. Mix lettuce with potatoes, eggs, and green peas. Chill. Mix oil, vinegar, mustard, salt, and sugar. Toss salad with salad dressing. Pour mixture into a salad bowl. Garnish with sliced tomatoes. Makes 4 servings.

SALAT (Lettuce, Norwegian Fashion)

2 heads Boston lettuce
½ cup dairy sour cream
1 tablespoon cider vinegar
1½ teaspoons sugar
½ teaspoon prepared mustard
2 hard-cooked eggs, shelled

Trim lettuce and separate leaves. Wash, drain, and crisp in the refrigerator. Mix sour cream with vinegar, sugar, and mustard. Toss lettuce with sour-cream dressing. Serve garnished with wedges of hard-cooked eggs. Makes 4 servings.

SAUCES

SENNEPSSAUS (Mustard Sauce)

¼ cup butter or margarine
¼ cup all-purpose flour
1½ cups beef bouillon
1½ cups water
½ teaspoon salt
1½ teaspoons powdered mustard
1 cup heavy cream
1½ teaspoons fresh lemon juice
4 egg yolks, well beaten

Melt butter and stir in flour. Gradually stir in bouillon and water. Stir in salt and mustard. Cook over low heat, stirring constantly, until smooth and thickened. Beat cream with lemon juice and egg yolks. Gradually beat hot sauce into egg mixture. Reheat but do not boil. Makes about 4 cups sauce.

PEPPERROTSAUS (Horseradish Sauce)

2 cups dairy sour cream
2 to 3 tablespoons grated prepared horseradish
2 teaspoons sugar

Combine all ingredients and blend well. Serve with lamb, veal, chicken, or fish. Makes about 2 cups sauce.

LØKSAUS (Onion Sauce)

4 onions, peeled and chopped
2 tablespoons butter or margarine
½ teaspoon salt
¼ teaspoon ground white pepper
1 teaspoon sugar
2 tablespoons all-purpose flour
1 cup meat bouillon or milk
2 teaspoons horseradish or vinegar

Sauté chopped onions in melted butter with salt, pepper, and sugar. Cook over low heat, stirring constantly, until onions are tender but not brown. Stir in flour. Gradually stir in bouillon and continue to cook, stirring, until smooth and thickened. Stir in horseradish. Serve with boiled meat. Makes about 2 cups sauce.

BREADS AND PANCAKES

RUGBRØD (Rye Bread)

2 packages active dry yeast or 2 cakes compressed yeast
1 cup lukewarm water*
1½ cups scalded milk
2 teaspoons salt
1 teaspoon sugar
6 to 7 cups sifted rye flour

Sprinkle or crumble yeast into water. *Use very warm water (105°F. to 115° F.) for dry yeast; use lukewarm (80°F. to 90°F.) for compressed. Let stand for a few minutes, then stir until dissolved. Cool scalded milk to lukewarm. Stir in salt, sugar, and dissolved yeast. Beat in enough flour to make a stiff dough. Pour remaining flour onto a board and knead dough for a few minutes. Put in bowl, brush with shortening, and let rise in warm place until doubled in bulk. Shape dough into 2 round loaves. Put loaves on lightly greased cookie sheets. Let rise until doubled in bulk. Bake in preheated moderate oven (350°F.) for 45 minutes, or until loaves when thumped give a hollow sound. Makes 2 loaves.

JULEKAKE (Christmas Bread)

1½ cups milk
1½ cups sugar
1 cup margarine
1½ teaspoons salt
4 packages active dry yeast or 4 cakes compressed yeast
1 cup warm water*
9 cups sifted all-purpose flour
2 teaspoons ground cardamom
1 cup raisins
1½ cups diced citron

Scald milk, mix in sugar, margarine, and

salt. Cool to lukewarm. Sprinkle or crumble yeast into water. *Use very warm water (105°F. to 115°F.) for dry yeast; use lukewarm (80°F. to 90°F.) for compressed. Let stand for a few minutes, then stir until dissolved. Stir dissolved yeast into milk mixture. Add 2 cups flour and the cardamom. Mix well. Add remaining flour, 2 cups at a time, mixing well after each addition. Turn out on floured board. Knead well for several minutes until smooth and elastic. Place in greased bowl. Turn over. Let rise, covered, in warm place for 1½ hours, or until doubled in bulk. Punch down. Turn out on floured board. Knead in raisins and citron. Form into 4 balls each about 6 inches in diameter, or 8 smaller ones. Place several inches apart on 2 greased cookie sheets. Let rise, covered, in warm place for 1½ hours, or until doubled in bulk. Bake in preheated moderate oven (375°F.) for about 30 minutes for the 4 round loaves, or for 15 to 20 minutes for 8 smaller ones. Cool on wire racks. Frost with confectioners'-sugar icing and decorate with additional citron, if desired.

KAFFEKAKE (Coffeecake)

4 eggs
¾ cup sugar
⅔ cup melted butter
1 teaspoon fresh lemon juice
1 teaspoon ground cardamom
3¾ cups sifted all-purpose flour
3¾ teaspoons baking powder

Beat eggs and sugar together until light. Add melted butter, lemon juice, and cardamom. Mix well. Sift flour and baking powder together. Add to egg mixture and mix well. Turn the dough out on a lightly floured board. Cut into 4 portions. Shape each into a long roll. Place rolls on greased and lightly floured cookie sheets. Bake in preheated hot oven (425° F.) for 20 minutes or a little longer. The top should be lightly browned. Remove from oven and let cool slightly. Cut into ½-inch slices while still warm. Spread out slices flat on a cookie sheet and return to hot oven (425°F.) for 5 minutes to brown slightly. It is much like rusk in flavor and texture, not soft but a little dry. Excellent with coffee. Makes 5 to 6 dozen pieces.

PLÄTTAR or PANNEKAKER (Tiny Pancakes)

1 egg, well beaten
1 cup milk
1 teaspoon sugar
⅔ cup sifted all-purpose flour
¼ teaspoon salt
Butter for frying

Mix first 5 ingredients as given. Heat *plättar* pan slowly and brush with melted butter. Put 1 tablespoon of batter into each round opening in the pan. Brown on one side, turn, and brown on other side. Brush *plättar* pan with butter each time before pouring batter into round openings. Serve hot with lingonberries. Makes 21 tiny pancakes, 3 servings.

Note: The pans for these can be bought in specialty hardware stores.

LEFSER (Griddle Cakes)

4 cups riced hot potatoes
2½ tablespoons light cream
2½ tablespoons lard
1½ tablespoons sugar
1 teaspoon salt
2 cups sifted all-purpose flour

Mix riced potatoes with cream and lard. Chill for 1 hour. Add sugar, salt, and flour. Blend thoroughly. Take about ⅓ cup of mixture and form into 2 balls. Continue with remaining dough. Chill balls for 1 hour. On a lightly floured board roll each ball into a paper-thin round about 5 inches in diameter. Cook on heated griddle over low heat until very light tan. Turn and cook on other side. Serve hot or cold. Makes 26.

VAFFLER (Waffles)

1 cup dairy sour cream, whipped
1½ teaspoons sugar
Pinch of salt
1 egg, well beaten
⅔ cup sifted all-purpose flour

Combine all ingredients in order given. Beat and blend well. Put 1 tablespoon of batter in hot Norwegian waffle iron. Cook until golden-brown. Makes 35 waffles. Makes 4 to 6 servings.

Note: Can be prepared in a regular waffle iron. Prepare a double recipe.

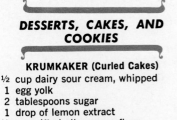

DESSERTS, CAKES, AND COOKIES

KRUMKAKER (Curled Cakes)

½ cup dairy sour cream, whipped
1 egg yolk
2 tablespoons sugar
1 drop of lemon extract
½ cup sifted all-purpose flour

Combine all ingredients in order given. Put 1 teaspoon of batter in the center of a preheated *krumkake* pan. Close the lid and cook for a few minutes, turning the pan once to brown on both sides. Roll the cake while still hot around the handle of a wooden cooking spoon. Makes 12 to 16.

Note: These pans can be bought in specialty hardware stores.

FATTIGMANN (Poor Man's Cake)

5 egg yolks
3 tablespoons confectioners' sugar
¼ cup heavy cream, whipped
1 tablespoon brandy
½ teaspoon ground cardamom
½ teaspoon grated lemon rind
2 to 2½ cups sifted all-purpose flour
Fat or lard for deep frying
Confectioners' sugar

Beat egg yolks until thick and lemon-colored. Stir in confectioners' sugar. Stir in whipped cream, brandy, cardamom, and lemon rind. Stir in flour until dough becomes stiff enough to knead. Chill overnight. Roll out on a lightly floured board to ⅛-inch thickness. Cut into shapes with pastry cutter. Fry in deep hot fat or lard (370°F. on a frying thermometer) for 2 or 3 minutes, or until golden-brown on both sides. Sprinkle with confectioners' sugar. Makes 2½ dozen cakes.

RABARBRAGRØT (Rhubarb Pudding)

1½ pounds rhubarb
1½ cups water
¾ cup sugar
1½ teaspoons vanilla extract
3 tablespoons cornstarch
1 cup heavy cream

Trim rhubarb and cut into ½-inch slices. Combine with water and ½ cup sugar and simmer until soft. Stir in ½ teaspoon vanilla. Blend cornstarch with a little cold water to make a smooth liquid. Gradually stir cornstarch into rhubarb. Cook over low heat, stirring constantly, until thickened and clear. Pour rhubarb into glass serving dish and chill. At serving time, whip cream. When frothy add remaining sugar and vanilla. Whip until stiff. Pipe whipped cream through a pastry tube in decorative swirls over top of pudding, or cover top of pudding with spoonfuls of whipped cream. Makes 4 servings.

TROLLKREM (Magic Cream)

3 egg whites
⅓ cup sugar
2 tablespoons fresh lemon juice
1 cup thick well-flavored applesauce or other puréed fruit

Beat egg whites until stiff but not dry. Gradually beat in sugar, 1 tablespoon at a time. Beat in lemon juice and continue beating until mixture is stiff and glossy. Fold in applesauce. Spoon into serving dishes and serve as soon as possible. Makes 4 to 6 servings.

SVISKEKOMPOTT (Baked Prune Custard)

1-pound box medium prunes (25 to 30)
Port
Whole blanched almonds
3 egg yolks
¼ cup sugar
1 teaspoon vanilla extract
1 cup light cream
½ cup heavy cream, whipped

Cover prunes with port and soak overnight, or simmer for 5 to 10 minutes. The prunes should still retain their shape. Drain and pit with a sharp pointed knife. Replace prune pits with whole almonds. Put prunes in 1½-quart baking dish (6 x 10 inches) in a single layer. Beat egg yolks with sugar until thick and light. Add vanilla. Heat cream and stir into egg-yolk mixture. Pour mixture over prunes. Bake in preheated slow oven (325°F.) for 30 to 40 minutes, or until custard is set. Chill. At serving time decorate with whipped cream, forced through a decorating tube if desired. Makes 4 to 6 servings.

JEG KAN IKKE LA VÆRE (Irresistible Dessert)

4 eggs, separated
½ cup sugar
1 envelope unflavored gelatin
¼ cup cold water
¼ cup fresh lemon juice
Whipped cream
Maraschino cherries
Macaroons

Beat egg yolks until thick and lemon-colored. Gradually beat in sugar. Soften gelatin in cold water and let stand for 5 minutes. Dissolve gelatin by placing over low heat and stirring until gelatin is dissolved. Add gelatin to egg-yolk mixture. Stir in lemon juice. Beat egg whites until stiff but not dry. Fold egg whites into egg-yolk mixture. Pour mixture into serving dish. Chill until firm. Garnish with whipped cream, maraschino cherries, and macaroons. Makes 4 servings.

KLEJNER (Fried Twists)

2 whole eggs
2 egg yolks
¾ cup sugar
½ cup melted butter or margarine
½ cup light cream
All-purpose flour (about 3 cups)
1 teaspoon baking powder
Fat or cooking oil for deep frying
Confectioners' sugar

Beat whole eggs with egg yolks until thick and lemon-colored. Gradually beat in sugar. Stir in melted butter and cream. Sift 2 cups flour with baking powder and stir into egg mixture. Then stir in enough additional flour so that dough cleans the

bowl. Roll on a lightly floured board until ⅛ inch thick. Cut dough into strips or diamonds 3 to 4 inches long and about 1½ inches wide. Cut a slit in center of each strip and pull one end completely through slit. Drop into deep hot fat (375°F. on a frying thermometer) and fry for 2 or 3 minutes, or until golden-brown on both sides. Drain on absorbent paper. Sprinkle with confectioners' sugar. Makes about 4 dozen.

BLÅBÆRKAKE (Blueberry Cake)

2 cups fresh blueberries, rinsed and drained
1½ cups fine cracker meal
½ to 1 cup sugar
½ cup melted butter or margarine
Heavy cream, whipped

Put half of blueberries in a greased casserole (1 quart). Top with half of cracker meal, half of sugar, and half of butter. Repeat the layering, ending with butter. Bake in preheated moderate oven (375°F.) for 1 hour. Serve warm, with whipped cream. Makes 4 servings.

TELEGRAFKAKE (Telegraph Cake)

3 cups sifted all-purpose flour
2 teaspoons baking powder
2 cups sugar
1 cup dried currants
½ cup chopped blanched almonds
¾ cup chopped mixed candied fruit
1 cup melted butter
1 cup milk
2 eggs, well beaten

Sift flour with baking powder and sugar. Add currants, almonds, and mixed candied fruit. Mix butter with milk and eggs. Add liquid ingredients to dry ingredients and stir until well blended. Pour mixture into greased and floured 9-inch tube pan. Bake in preheated moderate oven (375°F.) for 45 minutes to 1 hour.

KONG HAAKONSKAKE (King Haakon's Cake)

1 cup butter or margarine
1 cup sugar
1 teaspoon vanilla extract
4 eggs, separated
1 cup sifted all-purpose flour
1 cup potato flour or cornstarch
1 teaspoon baking powder
⅛ teaspoon salt
Chocolate Cream Filling
Marzipan

Cream butter until light and fluffy. Gradually beat in sugar and vanilla. Add egg yolks, one at a time. Sift both flours with

Goro Cakes

baking powder and salt. Stir dry ingredients into creamed mixture. Beat egg whites until stiff but not dry and fold into batter. Pour batter into well-greased 9-inch springform pan. Bake in preheated moderate oven (350°F.) for 25 to 35 minutes, or until top is golden-brown. Unmold and cool. When thoroughly cool, cut cake with sharp knife into 3 layers. Put layers together with Chocolate Cream Filling. Cover cake entirely with Marzipan. Garnish with King Haakon's initials H VIII and small Norwegian flags. Makes 12 servings.

Chocolate Cream Filling
3 egg yolks
¼ cup sugar
2 teaspoons all-purpose flour
3 tablespoons cocoa
1 cup heavy cream
2 ounces (2 squares) unsweetened chocolate, melted

Beat egg yolks; stir in sugar and flour. Beat in cocoa, ½ cup of cream, and melted chocolate. Cook over low heat, stirring constantly, until smooth and thickened. Cool. Whip remaining cream and fold it into chocolate mixture.

Marzipan
1½ cups finely ground blanched almonds
3½ cups (1 pound) confectioners' sugar
¼ teaspoon almond extract
1 to 2 egg whites, beaten until foamy
Food coloring (optional)

Mix almonds with confectioners' sugar. Add almond extract and egg white, 1 teaspoon at a time, until almonds can be kneaded into a paste. Tint, if desired.

MANDELTERTER
(Almond Tarts and Cookies)
½ cup butter or margarine
⅓ cup sugar
1 egg yolk, lightly beaten
½ cup very finely chopped blanched almonds
1½ cups sifted all-purpose flour
1 cup heavy cream, whipped and sweetened, or other fillings for tarts

Cream butter until light and fluffy. Beat in sugar. Add egg yolk, almonds, and flour. Mix well and chill. Rub small fluted muffin or tart pans lightly with butter or margarine. Roll dough on a lightly floured board to ⅛-inch thickness. Cut into rounds to fit pans and press dough lightly into pans. Bake in preheated moderate oven (325°F.) for 10 minutes. Let tarts cool in pans. Fill with sweetened

whipped cream or other tart fillings. Makes 3 dozen very small tart shells or 1 to 2 dozen larger shells.

Use same recipe to make cookies. Use cookie press, or roll lightly and cut into S shapes or crescents. Bake on lightly greased and floured cookie sheets in preheated moderate oven (325°F.) for 8 to 10 minutes. Let cool. Store between layers of wax paper in covered tin or jar. Makes 4 dozen or more small cookies.

GORO CAKES (Wafers)
1 cup butter
1 egg, well beaten
½ cup sugar
½ cup heavy cream, whipped
1 tablespoon brandy
2 teaspoons vanilla extract or grated lemon rind
2½ to 3 cups sifted all-purpose flour

Cream butter until light and fluffy. Beat in egg and sugar. Stir in whipped cream, brandy, and vanilla. Add enough flour to make a dough that can be rolled. Roll out on lightly floured board to ⅛-inch thickness. Cut out shapes that will fit the *goro* iron. Put dough in the preheated *goro* iron and cook until golden-brown. Trim edges and cut into sections immediately; cool. Makes 24 sections.
Note: *Goro* irons can be bought in specialty food stores.

MOR-MONSEN KAKER
(Mother Monsen Cakes)
1½ cups butter or margarine, melted
2½ cups sugar
4 eggs, well beaten
1 teaspoon vanilla extract
2½ cups sifted all-purpose flour
¾ cup chopped blanched almonds
⅓ cup dried currants

Melt butter and stir in sugar. Beat in eggs and vanilla. Add flour and stir until well blended. Spread dough in 2 greased and floured 8-inch square pans. Sprinkle dough with almonds and currants. Press into dough lightly. Bake in preheated moderate oven (375°F.) for 30 to 35

minutes, or until top is lightly browned. Cut with sharp knife into fingers, diamonds, or squares. Makes 30 to 36 cookies, depending on the shape.

SERINAKAKER (Serina Cakes)
2 cups sifted all-purpose flour
1 teaspoon baking powder
1 cup plus 2 tablespoons sugar
1 cup butter or margarine
1 egg, well beaten
1 teaspoon vanilla extract
2 egg whites
½ cup chopped blanched almonds

Sift flour with baking powder and 1 cup sugar. Cut in butter until mixture resembles coarse cornmeal. Add egg, vanilla, and 1 egg white, beaten until stiff and then beaten with 2 tablespoons sugar. Blend well. With floured fingers shape dough into small balls. Beat remaining egg white until foamy. Dip each ball into egg white, then roll in chopped nuts. Put on greased cookie sheets and flatten slightly. Bake in preheated moderate oven (350°F.) for 12 to 14 minutes. Makes about 4 dozen.

FIRE-SPECIEDALER-KAKER
(Four Specie Dollars)
1 cup butter or margarine
1½ cups sifted all-purpose flour
1½ cups sugar
1½ cups coarsely chopped blanched almonds

Cream butter until light and fluffy. Beat in flour and sugar. Stir in almonds and mix well. Shape mixture into long roll about 1½ inches in diameter. Wrap in wax paper and chill overnight. Cut into ¼-inch slices and put on greased cookie sheets, about 2 inches apart. Bake in preheated moderate oven (350°F.) for 10 to 12 minutes, or until lightly browned. Makes about 5 dozen.

PLESKENER (Spongecake Cookies)
4 eggs, separated
1⅓ cups sugar
1 teaspoon vanilla extract or grated rind of 1 lemon
1⅓ cups sifted all-purpose flour

Beat egg yolks until thick and lemon-colored. Beat in sugar and flavoring. Stir in flour. Fold in egg whites which have been beaten until stiff but not dry. Drop dough by teaspoonfuls onto greased cookie sheets, 2 inches apart. Bake in preheated moderate oven (350°F.) for 12 minutes, or until pale golden-brown. Makes about 4 dozen.

NOUGAT—A confection made with roasted nuts such as almonds or walnuts and sugar or honey. Sometimes egg white is added to bind the mixture. The word comes from the Latin *nux* or "nut."

Nougat of all kinds is a very old confection, possibly of Moorish origin. It has always been popular in Spain, Italy, and France. A variety of nougat much favored in these countries is *touron* in Spanish, or *torrone* in Italian, a chewy candy prevalent especially at Christmas time. There are a great many varieties of nougat: hard or soft, white or colored. Brown nougat, made from caramelized sugar and chopped almonds, is used by candymakers in their confections, or in professional fancy baking.

White nougat usually contains honey and sugar mixed, almonds, and white of egg. It is chewy rather than brittle.

FRENCH NOUGAT

Put 1 cup confectioners' sugar in heavy saucepan. Heat, stirring, until sugar is melted and golden-brown. Stir in 1 cup finely chopped blanched almonds. Put mixture on oiled platter and fold over and over with a spatula. When cool enough to handle, divide in four parts and, with hands, shape to form rolls about ½ inch in diameter. When hard, cut into 1½-inch pieces. Makes about ½ pound.

WALNUT NOUGAT

1 cup sugar
½ cup water
3 tablespoons light corn syrup
2 egg whites
¼ teaspoon salt
½ cup honey
1 cup broken walnut meats
1 teaspoon vanilla extract

Put sugar, water, and 2 tablespoons of the corn syrup in small, deep heavy saucepan. Bring to boil, stirring until sugar is dissolved. Continue cooking to 290°F. on a candy thermometer. Beat egg whites with salt until stiff. Gradually add syrup, beating constantly with electric beater. Continue beating while cooking honey and remaining corn syrup to a temperature of 290°F. Gradually add honey mixture to egg-white mixture, beating constantly. Add nuts and put mixture in top part of double boiler. Cook over simmering water, stirring frequently, for about 15 minutes, or until candy begins to dry out. Add vanilla and press into buttered pan (8 x 8 x 2 inches). Let stand until firm. Then cut into 1½- x ¾-inch pieces. Makes about 1 pound.
Note: Use candy thermometer in making this recipe.

NUT—The word is used to describe a large number of dry fruits which generally consist of a single kernel enclosed in a woody shell. Acorns, filberts, and hazelnuts are examples of true nuts. The Brazil nut represents another type of dry fruit popularly classed as a nut: it grows like the segments of an orange, eight to twenty-four of them within a single hard-walled husk. Some nuts are, botanically speaking, legumes. The peanut, for instance, is the pod of a vine of the pea family.

Some fruits whose kernels are not dry are called nuts because of their nutlike shells. The litchi nut, for example, is a fleshy raisinlike fruit enclosed in a shell. But not all the shells of true nuts are hard. The almond and pecan, for instance, come in more than one variety. Some have hard shells, some have soft ones, and some have paper-thin shells.

Nuts are one of man's oldest foods and one of the most useful. They may be eaten raw (usually dried), cooked, or in nut butters and pastes. Some nuts are dried and ground to serve as a coffee substitute or as a flour. Nuts are also used to feed livestock. Sometimes they are strung to make decorative necklaces and very hard nut shells are made into buttons.

Nuts were the traditional playthings of Roman children. They became so closely associated with childhood that it was customary for a bridegroom at his wedding to scatter nuts to the guests signifying that he had put away his childish pursuits.

Early Roman gourmets ate almonds, beechnuts, filberts, chestnuts, hazelnuts, pine kernels, and walnuts, and they were used in cooking. The Middle Ages and the Renaissance had many recipes for the use of nuts. Hugh Platt, an Englishman writing in 1609, tells how to make a sucket, a sort of conserve: "To make sucket of greene Walnuts. Take Walnuts when they are no bigger than the largest hasill nut, pare awaye the vppermost greene, but not too deepe, then seeth them in a pottle [2 quarts of water] till the water bee sodden away, then take so much more of fresh water, and when it is sodden to the halfe, put thereto a quart of vinegar and a pottle of clarified honie."

North America has always had a plentiful supply of nuts, welcomed by the early colonists as a relief from the meager diet on which they were forced to subsist. Many unusual ways of preparing nuts were practiced by the Indians and the colonists learned to copy them. Not only were nuts eaten out-of-hand, but they were roasted and added to various meat and vegetable stews. The Indians ground the dried kernels and used the meal to make breads and puddings much as they used corn. The hickory nut is native to America and an Indian milklike preparation was made from the boiled nuts. Chestnuts were also prepared in this way. The nuts the colonists found included the chestnut, hickory, pecan, black walnut, chinquapin, beechnut, and acorn.

Availability—The nuts available commercially are almonds, Brazil nuts, cashews, chestnuts, filberts, or hazelnuts, Macadamias, peanuts, pecans, pine nuts, pistachios, and walnuts. They are sold in the shell or shelled either by variety or as mixed nuts. Nuts are also sold chopped, ground, blanched or unblanched and in halves. Almonds alone come in the shell, shelled, either unblanched or blanched, chopped, slivered either plain or toasted, and ground either dry or into a paste. Nuts are sold in plastic bags, in boxes, in jars, and vacuum-packed in cans. They are sold dry-roasted (without additional fat), roasted in additional fat, toasted in hot deep fat or vegetable shortening, and either unsalted or salted. Some varieties are spiced, sugared, made into nut clusters, dipped into fondant, candy coating, or chocolate.

Many oils are extracted from nuts; peanut oil is the most popular. Some nuts are made into flour after oil is extracted. Available in health food stores are peanut and chestnut flour and almond meal. Some unripe nuts, such as green almonds and green walnuts, are sold pickled.

Purchasing Guide—If nuts are to be stored for a long period of time they should be purchased in the shell. A very general rule of thumb for the amount to buy is:
    1 pound nuts in the shell = ½ pound shelled nuts
When buying nuts in the shell, look for shells with no scars, cracks, or holes. Kernels should not rattle when nuts are shaken.

In shelled nuts, the nutmeats should be plump, meaty, crisp, and uniform in color and size.

Storage—Exposure to air, light, warmth, and moisture can cause rancidity in nuts. For long storage nuts should be kept unshelled. If shelled, do not chop or grind nuts until ready to use and keep as cool as possible; the colder they are the longer they will keep. Store in an airtight container to prevent absorption of foreign flavors and odors.

The length of time nuts can be stored varies greatly with the type of nut, but in general unshelled nuts can be kept at room temperature for about 1 year, and shelled nuts, in a moisture-proof wrapping, can be kept refrigerated for at least 4 months.

Nutritive Food Values—Although these vary with the specific nut, nuts are by

and large a good source of protein; and a fair source of phosphorus, iron, and thiamine. They have a high fat content.

Basic Preparation

☐ **To Salt**—In a large skillet heat about 2 tablespoons cooking oil for each cup of nuts. Cook, stirring, over medium heat until nuts are lightly browned, about 3 minutes. Sprinkle with salt and toss lightly to coat all nuts. Allow about ½ teaspoon salt for each cup of nuts. Other seasoning, such as curry powder, Worcestershire, etc., may be added at this point.

☐ **To Grate**—It is important to grate the nuts so that they will not be too oily when added to tortes or other preparations. Special nut graters are made for this. Nuts can also be ground in a blender, a small amount at a time.

☐ **To Blanch**—Cover them with boiling water and let stand for 5 minutes. Drain and cool slightly but rub the skins off with the fingers while they are still warm and moist.

☐ **To Roast and Toast**—Put nuts in pre-heated slow oven (300°F.) and bake until lightly browned. Nuts may be blanched or unblanched. Some nuts may be roasted in the shell.

☐ **To Deep Fry**—Heat the fat or oil to 360°F. on a frying thermometer. Fry nuts for 2 or 3 minutes, or until lightly browned. Sprinkle with salt or other spice or herb seasoning and store until needed in an airtight container.

NUT BUTTER—A spread made from finely ground nuts which may be blanched or unblanched. Particularly good for homemade nut butters are almonds, cashews, filberts, and peanuts. To produce the smooth oily texture needed to make a good nut butter, a food chopper or a blender is used to crush the nuts.

Nut butters made commercially include the most popular, peanut butter, and the less widely available almond and cashew butters.

Nut butters are used as is; or they may be blended with soft butter; or seasoned with a little salt, Worcestershire, or hot pepper sauce. In addition to their use as spreads, they are used as a flavoring for sauces, frostings, and other cooked dishes.

Nutritive Food Values—Nut butters are rich in fats, with good amounts of high-quality protein and carbohydrates and fair amounts of phosphorus and iron. They are a good source of thiamine.

Storage—Homemade nut butters should be stored in the refrigerator since fats at room temperature tend to become rancid. Commercially made nut butters have additives which prevent rancidity and they

may be stored on the kitchen shelf. Read label for proper storing instructions.

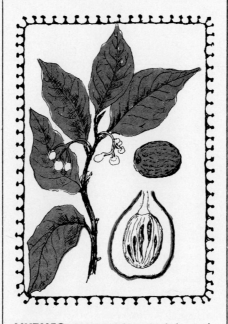

NUTMEG—The hard kernel of the apricotlike fruit of the different varieties of the nutmeg tree. This tree, *Myristica fragrans,* is a tropical evergreen, native to the Spice Islands, or Moluccas, of the East Indies, but now also raised in Grenada in the West Indies and in Brazil. It grows to a height of twenty to forty feet. In appearance it resembles the pear tree and it continues to bear fruit for some fifty years.

The fruit, which is intermingled with the flowers, is gathered with long hooked poles. The fruit is carefully split in half to expose the hard seeds, which is the nutmeg proper, covered by a false aril which is carefully removed, dried, and used to make mace, sister spice of nutmeg.

The nutmeg itself is also dried in the sun or over charcoal fires. It is oval in shape, gray-brown in color, and contains fat, volatile oil, acid, and starch. It is an aromatic spice, used a great deal in cooking.

Nutmegs were first traded to the Near East by the Arabs. In the 6th century they were used in the food at the court of Justinian in Constantinople. They became a favored and valuable spice in the Middle Ages. Chaucer, the greatest English poet of the Middle Ages, wrote in the 14th century: "Nutmegs, too, to put in ale, No matter whether fresh or stale." The oil taken from the nutmeg was used to flavor butter.

Nutmeg was one of the spices Columbus was looking for when he sailed west across the ocean from Spain in search of the East Indies. On his second trip in 1493 he was so eager to prove that he

had indeed found the Spice Islands that he thought many of the native plants were familiar spices. One of the members of the company, Dr. Chanca, a Spanish doctor, wrote home describing some of the territory of Hispaniola, the island which is present-day Haiti and the Dominican Republic: "We found other trees which I think bear nutmegs, because the bark tastes and smells like that spice, but at present there is no fruit on them." The reason there was no fruit was that they were not nutmeg trees.

Later, Magellan sailed off under the auspices of Charles V of Spain to find the Spice Islands and their riches. Although he died before he reached them, one of his crew, Pegafetta, has described some of the spices they found. The nutmeg, he says, "resembles our walnuts as well in the appearance of the fruit as in the leaves. The nutmeg when gathered is like a quince in shape, color, and the down with which it is covered, but it is smaller." The expedition had started out with five ships; it returned with one. Sebastian del Cano, the leader of the remaining ship, was awarded a coat of arms by Charles which included three nutmegs in its bearings.

Imported nutmegs were valued by the early settlers of America. Often traveling peddlers sold or bartered them. They were usually dipped into slaked lime before they were imported. This prevented them from being regrown by the buyer. It is said that once, when nutmegs without lime covering were sold in Connecticut, the housewives refused to buy because they feared the nutmegs were not real but imitations made of wood. This is the most likely story put forth to explain why Connecticut is called the Nutmeg State.

Nutmegs were used not only for flavoring in colonial America: because of their distinctive shape, they were sold as charms at country fairs.

Nutmeg is sold either whole or ground. Whole nutmegs are ground on a nutmeg grater which can be bought in hardware stores. The warm, sweet flavor of nutmeg improves many foods, particularly creamed dishes and fruit desserts, and is delicious sprinkled on custards and eggnogs.

NUTMEG CHEESE POTATOES

  2 pounds potatoes, boiled in skins
  1 to 2 tablespoons milk
1¼ teaspoons salt
 ¼ teaspoon pepper
 ¼ teaspoon ground nutmeg
  2 tablespoons butter or margarine
  3 eggs, beaten
 ¼ pound Gruyère cheese, grated

Peel potatoes. Add milk (amount depends upon dryness of potatoes) and beat until fluffy. Add remaining ingredients, reserving 2 tablespoons grated cheese. Turn into a shallow baking dish. Sprinkle with remaining cheese. Bake for 15 minutes in preheated hot oven (400° F.). Place under broiler for 2 or 3 minutes to brown lightly. Makes 6 servings.

CREAMY MUSHROOM SAUCE FOR PASTA

- 6 tablespoons butter or margarine
- 4 medium onions, thinly sliced
- 2 pounds fresh mushrooms, sliced
  Salt and pepper
- ¼ teaspoon ground nutmeg
- 1 to 1½ cups heavy cream
  Grated Parmesan cheese

Heat 3 tablespoons of the butter in heavy skillet. Over medium heat, cook onions in it until golden. Lower heat. Simmer, covered, for 20 minutes, or until onions are very soft. Stir occasionally. Melt remaining butter in another skillet. Cook mushrooms in it until tender. Season with salt and pepper to taste. Stir in nutmeg. Add mushrooms to onions; mix well. Keep sauce hot while pasta is cooking according to directions. Five minutes before serving time, add cream and heat thoroughly. Do not boil. Toss pasta and sauce together. Serve immediately with freshly grated Parmesan cheese. Makes enough for 1 pound of pasta.

OLD-FASHIONED APPLE TURNOVERS

- 1 egg
- ½ cup sugar
- ½ cup sour milk
- ½ tablespoon heavy cream
- 2¾ cups sifted all-purpose flour (about)
- ½ teaspoon each of baking soda, cream of tartar, and salt
- ⅓ teaspoon ground ginger
- ½ teaspoon ground nutmeg
- 2 cups applesauce, sweetened and spiced
  Confectioners' sugar

Beat egg; stir in sugar, then sour milk and cream. Sift 2 cups flour with soda, cream of tartar, salt, and spices and stir into first mixture. Add more flour, enough to make a soft dough that can be rolled without sticking. Turn out on floured board; divide into quarters, and roll 1 quarter at a time to about ¼-inch thickness. Cut into rounds 4½ inches in diameter and place a mound of applesauce on half of each round. Fold over other half of dough and press edges together with fork. Prick top with fork. Fry in deep fat (350°F. on a frying thermometer) until nicely browned on both sides. Drain on unglazed paper. Dust with sifted confectioners' sugar and serve warm. Makes 14 to 16.

STEAMED APPLE-PRUNE PUDDING

- ¾ cup soft butter or margarine
- ½ cup finely packed light brown sugar
- ¼ cup molasses
- 4 eggs, separated
- 1 cup unsifted all-purpose flour
- ½ teaspoon each of salt and baking soda
- ½ teaspoon each of ground nutmeg, cinnamon, cloves, and allspice
- 1 cup chopped uncooked prunes
- 1 cup chopped peeled tart apple
- ¼ cup diced citron
  Hard sauce

Cream butter and sugar until light and fluffy; beat in molasses. Add egg yolks, one at a time, beating after each addition. Add sifted dry ingredients. Stir in fruits. Then fold in stiffly beaten egg whites. Pack in greased 1½-quart pudding mold. Cover and steam for 3 hours, or until done. Serve warm with hard sauce. Makes 8 to 10 servings.

EGGNOG TARTS

- 1¾ cups fine graham-cracker crumbs
- 1⅓ cups sugar
- ½ cup soft butter
- 1 envelope unflavored gelatin
- 1¾ cups milk
- 4 eggs, separated
- ½ teaspoon salt
- 1 tablespoon cornstarch
- ¼ cup rum
- 2 tablespoons whisky
  Grated nutmeg
- 1 cup heavy cream, whipped
- ½ cup chopped candied fruit

Mix crumbs with ⅓ cup sugar and butter. Using back of spoon, press firmly on bottom and sides of 8 tart pans. Bake in preheated moderate oven (350°F.) for 5 minutes. Chill. Sprinkle gelatin on ¼ cup milk and let stand for 5 minutes. Scald remaining milk in top part of double boiler over boiling water. Beat egg yolks; blend in ½ cup sugar, the salt, and cornstarch; add hot milk slowly, stirring constantly. Return to double boiler and cook over simmering water, stirring constantly, for 5 minutes, or until mixture coats spoon. Remove from heat; add soaked gelatin and stir until dissolved. Chill until mixture begins to set. Stir in rum, whisky, and grated nutmeg to taste. Beat egg whites until stiff; gradually beat in remaining sugar; fold in custard mixture. Pour into lined tart pans. If there is more custard than needed to fill shells, keep remainder at room temperature. Chill tarts until almost set; then top with remaining custard; chill until set. Garnish with whipped cream and bits of candied fruit. Makes 8 tarts.

Note: For crust for 9-inch pie, use 1½ cups graham-cracker crumbs, ¼ cup sugar, and ⅓ cup butter. Use same amount of filling as for 8 tarts.

EARLY AMERICAN PEAR PIE

- ¾ cup sugar
- 2 tablespoons all-purpose flour
- ½ teaspoon each of ground nutmeg and cinnamon
- 6 cups thinly sliced peeled ripe pears
  Pastry for 2-crust 9-inch pie, unbaked
- 2 tablespoons butter

Mix first 4 ingredients; add pears and mix lightly. Line pie pan with half of pastry. Add filling and dot with butter. Adjust top crust. Bake in preheated hot oven (425°F.) for about 50 minutes. Serve warm or cold. Makes about 6 servings.

FRESH-PINEAPPLE PIE

- Pastry for 2-crust, 9-inch pie, unbaked
- 3 cups fresh pineapple chunks
- ¾ cup sugar
- 3 tablespoons all-purpose flour
- ½ teaspoon ground nutmeg
- 1 teaspoon ground cinnamon
- ¼ teaspoon salt
- 2 tablespoons butter or margarine

Line 9-inch pie pan with pastry. Mix remaining ingredients and cook, stirring until thickened; cool. Pour into lined pie pan. Adjust top crust and seal edges well. Bake in preheated hot oven (425°F.) for 25 to 30 minutes. Serve slightly warm or cold.

NUTMEG LOGS

- 1 cup soft butter
- 2 teaspoons vanilla extract
- 2 teaspoons rum flavoring
- ¾ cup sugar
- 1 egg
- 3 cups sifted all-purpose flour
  Ground nutmeg (2 to 3 teaspoons)
- ¼ teaspoon salt
  Rum-Flavored Frosting

Cream butter with flavorings; gradually beat in sugar until light. Blend in egg. Sift flour, 1 teaspoon nutmeg, and salt; add to butter mixture and mix well. Shape pieces of dough on a sugared board into long rolls ½ inch in diameter. Cut into 3-inch lengths and put on greased cookie sheets. Bake in preheated moderate oven (350°F.) for 12 to 15 minutes. Cool. Spread Rum-Flavored Frosting on top and sides of cookies; mark with tines of fork to resemble bark. Sprinkle lightly with remaining nutmeg. Makes 6 dozen.

Rum-Flavored Frosting

Cream ⅓ cup butter with 1 teaspoon vanilla extract and 2 teaspoons rum flavoring. Blend in 2 cups sifted confectioners' sugar and 2 tablespoons light cream; beat until smooth and creamy.

NUTRITION

by Fredrick J. Stare, M.D.
Professor and Chairman, Nutrition Department,
Harvard School of Public Health

A scientist would define nutrition as the sum total of all the processes by which our bodies get the materials (nutrients) they need for survival, growth, and repair. He might add that good nutrition comes from eating the right foods in the right amounts, in short, following a balanced diet.

All of which sounds more serious than it needs to be. Good nutrition is perfectly compatible with good eating, good companions, and good fun. Food can make or mar a day, or a holiday. Food can make life pleasant, and the enjoyment of food aids digestion. A person in normal health can eat the foods he likes, and keep in good trim, if he eats in moderation. And a working knowledge of foods and their best use will add to his happiness, health, and long life. Here are some of the essentials.

What is a balanced diet?

A balanced diet is achieved by eating a variety of foods—to furnish all the nutrients required for good health—in the proper amounts and in proper relation to each other. A group, or team, of nutrients functions more effectively than the same nutrients consumed individually. The nutrients are customarily placed in six food groups, depending on their chemical characteristics and the functions they perform in the body. They are: proteins, carbohydrates, fats, minerals, vitamins, and water. The body requires all of them in amounts that have been determined through research. A balanced diet provides better nutrition than an unbalanced one. There is no waste, the body uses the nutrients effectively, and better health results.

What does a balanced diet accomplish?

Most foods contain several of the nutrients which constitute a balanced diet, and it is important to know which ones, or the main ones. For example, oranges, lemons, and grapefruits are rich in vitamin C or ascorbic acid; and milk in protein, many B vitamins particularly riboflavin, calcium, and vitamin A.

What do the six groups of nutrients do?

Proteins have a main function of building and maintaining body muscles, glandular organs, arteries, skin—all living cells. The amino acids which make up proteins are often called, with reason, the "building blocks" of life. Of the twenty-two or more amino acids, eight are not synthesized or manufactured by the body and must be consumed in food from day to day for good health. Proteins, along with carbohydrates and fats, provide energy, or fuel, for body functions, and this energy is measured in calories which will be explained later. The main sources of proteins are meat, fish, poultry, eggs, milk and its products, and lesser amounts are to be found in the bread and cereal groups.

Carbohydrates (sugars and starches) are the most efficient sources of energy. We consume these in breads, cakes, cereals, rolls, rice, macaroni, noodles, potatoes, etc., which also give us worthwhile amounts of iron, several of the B vitamins, and energy in balanced proportion with that furnished by fats.

Fats provide twice as many calories as do the same amounts of protein or carbohydrate. Carbohydrates and fats are responsible for most of the total calories in the diet, and this permits the amino acids to do their vital building and maintenance work so that they are not burned for energy. Meat, eggs, cream, butter, oils, and margarine are a few of many fat sources.

Minerals—About fifteen to eighteen are now known to be essentials, and more may be found to be so in the future. They serve as catalysts to control the utilization of proteins, fats, and carbohydrates, and they function in essential structures on their own. Most persons are aware that they need calcium and iron, but it is now known that our bodies require many other minerals in trace amounts, including copper, chromium, manganese, selenium, zinc, fluoride, cobalt, molybdenum, etc. These are toxic in substantial amounts, but essential to health in minute amounts.

Vitamins are catalysts which enable the other nutrients to do their jobs. All are needed in small or trace amounts. With a balanced diet the normal, healthy person gets all the vitamins and minerals he needs.

Water is essential for the body's functions. Most of us should drink six to eight glasses of water a day, some of which can be in the form of tea, coffee, fruit and vegetable juices, soup, etc., depending on our body size, activity, and the type of climate we live in. Water may provide some of the minerals we need such as calcium, and, in some cases, fluorine which lessens dental decay. A large share of all body fluids are water, such as blood and urine. Water helps the body regulate its temperature and aids in the intestinal process.

While not ordinarily included in the six nutrient groups, *fiber* or *roughage* is another diet ingredient. Animal fiber, as found in meat, and vegetable fiber, such as cellulose, are not digestible, but help the intestinal muscles do their job. Bulk may be found in whole grain bread and cereals, and the skin and fibrous parts of fruits and vegetables.

Variety is essential

Nutrition authorities agree that a few simple rules will help one follow a balanced diet and enjoy many kinds of food.

Be sure to eat some of the "basic four" every day. These provide the "protective" foods, those rich in protein, minerals, and vitamins, and they are:

1. Meats, poultry, fish, eggs—at least two servings every day. Beans, peas, and nuts have good food values and can sometimes be substituted.

2. Milk and dairy products (directly or in cooking)—at least two to four cups of milk or the equivalent ice cream, cheese, or dairy food.

Children........3 to 4 cups milk
Teenagers....4 or more cups milk
Adults........2 or more cups milk

3. Breads and cereals—at least four servings every day—whole grain, enriched, restored. Remember: macaroni, rice, and grits are cereals, not vegetables.

4. Fruits and vegetables—at least four servings a day, including a dark-green or deep-yellow vegetable for vitamin A at least every other day, and a citrus fruit, or other fruit or vegetable for vitamin C every day. Some dark-green vegetables are: collards, kale, spinach, broccoli, cress, etc. Some deep-yellow vegetables are sweet potatoes, pumpkins, yellow squash. Apricots and cantaloupes are deep-yellow fruits.

Pastries, spreads, jellies, relishes, and the like, help to add zest to a meal. But be sure you first have your "basic four."

Desserts can have a few calories, or many, as you decide.

Eat a variety of foods at each meal. Monotony is the enemy of good nutrition. Changed combinations of foods and new methods of preparation make them more attractive. Some foods taste better hot, others cold. Nutritionally, either way is fine. Avoid noise, rush, and clatter when eating. Pleasant conversation and attractive surroundings aid good digestion. In the family, mealtimes should be fun, occasions for sharing amusing or stimulating experiences and strengthening family ties.

How many calories do you need?

Granted its limitations, the calorie is the unit of energy measurement in nutrition. If too few are eaten, weakness and hunger prevail; if too many, sluggishness and overweight result. The calorie is essentially a heat unit: the energy required to lift the temperature of a quart of water two degrees Fahrenheit. A diet calorie, or kilo calorie, is 1,000 times the calorie used as a unit of measurement by physicists, chemists, and engineers.

The calories expended depend on your body size, age, and physical activity. An adult of 100 pounds burns fewer calories than an adult of 150 pounds, assuming they are living on about the same pattern of physical activity. An average adult of 150 pounds uses up about sixty calories an hour just to live: in heart action, breathing, liver function, and the like. This is called his basal metabolism rate.

If he (or she) does some sedentary work such as writing, sewing, or reading he will burn up to eighty to 100 calories an hour. Cooking, dusting, ironing, handwashing, and rapid typewriting take about 110 to 160 calories per hour. Mopping, gardening, carpentry, or walking moderately fast use 170 to 240 calories an hour. Hanging out clothes, heavy scrubbing, waxing floors burn 250 to 350 calories per hour. Vigorous tennis, swimming, cycling, skiing, or dancing use 400 to 500 calories per hour.

It is just as important in weight control to know how many calories one expends in physical activity, as it is to know how many calories there are in one's foods. Exercise is frequently overlooked as a calorie "burner."

One's daily caloric requirements decrease each year after twenty-five as body processes tend to slow down and one's energy expenditure decreases. Actually the decrease averages about five per cent for each decade past twenty-five years; thus adults of forty-five or fifty years of age need about ten per cent fewer calories than they did when they were twenty-five or thirty and they must eat less to avoid overweight.

Weight control the healthful way

The best way to lose excess weight is to bring one's daily caloric *intake* below one's *output,* to continue on a balanced diet, and to secure adequate exercise. This permits sensible, healthy weight reduction, and avoids the nervousness, headaches, and short temper which usually go with extreme or crash diets. Establishing a total daily caloric intake at about 500 calories below the caloric output is a good working rule. On this basis the average healthy person will lose a pound a week, or fifty pounds a year. A pound of stored fat represents about 3,500 calories. Records show that the gradual loss of weight also offers a better chance for permanent loss. The subject of weight loss, however, may be more complicated than here described. Medical factors enter, since no two individuals assimilate their food in the same manner. This is one of the reasons why no diet aimed at reducing more than ten to fifteen pounds should be undertaken without a doctor's advice.

The writer, Alexander Woollcott, who was considerably overweight, once remarked that "The most interesting things in life are immoral, illegal, or fattening." Things aren't that bad. If you want to lose weight, don't go at it with a do-or-die attitude and try to cut out everything you like. Keep some of your favorites, but keep your daily caloric total in mind. Reduce the size of servings, and avoid extra helpings. You can substitute lower calorie foods for higher, still secure the nutrients you need, and not feel hungry all the time. For example, a serving of string beans has about twenty-five calories; Lima beans, 100. Half a grapefruit at thirty-five calories is but a fraction of the 350 calories in a substantial slice of pie or frosted cake.

Don't skip meals. The long periods between meals put the body out of balance. Passing up breakfast reduces one's morning output of work by as much as twenty per cent, and one may then overeat at lunch and dinner. Avoid "reducing drugs."

For most persons past their teens who wish to lose weight, a 1,400 calorie a day diet is recommended as being safe, within the capacity of most of us, and it will provide the energy needed for a normal day's work.

Individual food requirements

Each member of the family requires the same basic foods, but the quantities vary according to age, physical activity, and other factors.

Children require more food proportionately for energy and body growth than adults. They may need second helpings. They require adequate amounts of the basic four groups of foods, and milk products especially. Children require adequate vitamin C, so citrus fruits, tomatoes, cherries, and other sources can be served to meet this need. Youngsters also need exercise to help avoid overweight; in the United States overweight in children is a serious problem.

Good food habits can help many teenagers attain good complexions, attractive hair, skin, and teeth. Some teenage girls do not get enough vitamins A and C. The boys want to excel in sports, so they usually drink enough milk and citrus fruit juice, and do somewhat better than the girls. High calorie snacks with low nutritive value are to be avoided. Teenagers should be reminded that what they eat determines in large measure how they feel. Excess weight, put on in the teens, tends to stay on into young adulthood.

The modern mother knows the importance of sound diet during pregnancy and lactation, both for herself and her baby. She should increase, as a rule, her intake of the basic four or protective foods in accordance with her doctor's instructions. She will avoid eating too much or too little.

Older persons need a balanced diet and fewer calories. Variety becomes even more important, as taste, smell, and other sensations diminish somewhat with age. One danger for the older person is that it is "too much trouble" to go to the food store, or to prepare an adequate meal. This makes for meals that are really only snacks. With the tapering off of bodily functions such as chewing ability, a balanced diet of protective foods is imperative.

Therapeutic diets are prescribed by a physician to deal with a particular disease or condition, and should be followed carefully. One's health, and possibly one's life, may depend on obeying the doctor's orders.

Changing patterns of eating

Modern living calls for occasional flexibility in the times members of the family eat, because of different school and working hours. While it is advisable to have three balanced meals, some recent scientific evidence suggests that equally good health may come about from eating four, five, or six meals of smaller quantity. There is nothing the matter with snacks for adults or older people, providing they possess nutritional value and do not simply add to one's total daily caloric intake. If one is underweight, snacking may be helpful in increasing food consumption. What is a mistake is watching television by the hour in an easy chair and snacking at the same time.

There is nothing wrong nutritionally in substituting foods for the familiar or traditional ones at certain meals. At breakfast the tendency is toward certain standard items. If a teenager thinks he'd like a hamburger for breakfast, give it to him for a change. It's a perfectly good food. With the great variety of foods at the supermarket or food store the year round there is little excuse for mealtime boredom. Change should be welcomed. Increasingly, Americans and Canadians are trying the unfamiliar foods of other countries or of other sections of our own. For example, do you eat papayas, avocados, Chinese cabbage, black-eyed peas, artichokes, mangoes? Do you enjoy French, Italian, German, Mexican, and other national styles of cooking?

Conserving nutritional values

With the high quality of foods available today it is important that we use them so as to retain their palatability and nutritional values. A few reminders:

1. Many people keep their lettuce, carrots, cabbage, and other vegetables in the refrigerator too long before serving.

2. Despite the educational job that has been done, many people still cook vegetables and other foods in substantial quantities of water and then throw the water away, thus discarding valuable nutrients.

3. Even in a freezer, there is some loss of nutritional value and flavor over a period of weeks or months. Keep the foods moving toward the table.

4. Serving food as fresh as possible helps to keep it appealing to the eye as well as the palate.

5. Don't be timid about using new combinations of foods. You will be surprised at the difference in flavors when you find some new companions for your food favorites.

Food myths and facts

The Food and Drug Administration says that over half a billion dollars a year is wasted on food fads, myths, and misconceptions. These are fostered by promoters with "wonder" food products to sell at high prices. They are claimed to possess some miraculous nutritional or health building quality in themselves, or

as a result of the conditions under which they are grown. Neither of these viewpoints is accepted by responsible nutrition scientists.

Some of the myths are: (1) that all human diseases are due to a faulty diet, (2) that widespread soil depletion causes malnutrition in this country, (3) that prevailing methods of "overprocessing" destroy food values, and (4) that most Americans are in dire need of "food supplements" or vitamin pills. The Food and Drug Administration says that none of these assertions has any foundation, and that the American and Canadian food supply possesses high nutritive value, variety, abundance, and safety. The Food and Drug Administration, other government agencies, and professional organizations combat food myths and fads constructively and vigorously.

Standards of food safety and quality are set by professional and governmental bodies, including the U.S. Department of Agriculture, the Food and Drug Administration, the American Medical Association, the American Dietetic Association, the American Home Economics Association, and many other professional organizations. Many standards for the science of nutrition and for the guidance of the food industry are determined by the Food and Nutrition Board of the National Academy of Sciences—National Research Council. These standards are revised from time to time in the light of research done in university and other laboratories.

Nutrition Science

Nutrition is a "new" science in that the major developments in it have occurred in the past generation. Notable progress has been made toward a better understanding of (1) the complicated processes by which the body makes use of foods, (2) the nutritional qualities of food eaten singly and combined with other foods, and, more recently, (3) the role of diet in diseases of a metabolic character, such as diabetes. Nutrition science helps to treat and control diabetes and liver injury. It also prepares the body to withstand surgery and to recover properly afterward.

In the United States and Canada the diseases caused by vitamin deficiencies such as rickets (lack of vitamin D) and pellagra (lack of niacin, part of the B-complex) have been overcome. This is not true in the underdeveloped countries where protein and other deficiencies cause disease and high mortality.

In the United States, and Canada also, there has been an enormous scientific and technical improvement in the methods of growing, processing, distribu-

ting, and preserving foods. In recent years we have seen the development of the "convenience" foods, in which the labor of preparation has been performed before they reach the consumer. Quick freezing and freeze-dry methods have made many foods available in attractive form the year round. "Instant" and dehydrated foods save time and energy in the kitchen. Improvements in food containers and packages have resulted in the retention of higher nutritional qualities for longer periods of time.

However, the familiar phrase, "we have only scratched the surface," applies to nutrition research as well as to other fields of endeavor. Many questions await answers in the laboratories. It could aptly be said that we are in the midst of a biochemical revolution. Advances in scientific knowledge are being translated into nutritious foods for the dinner table and advances in human health. Those responsible for the advances in knowledge and human health are the nutrition scientist, food technologist, physician, public health official, dietician, home economist, teacher, food industry executive, and others.

Today, nutrition scientists are striving to keep people in good health, to lengthen the life span, and to extend one's peak of achievement. The degenerative diseases of later years, or some of them, now appear to have early beginnings. Scientists are endeavoring to find out when and how they start, and what role the diet can and should play at various periods in life. A healthy old age can be given a good start in youth with sound food habits.

Nutrition scientists have devoted a great deal of study of late to the role of fats. Fats may be associated with heart disease and atherosclerosis, along with genetic inheritance, overweight, lack of exercise, smoking, and stress, although no one has quite defined what stress is. Considerable information on the metabolic role of fats has been obtained, some of it conflicting. Agreement does not yet exist on the precise amounts of saturated or animal fats and unsaturated or vegetable fats which should be in the optimum diet. We need both for best health. Definitive information should be available on the subject in the next few years. Drastic dietary changes are not justified at this time, and can be harmful.

Meanwhile, research continues to find many dietary answers to matters of good health, for the individual who wants to feel and be at his best, and for the nation which wants its citizens to be in top physical and mental condition. Sound nutrition is indeed the most important environmental factor in the health of a person or a people.

COMMON TERMS USED IN NUTRITION

ALLERGY Hypersensitivity to a food, pollen, drug, or any other allergen, usually a protein. The skin, gastrointestinal tract, or respiratory tract may be affected.

AMINO ACIDS The "building blocks" of protein, about twenty-two in all, of which eight are essential to man: tryptophan, threonine, methionine, isoleucine, leucine, lysine, valine, and phenylalanine. The body is unable to produce these and must get them from food. The other amino acids may be synthesized in the body.

ANEMIA A condition of the blood characterized by a low hemoglobin content, or reduction in the amount of blood, or a reduction in the number of red blood cells.

ANOREXIA Lack or loss of appetite.

ARTERIOSCLEROSIS A condition of the arteries marked by thickening and hardening of the walls and a loss of elasticity; related to

ATHEROSCLEROSIS A type of arteriosclerosis characterized by the accumulation of cholesterol and other lipids in the artery walls, resulting in a narrowing of the passages.

CALORIE A unit of heat, used as a measure of the energy value of foods.

CARBOHYDRATE Food substances containing carbon, hydrogen, and oxygen, such as sugars, starches, cellulose, and gums. They furnish heat and energy and carry other nutrients.

CAROTENE A yellow or orange pigment found in green and yellow vegetables and fruits—obvious in carrots and masked by chlorophyll in green leaves. It is a precursor of vitamin A and can be converted to that compound in the body.

CHOLESTEROL A fatlike substance associated with atherosclerosis. It is normally synthesized in the body. Animal tissues are a source of cholesterol in food; however, the cholesterol in food consumed may or may not determine serum cholesterol levels.

DIETETIC FOOD Food processed commercially which may be used to meet diet restrictions. Consult physician before using. Many, if not most, diet modifications can be made using regular foods.

ENRICHED Food that has certain basic nutriments added to it.

ENZYMES Substances protein in nature that are produced by the body which facilitate chemical changes but are not themselves changed in the reaction (e.g., digestive enzymes aid in the breakdown of food).

FATTY ACIDS, ESSENTIAL Collective name for three unsaturated fatty acids, linoleic, linolenic, and arachidonic, found in many food fats, which are considered dietary essentials. They are poorly distributed in animal fats and occur mainly in vegetable oils.

LIPIDS Fats or fatlike substances.

METABOLISM The sum total of all the chemical changes that occur in the body by which food is converted into tissue, reserve nutrients are stored, and waste products are eliminated.

MINERALS Inorganic substances present in the body which have specific functions.

Calcium A mineral that helps to build sound bones and teeth; helps blood to clot, helps muscles and nerves react normally. Found in milk products and in dark-green vegetables.

Iron A mineral that combines with protein to make hemoglobin (the substance in the blood that carries oxygen to all body cells) and, in each cell, helps develop energy.

Sodium A mineral necessary for maintaining body neutrality and water balance. It is also associated with muscle contraction. The usual source in the diet is sodium chloride, table salt, and it is also obtained in other foods such as baking soda and baking powder.

Other Minerals:

Copper Works with iron in forming hemoglobin in the red blood cells.

Fluorine A constituent of bones and teeth. Fluoridation of water under controlled conditions is said to be effective in reducing the incidence of dental caries, but the matter is still under dispute.

Iodine Useful for the cure and prevention of nutritional goiters.

Magnesium Required for the utilization of amino acids in formation of proteins.

Phosphorus Constituent of bones and teeth; necessary for calcium utilization.

Potassium Necessary for muscle and nerve functions, carbohydrate metabolism.

Sulfur An essential mineral found in certain amino acids, vitamins, and in insulin.

Trace Elements Cobalt, zinc, manganese, molybdenum, selenium, etc.

OXIDATION The reaction in the body of oxygen and nutritionally useful compounds which results in the release of energy and the formation of various end products.

PROTEINS Essential constituents of all living cells, distinguished from carbohydrates and fats in that they contain nitrogen. Needed to build, maintain, and repair body tissues; help form antibodies to fight infection; supply energy.

VITAMINS General term for organic substances occurring in many foods, necessary for the normal metabolic functioning of the body.

Vitamin A Necessary for growth, skin health, vision, resistance to infection. Fat soluble, found in butter, Cheddar cheese, liver, kidney. Made in the body from carotene in green and yellow vegetables and fruit.

Vitamin B-Complex Water-soluble compounds which function with the enzymes in the body and are directly related to the production of energy. Included are: *thiamine* (B-1); *riboflavin* (B-2); *niacin; pyridoxine* (B-6); *cobalamin* (B-12); *biotin; folacin* (folic acid); *inositol; panthothenic acid*. Widely distributed in food; in the meat group, many fruits and vegetables, the milk group, and the bread-cereal group.

Vitamin C (Ascorbic Acid) Needed for the formation of intercellular cement, for maintaining the strength of the blood vessels; helps resist infection; helps insure more rapid healing of wounds. It is found in citrus fruits, strawberries, cantaloupes, tomatoes, cabbage, green peppers, broccoli, and other vegetables and fruit.

Vitamin D The sunshine vitamin, so named because ultra violet light from the sun converts a precursor located in the skin into the vitamin. Other forms of vitamin D are available in fish-liver oils, fish, egg yolk, and milk. It is necessary for growth. It aids in the absorption of calcium and phosphorus and helps to build bones and teeth.

Vitamin E (Tocopherol) It acts as an antioxidant to preserve the fat-soluble vitamins and the unsaturated fatty acids. It may be necessary for reproduction, and it is also effective against certain toxic agents. Seed oils and margarine are the best sources.

Vitamin K There are two natural forms: one may be obtained from food and the other is synthesized in the intestinal tract by bacteria. Food sources include pork liver, cabbage, cauliflower, spinach, soybeans, etc. It is essential for the synthesis of prothrombin and the normal clotting of blood.

Choline A nutritionally important substance necessary for transporting fat in the body. It is widely distributed in food and a deficiency is unlikely. Good sources include meat, egg yolk, bread, cereal, beans, and peanuts.

OAT, OATMEAL—Oats are the grains of a cereal-grass plant of the *Avena* genus, or the plant itself. Like the rest of the grains, oats consist of a soft inner part surrounded by a husk which is removed before being eaten by humans. Some varieties of oats, however, are hull-less. The grain is used to make rolled oats and oatmeal and as feed for livestock.

Most cultivated varieties of oats have a smooth-surfaced hull, although some wild varieties are hairy. Cultivated oats are thought to be the descendants of two kinds of wild oats, the common and the red which probably originated in western Europe. From there they spread to other parts of the world. They are now largely cultivated in northern Europe and North America since they can be grown more easily and more profitably than any other grain except rye in cold and damp climates. Oats will flourish as far north as the Arctic Circle, and a damp island climate suits oats precisely; that is why they flourish in Scotland and Ireland.

In manufacture, the grain is cleaned, sorted for size, kiln-dried to loosen the hull and develop the nutty flavor of the kernel, cleaned again, put through machines which remove the hulls, and then sterilized. To produce rolled oats, the husked sterilized grains are flattened, by heated rolls, into the flakes familiar to the consumer. To make oatmeal, the groats (edible portion of the oats with the hull removed) are steel-cut in three sizes and ground in grades from coarse to extra-fine. Even finer grinding produces oat flour or oatmeal flour. Although properly speaking the term "oatmeal" should only be applied to the ground meal of the grain, it is commonly used to describe both rolled and ground oats.

Oats are the most nutritious of cereals, containing a good amount of fat, proteins, and minerals. They are an excellent energy food for people who live an active outdoor life in cold weather. All the people of northern Europe depended on them for their diet until modern times, eating them as a meal in porridges, in baked foods such as bannocks, and as a food stretcher. Oats do not lend themselves to breadmaking since the protein material does not occur in the form of gluten; risen oatmeal bread, to be satisfactory, has to be mixed with other flour.

The highly processed rolled oats that we know today were first made by Alexander Hornby from Craigsville, New York, using a new precooking process developed by two Englishmen. H. O. Hornby Oats, as the new product was called, were baked raw oats steamed under pressure in rotating boilers. This process shortened the cooking considerably and made oatmeal more palatable to people who like a more refined product.

Availability and Purchasing Guide—Rolled oats, both quick-cooking and regular, are widely available. Scotch oatmeal (oat groats cut with stone rather than steel rollers, thus producing a more coarsely ground grain), oat groats, and oat flour are available in specialty or health-food stores.

Many uncooked and dry cereals made with oats are also available. Among the uncooked types are: oat cereal with toasted wheat germ and soy grits; maple-flavored instant-cooking oat flakes; oat granules, maple-flavored, instant-cooking; oat and wheat cereal. Ready-to-eat cereals include: shredded oats with protein and other added nutrients; oats (with or without corn) puffed, with added nutrients; oats (with or without corn or wheat) puffed, with nutrients and sugar-covered; oats (with soy flour and rice) flaked, and with added nutrients.

Storage

☐ Kitchen shelf: 2 to 3 months
☐ Refrigerator shelf, cooked: 3 to 4 days

Nutritive Food Values—Good source of vitamin B-1; fair source of vitamin B-2 and vitamin E.

The caloric values for 3½ ounces of the various oat products are:

☐ Oatmeal or rolled oats, cooked = 55 calories
☐ Oat and wheat cereal, cooked = 65 calories
☐ Oat granules, maple-flavored, quick-cooking, cooked = 60 calories
☐ Oat flakes, maple-flavored, instant-cooking, cooked = 69 calories
☐ Oat cereal with toasted wheat germ and soy grits, cooked = 62 calories
☐ Shredded oats with added nutrients = 379 calories
☐ Puffed oats (with or without corn or wheat) with added nutrients = 397 calories
☐ Flaked oats (with soy flour and rice) with added nutrients = 397 calories

Basic Preparation—Sprinkle cereal slowly into boiling salted water and stir while cooking to prevent lumping. Quick-cooking cereals should be prepared as directed on the package as one brand is more quick cooking than another. A quick-cooking cereal can be cooked over direct heat. Some quick-cooking oatmeal can be "cooked" right in the cereal bowl by adding boiling water and stirring.

With regular oatmeal, long slow cooking gives the best flavor. To prevent sticking and possible scorching, cook the cereal in the top part of a double boiler over boiling water.

OATMEAL BREAD
1 cup sifted all-purpose flour
2 tablespoons sugar
2 teaspoons baking powder
½ teaspoon baking soda
¾ teaspoon salt
¾ cup quick-cooking rolled oats
¼ cup butter or margarine
¾ cup buttermilk

Sift flour with sugar, baking powder, baking soda, and salt. Stir in rolled oats. Cut in butter until butter forms small particles. Add buttermilk all at once and stir until smooth. Pour mixture into well-greased 8-inch square pan. Bake in pre-

heated hot oven (400°F.) for 30 minutes. Cut while warm into squares. Makes 8 servings.

PLUM AND APPLE CRUMBLE
½ cup quick-cooking oats
2 apples, sliced
6 plums, halved and stoned
1 cup dark corn syrup
¼ teaspoon salt
¼ to ½ teaspoon ground allspice
1 tablespoon butter

Put oats on baking sheet and toast in moderate oven (375°F.) for about 10 minutes, until lightly browned. Put fruit into 1½-quart baking dish; pour syrup over fruit. Mix oats with salt, allspice, and butter; sprinkle over fruit. Bake in preheated moderate oven (375°F.) for about 30 minutes. Makes 4 servings.

FILLED OATMEAL COOKIES
2 cups quick-cooking rolled oats, ground very fine
1 cup soft butter or margarine
1 cup sugar
1 teaspoon vanilla extract
2 cups sifted all-purpose flour
¼ teaspoon baking soda
¾ teaspoon salt
½ cup buttermilk
Date-Nut Filling

Grind rolled oats twice if necessary, or chop in an electric blender. Cream butter until light and fluffy. Gradually beat in sugar and vanilla. Add oats and flour, soda, and salt alternately with buttermilk. Mix well. Chill for several hours. Roll out very thin and cut with fancy cutters. Arrange on ungreased cookie sheets and bake in preheated hot oven (400°F.) for 8 to 10 minutes. Put together in pairs with Date-Nut Filling the day cookies are served. Or fill, wrap, and freeze. Makes about 7 dozen small filled cookies.

Date-Nut Filling
Cut 1 pound pitted dates into small pieces. Put in saucepan with 1½ cups sugar, ½ teaspoon salt, 2 teaspoons grated lemon rind, and 2 cups water. Bring to a boil and cook for 10 minutes, or until thickened, stirring occasionally. Add 2 cups finely chopped nuts, and cool.

CHEESE-AND-OATMEAL SNAPS
1 cup sifted all-purpose flour
1½ teaspoons baking powder
½ teaspoon salt
1 cup quick-cooking rolled oats
¾ cup butter or margarine
½ cup shredded sharp Cheddar cheese
1 tablespoon milk

Sift together flour, baking powder, and salt. Add rolled oats; cut in butter; add cheese and milk. Mix to form a soft dough. Turn out on lightly floured board; roll thin and cut with small round cookie cutter. Bake on lightly greased cookie sheets in preheated moderate oven (375° F.) for about 12 minutes, or until

browned. Serve hot with soups or salads. Makes about 4 dozen.

OATMEAL DROP COOKIES
½ cup soft butter or margarine
1 cup sugar
1 egg
1½ cups sifted all-purpose flour
½ teaspoon each of salt and baking soda
¾ teaspoon ground cinnamon
½ teaspoon each of ground cloves and allspice
1¾ cups quick-cooking rolled oats
⅔ cup raisins, cut into small pieces
½ cup chopped nuts
⅓ cup milk

Cream butter until light and fluffy. Gradually beat in sugar. Add egg and beat until light. Sift flour with salt, baking soda, and spices; add oats, raisins, and nuts. Add to first mixture alternately with milk and mix well. Drop by teaspoonfuls onto greased cookie sheets. Bake in preheated moderate oven (350°F.) for about 15 minutes. Makes 3 dozen.

OIL—In cookery, this is an edible fatty or greasy substance occurring in the seeds of certain plants. Although there are some edible fats procured from mammals and fish, whale and cod-liver oils, for example, they are not used in cooking. The terms fat and oil are often used interchangeably but to be accurate the term "fat" applies to substances that are solid at normal temperatures, whereas oils are liquid at these temperatures.

Food oils are made from olives, cottonseed, corn, peanuts, coconuts, palm nuts, soybeans, rapeseed, sesame seed, poppy seed, safflower seed, sunflower seed, walnuts, hickory nuts, almonds, beechnuts, and others. Generally it is cottonseed or corn oil which is used in making the widely available cooking, salad, and vegetable oils.

The principal uses of oils in cookery are:

(1) *To give richness and flavor,* as in the addition of oil to mayonnaise or French dressing. Olive oil is much prized for the latter, where its unique flavor is particularly prominent.

(2) *To sauté, pan-fry, or deep fry foods.* In choosing a fat for sautéing or frying the physical and chemical qualities of the fat are as important as the flavor. The oils are particularly well suited for both purposes since most of them have high smoking points and negligible flavor. An exception is olive oil which tends to spatter over high heat. Nevertheless it is often used, especially in Italian cooking, because its flavor is desirable and blends well with the food being cooked.

(3) *For shortening (tenderizing),* as in cakes, pies, muffins, biscuits, etc. Oils can

be used with good results for shortening, but recipes specifying oil are necessary since the oils add more liquid. Oil is used in making chiffon cakes and is convenient for making tender, flaky pie crust.

Storage—Oils can be kept, tightly covered, on the kitchen shelf in a cool dry place away from foods with strong odors for 2 to 3 months. They should not be exposed to light as it fades them. When exposed to air they will become rancid if moisture is present. Cans are better for storage than bottles. If to be kept for longer periods of time, oils, with the exception of olive oil, should be refrigerated, tightly covered. They will keep this way on the refrigerator shelf for up to 1 year. Olive oil is an exception; it may solidify if refrigerated for long periods of time.

Nutritive Food Values—Oils are a highly concentrated form of food energy. One cup of pure oil yields about 2,000 calories. Fats and oils give a general satisfaction to food because they slow down the rate at which it is digested. They also contain certain fatty acids that are essential to good nutrition.

OKRA—A tall annual plant, *Hibiscus esculentus,* of the mallow family which yields an edible pod with a gooey, mucilaginous quality. Okra should be eaten when very tender; the pods, which grow extremely fast, should be cut often.

Okra, in America, is also often called gumbo since it is used mostly in the southern states to flavor and thicken the gumbos or soup-stews that are a specialty of the region.

Grown extensively in South America, the southern United States, and India, the plant is a native of tropical Africa, and is said to have come from the region that includes Ethiopia and the east-

ern, higher, part of the Sudan. Okra is of considerable antiquity, but relatively little is known about it. It was mentioned by a Spanish Moor who visited Egypt in 1216. Very likely, it was introduced into the Arab countries through traders and slave raiders from Ethiopia and the Sudan. The Arabs grew very fond of it, calling it *bâmiya.*

From Arabia, okra was taken west to North Africa and the Mediterranean and east to southwestern Asia. It was brought to the New World, specifically, to Brazil and the West Indies, around the middle of the 17th century. How okra came to Louisiana and other southern states we do not know; it may have been introduced by the Spanish or French colonists, or by the Negro slaves, or by both.

Okra was cultivated as far north as Philadelphia in 1748. Jefferson says that it was known in Virginia before 1781. Garden writers speak about it from 1800 on.

The ripe okra seeds yield an edible oil used in Mediterranean countries and in the orient. Sometimes they are ground and used as a coffee substitute or stretcher, like chicory.

Availability—Fresh okra is available year round in the southern United States and from April to November in the north. Peak months are June through October. Some varieties are long and thin. Others are short and chunky. The pods vary from whitish-green to green in color and may be smooth or ridged.

Okra is also available canned and frozen. It is an ingredient in canned chicken-gumbo soup.

Purchasing Guide—Look for young, tender, crisp, fresh pods, 2 to 4 inches in length. The pods should snap easily and be free from hard seeds.

Storage—Wash; store in a covered container in refrigerator.
- Fresh, or canned and opened, refrigerator shelf or vegetable compartment: 4 days
- Fresh, prepared for freezing; or frozen, refrigerator frozen-food compartment: 1 month
- Fresh, prepared for freezing; or frozen, freezer: 1 year
- Canned, kitchen shelf: 1 to 2 months

Nutritive Food Values—Fair source of vitamins A and C.
- 3½ ounces, boiled and drained = 29 calories

Basic Preparation—Scrub pods. If pods are large, cut off stems and slice into ½- to 1-inch slices. Small pods may be left whole.
- **To Cook**—Cook, covered, in ½ to 1 inch of boiling salted water for 10 to 15 minutes, or until tender. (If overcooked,

okra may have a gummy consistency.) May also be steamed until just tender. Season with salt, pepper, and butter or margarine.

Boiled or steamed okra may be served with individual dishes of melted butter or margarine or hollandaise sauce. Pods are picked up by the stems and dipped into the butter sauce. Okra may be added to soups.

- **To Fry**—Dip crosswise slices into a mixture of egg and 1 tablespoon water, then roll in seasoned flour, crumbs, or cornmeal. Panfry or deep fry for 2 to 5 minutes.
- **To Freeze**—Wash; remove stems with a sharp knife. Blanch in boiling water, 2 or 3 minutes for small pods, 3 or 4 minutes for large pods. Chill in ice water for 3 to 5 minutes. Drain. Pack whole or slice crosswise. Pack into containers, leaving ½-inch headspace. Seal.

Okra
by Margaret M. Thornburgh

People who like okra and people who think they don't are as violently partisan as candidates before election. In our family, we are all okra addicts. It shows, too, especially in our garden.

As gardeners, we have always been a little on the casual side, except for a neat plot that we plant with gusto and tend with care. In it grow four kinds of vegetables: okra, tomatoes, green peppers, and onions, the necessary ingredients for okra stew.

If you are a gardener, try a row or two of gumbo, as this delectable is sometimes called. It's a warm-weather plant, so wait until the winter's chill is out of the ground and all danger of frost is past. It will grow well in any good, well-drained garden soil, but prefers a rich, sandy loam.

Sow seed a half inch deep, and space rows three-and-a-half feet apart for the dwarf varieties; a foot or more farther apart if you try the mammoth, long-pod plants that reach a height of six or seven feet. When seedlings are about four inches tall, thin each row to provide one or two feet between plants.

Okra grows rapidly in warm temperatures, and in a little less than two months you will be harvesting the first pods. Watch for the plants to blossom, pale-yellow flowers, red at the throat, resembling the mallow or a small, single hollyhock bloom. Four to six days later, the pods should be about three inches long and ready for your table. Always cut them off promptly, for two reasons:

young pods are tender and have the best flavor, and if they are not allowed to mature, the plant will continue to bear until frost.

It's surprising how quickly pods become tough and fibrous, so cut them every second day, at least. Cook them promptly, or if you must keep them a few days, store (spread out or pack very loosely) in refrigerator. Never cut into pods until you are ready to use them.

In buying okra, always choose pods that are crisp-looking and two to four inches long; avoid those that look limp and old or are streaked with brown.

Packaged frozen okra lends itself handily to combinations with other frozen vegetables. Such combinations are standard fare at our house for Sunday suppers and for early, hurry-up dinners that precede an evening out. Try frozen okra with frozen corn, cooked separately according to package directions. Transfer to casserole; pour a buttery cream sauce over the vegetables, and sprinkle with grated Parmesan cheese. Brown in preheated hot oven (425°F.) for 10 minutes.

A new canning method, in which freshly harvested pods are quickly placed in a precanning solution, results in okra that is tender yet firm. Of course, canned or frozen okra can be used in any recipe that calls for fresh okra.

Gumbo can be many things to a versatile and imaginative cook. It is delicious prepared whole. Just remove the little fringe of "beard," and cook, tightly covered, with very little water, until the pods can be cut with a fork—about 12 to 15 minutes. Season with butter, lemon juice if you like, salt, and pepper.

Or remove stems, dip pods in cornmeal, and fry.

For French-fried okra, dip pods in beaten egg and fine cracker crumbs; then dry in deep fat.

For a delicious chilled green salad, add cooked okra pods to tomato wedges; spoon finely diced radishes and celery over them, and serve on crisp salad greens with French dressing. We prefer a simple dressing of oil, red-wine-tarragon vinegar, salt, and black pepper.

Give okra a south-of-the-border touch with chili sauce. Just add ⅓ cup water and 1 teaspoon minced onion to a 15½-ounce can okra, and simmer for 10 minutes. Add 2 tablespoons chili sauce; heat.

Use okra in soups or stews, with chicken, with rice and tomatoes. Southern cooks recommend it as a seasoning in other vegetables—for instance, 3 or 4 pods in a batch of butter beans, in fried corn, or with purple-hull black-eyed peas. There are almost as many ideas for ingredients and preparation as there are good cooks in the South.

Don't overlook the possibilities of **Baked Okra.** To 2 cups cooked okra add 1 well-beaten egg, ½ teaspoon salt, 1 cup cream (or ½ cup each cream and milk), and 1 cup well-buttered, soft bread crumbs. Pour mixture into buttered pan or custard cups. Set in pan of water. Bake in preheated moderate oven (350° F.) until set, about 45 minutes. For a good variation, 1 cup drained, whole-kernel corn can be added. Makes 4 to 6 servings.

Our favorite **Okra Stew** is prepared without hard-and-fast rules. Proportions and ingredients vary according to the current stage of the garden. Sometimes we add bacon, sometimes we don't. You can prepare it to suit yourself. Here is a starter: Sauté chopped onion and green pepper in a little bacon fat or butter until tender. Add tomatoes, fresh or canned, and okra, whole (with stem end removed) or sliced, salt, and pepper. Simmer over low heat only until okra is tender. Top with bacon bits. Serve on triangles of buttered whole-wheat toast, or add croutons browned in butter. A thicker mixture may be topped with bread crumbs and browned in the oven. We like to season it with a little rosemary or thyme. You may prefer to season with chili powder, celery salt, or a hint of garlic. Serve with an ample supply of spoon bread (made, of course, with stone-ground cornmeal), followed by a light dessert and coffee, and there's a meal!

A similar combination can be the basis for a delicious **Chicken Gumbo.** First disjoint a medium-size hen, and simmer until tender. Remove chicken; dice meat, and return to broth. Add okra, cut in 1-inch pieces, tomatoes, celery, green pepper, onion, and parsley, all cut rather fine. Simmer until vegetables are tender. Season to taste with salt, black pepper, and a pinch each of thyme and marjoram. Next, put cooked rice in a well-greased baking dish; pour the chicken gumbo over it; cover generously with buttered crumbs, and bake for 30 minutes in preheated moderate oven (350°F.).

Beef-and-Okra Stew makes a hearty main dish. For 6 servings: Melt 4 tablespoons fat in heavy pan. Add 1 pound lean beef, cut in small pieces (round steak is good), and 2 onions, chopped. Cook slowly, stirring, until onions start to brown. Add 2 tablespoons flour, and blend. Add ½ cup beef broth or canned bouillon and 1 cup water, stirring until mixture thickens a little. Add 1 green pepper, chopped, 2 cups sliced carrots, 2 cups or 15½-ounce can okra, sliced, 1 teaspoon salt, black pepper, and 1 teaspoon Worcestershire. Simmer about 1 hour, stirring frequently. Serve over rice or with corn bread.

Vegetables, it seems to me, are the problem children of cookery. We serve them dutifully, and although we try to vary the cycle as much as possible, they do tend to become routine—a little monotonous, in fact. So why not try something new? Why not try okra?

OLEOMARGARINE—A smooth-textured fat used as a spread and in cooking. The name comes from elo-, a combining form meaning "oil," and from margaric acid, a constituent of animal fat. It was first devised in 1870 by the French chemist Mège-Mouriès. He used beef oil, milk, and water in proportions of ten, four, and three, churning together with annatto for yellow coloring.

Oleomargarine, or margarine as it is more commonly called nowadays, has come a long way since its introduction and has evolved in many types containing a variety of ingredients differing greatly from the original.

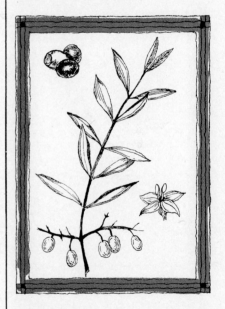

OLIVE—The fruit of a twenty-five- to forty-foot subtropical evergreen tree (*Olea europea*) with thin silvery, willowlike leaves and whitish flowers. Olives are among the world's oldest fruits and have been cultivated in the Mediterranean area since about 3,000 B.C.

The olive tree probably originated in Asia or Asia Minor. The name is so old that its origins remain obscure. The original root is related to the Armenian word *eul* which means oil.

Olives, and the olive tree, have had a long and colorful history. In their warm home countries, where the dairy products of temperate regions did not exist, olives provided the essential fat in man's diet. Mediterranean man could not have lived without them. They are indeed the fruit of civilization. To this day in Spain, France, and Italy, which lie partially in the subtropical zone, cookery is divided into butter and oil cooking, and until fairly recently the twain seldom met.

Olive trees, which grow to a gnarled old age, do not start fruit until the age of eight years, so that an olive grove represented a considerable investment; thus, the ancients reckoned wealth by the number of olive trees owned. Cutting down olive trees was a serious crime; from this comes the origin of the olive as a symbol of peace, for war destroyed the sacred trees. Olive oil was held as sacred as bread, as we know from Egyptian records that go as far back as the 17th century B.C. The Sumerians used olive oil around 3,000 B.C. for cooking, and for anointing their hair and bodies. The Bible mentions olives many times: the dove that announced the ebbing of the flood to Noah carried an olive leaf in its beak, but perhaps the most moving reference is found in Psalm 23 verse 5: "Thou preparest a table before me in the presence of mine enemies; thou anointest my head with oil; my cup runneth over."

In classical mythology the olive tree is said to have been created by Athena, the Greek goddess of wisdom. A new city in Greece was to be named, and Athena and Poseidon, god of the sea, competed for the honor of giving the city a name. The one who produced the best gift for the welfare of the new city was to be the winner. Poseidon offered a war horse, Athena an olive tree. The new city was named Athens.

There is no lovelier sight in the world than a grove of ancient, gnarled olive trees, thickly covered with silvery shimmery leaves, trembling in the breeze, seen against the deep blue of the water, as one can see in Spain, southern France, on Capri, and in the Greek islands. It is a sight to put the mind and senses at rest, in tune with the civilizations of the past.

Jesuit missionaries introduced olive trees into Mexico in the 17th century, and took them from there into southern California where they flourished.

In the United States olives are grown for their fruit but elsewhere they are grown primarily for oil. The olive itself is a hard-stoned fruit used as a condiment, for seasoning, and as an appetizer. Olives are also delicious when added to many meat dishes and stews. Because they are one of the prime foods of the Mediterranean, they are a frequent ingredient in many spicy dishes originating in these countries.

Olives, as they grow on the tree, are

pale green. When they begin to turn straw-colored, they are picked and prepared in various ways for eating. Fresh olives are very bitter. The bitterness is removed in the preparation.

Green fermented olives, the well-known Spanish-style olives, are soaked in lye for a short time, washed, and then kept in barrels of salt solution for six to twelve months. This causes a lactic-acid fermentation and gives them their astringent taste. Sugar is added from time to time to keep fermentation going. When the olives are properly fermented, they are packed in a weak salt brine and bottled.

As the olive becomes riper it develops more oil. Ripe olives are either green or black. Both are picked later than the early light-green olives but before they turn jet-black, as they do when ready to be picked for their oil. These "ripe" olives are heated and soaked in lye, then packed in brine. The black color of the "ripe" olive is developed during the lye treatments. Between treatments they are exposed to the air to develop the characteristic dark color.

If the olive is left on the tree until it is fully ripe and ready to be pressed for oil, it turns jet-black. If used for eating, the olives are picked and mixed with salt. This removes some of the bitterness and most of the moisture. These olives, popular in France, Spain, Italy, and Greece, are wrinkled and shriveled and very nutritious. They are often packed in oil or eaten after being dipped into oil.

Availability and Purchasing Guide—Olives, available year round, are graded by size as small, medium, large, extra large, mammoth, giant, colossal, and super colossal. Green olives are sold in jars, pickled: Pitted; unpitted; stuffed with pimientos, almonds, capers, onions, or celery.

Ripe olives are available in jars and cans, pitted or unpitted, whole, sliced, or chopped.

Dried and salt-cured olives, also known as Greek or Italian olives, are available canned and in bulk.

Olive condite, or salad, is available in jars and is also included with canned antipasto. Olive spread, or butter, made from green or ripe olives, is available canned. Chopped olives mixed with cream cheese and with process cheese spreads is available.

Storage—Olives in cans or jars can be stored unopened at room temperature indefinitely. Once opened they should be refrigerated in their own liquid and can be stored thus indefinitely. If any white scum forms on top of the liquid in which the olives are packed, rinse olives before using. They should not be used if they are

no longer firm.

Caloric Values
- [ ] Green, 1 large = 7 calories
- [ ] Ripe, 1 large = 11 calories
- [ ] Dried and salt-cured, 1 large = 20 calories

OLIVE-AVOCADO APPETIZER
1 large ripe avocado
1 cup highly seasoned French dressing
1/3 cup chopped stuffed olives

Peel avocado. Cut into halves; remove seed. Cut into 1/4-inch lengthwise slices. Immediately cover slices with French dressing and let stand in refrigerator for 30 minutes. Drain (reserve dressing for future salads). Sprinkle with olives. Makes 4 servings.

OLIVE SURPRISES
1/4 cup soft butter or margarine
1 cup grated sharp Cheddar cheese
1/4 teaspoon each of salt and paprika
1/2 cup sifted all-purpose flour
3 dozen medium-size stuffed olives

Cream butter and cheese until blended. Add remaining ingredients except olives and mix well. Chill for 15 to 20 minutes. Shape a small portion of dough around each olive. Bake in preheated hot oven (400°F.) for about 15 minutes. Good hot or cold. Makes 36.

HAKE FILLETS WITH OLIVES
2 pounds hake fillets
Salt and pepper to taste
1/4 cup butter or margarine, softened
1 small onion, minced
1 tablespoon vinegar
1/3 cup chopped olives

Season fish lightly with salt and pepper. Put in shallow baking dish. Combine remaining ingredients and spread on fish. Bake in preheated moderate oven (350° F.) for 30 minutes, or until fish flakes easily with fork. Makes 4 servings.

SPANISH MEAT LOAF
1 1/2 pounds ground meat
1 cup drained canned chick-peas
1/4 cup tomato sauce
1/4 cup seedless raisins
1/4 cup sliced stuffed olives
1 large onion, chopped
1 small green pepper, seeded and chopped
1 small garlic clove, chopped
2 eggs
Oregano, salt, and pepper

Toss together lightly but thoroughly meat, chick-peas, tomato sauce, raisins, olives, onion, green pepper, and garlic. Add eggs to bind and season with oregano, salt, and pepper to taste. Pack into loaf pan or 1 1/2-quart casserole greased with bacon fat. Bake in preheated moderate oven (350°F.) for 1 1/4 hours. Makes 4 to 6 servings.

STEAK-AND-OLIVE CASSEROLE
1 1/2 pounds beef round steak, cut into 1/2-inch cubes

2 tablespoons shortening
1 teaspoon salt
¼ teaspoon pepper
½ teaspoon crumbled dried marjoram
1 can (8 ounces) tomato sauce
¼ cup (one 2-ounce bottle) stuffed olives, sliced
2 tablespoons liquid from olives
Garlic

Brown steak in shortening. Add next 6 ingredients. Pour into 2-quart casserole that has been greased and rubbed with garlic; cover. Makes 6 servings.

CORN, EGG, OLIVE, AND RAISIN CASSEROLE

1 medium onion, minced
1 medium green pepper, minced
½ cup butter or margarine
1 can (17 ounces) cream-style corn
1 medium tomato, chopped
½ teaspoon pepper
1 teaspoon sugar
2 egg yolks
½ cup chopped green or ripe olives
½ cup seedless raisins
2 hard-cooked eggs, chopped
¼ teaspoon powdered thyme
Salt to taste

Cook onion and pepper in butter for 3 or 4 minutes. Reserve half of mixture. To remainder add corn and tomato; cook for 5 minutes. Add pepper, sugar, and egg yolks and cook for 10 minutes, stirring occasionally. To reserved onion and pepper mixture, add olives, raisins, hard-cooked eggs, thyme, and salt. Spread half of corn mixture in shallow baking dish (1½ quart). Top with olive mixture and remaining corn. Bake in preheated moderate oven (350°F.) for about 20 minutes. Makes 4 to 6 servings.

CRABMEAT OLIVE SANDWICHES

1 can (6½ ounces) crabmeat, drained, boned, and flaked
1½ cups grated process American or mild Cheddar cheese
1 tablespoon instant minced onion
⅓ cup sliced pimiento-stuffed olives
1 cup dairy sour cream
12 slices of rye bread

Mix all ingredients except bread. Spread between bread slices. Makes 6 sandwiches.

CHEESE-OLIVE-RAISIN SANDWICHES

2 packages (8 ounces each) cream cheese, softened
2 tablespoons French dressing
¼ cup chopped pimiento-stuffed olives
½ cup seedless raisins
16 slices of bread, buttered

Mix cheese and dressing until smooth. Add olives and raisins. Spread on 8 bread slices. Top with remaining slices. Makes 8 sandwiches.

GARLIC BLACK OLIVES

1 large or 2 small cans black ripe olives, drained
Olive oil
2 medium garlic cloves, halved
Cracked ice, about ½ cup

Put olives in bowl. Cover to a depth of ¼ inch with olive oil. Stir in garlic and ice. Cover and let stand at room temperature for 2 to 3 hours. Drain.

OLIVE OIL—A product obtained by crushing tree-ripened olives, then extracting the liquid by pressing the pulp or by centrifugal separators. The first "crude olive oil" is obtained from this liquid by settling and skimming or by "washing" by a continuous flow of clear water. Refining produces the clear oil which we use for salads and cooking. The best olive oil is golden or straw-yellow in color. Greenish-colored oils are of an inferior quality. Olive oil is imported from France, Italy, Spain, and Greece. Fine quality California olive oil is also obtainable.

Olive oil should not be exposed to extremes of light or temperature. Light will fade its color and cold will cause it to congeal and separate. It is sold in bottles or cans by liquid measure.

Olive oil has a more distinctive flavor and a lower smoking point than other edible oils. It is used for salad dressings, seasoning vegetables, and sautéing over low heat where its special flavor is desired. Its use is characteristic of Mediterranean cookery.

OMELET—A combination of eggs, milk or water, and seasonings, cooked in a skillet until firm. Omelets generally are of two different types: puffy, in which the yolks and whites are beaten separately, resulting in a fluffier omelet; and French, in which the yolks and whites are beaten together, producing a firmer, less-fluffy omelet. All other omelets are variations of these basic types.

PUFFY OMELET

6 eggs, separated
½ teaspoon salt
⅛ teaspoon pepper
1½ tablespoons all-purpose flour
1 tablespoon water
2 tablespoons butter or margarine

Beat egg whites with salt until stiff but not dry. Beat egg yolks with pepper, flour, and water until fluffy. Fold yolk mixture into whites gently but thoroughly. Melt butter in 10-inch skillet. Tip skillet to spread butter over bottom. Pour in omelet mixture, level surface gently, and cover. Cook over very low heat until surface of omelet is dry and knife, when inserted, comes out clean. Fold and serve at once. Makes 4 servings.
Note: To cook in an electric skillet, heat butter at 320°F. and pour in omelet mixture. Reduce heat to 240°F. for cooking.

FRENCH OMELET

3 eggs
3 tablespoons water
¼ teaspoon salt
Dash of pepper
1 tablespoon butter or margarine

Mix eggs, water, salt, and pepper with fork. Heat butter in 8-inch skillet and pour in egg mixture. It should set at edges at once. As mixture at the edges thickens, draw these portions toward the center with the fork so that the uncooked portions flow to the bottom. Tilt skillet as necessary to hasten flow of uncooked egg. When egg is set and surface is still moist, increase heat to brown bottom quickly. Fold and serve at once. Makes 2 servings.

SPANISH OMELET

1 small onion, chopped
½ cup canned tomatoes
1 small green pepper, chopped
1 small garlic clove, minced
2 tablespoons olive oil
Salt and pepper to taste
1 recipe for French Omelet, above

Put onion, tomatoes, green pepper, garlic, and olive oil in saucepan. Bring to boil and simmer for 10 minutes. Season with salt and pepper. Make French Omelet, filling it, before folding, with half the mixture. Fold omelet, put on hot serving plate, and pour the remaining mixture around it. Makes 2 servings.

HAM OMELET

1 cup minced cooked ham
½ teaspoon prepared mustard
1 teaspoon minced onion
1 recipe for Puffy Omelet, at left

Mix ham, mustard, and onion. Make Puffy Omelet. Spread ham mixture on omelet before folding. Fold and serve at once. Makes 4 servings.

CHEESE OMELET

4 eggs
¼ cup water
½ teaspoon salt
⅛ teaspoon pepper
¼ cup grated Gruyère or Cheddar cheese
2 tablespoons butter or margarine

Beat eggs slightly. Add water, salt, pepper, and cheese. Melt butter and heat just until it sizzles. Add eggs and reduce heat slightly. As omelet cooks, lift it with a spatula to allow the uncooked part to run under. Increase heat slightly to brown underside. When omelet is of desired doneness, fold over and serve at once. Makes 2 or 3 servings.

ONION OMELET

Sauté 2 large mild onions, sliced, in 2 tablespoons olive oil. Season 6 eggs to taste with salt and pepper, and beat lightly. Stir in onion. Add 2 tablespoons oil to pan; add eggs and cook over low heat until set. Turn carefully to other side; brown lightly. Makes 4 servings.

Chives

Leek

Red Globe Onions

Yellow Onions

Green Onions,
often called Scallions

White Onions

Spanish Onions

Shallots

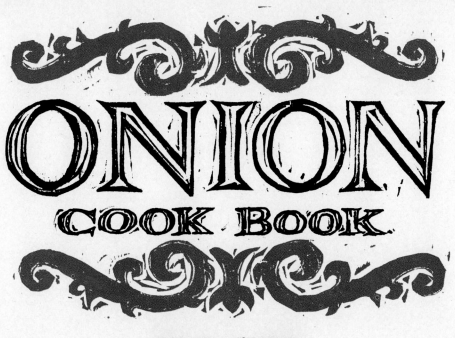

ONION COOK BOOK

The versatile onion, pungent and aromatic, is a culinary jewel that imparts an incomparable flavor to roasts, casseroles, salads, vegetables, soups, stews; a gourmet taste to any dish.

ONION—The underground bulb of the plant *Allium cepa.* There are many kinds of onions with different-colored skins, and in size they vary from the very small bulbets of the spring or green onions, also known as scallions, to the huge round red Italian onions. A pungent volatile oil, rich in sulphur, is the cause of the onion's strong smell and flavor, and the warmer the climate in which onions are grown, the milder and sweeter they tend to be.

Onions are a member of the lily family which includes such flowers as the tulip, hyacinth, and lily-of-the-valley as well as the edible leek, garlic, garlic chive, chive, and shallot. All have a bulb growing under the ground and a stalk, leaves, and flowers above.

The word "onion" comes through French from Latin, probably from the Latin word unus, meaning "one." Perhaps because the onion is a single bulb with a spherical shape it was considered a symbol of the universe by the Egyptians. Today we do not associate the onion with such symbolism, but it does have a practically universal use; much cooking would be flavorless without it.

The versatile onion, a native of western Asia, has been cultivated from earliest times. In the 4th millenium B.C., Egyptian slaves working to build the gigantic Great Pyramid at Gizeh are said to have subsisted largely on onions, radishes, and garlic. The children of Israel were loath to leave the onions they had enjoyed in Egypt and cried out bitterly when they were deprived of this delicacy, resisting even the substitution of manna. The American Indians ate a type of wild onion which was powerful to the taste, and also used it in cooking stews.

The ancient Greeks and Romans used onions medicinally as well as in cooking. Hippocrates, the Greek physician of the 3rd and 4th centuries B.C., declared onions to be good for the sight but bad for the body. In the Middle Ages onions were used to help cure dog bites, adder bites, and the bites and stings of "venomous worms."

A 14th-century Icelandic manuscript states: "It is good for them that have cold and wet natures, and it does good in the stomach, and gives good complexion. If one mixes onion's juice and paunch fat of chickens, it is good to rub on shoes that cut." Through the centuries onions and onion juice were recommended to cure earache, colds, fever, laryngitis, and warts: an onion, cut into halves, rubbed on a wart, tied together again and buried, was supposed to make a wart disappear while the onion decayed in the ground.

The amount of onion to be used was often a subject of controversy. A very popular late 19th-century American cook book, *Practical Housekeeping,* advised its readers in rhyme as to the exact amount of onion needed for a perfect salad: "Let onion atoms lurk within the bowl, And half-suspected, animate the whole."

Availability—The more strongly flavored domestic onions, available year round, are globe-shape and have white, yellow, or red skins. The white-skinned onion has the mildest flavor in this group.

More mildly flavored still are the Bermuda, Spanish or Valencia, and Italian onions. Bermudas, large, flat, and white or yellow in color, are available from March to June. The very large Spanish onions, brown or yellow in color, are available from August through April. The large red Italian onions are available year round.

Green onions, or scallions, are available year round.

Available in cans or jars are boiled whole onions, pickled onions, onion juice, and onion soup.

Chopped onions, pearl onions mixed with peas, and creamed onions are available frozen.

Dried or freeze-dried onion products include instant onion, onion flakes, scallions, onion-soup mixes, onion bouillon cubes, and some onion-gravy mixes.

Onion powder, made by grinding dehydrated onion into a fine powder, and onion salt, a combination of onion powder and salt, are also available.

Purchasing Guide—Most onions are slightly dried before they come to market and this accounts for their characteristically dry paper-thin skin. They are sold by weight, but very large Bermudas or Spanish types often are sold by unit. They should be firm with a dry skin which is bright and smooth.

All types of green onions are sold in bunches. They should have fresh green tops and medium-size necks 2 to 3 inches in length. Necks should be young, tender, and crisp, and roots should not be too long.

Storage—Dry onions should be kept in a cool dry well-ventilated place in a single layer. Green onions should have wilted parts and roots discarded. Wrap in moisture-proof wrapping and refrigerate.

☐ Dry, room temperature, uncooked: 1 to 4 weeks
☐ Green, refrigerator shelf or vegetable compartment, uncooked: 1 to 4 months
☐ Refrigerator shelf, cooked: 4 to 5 days
☐ Frozen, refrigerator frozen-food compartment: 2 to 3 months
☐ Frozen, freezer: 1 year
☐ Canned, kitchen shelf: 1 year
☐ Dried instant onion, kitchen shelf: 6 to 8 months

Nutritive Food Values—Onions contain some vitamin C with small amounts of other vitamins and minerals. Green parts of the onion yield some vitamin A.

☐ Dry, 3½ ounces, raw = 38 calories
☐ Dry, 3½ ounces, boiled and drained = 29 calories
☐ Green, 3½ ounces, raw, bulb and entire top = 36 calories
☐ Green, 3½ ounces, raw, bulb and white portion of top = 45 calories
☐ Green, 3½ ounces, green portion of tops only = 27 calories

Basic Preparation

☐ **To Peel**—Peel under running water to avoid tears. Onions can be more easily peeled by pouring boiling water over them and letting them stand for a few minutes.

☐ **To Chop**—Cut into halves crosswise. With a sharp knife, cube the top cut surface of the onion, then cut onion crosswise to release all the cubes. To cut onion into rings, cut onions into crosswise slices and carefully separate the slices into rings.

☐ **To Cook Whole**—Drop peeled onions into boiling salted water; cook for 20 to 35 minutes depending on the size of the onion, or until onion is transparent and can be easily pierced with a fork. Sliced onions can be cooked in the same way but require less time. Drain and season with salt and pepper to taste and add butter.

Odor can be removed from a knife by rubbing with a raw potato. Odor can be removed from the hands by rubbing with salt, lemon, or celery salt.

FRENCH ONION SOUP

1½ pounds onions (about 5 cups sliced)
¼ cup butter or margarine
6 cups beef bouillon
Salt and pepper
Toasted slices of French bread
Grated Parmesan cheese

Peel onions and slice thin. Brown lightly in butter. Add to bouillon and simmer, covered, for about 30 minutes. Season to taste. Put into large casserole or individual casseroles. Top with toast and sprinkle with cheese. Makes 4 to 6 servings.

ONION AND CHEESE SOUP

1 cup chopped onions
2 tablespoons butter or margarine
2 tablespoons flour
6 cups rich milk, scalded
Salt and pepper to taste
2 cups grated sharp Cheddar cheese
Paprika and minced chives

Sauté onions in butter until soft. Add flour and mix; add milk gradually, stirring all the while, and heat to just below boiling. Season and stir in cheese. Serve sprinkled with paprika and chives. Makes 2 quarts.

SOUTH AMERICAN ONION SOUP

6 onions, thinly sliced
3 tablespoons butter or margarine
2 quarts rich bouillon or 3 cans (10½ ounces each) condensed consommé with 3 cans water
1½ cups almonds, blanched and chopped fine
Salt and pepper to taste
Rounds of crusty bread, toasted
1 cup grated Gruyère cheese

Sauté onions in butter slowly until soft. Add bouillon and nuts and simmer for 30 minutes. Season and serve with toast rounds sprinkled with cheese. Makes about 2½ quarts.

BEEF AND ONION PIE

3 pounds boneless beef chuck
2 tablespoons shortening

Salt and pepper to taste
2 cups water
2 cups (one 16-ounce can or jar) cooked onions, undrained
¼ cup cornstarch
Special Pastry for Meat Pies, baked (page 1304)

Cut meat into 1½-inch cubes. Brown meat in shortening in kettle. Sprinkle with salt and pepper. Add water. Bring to boil, cover, and simmer for 2 hours, or until tender. Drain, reserving broth. Put meat in shallow baking dish. Measure broth and add onion liquid to make 3 cups. Add cornstarch blended with a little cold water. Cook until slightly thickened. Season to taste. Add onions and gravy to meat. Bake in preheated hot oven (425°F.) for 10 minutes. Reduce heat to moderate (350°F.) and bake for 20 minutes longer. Put baked Pastry on top of meat and serve. Makes 6 servings.

Beef-Pie Pastry

Sift 2 cups all-purpose flour and 1 teaspoon salt. Cut in ⅔ cup shortening until mixture resembles coarse cornmeal. Mix 1 egg yolk with 3 tablespoons water. Mix lightly into flour mixture. Roll to ¼-inch thickness. Cut into diamonds or other desired shapes. Put on ungreased cookie sheet. Prick tops with fork and brush with slightly beaten egg white. Bake in preheated moderate oven (350°F.) for 20 minutes.

PORK CHOPS WITH ONIONS
Salt
6 thick lean pork chops
1½ cups sliced onions
½ teaspoon dried thyme
1 can (10½ ounces) beef consommé, undiluted
¼ teaspoon pepper
Dash of cayenne
¾ cup dairy sour cream
2 tablespoons flour
12 small potatoes, boiled
Parsley

In salted hot skillet brown chops; pour off any fat. Add onions, thyme, consommé, pepper, and cayenne. Cover and simmer slowly for about 45 minutes. Remove chops and add sour cream; thicken with flour and a little cold water. Season to taste and pour over chops. Garnish with potatoes and parsley. Makes 6 servings.

FRENCH STUFFED ONIONS
6 Bermuda onions, peeled
½ pound raw veal or ham, ground (if ham, substitute 2 tablespoons butter for bacon below)
2 bacon strips, diced
Salt and pepper
Cayenne
½ cup dairy sour cream
1 tablespoon finely chopped celery
2 tablespoons each of chopped chives and parsley
1 cup soft bread crumbs
Butter or margarine

1 cup meat bouillon or consommé

Parboil onions for 10 minutes. Scoop out centers. Sauté chopped centers, veal, and bacon. Add remaining ingredients except butter and bouillon and stuff onions. Dot with butter. Bake with bouillon in shallow baking dish in preheated hot oven (400°F.) for 45 minutes. Makes 6 servings.

ONIONS WITH CHICKEN
6 large mild onions, peeled
½ cup chopped mushrooms
½ cup chopped cooked chicken
2 tablespoons soft butter or margarine
½ cup soft bread crumbs
Salt and pepper
½ cup chicken bouillon
Paprika
½ cup dairy sour cream

Parboil onions for 30 minutes. Scoop out centers and make stuffing of chopped centers and remaining ingredients except bouillon, paprika, and sour cream. Stuff onions. Put in buttered baking pan. Add bouillon, sprinkle with paprika, cover, and bake in preheated hot oven (400°F.) for about 30 minutes. Remove cover for last 10 minutes. Remove onions; add sour cream to pan; serve over onions. Makes 6 servings.

FRENCH ONION QUICHE
1 cup sliced mild onions
2 tablespoons butter or margarine
½ pound Swiss cheese, grated
Pastry for 1-crust, 9-inch pie, unbaked
3 eggs, beaten
1 cup each of milk and light cream
1 teaspoon salt
¼ teaspoon pepper
Dash of ground nutmeg
3 crisp bacon strips, crumbled

Sauté onions in butter until golden and soft. Put with cheese in pastry-lined pie pan. Combine rest of ingredients and pour over cheese and onions. Bake in preheated moderate oven (375°F.) for 45 minutes, or until a knife blade, when inserted, comes out clean. Cool slightly. Makes 6 servings.

GERMAN ONION TART
3 cups thinly sliced onions
3 tablespoons butter or bacon fat
2 cups dairy sour cream
2 eggs, slightly beaten
1½ teaspoons salt
¼ teaspoon pepper
⅛ teaspoon each of ground nutmeg and ginger
9-inch pie shell, baked in very hot oven (450°F.) for 10 minutes
Caraway seeds and paprika

Sauté onions in butter slowly until soft and golden. Add all except last 3 ingredients to onions; turn into pie shell. Sprinkle with caraway seeds and paprika. Bake in preheated very hot oven (450°F.) for 10 minutes; reduce heat to moderate (350°F.) and bake for 30 minutes longer, or until a knife blade in-

serted in the tart comes out clean. Makes 6 servings.

STUFFED ONIONS, ITALIAN STYLE
6 chicken livers
½ cup butter or margarine
2 mushroom caps, chopped
Salt and pepper
6 large onions, cut in half crosswise
1 tablespoon all-purpose flour
¼ teaspoon bottled gravy sauce
1 cup chicken bouillon
Chopped parsley

Brown chicken livers in ¼ cup of the butter; chop livers. Add chopped mushrooms and salt and pepper to taste. Parboil onions in small amount of boiling water for 10 minutes. Drain and hollow out centers. Put in shallow baking dish and fill centers with liver mixture. Cover and bake in preheated moderate oven (375°F.) for 15 minutes. Melt remaining butter and blend in flour, salt and pepper to taste, and gravy sauce. Add bouillon and cook, stirring constantly, until slightly thickened. Pour over onions and bake for 20 minutes longer. Sprinkle with parsley. Makes 6 servings.

ONIONS AND NOODLES, MEXICANOS
3 cups finely chopped mild onions
¼ cup butter (Mexicans use lard)
8 ounces fine noodles
2 cups rich beef bouillon or consommé
Salt and pepper
Chopped parsley

Sauté onions in butter for a few minutes; add uncooked noodles and stir. Cook for 5 minutes. Add bouillon; cover and simmer until cooked, about 30 minutes. Add salt and pepper to taste. Garnish with parsley. Makes 6 servings.

SPICED ONIONS AND BEETS
2 cups thinly sliced mild onions
2 cups peeled and sliced cooked beets
½ cup white vinegar
¾ cup water
1 cinnamon stick
4 cloves
1 tablespoon sugar
½ teaspoon salt
⅛ teaspoon pepper

Place onions and beets in pan with rest of ingredients. Bring to boil and simmer gently for 10 minutes. Serve cold as a relish or hot, with 1 tablespoon butter added, as accompaniment to meat. Improves with time and will keep for weeks in refrigerator. (Add just a touch of garlic salt for extra flavor.) Makes 4 servings.

DUTCH ONION PIE
3 cups thinly sliced onions
2 tablespoons butter or margarine
1 pound cottage cheese
¼ cup heavy cream
9-inch pie shell, baked
Salt and pepper to taste
Dash of cayenne

Fry onions in butter until soft. Moisten cheese with cream and pour into baked

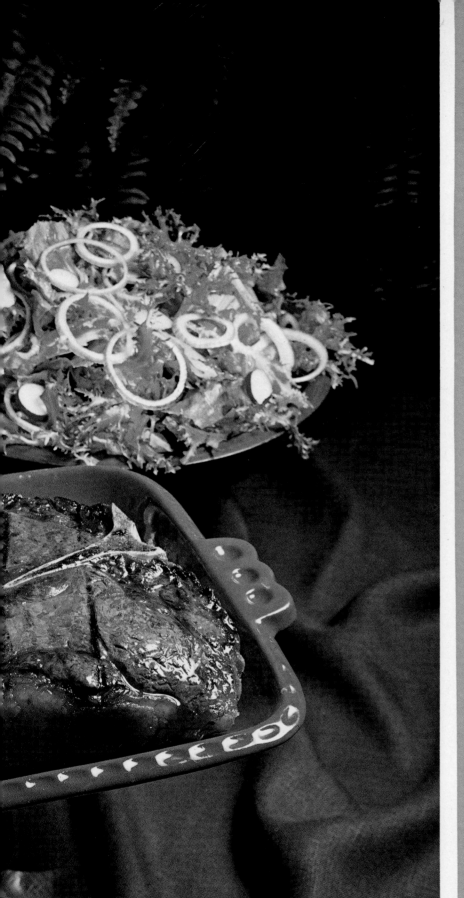

French Onion Soup, French-Fried Onions, and a green salad with onion rings and radishes

pie shell; season lightly with salt and pepper. Cover with onions. Add more salt and pepper and the cayenne. Bake in preheated hot oven (400°F.) for 15 minutes. Makes 6 servings.

BERMUDA CASSEROLE

- 2 large Bermuda onions, sliced
- 4 slices of stale white bread (without crusts), cubed
- ¾ cup grated sharp Cheddar cheese
- ¾ cup rich milk
- 2 eggs, beaten
- ¾ teaspoon salt
- ⅛ teaspoon pepper
  Butter or margarine
  Dash of cayenne

Parboil onions for 10 minutes. Place them in a buttered shallow baking dish in layers with bread and cheese. Combine milk, eggs, and salt and pepper; pour over top layer; dot with butter. Sprinkle with cayenne. Set dish in pan of hot water, and bake in preheated moderate oven (375°F.) for 40 minutes. Makes 4 servings.

RUSSIAN ONIONS AND MUSHROOMS

- 1½ cups chopped onions
- 2 tablespoons butter or bacon fat
- 1 pound mushrooms, sliced
- 1½ teaspoons salt
- ¼ teaspoon pepper
- ½ teaspoon paprika
- 1 tablespoon flour
- 2 cups dairy sour cream

Simmer onions in butter until golden. Add mushrooms and seasonings and cook slowly for 10 minutes. Add flour, stir; add sour cream slowly and simmer for another 10 minutes. Serve with steak or roast beef as a luncheon dish. Also good in tiny cream-puff shells as hot appetizers. Makes 6 luncheon servings.

ONIONS AND POTATOES, CHARLENE

Peel and quarter enough onions and potatoes to make 3 cups of each. Simmer them in just enough salted water to cover until cooked. Drain off liquid and replace with 1½ cups rich milk and ½ cup cream. Add 3 tablespoons butter; season to taste with salt and pepper and dash of cayenne. Simmer until thoroughly heated. Makes 6 servings.

ONIONS AND TOMATO, AMERICAN

- 18 small white onions, peeled and cooked
- ¼ teaspoon pepper
- 1 tablespoon butter
- 1 tablespoon cooking oil
- 1 can (10½ ounces) condensed tomato soup
- 1 cup meat bouillon (or bouillon made with cube and onion water)

Put all ingredients in 1½-quart casserole. Mix well, cover, and bake in preheated moderate oven (375°F.) for about 30 minutes. Makes 6 servings.

ONIONS AND EGGS, FAUST

- 6 hard-cooked eggs
- 2 cups chopped onions

2 tablespoons butter or margarine
½ cup dry white wine
¾ teaspoon salt
¼ teaspoon pepper
   Paprika and powdered mustard to
   taste
¼ cup chili sauce
¼ cup buttered fine dry bread crumbs

Slice eggs and place them in buttered baking dish. Brown onions lightly in butter and add mixture of remaining ingredients except crumbs. Pour over eggs. Sprinkle with crumbs and bake in preheated hot oven (425°F.) for about 15 minutes. Makes 4 to 6 servings.

ONIONS AND APPLES
2 cups sliced onions
3 cups peeled apple slices
2 tablespoons butter or bacon fat
   Salt to taste
2 tablespoons brown sugar

Put onions and apples in skillet with fat; cover and simmer over low heat, stirring, until apples are soft and onions tender but not too brown, about 10 minutes. Season with salt, add sugar, stir, and serve with meat. Makes 4 servings.

ONION AND ORANGE SALAD
Peel oranges and slice about ½ inch thick. Peel red Italian onions and slice thin. Separate into rings. Arrange orange slices and onion rings on bed of salad greens and watercress. Pour French dressing over top.

MARINATED ONIONS AND
BLUE CHEESE
½ cup olive oil
2 tablespoons fresh lemon juice
1 teaspoon salt
   Dash each of pepper and paprika
½ teaspoon sugar
¼ cup crumbled blue cheese
2 cups thickly sliced large red or
   yellow onions

Mix oil, lemon juice, seasonings, and sugar. Stir in cheese; pour over onions, cover, and chill for at least 2 days. Makes 6 to 8 servings.
Note: These are delicious with thin buttered slices of pumpernickel.

GLAZED ONIONS
2 dozen small white onions, peeled
¼ cup butter or margarine
2 tablespoons molasses
   Dash of hot pepper sauce

Cook and drain onions. Put in skillet with remaining ingredients. Cook slowly, turning to brown and glaze. Makes 6 servings.

GLAZED ONIONS AMANDINE
36 tiny silver-skinned onions
2 tablespoons butter or margarine
½ cup slivered blanched almonds
2 teaspoons sugar

Peel onions. Cook in boiling salted water for 15 minutes. Drain. In a skillet melt butter and add onions and almonds. Add 1 teaspoon sugar and toss. Add remaining sugar and cook slowly until onions and almonds are glazed and browned, about 15 minutes. Toss or shake pan often. Delicious with turkey or chicken. Makes 4 to 6 servings.

HONEY-GLAZED ONIONS
2 dozen small white onions, peeled
2 tablespoons honey
2 tablespoons ketchup
3 tablespoons butter or margarine
¼ cup hot water
   Dash each of salt and cayenne

Cook onions in salted water for 20 minutes. Drain and place in buttered baking dish. Make a sauce of remaining ingredients, pour over onions, and cover. Bake in preheated moderate oven (350°F.) for 1 hour, or until onions are mellow and glazed, basting occasionally. Makes 4 servings.

BERMUDAS GLACÉS
6 Bermuda onions
2 tablespoons butter or margarine
¼ cup honey
½ teaspoon paprika
½ teaspoon salt
⅛ teaspoon pepper
3 tablespoons water

Halve onions and put cut side up in large covered casserole. Top with remaining ingredients and cover. Bake in preheated moderate oven (350°F.) for 1½ hours, basting with sauce. Makes 6 servings.

CREAMED ONIONS
2 dozen small white onions, peeled
¼ cup butter or margarine
¼ cup all-purpose flour
1½ cups light cream
   Salt and pepper
   Dash of cayenne
½ cup buttered soft bread crumbs, or
   grated sharp Cheddar cheese

Cook onions until tender. Drain, reserving ½ cup liquid. Melt butter and blend in flour. Gradually add reserved liquid and cream, stirring constantly. Cook, stirring, until smooth and thickened. Add salt and pepper to taste and cayenne. Add onions and mix lightly. Pour into shallow baking dish, and top with crumbs. Cover, and bake in preheated moderate oven (350°F.) for 45 minutes. Uncover during last 20 minutes of baking to brown the top. Makes 6 servings.

FRENCH-FRIED ONIONS
Peel Spanish or Bermuda onions and cut into ¼-inch slices. Separate into rings, dip into evaporated milk, then into flour. Fry in hot deep fat. Drain on paper towels and sprinkle with salt.

CURRIED ONIONS
Cut 3 large Bermuda or Spanish onions into thick slices. Cook in salted water until tender, drain, and add 2 cups hot cooked rice. Stir in 1 cup light cream or evaporated milk, 2 tablespoons butter or margarine, ¼ teaspoon ground mace, ¾ teaspoon salt, and 1 tablespoon curry powder. Heat and serve. Makes 4 to 6 servings.

TURK'S ONION DELIGHT
¼ cup chopped onion
2 tablespoons olive oil
4 eggs
   Salt and pepper to taste
   Grated sharp Cheddar cheese
   Yogurt seasoned with dash each of
   garlic salt and paprika

Simmer onions in olive oil until golden; place in buttered shallow baking dish. Break eggs gently on top, sprinkle with salt, pepper, and cheese, and bake in preheated moderate oven (375°F.) for 15 minutes. Serve with heated seasoned yogurt. Makes 4 servings.

SPANISH ONION BAKE
6 Spanish or Bermuda onions
¼ cup water
   Salt, pepper, and paprika to taste
¼ cup melted butter or margarine

Clean and wipe but do not peel onions. Cut off root end to just beyond skin joint. Put in buttered baking dish with water and bake in preheated moderate oven (375°F.) 1¼ hours. Remove skin by grasping top and slipping it off. Return to dish, season, pour butter over, and return to oven for 5 minutes. Serve in same dish. Makes 6 servings.

ONIONS, SWISS STYLE
2 mild onions, sliced thin
2 tablespoons butter or margarine
   Salt and pepper to taste
2 cups grated Swiss cheese
1 can (10½ ounces) condensed
   cream-of-chicken soup
1 cup rich milk
1 cup buttered bread crumbs
   Crisp toast

Separate onion slices into rings and sauté in butter until golden; then cover pan and simmer for 10 minutes. Put in buttered baking dish, season, and cover with cheese. Dilute soup with milk and pour over cheese. Top with crumbs. Bake in preheated moderate oven (375°F.) for 30 minutes. Serve as a dunk with crisp toast. Makes 4 servings.

PEANUT CREAMED ONIONS
18 small white onions, peeled
½ cup salted peanuts, chopped fine
1 cup rich white sauce
   Salt and pepper to taste
   Dash of ground mace

Cook onions in salted water until tender. Drain and add with half of peanuts to white sauce. Season; top with remaining nuts. Bake in preheated moderate oven (375°F.) for 20 minutes. Makes 4 servings.

ONIONS CONSTANTINE
16 small white onions, peeled
¼ cup olive oil
1 garlic clove, crushed
½ cup tarragon vinegar

Salt and pepper
½ teaspoon powdered mustard
3 cloves
¼ cup large seeded raisins

Put onions in skillet with oil; sauté until lightly browned. Add rest of ingredients except raisins and simmer until onions are just tender. Add raisins. Chill. Makes 4 servings.

DANISH ONIONS
8 medium onions, peeled
¼ cup crumbled blue cheese
2 cups rich white sauce
Salt, pepper, and cayenne to taste

Boil onions in salted water until tender. Drain; mix with cheese in white sauce. Season; simmer for 5 minutes. Serve on potatoes. Makes 4 servings.

SOUTHERN ONION BREAD
2 tablespoons butter or bacon fat
¾ cup uncooked white cornmeal
1 egg, beaten
¼ cup chopped onion
1½ cups buttermilk or sour milk
½ teaspoon baking soda
1 teaspoon salt
⅛ teaspoon pepper

Put butter in 1-quart casserole and heat in preheated oven. Mix rest of ingredients until smooth and put in hot casserole. Bake in hot oven (425°F.) for 30 minutes, or until barely set. Serve as you do spoon bread. Makes 4 to 6 servings.

ONION GRAVY
2 cups sliced onions
¼ cup meat fat and drippings
¼ cup flour
2 cups meat broth
Salt and pepper
Dash of garlic salt
1½ teaspoons Worcestershire
Dash of bottled sauce for gravy

Sauté onions in fat until soft and golden. Add flour, stir, and add remaining ingredients. Stir, cover, and simmer for 5 minutes. Makes 3 cups.

GOURMET RELISH
4 cups thinly sliced peeled Bermuda onions
1 teaspoon salt
⅛ teaspoon pepper
2 cups dry white wine
½ cup chopped parsley

Put onions and seasonings in wine and chill for several hours. Add parsley. Serve cold with rye-bread rounds and cheese for a late buffet. Makes 8 servings.

EGGS IN SCALLION AND MUSHROOM SAUCE
1½ cups diced scallions, including tops
2 tablespoons butter or margarine
1 package (10 ounces) frozen peas
1 can (10½ ounces) cream-of-mushroom soup
6 hard-cooked eggs, sliced
½ cup dairy sour cream
1 tablespoon fresh lemon juice
Salt and pepper to taste
Dash of ground nutmeg or mace
Hot cooked rice

Sauté scallions in butter until golden.

CLEAN:

**BERMUDAS GLACÉS
ONION AND ORANGE SALAD**

Cook peas and reserve ¼ cup cooking liquid. Thin soup with this liquid and add soup plus all remaining ingredients except rice to scallions. Heat and serve with rice. Makes 6 servings.

GREEN HEAVEN IN A POT

1 box frozen artichoke hearts
1 bunch of green onions
4 eggs
½ cup medium cream
Salt and pepper
Grated Parmesan cheese

Cook artichoke hearts as directed on the label. Drain and dice. Wash green onions and cut fine, including tops. Divide artichokes and onions among 4 small ramekins. Break an egg into each. Pour cream over eggs, season with salt and pepper to taste, and sprinkle with cheese. Bake in preheated moderate oven (350°F.) for 45 minutes, or until eggs are of desired doneness. Makes 4 servings.

Note: Good as a lunch dish with crusty French bread.

GARDEN RAGOUT

1½ cups diced scallions, including tops
2 medium cucumbers, peeled and diced
¼ pound mushrooms, sliced
2 tablespoons butter or bacon fat
Salt, pepper, and garlic salt to taste
Dash of soy sauce
1½ cups rich white sauce
1 egg yolk, beaten
Chopped chives
Hot cooked rice

Boil scallions and cucumber in salted water until tender. Sauté mushrooms in butter, combine with drained vegetables, and season. Add to hot white sauce. Add some of sauce to egg yolk, then return egg to sauced vegetables. Garnish with chives and serve with rice. Makes 6 servings.

SCALLIONS AND BEANS

1 pound dried white beans, washed
4 scallions, including tops, chopped
2 garlic cloves, peeled and pressed
¼ cup fresh lemon juice
½ cup olive oil
Salt and pepper to taste
Chopped parsley

Soak beans overnight, drain, and simmer in water to cover until done, about 2 hours. Drain and cool. Make dressing of scallions, garlic, lemon juice, olive oil, and salt and pepper. Pour over beans; top with parsley. Chill for several hours. Makes 8 servings.

OPOSSUM—A small marsupial animal found in the southern and midwestern United States. The common, or Virginia, opossum is about the size of a cat, with grayish fur and black ears and feet. Opossum is often used for food, the flavor resembling young pig. It can be prepared in the same manner as for roast suckling pig.

ORACHE, ORACH—An annual herb plant, *Atriplex hortensis,* native to the Tatary region of Asia, which is now extensively grown as a potherb in France. It is also known as Garden orache, Mexican spinach, French spinach, and sea purseane. Orache grows to a height of five to six feet. Its leaves vary in color from a pale yellowish-green to dark red, are arrow-shape, slightly crimped, and very tender. Orache is prepared for the table in the same way spinach is. The wild orache, commonly called mountain orache, is considered a weed, but is edible. In some English country districts it is known by the curious name fat hen.

ORANGE—This popular citrus fruit grows on an evergreen tree with shiny, rather narrow leaves and wonderfully fragrant white flowers. There are many varieties of oranges, but the three principal species are the sweet, common, or China orange, *Citrus sinensis;* the loose-skinned or "kid-glove" orange, *Citrus nobilis;* and the sour, bitter, Seville, or bigarade orange, *Citrus aurantium.*

The sweet orange is the most important species, and is the one from which most edible varieties have developed. The tree may reach a height of thirty-five or forty feet; the fruits are globular or oval, with a sweet and juicy pulp. Far and away most of the oranges grown in the United States are some variety of this species.

The best-known sweet oranges are the golden-yellow Valencia, or Spanish, heavy and juicy, with large coarse-grained fruit; Mediterranean oranges, which have a fine-grained fruit; blood oranges, with a red, or red and white streaked, pulp; and the seedless navel, or Washington navel oranges.

The trees producing the loose-skinned oranges are smaller, growing to perhaps twenty feet. Included among them are mandarins and king oranges, names often used to describe the entire species; the temple; and the tangerine. The flesh of these oranges divides easily into segments and they got the name "kid-glove" because of the ease with which their skins can be removed. They are grown extensively in Japan, southern Europe, and, in this country, in the Gulf states.

Sour orange trees seldom grow larger than twenty-five feet. The orange itself is large, with a rough, red-orange skin. Its pulp is too acid to be eaten raw. These trees are cultivated to a small extent in the United States for ornamental purposes. Spain grows them commercially: they are used for making marmalade; the peel is candied; the oil is used for food

flavorings, in the liqueur Curaçao, and for medicinal and cosmetic purposes. The bergamot orange, probably a hybrid of the sour orange, is a golden-yellow pear-shape fruit, which grows on a spiny tree and is cultivated in the Mediterranean area, chiefly in Italy, where the peel is used to make oil of bergamot, for perfumes.

Oranges are thought to have originated somewhere in southeastern Asia, northeastern India, or southern China. The first species introduced into Europe, through the agency of the Arabs, was the sour orange which they had brought across North Africa and into Spain by the 11th century. Loose-skinned oranges were not known in Europe until the end of the medieval period. Records tell us that the sweet orange was first cultivated in southeastern Asia between 1,500 and 1,000 B.C. Very early in its history the orange reached India, and from there either Portuguese explorers or early Genoese traders brought it into southern Europe in the 15th century. The Spaniards carried oranges to Florida in 1565 and to California in 1769.

We think of "orange" as a color, but in fact the word originally referred to the smell of the fruit. It is derived from Sanskrit, the classical language of India. The Sanskrit *naranga* is akin to the word *naru* of another Indian language, Tamil. *Naru* means "fragrant."

In classical mythology Juno gave Jupiter "Golden Apples" on the day of their marriage. Two of the most famous English poets, Spenser and Milton, have claimed that this golden apple was in fact the orange. Milton says the orange was "fruit, burnished with golden rind . . . of delicious taste." Spenser describes the golden fruit of the orange tree: "The fruit were golden Apples glistening bright, /That goodly was their glory to behold; /On earth no better grew, nor living wight; /E'er better saw."

Traditionally oranges have been associated with marriage. This may be because the tree produces at the same time foliage, flowers, and fruit, and hence is a symbol of great fertility. Orange blossoms were worn by brides among the Saracens, who regarded the flower as a token of a happy and prosperous marriage. Cretan couples were sprinkled with orange-flower water on their wedding day. Sardinians attached oranges to the horns of oxen pulling the cart that drew the newly married pair.

The orange arrived in England by courtesy of the Portuguese shortly before it began to be cultivated in southern Europe. When Henry IV was crowned in 1399, oranges were served at his coronation banquet and much admired as a strange and wonderful treat.

Oranges grew wild in great profusion in Florida. Columbus, on his second voyage to the New World, had planted the slips in the West Indies and from there they were brought to Florida. The Seminole Indians were quick to take advantage of the juicy fruit. John Bartram, an 18th-century naturalist, tells of the Indian custom of slicing off the top, filling the middle with wild honey, and then eating the delicious middle. John Bartram's son, William, reported of his journeys through Florida that a favorite dish was trout stewed in orange juice. This, he remarked "with boiled rice, afforded me a wholesome and delicious supper."

Benjamin Franklin had a special recipe for orange shrub: "To a Gallon of Rum two Quarts of Orange Juice and two pounds of Sugar—dissolve the Sugar in the Juice before you mix it with the Rum—Put all together in a Cask & shake it well—let it stand 3 or 4 weeks & it will be very fine & fit for Bottling." Franklin was so fond of this drink that he was careful to explain how to filter the dregs so "that not a drop may be lost."

Thomas Jefferson, the third American president, and a great experimenter, tried to grow orange trees, imported from Italy, at Monticello.

Today, of course, the United States is the largest orange grower in the world, producing half of the world supply.

Oranges can be grown on fertile and well-irrigated soil, wherever the climate is warm and dry. They do not tolerate frost. Oranges can be grown from seed, but commercially grown oranges are budded or grafted. Florida and California are leaders, followed by Texas, Louisiana, Arizona, and Mississippi. Orange growing in Florida and California is a most scientific enterprise. The maturing time, quality, and even the sweetness of the oranges is controlled. The oranges, to prevent bruising, are picked by gloved workers. They are washed and scrubbed in soap and water, borax solutions, and clean water. They are dried and often colored artificially, because many oranges, especially in Florida, are picked green although ripe, and do not have the glowing golden color we associate with them. The added coloring is entirely harmless.

Oranges are eaten raw, or used in cooking and for making candied fruit. The yellow part of the rind is often shredded or grated to add to both non-sweet and sweet dishes, for it gives a delicious flavor. But the majority of American oranges are consumed in the form of juice at breakfast. Orange juice, as distinct from orangeade, is an Ameri-can custom, although oranges have been eaten all over the world for many centuries. The American custom of drinking orange juice has been taken up recently in Europe, but it is still thought of as rather dashing and "American." The peel of oranges is candied, for baking and confectionery. The essential oil pressed from the skins is used for cosmetics, medicine, and food flavorings. In Brazil, oranges are eaten in huge quantities, either by sucking or peeled, or, most deliciously, placed on a slice of fresh pineapple, and eaten with knife and fork. The skins are utilized as kindling wood for the kitchen stove. The oranges are peeled in one long strip which is left to dry on the backyard fence. When dried, the peel catches fire with great ease and fragrance.

Availability—A certain number of fresh oranges are available year round but they are at their peak during the fall and winter months. Among the sweet oranges available are: the *Hamlin,* a thin-skinned orange, good for juice and marmalade, in season from October to December; the *Indian River,* a thin-skinned variety with a rich juicy pulp, in season from December through April; the *navel,* or *Washington navel,* a large thick-skinned seedless orange, used for eating out-of-hand, for sections, slices, for crystallized peel, and marmalade, in season from October to December; the *Parson Brown,* a rough-skinned orange, good for eating, juice, and for marmalade, in season from October to December; the *Valencia,* a large and heavy golden-yellow orange, excellent for juice and flavor, easy to peel and section. It freezes well and makes a good marmalade, is in season from March to July. The Valencia variety accounts for about half the orange production of the United States.

Among the loose-skinned oranges available are: the *King* or *Satsuma,* a large thick- and rough-skinned orange, resembling the tangerine, which peels easily, is very sweet, and is best for eating out-of-hand, in season March to July; the *Ponkan,* a large tangerinelike variety, peels easily, best for eating out-of-hand, in season from December through March; the *tangerine,* easily peeled and segmented, sweet flavor, best for eating out-of-hand, in season from December through April; the *Temple,* a bright orange with a rough thick red skin, peels and segments easily, very sweet flavor, in season from December through March. A few *Mandarin* oranges, small, round, easily peeled and segmented, are grown in California. The *tangelo,* a cross between a loose-skinned orange and a grapefruit, is generally yellowish-orange in color and medium to large in size. Two of the most successful varieties differ considerably in shape (pear or round) and in peel (smooth and thin, or rough and thick). It is easy to peel and segment, its flavor is a pleasing and distinctive combination of the sweetness and tartness of its parents, and is in season December through March.

Chilled containers of orange juice and orange segments mixed with other fruits are available in food stores.

Canned orange juice, orange and grapefruit juice, tangerine juice, orange and grapefruit segments, and Mandarin orange segments are available. Available frozen are concentrated orange juice, orange juice blended with other juices, and tangerine juice; and frozen orange and grapefruit segments.

Other orange products available are orangeade, orange drinks, candied orange peel, orange-flavored gelatin desserts and puddings, orange-flower water, oil of orange, orange extract, and marmalades.

Purchasing Guide—Select fresh oranges that are firm and heavy for their size, free from soft spots or mold. Skin color does not indicate ripeness as regreening sometimes occurs in the ripe fruit. Russeting does not affect flavor, either. Sometimes oranges are artificially colored with a harmless dye to improve the appearance. Such fruits must be stamped "color added." Oranges are sold by the piece or by weight and are graded according to size.

Storage—Store in refrigerator or cool dry well-ventilated place. Oranges can be kept at room temperature if they are to be used in a very short time.

☐ Fresh, refrigerator shelf: 1 to 2 months
☐ Canned, kitchen shelf: 1 year
☐ Canned, refrigerator shelf, opened: 5 to 6 days
☐ Frozen, refrigerator frozen-food compartment: 3 weeks
☐ Frozen, freezer: 1 year

Nutritive Food Values—Excellent source of vitamin C and some vitamin A. Freezing destroys some of the vitamin C. Once juices are squeezed or canned juices are opened, vitamin C combines with air and forms a new compound which has no vitamin value. After 24 hours in refrigerator: 20 per cent vitamin C loss; after 24 hours at room temperature: 60 per cent vitamin C loss.

3½ ounces, approximately ½ cup, has the following caloric values:

☐ Peeled raw oranges = 49 calories
☐ Orange juice, fresh or frozen = 45 calories
☐ Orange juice, canned, unsweetened = 48 calories

☐ Orange juice, canned, sweetened = 52 calories

☐ Candied orange peel = 316 calories

Basic Preparation—Wash before using. Serve peeled or unpeeled. Oranges may be cut into various shapes, slices, chunks, or sections.

☐ **To Eat Out-of-Hand**—Cut into quarters. They may also be peeled by hand and split with the fingers into segments.

☐ **To Serve Whole**—Slit the outer skin into 8 wedges cut from top to bottom. Carefully peel the skin away from the orange, leaving the skin attached to the bottom of the fruit. Tuck the skin points underneath the orange. (A tangerine may be prepared in the same way, snipping the skin with scissors at ½-inch intervals almost down to the bottom of the tangerine. The tangerine will then resemble a chrysanthemum.)

☐ **To Cut Sections**—Remove the rind and the white inner rind with a sharp knife. Cut in between the membranes, releasing sections.

☐ **To Cut Shells**—Cut fruit into halves and with a sharp knife cut out the pulp, leaving a shell about ½ inch thick. Cut up pulp and use with other fruits to refill shell. Shell edge may be scalloped by cutting diagonal slits into the fruit instead of cutting into straight halves.

☐ **To Squeeze**—Leave them at room temperature to make them easier to squeeze.

☐ **To Grate Rind**—Rub in short strokes across small area of grater and grate only the outermost portion.

☐ **To Freeze**—Use firm fruit. With a sharp knife peel fruit, removing fruit peel and white membranes. Section fruit, removing inner membranes and seeds. Pack fruit into containers. Cover with syrup. For every 4 cups water use 3 or 4 cups sugar, depending on sweetness of fruit. Allow ½-inch headspace. Cover.

ORANGE-STUFFED VEAL
3 cups toasted bread cubes
1 teaspoon grated orange rind
1 cup chopped celery
1 teaspoon ground mace (optional)
½ cup chopped onion
    Butter (about ¾ cup)
2 cups fresh orange juice
3 to 4 pounds breast of veal with pocket
    Salt and pepper

Combine first 5 ingredients and ½ cup each of butter and orange juice in large bowl. Blend thoroughly. Stuff meat and secure edges with small skewers or toothpicks. Rub meat with salt and pepper. Heat enough butter to cover bottom of skillet. Brown meat on all sides. Add remaining orange juice and cover tightly. Simmer gently on top of stove or bake in preheated moderate oven (325°F.) for about 2½ hours, or until meat is tender. Check for dryness; if necessary, add hot water, 1 tablespoon at a time. Makes 4 servings.

DRIED BEEF WITH ORANGE SAUCE
½ pound dried beef
2 tablespoons butter or margarine
1½ tablespoons all-purpose flour
1 cup fresh orange juice

Pour boiling water to cover over beef. Let stand for 10 minutes; drain. Heat butter, and cook beef in it for 3 minutes. Stir in flour and orange juice. Cook until thickened, stirring constantly. Makes 4 servings.

CHICKEN BAKED IN ORANGE SAUCE
1 frying chicken (about 3 pounds), cut into pieces
¼ cup olive oil
1 cup fresh orange juice
1 cup dry white wine
½ cup seedless raisins
½ cup blanched almonds, ground fine
1 tablespoon sugar
½ teaspoon ground ginger
1 teaspoon salt
½ teaspoon pepper

Brown chicken in hot oil. Place in shallow baking pan. Combine other ingredients and pour over chicken. Bake in preheated moderate oven (350°F.) for 45 minutes, or until tender, basting often. Makes 4 servings.

ORANGE CHICKEN SALAD
4 cups diced cooked chicken (white meat only)
2 cups thinly sliced celery (white stalks only)
1 cup California walnuts, chopped
½ cup seedless green grapes
1 cup orange sections
    Orange Cream Dressing
    Salad greens

Combine all ingredients except dressing and greens, and chill. Toss with enough Orange Cream Dressing to moisten. Serve on a bed of greens. Makes 4 to 6 servings.

Orange Cream Dressing
Combine ¼ cup thawed frozen concentrated orange juice, ¼ cup mayonnaise, grated rind of 1 orange, ¼ teaspoon hot pepper sauce, and 1 cup heavy cream, whipped, just before serving. Makes about 2½ cups.

ORANGE AND BELGIAN-ENDIVE SALAD
4 navel oranges
8 heads Belgian endive
¾ cup olive oil
¼ cup mild cider vinegar
1 teaspoon salt
2 teaspoons mild prepared mustard
¼ cup fresh orange juice
½ pound Swiss cheese, cut into ½-inch cubes (optional)

Peel oranges and remove all white membrane. Separate sections and remove seeds and membrane between sections. Chill. Cut Belgian endive into rounds and chill. Make dressing by combining remaining ingredients except cheese. Chill. At serving time, combine oranges, Belgian endive, and cheese. Stir dressing well and toss salad in it. Makes 6 servings.

ORANGE AND ONION SALAD
¼ head curly endive
½ small head lettuce
½ head romaine
3 fresh oranges
½ cup mild white onion rings
3 tablespoons fresh lemon juice
¼ cup salad oil
½ teaspoon garlic powder
¾ teaspoon salt
½ teaspoon powdered mustard
1 teaspoon sugar

Wash salad greens and dry thoroughly. Tear into bite-size pieces and place in a salad bowl. Peel oranges and cut into crosswise slices. Place as desired over salad greens and top with onion rings. Combine fresh lemon juice, salad oil, garlic powder, salt, mustard, and sugar. Add to salad just before serving. Toss lightly. Makes 8 to 10 servings.

ORANGE COTTAGE-CHEESE CUPS
1 envelope unflavored gelatin
¼ cup water
1 pound creamy cottage cheese
1½ cups diced fresh oranges
½ teaspoon salt

Soften gelatin in cold water. Let stand for 5 minutes in pan of hot, not boiling, water to melt. Stir into cottage cheese along with diced fresh oranges and salt. Rinse 4 to 6 individual salad molds with cold water. Fill with fresh orange cottage-cheese mixture. Chill. Unmold and serve on lettuce beds. Makes 4 to 6 servings.

ORANGE AND WATERCRESS SALAD
Rub a clove of garlic around inside of wood salad bowl. Combine sections from 2 or 3 oranges with the picked-over leaves of 2 bunches of watercress. Toss in salad bowl with a plain French dressing. Makes 4 servings.

ORANGE RICE FOR DUCK OR HAM
3 tablespoons butter or margarine
⅔ cup diced celery with leaves
2 tablespoons chopped onion
1½ cups water
1 cup fresh orange juice
    Grated rind of 1 orange
1¼ teaspoons salt
¼ teaspoon thyme
1 cup uncooked rice

Melt butter in heavy saucepan. Add celery and onion, and cook until onion is soft and golden. Add water, orange juice, orange rind, salt, and thyme. Bring to a boil. Add rice slowly, stirring constantly. Cover; reduce heat and cook for 25 minutes, or until rice is tender. Makes 4 to 6 servings.

FRESH BEETS IN ORANGE SAUCE
2 tablespoons grated orange rind
2 tablespoons fresh lemon juice
1 tablespoon fresh orange juice
¼ teaspoon salt
    Pinch of pepper
⅛ teaspoon ground nutmeg

Italian Orange-Rum Cake, Orange Chicken Salad with Orange Cream Dressing

¼ cup butter or margarine
4 cups sliced peeled cooked fresh beets

Combine orange rind, lemon juice, orange juice, salt, pepper, and nutmeg in top part of double boiler. Add butter and beets. Heat well. Makes 8 servings.

GLAZED ORANGES
6 seedless oranges
¾ cup sugar
½ cup water
3 tablespoons light corn syrup
6 cloves
One 2-inch piece gingerroot (optional)

Peel oranges, remove all white membrane, and cut oranges into sections. Combine all other ingredients and boil for 2 or 3 minutes. Add orange sections and simmer over low heat for about 5 minutes. Before serving, remove cloves and gingerroot. Makes 6 servings.
Note: Good with cold roast duck, ham, or goose.

ORANGE FRENCH DRESSING
1¼ teaspoons salt
1 teaspoon celery seeds
½ teaspoon paprika
⅛ teaspoon white pepper
1 teaspoon finely chopped onion
1 garlic clove, crushed
2 tablespoons sugar
1 cup salad oil
⅔ cup fresh lemon juice
⅔ cup fresh orange segments, juice and all

Combine first 8 ingredients and let stand for 1 hour. Add remaining ingredients and mix well. Serve over apple salad. Makes 2 cups.

APPLES BAKED IN ORANGE JUICE
Pare and core 6 apples. Drop in lightly salted cold water to prevent discoloring. Cook together juice of 6 oranges, ¼ cup sugar, and 2 tablespoons butter or margarine until clear and thickened. Drain apples. Fill centers with seedless golden raisins and put in baking dish. Cover with orange sauce; bake in preheated moderate oven (350°F.) for 30 minutes to 1 hour, or until easily pierced with a fork, basting occasionally with orange sauce. Time varies with apples. Serve warm with pork or ham. Makes 6 servings.

ORANGES IN RED WINE
¾ cup sugar
1 cup dry red wine
1 cup water
2 whole cloves
½ teaspoon ground cinnamon
2 lemon slices
4 oranges

Mix sugar, red wine, and water in saucepan. Tie whole cloves, cinnamon, and 2 lemon slices in a small piece of cheesecloth. Put in saucepan. Bring to boil and simmer for 10 minutes, or until syrupy. Remove spice bag. Remove rind from oranges; reserve. Add segments to syrup. Chill. Serve with garnish of slivered orange rind. Makes 4 servings.

SLICED ORANGES AND APPLES WITH WINE
Peel oranges and remove all white membrane. Slice into thin slices and remove seeds. Core but do not peel apples and slice into rounds. Arrange in alternate layers in glass serving dish. Sprinkle each layer with sugar to taste. Pour Marsala or sweet sherry over fruit barely to cover. Chill for at least 4 hours before serving. Use 1 orange and 1 apple to make 2 servings.

ORANGE DELIGHT
1 envelope unflavored gelatin
¼ cup water
3 cups fresh orange juice
3 tablespoons sugar
2 tablespoons fresh lemon juice
¼ teaspoon salt
½ teaspoon vanilla extract
½ cup diced fresh oranges
Fresh orange sections

Soften gelatin in water. Let stand for 5 minutes. Place over hot, not boiling, water to melt. Add to orange juice. Stir in sugar, lemon juice, salt, and vanilla. Chill until the mixture is a little thicker than unbeaten egg whites. Fold in diced fresh oranges. Refrigerate until ready to serve. Serve in sherbet glasses. Garnish with fresh orange sections. Makes 6 servings.

ORANGE SOUFFLÉ
1 can (6 ounces) frozen orange juice
3 tablespoons butter
3 tablespoons all-purpose flour
4 eggs, separated
Pinch of salt
Butter
Sugar
Rich custard sauce or whipped cream flavored with orange liqueur

Thaw orange juice and add ¼ cup water, or enough to make 1 full cup of liquid. Melt butter and blend in flour. Slowly stir in orange juice. Cook over low heat, stirring constantly, until mixture thickens. Beat egg yolks until light and lemony and add to slightly cooled orange mixture. Beat egg whites with salt until they are stiff but still moist. Fold half of beaten whites into orange mixture rather thoroughly; then fold rest in very lightly. Butter a 2-quart soufflé dish and sprinkle bottom and sides lightly with sugar. Pour in orange mixture and bake in preheated moderate oven (375°F.) for about 30 minutes. Serve with rich custard sauce. Makes 4 to 6 servings.

ORANGE FLUFF PUDDING
5 eggs, separated
½ cup sugar
1 envelope unflavored gelatin
Juice of 1 lemon
Juice of 1 orange
½ cup boiling water
Grated rind of 1 orange
⅛ teaspoon salt
Orange slices
Green grapes

Beat egg yolks until thick and lemon-colored; gradually beat in sugar. Soften gelatin in fruit juices and dissolve in boiling water; add to egg-yolk mixture with grated orange rind. Refrigerate until mixture just starts to congeal. Fold in the egg whites, beaten with salt until stiff. Pour into 2-quart ring mold. Refrigerate for at least 4 hours. Unmold and decorate with orange slices and green grapes. Makes 6 to 8 servings.

ORANGE VELVET ICE CREAM
2 egg yolks
1 cup light cream
¼ teaspoon salt
2 cups sugar
1 cup water
2 cups fresh orange juice
1 cup heavy cream, whipped
¼ cup finely diced or shredded candied orange peel

In top part of small double boiler beat egg yolks, light cream, and salt with rotary beater. Put over simmering water and cook, stirring constantly, until mixture is slightly thickened and coats a metal spoon. Cool. Boil sugar, water, and juice for 5 minutes; cool. Combine mixtures and fold in cream. Partially freeze in crank-type freezer. Then add orange peel and finish freezing. Makes about 2 quarts.

JELLIED MANDARIN ORANGES
2 cups canned tangerine juice
1 box (3 ounces) orange-flavored gelatin
About 1¼ cups (one 11-ounce can) mandarin oranges, drained

Heat 1 cup juice; pour over gelatin and stir until dissolved. Add remaining juice. Chill until thickened but not firm. Add oranges and chill until firm. Makes 4 servings.

JELLIED ORANGE AMBROSIA DESSERT
1 cup hot water
1 box (3 ounces) lemon-flavored gelatin
¼ cup sugar
Dash of salt
1 tablespoon grated orange rind
¼ cup fresh orange juice
1 cup heavy cream
½ cup shredded coconut, cut with scissors
½ cup drained orange pieces
4 ladyfingers, split

Add water to gelatin and stir until dissolved. Stir in sugar, salt, rind, and juice; chill until mixture begins to set. Whip cream with rotary beater or electric mixer. Fold into gelatin mixture with coconut and orange pieces. Line a 1-quart mold with ladyfingers. Pour in mixture and chill until firm. Unmold. Makes 4 servings.

FRESH ORANGE CHIFFON PIE
5 graham crackers
5 tablespoons sugar
2 teaspoons butter or margarine, melted
1 envelope unflavored gelatin
1½ cups fresh orange juice
2 egg yolks
¼ teaspoon salt

Orange Soufflé

1 tablespoon fresh lemon juice
1 teaspoon vanilla extract
3 egg whites
Fresh orange sections

Roll graham crackers into fine crumbs. Blend in 1 tablespoon sugar and melted butter. Save 1 tablespoon of crumb mixture to sprinkle over top. Sprinkle remaining crumbs over bottom and sides of a buttered 9-inch pie pan. Bake in preheated moderate oven (375°F.) for 10 minutes. Remove from oven. Cool. Soften gelatin in ½ cup of the orange juice. Let stand for 5 minutes. Beat egg yolks lightly. Stir in remaining sugar and the salt. Add remaining orange juice and the lemon juice. Mix well. Cook over hot water or low heat for 10 minutes, stirring constantly, or until thoroughly hot.

Remove from heat and stir in softened gelatin and vanilla. Chill over ice water until mixture is about as thick as unbeaten egg whites. Beat egg whites until they stand in soft peaks. Fold into mixture. Turn into crumb-lined 9-inch pie pan. Chill until firm. Sprinkle remaining crumbs over top; garnish with fresh orange sections. Makes 6 servings.

ORANGE CREAM PIE

⅔ cup sugar
¼ cup cornstarch
¼ teaspoon salt
1 cup evaporated milk, undiluted
1 cup mixed fresh orange juice and water
  Grated rind of 1 orange
1 tablespoon fresh lemon juice
2 egg yolks or 1 egg
9- inch pie shell, baked

Mix dry ingredients in top part of double boiler. Stir in milk, fruit juice, and water. Cook over direct heat, stirring constantly, until thickened. Combine orange rind and lemon juice with egg yolks; add cooked mixture gradually. Cook over hot water until thickened again, about 5 minutes. Cool; strain into pie shell. Makes 6 to 8 servings.

ORANGE TARTLETS

⅔ cup shortening
2 cups sifted all-purpose flour
1 teaspoon salt
2 teaspoons grated orange rind
5 to 6 tablespoons fresh orange juice
  Orange marmalade
  Chopped nuts

Cut shortening into flour and salt. Add rind and enough orange juice to hold mixture together. Roll out tiny pieces of dough to ⅛-inch thickness on floured board. Fit pieces over backs of tiny scalloped tart pans. Put on cookie sheet and prick bottoms with fork. Bake in preheated hot oven (425°F.) for about 10 minutes. Cool slightly and remove gently from pans. Cool; put 1 teaspoon marmalade in each. Sprinkle with nuts. Makes 4 dozen.

ORANGE CHIFFON TARTS
1 package (3 ounces) orange-flavored gelatin dessert
1 cup boiling water
1 cup fresh orange juice
Grated rind of 2 oranges
2 oranges, sectioned
6 Orange-Pastry Tart Shells

Add gelatin to water, stirring until dissolved; add orange juice; chill. When gelatin is almost set, beat thoroughly with egg beater until fluffy. Add orange rind and sections. Fill cooled Orange-Pastry Tart Shells with gelatin mixture and chill in refrigerator to set before serving. Makes 6 tarts.

Orange-Pastry Tart Shells
1 cup sifted all-purpose flour
½ teaspoon salt
Grated rind of 1 orange
¼ cup lard
2 to 3 tablespoons fresh orange juice

Sift flour and salt. Add orange rind. Cut in lard to the size of large peas. Add just enough orange juice to make dough hold together. Roll out thin and make 6 tart shells using backs of 2-inch muffin tins. Prick all over with fork. Bake in preheated very hot oven (500°F.) for 10 minutes. Cool.

ORANGE PIE WITH WHIPPED CREAM
1 envelope unflavored gelatin
¼ teaspoon salt
⅔ cup sugar
1¼ cups fresh orange juice
2 eggs, separated
2 tablespoons fresh lemon juice
Grated rind of 2 oranges (about 2 tablespoons)
¼ teaspoon cream of tartar
1 cup heavy cream, whipped
9-inch pie shell, baked
Whipped cream
Shaved chocolate

Combine gelatin, salt, and ⅓ cup of the sugar. Beat together orange juice and egg yolks and add to gelatin mixture. Cook over low heat, stirring constantly, until gelatin is melted and mixture is slightly thickened, about 5 minutes. Remove from heat and stir in lemon juice and orange rind. Chill, stirring occasionally, until mixture is just beginning to set. Beat egg whites until foamy. Add cream of tartar and beat until stiff. Gradually beat in remaining sugar. Beat until very stiff. Fold into gelatin mixture. Fold in cream. Blend thoroughly. Pour into pie shell and chill until firm. Garnish with addi-

tional whipped cream, forced through a pastry tube. Sprinkle with shaved chocolate. Makes 6 to 8 servings.

ITALIAN ORANGE-RUM CAKE
3 eggs
1 cup sugar
3 tablespoons fresh orange juice
2 teaspoons grated orange rind
1 cup sifted all-purpose flour
2 teaspoons baking powder
Orange-Rum Topping
Orange slices, candied cherries, and whipped cream rosettes

Beat eggs until light. Gradually beat in sugar and continue to beat until mixture is thick and lemon-colored. Use an electric beater if possible, and beat at high speed for about 5 minutes. Stir in orange juice and rind. Sift flour with baking powder 3 times and fold into batter. Pour into buttered and floured 9-inch springform pan. Bake in preheated moderate oven (350°F.) for 30 minutes, or until cake tests done. Cool in pan. Pour Orange-Rum Topping over cooled cake and chill until serving time. Remove from pan. Decorate with oranges, cherries, and whipped-cream rosettes.

Orange-Rum Topping
1 envelope unflavored gelatin
¼ cup cold water
1 cup hot milk
¾ cup sugar
4 egg yolks, lightly beaten
⅓ cup dark rum
1 large orange, peeled and sectioned
1 cup heavy cream, whipped

Soften gelatin in cold water. Stir in hot milk and sugar. Cook over low heat until mixture is hot. Do not let boil. Gradually pour over egg yolks, stirring constantly. Add the rum. Set in bowl of cracked ice and stir constantly until cool and beginning to set. Fold in orange sections and whipped cream.

ORANGE-MARMALADE CAKE
¾ cup butter
1 cup sugar
3 eggs
3 tablespoons orange marmalade
2½ cups sifted cake flour
3 teaspoons baking powder
¾ teaspoon salt
½ cup fresh orange juice
Grated rind of 2 oranges

Cream butter; add sugar gradually; beat until light and fluffy. Add eggs, one at a time, beating thoroughly; then add marmalade. Add sifted dry ingredients alternately with orange juice and grated rind. Beat until smooth. Bake in well-greased paper-lined pan (8 x 8 x 2 inches) in preheated moderate oven (350°F.) for 30 to 40 minutes. Makes 6 to 8 servings.

BRAZILIAN ORANGE CAKE
⅔ cup butter
2 cups sugar
Grated rind of 2 oranges
3 egg yolks, well beaten
Juice of 2 oranges and water to equal

1 cup
3 cups sifted cake flour
3 teaspoons baking powder
½ teaspoon salt
3 egg whites, stiffly beaten
Orange Boiled Frosting

Cream butter, add sugar, and beat until fluffy. Add rind and beat in egg yolks, one at a time. Add orange juice and water alternately with mixed and sifted dry ingredients. Fold in egg whites. Spoon into 2 greased paper-lined 9-inch layer-cake pans. Bake in preheated moderate oven (375°F.) for 25 minutes. Turn out on racks and cool. Spread Frosting between the layers and on top and sides of cake. Makes 8 to 10 servings.

Orange Boiled Frosting
1½ cups sugar
1 tablespoon light corn syrup
⅔ cup boiling water
¼ teaspoon salt
2 egg whites, stiffly beaten
Grated rind of 1 orange

Cook sugar, corn syrup, and water together until small amount of syrup forms a soft ball in cold water, or until it reaches 242°F. on a candy thermometer. Pour gradually over salted egg whites, beating constantly until frosting has right consistency to spread. Fold in rind.

ORANGE-AND-DATE TEA LOAF
3 cups sifted all-purpose flour
3 teaspoons baking powder
1 teaspoon salt
2 tablespoons sugar
1 cup sliced pitted dates
1 package (3 ounces) candied orange peel
1 egg, slightly beaten
1½ cups milk

Mix and sift dry ingredients. Add dates and orange peel. Combine egg and milk; stir into dry ingredients. Pour into well-greased loaf pan (9 x 5 x 3 inches). Bake in preheated moderate oven (325°F.) for 1 hour. Cool on rack; wrap in wax paper and store for 24 hours before slicing. Makes 1 loaf.

FLORENTINES
½ cup heavy cream *add some lemon juice*
3 tablespoons butter
½ cup sugar
1¼ cups finely chopped almonds
⅓ cup sifted all-purpose flour
¾ cup finely chopped candied orange peel
Melted chocolate *add some grated orange peels to chocolate*
Tiny colored candies

Combine cream, butter, and sugar in saucepan and bring to boil. Remove from heat and stir in almonds, flour, and orange peel. Drop by tablespoonfuls onto greased and floured cookie sheet, keeping cookies 3 inches apart. Bake in preheated moderate oven (350°F.) for about 10 minutes. Cool for 5 minutes. Remove carefully with spatula to cake rack. Cool. Spiral melted chocolate over cookie tops

Bake at 300°F

and decorate with candies. Makes about 2 dozen 3-inch cookies.

SPICED ORANGE PEEL
    1 quart orange peel, cut into strips
      ½ x 2 inches
      Water
 1¾ cups sugar
  ⅓ cup vinegar
    1 tablespoon whole cloves
    3 sticks cinnamon

Cover peel with water and let stand in refrigerator overnight. Drain, put in kettle, and cover with water. Bring to boil, drain, and again cover with water. Bring again to boil and drain. Cover with water, bring to boil for a third time, and simmer for 10 minutes, or until tender. Drain. Put peel and remaining ingredients in kettle and simmer for 5 minutes to form a thick syrup. Add peel and simmer, stirring frequently, for 5 minutes. Pour into hot sterilized ½-pint jars and seal. Makes about three ½-pint jars.

HONEYED ORANGE PEEL
      Peel from 3 large oranges
      Water
  ½ teaspoon salt
  ½ cup sugar
  ½ cup honey

Cover peel with water and add salt. Simmer for 30 minutes. Drain. Cover again with water and simmer until tender. Drain. Remove white inner portion of peel. Cut outer peel into strips. Bring sugar, honey, and ¼ cup water to boil. Add peel and simmer until clear. Cool in syrup for several hours. Reheat; then drain and spread out to dry on wax paper or foil. Roll in additional sugar if desired. Makes about ¾ pound.

JAMAICAN GOLD DOUBLOONS
    4 ounces (½ cup) Jamaica rum
  ¾ cup fresh orange juice
      Juice of 1 lime
    1 teaspoon sugar
  ¼ cup orange liqueur
    4 cups finely crushed ice
      Mint sprigs

Mix all ingredients, except mint sprigs. Pour into 6 old-fashioned glasses. Decorate each with a mint sprig. Makes 6 servings.

ORANGEADE—Fresh, frozen, canned, or dehydrated orange juice mixed with water and flavored with sugar to taste. Lemon juice can be added to give the drink a tart-sweet flavor. Orangeade should be served chilled or with ice cubes. It can be garnished with a variety of fruits, mint leaves, etc.

Commercially made orangeade is available bottled and canned, with or without sugar; frozen concentrated, with or without sugar; and as a powder, also with or without added sugar.

ORANGEADE
Fill tall glasses half full of crushed ice. For each serving, prepare ¾ cup fresh orange juice or use frozen concentrated orange juice. Add sugar syrup or lemon juice to taste and pour over ice. Stir well.

OREGANO (Origanum vulgare)—This popular herb, also called wild marjoram, is one variety of the aromatic plant origanum which is native to the Mediterranean region, but nowadays grows widely in northeast Canada and the United States. Oregano is a beautiful plant that grows in clumps with purplish, pink, lilac, or white flowers and reaches a height of two to three feet. It is the dark-green leaf, shaped like a roundish egg, that is used as a culinary herb. Leaves may be used fresh or dried. The tops of the plant may also be used. The flavor is similar to that of sweet marjoram or thyme, all belonging to the mint family. Oregano is considerably more bitter and pungent, and should be used with discretion. Vegetable-juice cocktails and bean, beef, game, or tomato soups may be flavored with oregano. The herb adds pungency to beef, lamb, pork, veal, sausages, Swiss steak, poultry, fish, cheese spreads, or omelets, and it is essential to pizza. Oregano is often used as a seasoning in Mexican and Italian dishes. Fish, butter, cream, meat, spaghetti, or tomato sauces are improved by the addition of the herb, as are marinades for game. Oregano is good for seasoning many vegetables including broccoli, beans, carrots, Lima beans, mushrooms, onions, peas, potatoes, tomatoes, and aspic or potato salads. In short, like any other herb, it is to be used to taste, and with discretion. It is not only useful as a culinary herb for flavoring, but may be boiled alone as a potherb.

Oregano is sold in dried crumbled form, and is occasionally available ground. Fresh oregano, when in season, can be found in Italian, Spanish, and Greek neighborhood food stores.

MEXICAN MEATBALLS
    1 pound ground beef
  ¼ cup white cornmeal
    1 egg
    1 garlic clove, minced
    1 small onion, minced
  ½ teaspoon crumbled dried oregano
 1¼ teaspoon salt
  ½ teaspoon pepper
      Chili-Tomato Sauce

Mix beef, cornmeal, egg, garlic, onion, and seasonings. Shape into tiny balls about ½ inch in diameter. Drop into boiling Chili-Tomato Sauce; cover and simmer for 5 minutes. Makes 4 servings.

Chili-Tomato Sauce
    1 tablespoon shortening
    1 small onion, chopped
    1 garlic clove, minced
    2 to 3 tablespoons chili powder
    3 cups tomato juice
      Salt

Melt shortening in large saucepan. Add onion and garlic and cook slowly until lightly browned. Add chili powder, tomato juice, and salt to taste. Cook for 10 minutes. Makes about 3 cups.

VEAL WITH MUSHROOMS
    2 pounds veal steak, cut ¾ inch thick
  ½ cup red wine
    2 tablespoons white vinegar
  ¼ cup chopped onion
    1 garlic clove, mashed
    1 teaspoon crumbled dried oregano
  ¼ cup olive oil
  ¼ cup butter or margarine
    1 teaspoon salt
  ½ pound sliced mushrooms

Cut meat into serving pieces. Mix red wine, vinegar, onion, garlic, oregano, and olive oil and pour over meat. Let stand in refrigerator overnight. Remove meat from marinade and reserve marinade. Brown meat on all sides in hot butter. Put meat in shallow baking pan and cover with marinade. Top with salt and sliced mushrooms. Cover. Bake in preheated moderate oven (350°F.) for 1 hour and 20 minutes. Makes 6 servings.

HAMBURGER PIZZA PIE
    1 pound beef chuck or round, ground
    1 teaspoon instant seasoned meat tenderizer
    1 small garlic clove, minced
    1 can (8 ounces) tomato sauce
  ¼ teaspoon garlic salt
  ½ teaspoon sugar
  ¼ teaspoon Italian herb seasoning
    1 sweet onion, thinly sliced
  ¼ pound Italian salami, thinly sliced
  ½ pound Mozzarella cheese, thinly sliced
    1 can (6 ounces) chopped mushrooms, drained
  ¼ teaspoon crumbled dried oregano
  ¼ cup grated Parmesan cheese

Mix first 3 ingredients and pat into 12-inch pizza pan. Mix next 4 ingredients and spread on beef. Arrange next 4 ingredients on beef in order given. Sprinkle with oregano and grated cheese. Bake in preheated very hot oven (450°F.) for about 15 minutes, or until Mozzarella is bubbly. Makes 4 to 6 servings.

INDIVIDUAL PIZZAS

Split English muffins; rub with garlic; brush with oil. Top with tomato sauce, slice of Mozzarella, an anchovy, and dash of oregano. Heat in preheated moderate oven (375°F.) for 8 minutes.

NEAPOLITAN RIGATONI

1 pound rigatoni
⅓ cup olive oil
1 garlic clove, minced
  About 1¾ cups (one 14½-ounce can) stewed tomatoes
½ teaspoon salt
1 can (8 ounces) tomato sauce
¼ teaspoon coarse black pepper
1 teaspoon crumbled dried oregano
2 tablespoons chopped parsley

Cook and drain rigatoni; while pasta is cooking, make sauce. Heat olive oil in heavy saucepan. Add garlic and cook for 3 or 4 minutes. Add all other ingredients. Cook, stirring constantly, for 10 to 15 minutes. Makes 6 servings.

EGGS BAKED IN TOMATOES

8 medium tomatoes, not too ripe
2 tablespoons olive oil
⅛ teaspoon salt
⅛ teaspoon pepper
8 eggs
½ teaspoon ground oregano
8 thick slices of Italian bread, fried in butter

Without peeling cut off tops of tomatoes; remove seeds. Place tomato shells in shallow greased casserole and sprinkle with oil, salt, and pepper. Break 1 egg into each tomato. Sprinkle a little more oil, salt, pepper, and some of the oregano on each egg. Bake in preheated hot oven (425°F.) for 20 minutes, or until egg is set and tomato cooked. Serve on slices of fried bread. Makes 4 servings.

SAVORY MUSHROOMS WITH OREGANO

1 pound large mushrooms
3 tablespoons olive oil
1 garlic clove, mashed
1 teaspoon crumbled dried oregano
  Salt and pepper

Cut mushrooms into thick slices, splitting the stems once. Heat olive oil in large skillet. When just below smoking, add mushrooms. Cook for 10 minutes, stirring frequently. Add garlic, oregano, and salt and pepper to taste. Serve as a vegetable, or as an entrée with buttered hot French bread and a tossed green salad. Makes 2 to 4 servings.

ORGEAT—A syrup used in France, Spain, Italy, and other Latin countries as a refreshing drink when mixed with water, or as a flavoring for frostings and fillings. Originally orgeat was made from barley mixed with almonds, but today the syrup is made from an emulsion of almonds and sugar with a little rosewater or orange-flower water added. The origin of the drink is probably Arabic or Persian.

Orgeat is imported and sold bottled in gourmet food stores.

ORTOLAN—A central and southern European bunting about six inches in length. The bird frequents orchards and its name is derived from the Latin *hortulanus* or "gardener." Although now almost extinct, the ortolan was long considered a great delicacy, and large numbers were netted and fattened for the table, with gourmets maintaining that the best method of preparation was to roast the birds in the oven or on a spit, and only in their own fat.

OSSOBUCO or OSSO BUCO—An Italian dish made with veal shanks, skin, or knuckle; white wine; olive oil; tomato purée; chopped anchovies; etc., and served on saffron-colored rice. The literal translation is "hollow bone."

OSSOBUCO

4 meaty veal shanks, about 2 inches thick
  All-purpose flour
  Salt and pepper to taste
¼ cup olive oil
1 garlic clove, minced
½ cup dry white wine
½ cup tomato purée
1 anchovy fillet, minced
  Few sprigs of parsley, chopped
  Grated rind of 1 lemon
  Hot cooked rice
  Pinch of saffron

Dredge veal shanks with flour seasoned with salt and pepper. Brown on all sides in hot olive oil. Add garlic, wine, and tomato purée. Bring to boil, cover, and simmer for 1 hour, or until meat is tender. Add anchovy, parsley, and lemon rind. Heat well, and serve on rice lightly mixed with the saffron. Makes 4 servings.

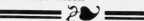

OUTDOOR COOKING AND EATING

by Craig Claiborne

Everything tastes better out-of-doors. If I have heard that once, I have heard it a hundred times within the past few months. For me "out-of-doors" is a little over 100 miles from New York City as the sea gull flies. It is light years away from the subway and Times Square and the oppressive heat of Manhattan. It is blue sky and a pebbly beach and good friends who love to cook both indoors and out.

"Out-of-doors" is in reality a small plot of ground less than an acre on which is set a somewhat small, prefabricated house that is far more endearing than a castle in Spain. It is a house surrounded by fruit trees, apples, wild cherry and pear, by cedar and an underbrush of bayberry and beach plum. The front lawn, so to speak, is Gardiners Bay, and with a small boat during the summer there is a constant harvest of sea bass and striped bass, blowfish, porgies, weakfish, mussels and clams. With a net we can haul in whitebait for dredging with flour and cooking in fat for the keenest first course imaginable.

In addition to myself, we are the Pierre Franeys and the Auguste Chardenets, good neighbors who enjoy good food and good fishing. In summer there is rarely a meal that doesn't begin with clams on the half shell or with steamed clams or mussels. During the summer when the Franey children are free from school the charcoal grill does yeoman work at least twice a day and sometimes more often if hungry guests drop by unexpectedly.

Since I am a professional food man whose closest friends have a professional interest in food, the meals in my house may run a fairly fancy gamut. When fancy city folk arrive for a weekend the kitchen may produce such elegant dishes as creamed sweetbreads in patty shells, fresh asparagus with hollandaise, or chicken with an egg-and-cream sauce supreme. Then there comes a time when the appetite cries for the simplicity of a grilled steak or hamburger, fresh corn on-the-cob, or a summer casserole with all the good things the small garden to the side of the house has to offer (tomatoes, Italian squash, green peppers, eggplant), and then, for a final touch, fresh watermelon dripping with honeyed sweetness. The refrigerator is stocked throughout the summer with an unending supply of iced tea, beer, cola drinks, and for serious occasions chilled white wine. A serious occasion can happen at almost any time. In late afternoon, for example, with fresh-caught sea bass cooked in a skillet on the beach.

Food is something to be treated seriously, or at least it should be if we are to believe Arnold Bennett who observed that "A man of 60 has spent more than three years of his life in eating." A hamburger or a sparerib is just as important as a soufflé and deserves as much care. All things should be done in moderation but if eat we must, then let us feast and enjoy it to the fullest. Pleasure is good for digestion.

Attractive service pieces, sparkling glasses, and decorative plates add to the pleasure. To me they are as important outdoors as they are at a formal dinner. I do not mind washing dishes. I do not mind washing them after breakfast, lunch, or dinner. Unfortunately, I am not for hire.

It has become increasingly popular with some food writers to decry charcoal broiling on the grounds that they cannot take another bite of all that smoke. I am an addict of charcoal-grilled foods and always will be. Food rarely tastes better than when it is cooked properly over hot coals and part of it is because the open air and the whole atmosphere of cooking out-of-doors whets the appetite and sharpens the taste buds.

It is certainly not necessary to have elaborate equipment in order to use charcoal successfully. I happen to own a grill with a large fire basket that can be raised or lowered with the greatest of ease; it has a hood; it has an electric spit; it does the job.

Such a grill is a convenience but not essential. Food can be grilled with great success on an improvised one made of stones or bricks with a sturdy metal grill laid across. Ideally, it should be possible to raise or lower the grill from the fire or raise or lower the fire. The reason is obvious: to adjust the cooking temperature by altering the distance between the source of heat and the food being grilled. Some manufacturers of grills disagree with me that the amount of charcoal used in grilling is not of the essence. There are those who believe they do not enjoy the full flavor of smoke from a grill and I do. I believe in a full fire-basket of hot coals and by hot I mean that the coals should not be used for cooking until white ash forms. That is more or less standard procedure in all books. It may be commonplace to add that the smoked flavor of charcoal-grilled foods does not come from the taste of charcoal itself. White-hot charcoal is tasteless. The smoke and resultant flavor come from the fat that falls into the fire. And now without further ado let us proceed to the menus and recipes which I have found to be splendid fare to serve out-of-doors.

CASSEROLE BUFFET

If there is one single request that crosses my desk as a professional food writer, it is for dishes that can be made ahead and then reheated. Another that is commonplace is the request for dishes to be cooked for large gatherings. The best recipe that I know that meets both requirements is for a spaghetti casserole with chicken and *chorizos,* which are Spanish sausages. These sausages have a wonderful flavor and are available in Spanish markets in metropolitan areas. This spaghetti dish will require the better part of a morning to prepare, but it can be made several hours in advance, and rest assured that in this case the game is worth the candle. For those who do not have access to the sausages, it may be made without them.

MENU
SHRIMPS WITH ANCHOVY BUTTER
CHICKEN AND CHORIZO SPAGHETTI
GARLIC OLIVES
TOSSED GREEN SALAD
WITH FRENCH DRESSING
PARSLEY AND GREEN-ONION
STUFFED BREAD
LOTUS ICE CREAM
ICED TEA

SHRIMPS WITH ANCHOVY BUTTER
5 pounds raw shrimps
2 cups butter, melted
3 tablespoons anchovy paste
Juice of 1 lemon
Cayenne to taste

Using a pair of kitchen shears split shrimps down the back shell but do not cut through the last tail segment. Peel off the shell but leave the last tail segment intact. Rinse and dry shrimps. Arrange them on 6 skewers and place over charcoal. Brush lightly with butter and broil for about 3 minutes to a side. Cooking time will depend on size of shrimps, heat of coals, and distance of shrimps from coals. Turn once; brush with butter. To the remaining butter add remaining ingredients. Beat lightly with a fork to blend. Serve as a dip for the shrimps. Makes 16 servings.

CHICKEN AND CHORIZO SPAGHETTI
2 roasting chickens (about 4 pounds each)
2 onions
1 large carrot, scraped and cut into 1-inch lengths
2 celery stalks with leaves, halved
Salt
3 parsley sprigs
10 peppercorns
Water
About 4½ cups (one 2-pound, 3-ounce can) tomatoes, preferably Italian plum variety
¾ cup butter

2 cups finely chopped celery
2 cups finely chopped green peppers
3 cups finely chopped onions
8 to 10 garlic cloves, finely minced
1 pound mushrooms, thinly sliced, or 1 cup drained canned button mushrooms
7 chorizos (about 1½ pounds)
1 pound round steak, ground
1 bay leaf
½ teaspoon crushed red pepper
¼ teaspoon ground thyme
Freshly ground black pepper
1 cup all-purpose flour
6 cups broth in which chicken cooked
½ cup heavy cream
2 pounds thin spaghetti
1 pound shredded sharp Cheddar cheese
2 or more cups grated Parmesan or Romano cheese

Place chickens in a kettle and add onions, carrot, celery stalks and leaves, salt to taste, parsley, peppercorns, and water to depth of about 1 inch. Bring to boil and simmer until tender, 1 to 1½ hours. (If stewing chickens are used, it will take longer.) Let chickens remain in broth until ready to use. Put tomatoes in a large kettle.

Melt 2 tablespoons butter in a large skillet and add chopped celery, chopped green peppers, chopped onions, and garlic. Cook, stirring, until onions are translucent. Add to tomatoes. Melt 2 tablespoons butter in same skillet and cook mushrooms; add to tomatoes.

Slice chorizos and cook them in skillet until they are slightly browned. Pour off most of the fat and add chorizos to tomatoes. Cook ground meat in same skillet until it loses its red color. Add bay leaf, crushed red pepper, thyme, and salt and pepper to taste. Add to tomatoes. Simmer for 20 to 30 minutes, stirring occasionally so it will not stick to the skillet.

Melt remaining butter in saucepan and add the flour, stirring preferably with a wire whisk. Add 6 cups broth in which the chicken cooked and when the mixture is thickened and smooth, continue cooking, stirring, for 5 minutes or longer. Stir in heavy cream and combine with tomato sauce. Add a little more salt if necessary.

Meanwhile remove skin and bones from chicken and tear or cut into large bite-size pieces. Cook spaghetti in a large container of boiling salted water. The water should be boiling vigorously and the spaghetti should be immersed in it. Stir with a 2-prong fork until all strands are wilted and under water. Continue stirring until a roaring boil is reached again. This is important: cook the spaghetti only until it is barely tender. Do not cook as long as the package directions say because the spaghetti will be reheated later. Drain spaghetti and rinse it to prevent strands from sticking together.

To assemble the dish, cover the bottom of a large heatproof casserole or roasting pan with a little sauce. Add a layer of spaghetti, then of chicken, Cheddar cheese, and more sauce. Continue building up layers until all the ingredients are used, ending with a final layer of cheese. It may be necessary to add more broth if, as the casserole stands, it seems to become dry. The sauce should be a little, but not too, soupy. Set aside until ready to serve.

When ready to serve, preheat the oven to hot (400°F.). Place casserole in the oven and bake without cover until spaghetti is piping hot and bubbling on top. Do not overcook or spaghetti will become mushy. Serve with grated Parmesan on the side. Makes about 16 servings.
Note: The chorizo can be omitted or pepperoni can be substituted.

GARLIC OLIVES
2½ cups (one 1-pound, 5-ounce jar) large green olives or 4 cups (two 1-pound jars)
2 cups (one 1-pound can) black olives
3 tablespoons wine vinegar
Juice of ½ lemon
1 to 3 garlic cloves, crushed
¾ cup olive oil
10 peppercorns, crushed
Crushed red pepper (optional)

Drain olives and crush them slightly. Put them in a mixing bowl or other container. Add remaining ingredients and stir well to coat all the olives. Chill, stirring occasionally, for several hours or overnight. Serve as an appetizer. These olives keep well in the refrigerator. Makes about 3 pounds.

TOSSED GREEN SALAD
There is a lot of nonsense at large about salad making. Some say the greens should be torn apart with the fingers. I say it bruises the lettuce. Preferably, the greens should be cut into bite-size pieces with a knife or scissors. In the same vein, salad dressing should never be made far in advance and refrigerated, particularly if it contains a garlic clove. Overnight the garlic loses its freshness and gives indigestion. It is also true that salad bowls should not only be washed, they should be scrubbed after each use. An unwashed salad bowl becomes rancid and the subsequent salads not only have a questionable taste but a questionable odor.

FRENCH DRESSING FOR SALAD
This is the best standard recipe for a French dressing I know.
Salt
1 garlic clove (optional)
2 tablespoons prepared mustard, preferably Dijon or Dusseldorf
3 tablespoons wine vinegar
2 tablespoons finely chopped shallots or green onions
¾ cup olive or salad oil
Freshly ground black pepper to taste

Sprinkle the bottom of a salad bowl with salt and rub it with a garlic clove. Add mustard and stir in vinegar with a fork. Add shallots and oil and salt and pepper to taste. Stir well before adding crisp greens. Makes about 1 cup.

PARSLEY AND GREEN-ONION STUFFED BREAD
3 long crusty loaves of French or Italian bread
1 cup butter or margarine
¾ cup finely chopped parsley
¾ cup finely chopped green onions (green part and all)

Split loaves lengthwise but do not cut through both sides of the bread. Leave one side as a "hinge." Melt butter and stir in parsley and onion. Spoon the mixture into the center of split loaves. Wrap each loaf in heavy-duty aluminum foil and place over hot coals until heated through. Or bake in preheated hot oven (400°F.) for about 10 minutes. Slice bread and serve piping hot. Makes about 16 servings.

LOTUS ICE CREAM
12 lemons
6 cups sugar
12 cups light cream
6 cups milk

Slice away and discard the ends of 3 lemons. Cut into thin, almost transparent slices. Remove seeds and cut slices into halves to make crescent shapes. Squeeze remaining lemons and combine the juice with the sugar. Add the lemon slices, cover, and refrigerate overnight. Stir.

Combine cream and milk and pour into the churn of an ice-cream freezer. Cover and if possible place the churn in an electric freezer for about 10 minutes. Do not freeze at this point. Add lemon mixture to the cream and place churn in the ice-cream freezer. Freeze according to the directions and keep frozen until ready to use. Makes 18 servings.

● FISH PICNIC ●

My dear friend Pierre Franey is probably the greatest chef alive, although I may be prejudiced since I have been for years almost part and parcel of his family. He was chef at Le Pavillon for twenty-five years and is now a vice president of Howard Johnson's. He is the one who first introduced me to the pleasures of fish with rosemary, a splendid combination particularly if the fish are straight from Gardiners Bay and if they are cooked over an open fire on the beach.

MENU
COCKTAIL SAUSAGES
WITH WHITE WINE
GRILLED FISH
WITH MUSHROOMS AND ROSEMARY
CORN ON-THE-COB
WITH PEPPER BUTTER
CUCUMBERS WITH SOUR CREAM
PICKLED BEETS
TOMATOES VINAIGRETTE
ROLLS
FRUIT WITH CHEESE
BEER   COLA   COFFEE

COCKTAIL SAUSAGES WITH WHITE WINE
24 cocktail sausages
2 tablespoons butter, melted
Dry white wine

Put sausages on skewers and brush with melted butter. Place over charcoal and brown lightly. Brush with a little dry white wine. Do not overcook. Serve immediately with assorted hot mustards including English Mustard. Makes 6 to 8 servings.

English Mustard
Spoon 2 tablespoons powdered mustard into a small mixing bowl and add beer, milk, or water, a little at a time, to make a smooth paste. Thin the mustard to the consistency of heavy cream. Cover and let stand for 10 minutes to develop flavor.

GRILLED FISH WITH MUSHROOMS AND ROSEMARY
6 small whole sea bass or other fish suitable for frying
Sprigs of fresh rosemary or 6 teaspoons dried rosemary
Salt and pepper to taste
All-purpose flour
Peanut oil
¾ cup butter or margarine
1 pound mushrooms, thinly sliced
Juice of 1 lemon
Lemon wedges
3 tablespoons chopped parsley

Clean the fish and rinse under cold water. Dry inside and out. Put 1 sprig of fresh rosemary or 1 teaspoon dried in the cavity of each fish. Sprinkle fish inside and out with salt and pepper and dredge with flour. Heat ¼ inch of oil in a large skillet. When it is hot, brown the fish quickly on one side, then on the other. Do not overcook. Immediately transfer the fish to a hot serving platter or another skillet and wipe out the skillet with a cloth or paper towel. Quickly add the butter to the skillet, heat quickly, and add the mushrooms. Stir; when the mushrooms are wilted, sprinkle with lemon juice. Do not burn the butter. Pour the mushrooms and sauce over the fish. Garnish with wedges of lemon sprinkled with chopped parsley. Serve immediately. Makes 6 servings.

CORN ON-THE-COB

12 ears of fresh corn on-the-cob
Water to cover
Pepper Butter

Do not shuck the ears until they are ready to be cooked. Bring enough water to cover the corn to a boil in a large kettle and when it is boiling vigorously add the shucked ears of corn, one by one. When the water returns to the boil, cover the kettle and turn off the heat. Let the corn rest in the water for 5 to 10 minutes and serve immediately with Pepper Butter. Makes 6 servings.

Pepper Butter

½ cup butter
Coarsely cracked black pepper to taste

Cream the butter with pepper, roll into a sausage shape in wax paper, and chill until ready to use. Unwrap and serve with hot corn on-the-cob.

CUCUMBERS WITH SOUR CREAM

2 large cucumbers, washed and dried
1½ cups dairy sour cream
1 tablespoon wine vinegar
Salt and pepper to taste
¼ cup chopped chives, green onion, or dill, or any combination of these

Run the tines of a fork down the sides of the cucumbers. Slice them thin. Combine remaining ingredients in a mixing bowl and toss gently with cucumbers. Chill. Serve sprinkled, if desired, with additional chopped herbs. Makes about 6 servings.

PICKLED BEETS

8 to 12 medium-size beets (1 quart sliced)
Water
Salt
1 tablespoon pickling spices
2 tablespoons sugar
Freshly ground black pepper
1 cup wine vinegar

Cut tops from the beets but leave 1 inch of stem. Wash beets and put them in a kettle. Add water to cover to the depth of 1 inch and salt to taste. Bring to the boil and cook for 1 to 2 hours depending on size and age of beets, until beets are tender. Drain; when cool enough to handle, peel them. Slice the beets and put them in a mixing bowl. Add remaining ingredients, and chill. Serve cold. The beets will keep for several days in the refrigerator. Makes 8 or more servings.

TOMATOES VINAIGRETTE

3 to 6 red ripe tomatoes, depending on size
Salt and pepper
¾ cup finely chopped sweet onions (Bermuda or Italian)
½ cup finely chopped parsley
¼ cup wine vinegar
½ cup olive oil

Wash and dry the tomatoes and pare away the cores. Peel them, if desired, and cut them into fairly thick slices. Arrange them on a serving dish and sprinkle liberally with salt and pepper. Scatter the onions and parsley over the tomatoes and sprinkle with vinegar and oil. Serve immediately. Makes 6 servings.

🍗 CHICKEN DINNER 🍗

Perhaps it is because I am a child of the South (Mississippi) or a child of the Depression, but I have an absolute passion for chicken in almost any form. During my early youth chicken appeared on the table once a day and more often than not twice a day. I like cold fried chicken and hot fried chicken. Even more (a taste developed perhaps during a period when I studied in France), I have a boundless appetite for roast chicken, either hot or cold. They will never invent the dish, perhaps, more delicious than cold roast chicken for a picnic. A loaf of bread, a bird, and a bottle and that is paradise, enow.

MENU

KING'S POINT PÂTÉ
COLD ROAST CHICKEN ON BED OF CHICORY
GARDINERS BAY POTATO SALAD
HARD-COOKED EGGS
FRENCH BREAD
WATERMELON
ESPRESSO

KING'S POINT PÂTÉ

2 pounds salt pork
2 pounds chicken livers
1 pound lean pork
1 pound lean veal
Boiling water
1 cup dry white wine
2 tablespoons brandy
¼ teaspoon each of ground allspice, bay leaf, and thyme
2 teaspoons salt
2 black truffles, coarsely chopped
1 cup heavy cream
4 egg yolks, lightly beaten
Sliced red pepper
Parsley or watercress

Remove rind from salt pork and tough membranes from chicken livers, pork, and veal. Cut all the meats into 1½-inch cubes. Place salt pork in a pan, cover with boiling water, and bring to the boil. Simmer for 5 minutes, drain, and add to the livers, pork, and veal. Combine wine and brandy, allspice, bay leaf, thyme, and salt and pour mixture over the meats. Let stand for 1 day, covered, in the refrigerator. Turn the meats occasionally to marinate on all sides. Preheat the oven to slow (325°F.). Drain meats, reserving the marinade. Grind meats twice, using first the coarsest and then the finest blade

of food grinder; then add the marinade and truffles. Add cream and egg yolks and blend well.

Turn mixture into 2 bread pans (9 x 5 x 3 inches). Place them in a pan of hot water and bake for 2 hours, or until done. Remove pans from water and let stand at room temperature for 2 hours. Loosen the loaves with a sharp knife, cover with a platter, and invert to unmold. Chill. Garnish the top with sliced red pepper and the base of the loaves with parsley or watercress. Slice and serve with French bread or buttered toast. Makes 2 loaves, or about 30 servings.

COLD ROAST CHICKEN

3 frying chickens (3 pounds each)
Salt and pepper
3 small onions
1½ bay leaves
Ground thyme
½ cup butter or margarine
3 celery stalks, coarsely chopped
3 carrots, coarsely chopped
2 parsley sprigs

Preheat oven to very hot (450°F.). Sprinkle chickens inside and out with salt and pepper. Place 1 onion, ½ bay leaf, pinch of thyme, and approximately 1 teaspoon butter in the cavity of each. Tie legs of chickens together securely. Heat butter in a large open heatproof skillet or roasting pan and place the chickens in it on their sides. Scatter the vegetables around them and place the skillet in the oven. Cook for 15 minutes; baste with a large spoon. Turn chickens to the other side and baste. Cook for 15 minutes longer and place the chickens on their backs. Continue basting and cooking for about 30 minutes, or until done. The chickens, when done, should be golden-brown and when the thigh is pierced with a fork the liquid should run clear. Remove chickens from the oven and let stand at room temperature. Chill until ready to serve. Cut into halves. Makes 6 servings.
Note: The recipe was doubled for the photograph on the facing page.

GARDINERS BAY POTATO SALAD

3 pounds potatoes
Water
Salt to taste
½ cup oil and vinegar dressing
¾ cup finely chopped seeded peeled cucumber
3 shallots or green onions, finely chopped (green part and all)
1 cup mayonnaise
1 teaspoon celery seed
3 tablespoons fresh lemon juice
3 tablespoons chopped fresh basil
Freshly ground black pepper to taste

Wash potatoes and place them in a small kettle or saucepan. Add water to cover and salt and simmer until done, 20 min-

utes or longer depending on size. Drain and peel the warm potatoes and slice into a mixing bowl. Pour oil and vinegar dressing over them, and chill. Before serving add remaining ingredients and toss lightly; garnish with hard-cooked eggs and parsley, if desired. Makes 6 servings.

●● STEAK PARTY ●●

One of my favorite quotations belongs to Alice B. Toklas, best known as the companion of Gertrude Stein. A resident of Paris, she is highly knowledgeable about fine cuisine and when someone once asked, "How many does this recipe serve?", she answered with admirable candor, "How should I know how many it serves? It depends—on their appetites —what else they have for dinner—whether they like it or not."

The thought could be turned to good purpose to answer those who ask how to charcoal-grill a steak. How thick, for example, is the steak? How close will it be to the coals? How hot are the coals and is the steak at room temperature or is it chilled from the refrigerator? Is there a breeze blowing?

There is no one on earth who could formulate an inviolate rule of thumb for grilling steak because there are so many variables involved. For those who insist, however, this is as good as any. With a hot fire to cook a 1-inch-thick steak very rare, try 3 or 4 minutes to a side. For well done, 10 minutes to a side or more. If the steak is nearly 3 inches thick, cook it for 10 to 15 minutes to a side for rare, and for well done for 20 to 25 minutes to a side, but not according to conscience. Anyone with a conscience would have no appetite for a well-done steak. In the end, the best timetable to use is personal judgment if not trial and error. Let us profit, praise be, by yesterday's mis-steaks.

MENU
BIG 3-INCH-THICK
SIRLOIN TO SLICE
THREE SAUCES:
MUSTARD, SHALLOT OR
GREEN-ONION, AND MUSHROOM
BAKED POTATOES WITH CORIANDER
FIREPLACE ROAD SUCCOTASH
TWISTED BREAD OR HARD ROLLS
STRAWBERRY AND
ALMOND CHEESECAKE
COFFEE

MUSTARD SAUCE
1 tablespoon powdered mustard
  Water
2 tablespoons finely chopped shallots
  or onion
3 tablespoons butter or margarine
¼ cup dry white wine
1 cup brown sauce or canned beef
  gravy

Salt to taste
Freshly ground black pepper
to taste
1 tablespoon fresh lemon juice

Place mustard in a cup and add enough water to make a thin paste. Let stand for 10 minutes to develop flavor. Cook shallots in 2 tablespoons butter, stirring, for about 1 minute. Add wine and cook until liquid is reduced by half. Add brown sauce and salt and pepper and simmer for about 15 minutes. Add lemon juice and remove sauce from the heat. Stir in mustard and swirl in remaining butter. Do not cook after mustard is added. Serve hot. Makes about 1 cup.

SHALLOT OR GREEN-ONION SAUCE

¼ cup finely chopped shallots or green onions
¼ cup plus 1 tablespoon butter or margarine
2 tablespoons tarragon vinegar
½ cup dry white wine
Salt and freshly ground black pepper
1 tablespoon bottled steak sauce

Cook shallots in ¼ cup butter, stirring frequently, over moderate heat for about 1 minute. Add vinegar and continue cooking for about 2 minutes. Add wine and simmer for 5 minutes. Add salt and pepper to taste and the steak sauce. Remove from heat and swirl in remaining butter. Serve immediately. Makes about 1 cup.

MUSHROOM SAUCE

1 tablespoon chopped shallots or green onions
¼ pound mushrooms, sliced thin
3 tablespoons butter or margarine
1 teaspoon fresh lemon juice
1½ cups brown sauce or canned beef gravy

Cook shallots and mushrooms in butter for 5 minutes, stirring occasionally. Add lemon juice and brown sauce and blend well. Bring to boil and serve hot. Makes about 2 cups.

BAKED POTATOES WITH CORIANDER

12 large potatoes for baking, washed and dried well
Bacon fat or shortening
¾ cup butter
Salt and freshly ground black pepper to taste
About 20 coriander seeds, crushed in a mortar with pestle or under a heavy skillet

Preheat the oven to hot (425°F.). Rub outside of potatoes with bacon fat and place on a rack in the oven. Bake for 40 minutes to 1 hour, depending on the size. To test for doneness, press fingers into the sides of potatoes, guarding fingers with a heavy cloth. Make a large deep gash down the center of potatoes, loosen pulp with a fork, and fill opening of each with 1 tablespoon butter. Sprinkle with salt, pepper, and coriander and serve immediately. Makes 12 servings.

Note: Other ground spices such as cuminseed and nutmeg are also good in baked potatoes.

FIREPLACE ROAD SUCCOTASH

⅓ cup olive oil
3 garlic cloves, peeled and chopped
2 cups thinly sliced onions
1 medium-size eggplant, peeled and cut into large cubes
¼ cup flour
6 zucchini (about 2 pounds), scrubbed and cut into 1-inch slices
3 green peppers, seeded and cut into strips
Salt and freshly ground black pepper
5 red ripe tomatoes, peeled and chopped
2 cups fresh corn, cut from the cob

Heat oil and cook garlic and onion until onion is translucent. Transfer garlic and onion to a flameproof casserole. Dredge eggplant with flour and brown it lightly in the skillet. It may be necessary to add more oil. Add zucchini and green peppers. Stir them around in the skillet and add salt and pepper to taste. Pour mixture into a casserole, cover, and simmer gently for about 1 hour; add a little water if necessary. Add tomatoes, stir gently, and simmer, uncovered, until thickened, 20 to 30 minutes. Ten minutes before the dish is done, stir in the corn. Makes about 12 servings.

STRAWBERRY AND ALMOND CHEESECAKE

2 cups graham-cracker crumbs
5 tablespoons melted butter
11 ounces cream cheese
2 eggs
¾ cup sugar
½ teaspoon vanilla extract
2 cups dairy sour cream
¼ cup toasted whole almonds
Whole strawberries
¼ cup currant jelly
1 tablespoon water

Combine crumbs and butter and press into a 9-inch pie pan. Preheat oven to moderate (350°F.). Place cream cheese in a large mixing bowl and blend slowly with an electric mixer. When cream cheese is fairly smooth, add eggs, one at a time, beating mixture well after each addition. Continue beating on low speed. Gradually add ½ cup sugar and vanilla. Pour mixture into prepared crust. Bake for 20 minutes.

Blend sour cream with ¼ cup sugar and almonds. Spread mixture evenly over top of pie. Turn off oven heat. Return pie to oven for 4 minutes. Cool pie briefly, then chill until set. Before serving garnish top with whole strawberries. Glaze with currant jelly melted with water and heated to dissolve. Makes 6 servings. Make 2 pies for 12 servings.

● HAMBURGERS SUPREME ●

Whether you are thinking of a backyard cookout or have a picnic site in mind by some secluded stream, hamburgers are always good. Here is a menu which is supreme.

Again, harkening back to my childhood, one of the delights of youth was driving to a combination service station and sandwich shop. This was, in fact, a principal diversion for the entire town: going to "Charlie Labella's for a hamburger and a Coke." One of the great mysteries of the town was how Labella made anything as delicious as those hamburgers, served with a sauce containing chili powder. Years later in doing research on Romanian cuisine I found a recipe for a grilled meat dish with garlic and discovered what I believe to be the closely guarded secret of the Labella family. It was the simple addition of garlic to the meat before it was grilled, rather than to the sauce.

In any event, garlic hamburgers are delicious for those who enjoy garlic. And chili is good anytime.

MENU
HOT CLAM-JUICE COCKTAIL
GARLIC HAMBURGERS
ON TOASTED BUNS
CHILI CON CARNE SAUCE
SHAVED LETTUCE
MEXICAN POTATO CHIPS
PICKLES
ANISE FRUIT CUP

HOT CLAM-JUICE COCKTAIL

4 to 6 cups fresh or bottled clam juice
Celery salt
Fresh lemon juice

Bring clam juice to the boil and sprinkle with celery salt. Ladle into 6 hot cups or mugs and sprinkle a little lemon juice over each serving. Makes 6 servings.

GARLIC HAMBURGERS ON TOASTED BUNS

2 pounds round steak or sirloin, freshly ground
1 garlic clove, finely minced, or more to taste
Salt and pepper to taste
6 to 8 hot toasted buns
6 to 8 pats of butter
2 cups Chili Con Carne Sauce
Shaved lettuce

Place meat in a mixing bowl and add garlic, salt, and pepper. Mix lightly but thoroughly and shape into 6 to 8 patties. Grill to the desired degree of doneness and place each on a hot toasted bun. Top each with a pat of butter and shaved lettuce. Serve the sauce separately. Makes 6 to 8 servings.

Chili Con Carne Sauce

½ pound pork or veal, ground twice
½ cup minced onion

½ garlic clove, finely minced, or more to taste
2 tablespoons olive oil
1 cup tomato purée
½ cup water
3 tablespoons tomato paste
½ teaspoon ground cuminseed
½ bay leaf
Salt to taste
1 tablespoon chili powder, or more to taste

Cook meat, onion, and garlic in olive oil until meat loses color. Add remaining ingredients and stir to sauce consistency. Simmer, stirring occasionally, for about 30 minutes. When finished, the sauce should have the consistency of thick soup. If necessary, thin with additional tomato purée. Makes about 2 cups.

MEXICAN POTATO CHIPS
Potato chips
1 lime
Hot pepper sauce
Salt
Bottled steak sauce

Use enough potato chips to fill a 2-quart bowl. Sprinkle the chips lightly with lime juice, tossing gently. Sprinkle with hot pepper sauce, salt, and steak sauce to taste. Serve immediately. Makes 6 servings.

ANISE FRUIT CUP
½ cup sugar
¾ cup water
2 tablespoons fresh lemon or lime juice
½ teaspoon aniseed
Pinch of salt
2 cups fresh orange sections
2 cups fresh strawberries
1 cup diced pears
1 cup seedless grapes

Combine sugar, water, lemon juice, aniseed, and salt in a saucepan and cook for 2 minutes. Bring to the boil and simmer for 10 minutes. Cover; leave for 10 minutes. Chill. Prepare fruits. Place in bowl; pour syrup over. Chill. Makes 6 servings.

SPARERIBS
Elena Zelayeta, the famed Mexican cookbook author and hostess, introduced me to the put-it-in-the-oven-and-leave-them-alone method of cooking spareribs. That is, to cut the spareribs into individual servings and place them in the oven for 1½ hours or more until crisp. With a little salt and a sauce of anyone's choosing they are delicious. I like the method and use it frequently since it is a fine way of cooking spareribs that are to be grilled before serving. After they are almost cooked, I transfer them to a grill, smear

them with sauce, and let them finish to accumulate a small amount of smoky flavor. Serve as an appetizer or a main course.

BARBECUED SPARERIBS
2 racks of spareribs (3 to 4 pounds each)
Salt and pepper to taste
Juice of 1 lemon
1 tablespoon Worcestershire
1 cup tomato ketchup
½ cup honey
½ cup butter or margarine
1 garlic clove, finely minced
½ teaspoon ground cuminseed

Preheat the oven to moderate (350°F.). Cut spareribs into individual ribs and rub with salt and pepper. Place ribs on a rack in a baking pan and bake for 1½ to 2 hours. Baking time will depend on the size of the ribs. When done, ribs should be crisp or almost crisp, although they will be cooked further over coals.

Combine remaining ingredients, season with salt and pepper, and bring to the boil. Place ribs on a grill over hot charcoal and baste with the sauce. Continue to baste and cook for 10 to 15 minutes, or until ribs are well glazed. Serve hot. Makes 6 to 8 servings, or more if they are used as an appetizer.

OVEN—In simplest terms, an oven is a box which can be heated. It may be part of a range, built into a wall, or portable. It may use gas or electricity as its source of heat. It has one, or sometimes two, doors, shelf supports, and racks which are usually movable, varying degrees of insulation, as well as different combinations of controls, timers, thermostats, and thermometers. It may have a vent and/or a hood and fan. It is used to broil, bake, roast, or cook (as in casseroles).

Electronic ovens are exceptional in that, although they use electricity, no heat is created in the oven except in the food to be cooked. Since it is a rapid method of cooking it is used to cook the foods more frequently cooked on the top of the range in addition to being used to prepare the conventional oven foods.

A Dutch oven is a heavy saucepot with tight-fitting lid used for cooking pot roasts, stews, soups, or other dishes which require long cooking.

OXFORD SAUCE—An English sauce, also known as Cumberland sauce, which is traditionally served with cold venison. It can be used with other game and meats.

OXFORD SAUCE
3 shallots, minced
1 orange
1 lemon
¼ teaspoon sugar
Dash of cayenne
⅓ cup red currant jelly, melted
⅓ cup port wine
½ teaspoon prepared mustard
Dash of ginger

Cook shallots in a little water for 1 or 2 minutes. Drain. Cut off thinnest possible peeling from the orange and lemon. Cut peeling into fine julienne strips, and simmer in water to cover for 10 minutes. Drain. Put shallots, orange and lemon peelings, juice from the orange and from half the lemon, and remaining ingredients in bowl. Mix well. Makes about 1 cup.

OXTAIL—A beef tail, weighing one-and-a-half to two pounds. This is an extremely bony cut, but it is very flavorful when braised or used as the basis for oxtail soup, a favorite of English cookery.

OXTAIL AND VEGETABLE SOUP
2 oxtails
All-purpose flour
3 tablespoons shortening
2 quarts water
1 teaspoon salt
½ teaspoon peppercorns
Dash of cayenne
1 bay leaf
1 celery stalk, diced
1 medium onion or leek, chopped
1 carrot, diced
½ cup tomato purée
1 teaspoon Worcestershire
Chopped parsley
Salt and pepper

Have oxtails cut into pieces; roll in ½ cup flour. Brown in 2 tablespoons shortening in large kettle. Add water, salt, peppercorns, cayenne, and bay leaf. Bring to boil; skim; cover and simmer for 3 hours, or until meat is tender. Strain broth; cool, and remove fat. Separate meat from bones. To broth and meat add celery, onion, and carrot. Bring to boil and simmer for 30 minutes. Add tomato purée and simmer for 10 minutes. In skillet brown 2 tablespoons flour; blend in remaining shortening. Add to soup and bring to boil. Add Worcestershire, parsley, and salt and pepper to taste. Makes 6 servings.

OYSTER—A bivalve mollusk of the family *Ostreidae,* genus *Ostrea,* found mainly between the tidal levels or in shallow waters along the coasts of all continents except those bordered by polar seas. The common oysters of Europe are the *O. edulis;* of the eastern and Gulf coasts of the United States, *O. virginica;* of the California coast, *O. conchophila;* and farther north along the Pacific coast, *O. lurida.*

Oysters have an irregular, two-part shell, held together at the hinge by an elastic ligament. The oyster itself is found in the concave lower half of the shell, protected by a thin membrane, called a mantle, which lies against the inner side of the shell.

Oyster fishery is an important industry in the United States, France, the Netherlands, the United Kingdom, and Australia, with the United States leading in the quantity grown for market and the value of the product. Many famous oyster varieties come from Chesapeake Bay; others from New York, Mississippi, Louisiana, and all the seaboard states. At one time, such names as Blue Point, Lynnhaven, and Cape Cod meant oysters from those specific regions. To some, they still do. But to market experts, Blue Point now indicates any oyster from two to four inches long and from two to two-and-a-half inches wide, no matter where it is produced. Lynnhaven has become a general name for any larger, angular-shape oyster. On the Pacific coast, the supply is chiefly of the native oyster, the Olympia (*O. lurida*), generally much smaller than the eastern, and the eastern type grown from baby or "seed" oysters shipped from eastern beds. The three chief sizes recognized in the oyster trade are "half-shells," the smallest, usually preferred for eating raw; "culls," of medium size, for eating raw and for stewing, etc.; and "box," the largest, generally used for frying.

Availability—Fresh oysters are available from September to April in the shell or shelled. Eastern oysters are graded as:

Counts or Extra Large—Not more than 160 per gallon, or 44 in a quart.

Extra Selects or Large—From 161 to 210 per gallon. A quart of the smallest oysters from this gallon contains 36.

Selects or Mediums—From 211 to 300 oysters per gallon. A quart of the smallest oysters from this gallon may have 83 oysters and a quart of the largest has over 46 oysters.

Standards or Small—From 301 to 400 oysters per gallon, and a quart of the smallest of these cannot contain more than 138 oysters; a quart of the largest holds more than 68.

Very Small—Over 500 to a gallon, and a quart of the larger of these oysters contains more than 112.

Pacific oysters are generally larger than the eastern variety, with the exception of the Olympia *(Ostrea lurida)* which is often identified as such, and is much smaller. Other Pacific oysters are graded as:

Large Pacific—Under 65 per gallon

Medium Pacific—From 65 to 96 oysters per gallon

Small Pacific—From 97 to 144 oysters per gallon

Extra Small Pacific—More than 144 oysters per gallon

Canned oysters are sold packed in water or oyster liquor, whole or in pieces. Frozen oysters and oyster stew are available.

Purchasing Guide—If buying fresh oysters in the shell, make sure oysters are alive, with shells tightly closed. Shucked oysters should be plump, with no shell particles, and with clear liquor. Oysters should have a grayish color and a fresh sea odor.

Storage—Refrigerate fresh oysters and plan to eat or cook as soon as purchased.

☐ Fresh, cooked; or canned, opened, refrigerator shelf: 1 to 2 days

☐ Canned, kitchen shelf, unopened: 1 year

☐ Frozen, refrigerator frozen-food compartment: 2 months

☐ Frozen, freezer: 1 year

Nutritive Food Values—Oysters are a good source of protein, high in calcium, niacin, and iron, a fair source of thiamine and riboflavin, and low in fat.

☐ Eastern, 3½ ounces, raw, meat only = 66 calories

☐ Pacific and Western (Olympia), 3½ ounces, raw, meat only = 91 calories

☐ Canned, 3½ ounces, solids and liquid = 76 calories

☐ Oyster stew, homemade, 3½ ounces, prepared with 1 part oysters to 2 parts milk by volume = 97 calories

☐ Oyster stew, commercial, 3½ ounces, prepared with equal volume of water = 51 calories

☐ Oyster stew, commercial, 3½ ounces, prepared with equal volume of milk = 84 calories

Basic Preparation

☐ **To Open Oysters in the Shell**—Scrub shells well and rinse in cold water. Insert point of sharp thin knife into hinged end of oyster and push blade between shells until muscle at center is cut and valves begin to separate. Run knife around shell, separate valves, and loosen oyster from shell.

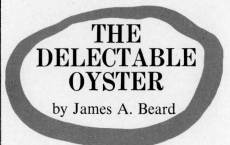

THE DELECTABLE OYSTER
by James A. Beard

The author of *Gulliver's Travels* said some two centuries ago: "He was a bold man that first ate an oyster." We can only wonder now how it happened. Was it on a dare? By mistake? Out of curiosity? Once in an old copy of *Harper's Weekly* I saw a cartoon of a prehistoric man tackling an oyster. The expression on his face was dazed, frightened.

There is a legend that the first prehistoric eater of oysters got his taste for the bivalve as follows: He was strolling on the shore and spied an oyster, shell open, gaping at the world. On impulse, the caveman stuck his fingers into the opening. As the shell snapped shut he pulled his hand away and with his fingers dragged the oyster out. Naturally he put his fingers to his mouth and, mm-m! What flavor!

My own theory is that the Chinese were the first, or surely among the first, oyster eaters. Long ago they perfected a method of drying the bivalve and stringing it on bamboo sticks to keep for future use. Chinese cuisine includes scores of dishes using oysters and delectable oyster sauces. As for the Romans, we know from Apicius that they cherished the oyster and served it in many ways. One Roman recipe called for stewing oysters in honey! This I don't recommend. The ancient Greeks, who had more conservative tastes than the Romans, were particularly fond of oysters baked in their shells in charcoal or coals just until the shells opened. These they seasoned lightly with lemon and butter. This is still one of the choice ways to cook oysters. Modern cooks sometimes serve baked oysters with Béarnaise sauce, a thoroughly delicious combination.

The French, Spanish, and Portuguese, all living near the sea, learned to appreciate oysters in ancient days. The English also loved oysters but, sad to say, served these delicate morsels with vinegar. Dickens in *Pickwick Papers* tells how Sam Weller's friend consumed a half pint of vinegar with a plate of oysters. This mistreatment is doubly horrifying since English waters produce two of the finest oysters in the world, Colchesters and Whitstables. These, along with the French Marennes, are greatly prized by connoisseurs.

Oysters vary in size, looks, and taste because the water, climate, and even the exact location of an oyster bed have profound effects on their growth. They range from plump and grayish with a bland taste, to greenish or even coppery with a definite metallic taste. Some are as small as your fingernail and others, such as the Japanese or the Malpeques from Prince Edward Island, as big or bigger than the palm of your hand. The Pacific Northwest, where I grew up, is noted for its tiny Olympia oysters from Puget Sound. These delectable tidbits, not fatty but coppery in flavor, are such midgets that it takes over 2,000 of them to make a gallon. An oyster lover can consume at least 250 at a sitting. Olympias command a premium price. Shucking them is a tedious job. Also, as with much of our finest seafood, the harvest grows less each year. We greedy eaters have helped to deplete the beds, and the pollution of our waters has taken its toll.

On the East Coast, the Chincoteagues are the nearest to the Olympias. The Cape Cod oysters were probably the first to attain popularity in America. They were an important food for the Pilgrims. The small oysters from Delaware Bay pleased William Penn and other Quakers of the Pennsylvania colony. Philadelphians are great oyster fans to this day. Elizabeth Robins Pennell wrote in her delightful book *A Guide for the Greedy:* "But the glory of Penn's town is the oyster croquette—from Augustine's by preference. A symphony in golden brown and soft fawn grey, it should be crisp without, within of such delicate consistency that it will melt in your mouth like a dream. Pyramidal of shape, it is of itself so decorative that only with the rarest blue and white china, or the most fairy-like Limoges, will it seem in perfect harmony."

The famous Lynnhavens from Virginia are no longer easy to come by. Man has stripped the beds. Nearby are ancient kitchen middens containing over three million shells, a testimonial to the quality of these great bivalves.

New Orleans oysters have been famed since the city was founded, and the local cuisine boasts many oyster specialties,

The author, James A. Beard, preparing Oyster Stew. In the foreground another of his favorites, oysters on-the-half-shell.

among them the well-known Oysters Rockefeller.

When I was young, a family friend in the west transplanted several well-known eastern varieties to the Toke Point area in Washington. We summered at the coast, and each week we received a great sack of these oysters. I can remember the wonderful pyramids of fried oysters my mother used to make with them. This was a breakfast specialty on the mornings when we went clamming and crabbing at dawn. Back we would come, tired, hungry, and cold. My mother was always in the kitchen ready for us. On the stove were two huge iron skillets partly filled with melted sweet butter, bubbling but not the least bit colored. The oysters, about a dozen to a person and a few for the pot, were opened and lined up. The moment we came in, the first lot would be quickly rolled in flour, dipped into beaten egg and milk, and then rolled in freshly crushed cracker crumbs. Then the oysters were slowly lowered into the hot butter and allowed to turn a golden-brown, no more. They were whisked to the table to be eaten with hot buttered toast and plenty of hot coffee. We bit through the crisp outside into the soft rich center. The coating of crumbs insulated the flesh so that these oysters were always delicate and tender, never tough.

This to me is still a great breakfast dish. Of course, most oyster fans insist that the delicacy is at its best served raw on-the-half-shell. Generally I agree. And in this form they need little or no embellishment. A dash of lemon juice and maybe a touch of freshly ground black pepper. But no vinegar, no chili sauce, and no cocktail sauce. With oysters on-the-half-shell serve thin sandwiches of rye bread lavishly buttered and a good wine or beer or stout. Dry white wines such as Chablis or Pouilly-Fuissé have a strong affinity for oysters.

Here are some ways to vary oysters on-the-half-shell:

■ Serve them with lemon juice and black pepper and piping-hot grilled or sautéed pork sausages; or with slices of garlic sausage. Be sure the sausages are hot and served on a hot plate and the oysters freshly opened and well chilled.

■ For a glamorous party dish, serve oysters on a bed of ice with a dab of fresh caviar and a squirt of lemon juice atop each one. Don't forget the rye-bread sandwiches with plenty of sweet butter.

■ Serve oysters-on-the-half-shell and pass bowls of chopped chives and parsley. Lemon juice and black pepper go along too. You'll find the tang of these fresh herbs an interesting variation.

■ Serve oysters-on-the-half-shell with cocktails. Pass large trays of the oysters with lemon quarters, caviar if you like, and piping-hot tiny sausages.

OYSTER STEW I

If there is any traditional Christmas Eve dish in this country, I guess it is probably oyster stew. Surely it is one of the more delicious morsels when hot and rich and served with piles of crisp, buttered toast.

You may go as rich as you please here. Try it with milk, with milk and cream, or, to be utterly fabulous, with heavy cream.

- 5 tablespoons butter
- 1 cup milk
- 2 cups heavy cream
- 1½ pints oyster liquor and oysters
  Salt, pepper, cayenne to taste
  Chopped parsley or paprika

Heat your bowl first. Add a good pat of butter to each bowl. Keep them piping hot. Heat milk, cream, and oyster liquor to the boiling point. Add the oysters and bring again to the boiling point. Season with salt, pepper, and cayenne. Ladle into the hot bowls and add a little chopped parsley. Makes 4 to 6 servings.

OYSTER STEW II

Combine oysters and butter in a skillet and cook until the edges curl. Add hot cream and heat to the boiling point; ladle into hot bowls. Season with salt and cayenne and serve with crisp biscuits or buttered toast.

CREAMED OYSTER PATTIES

My mother always served Creamed Oyster Patties in season for late supper parties. They were rich and delicious and beautiful to look upon. Serve them with a delicately tossed salad, or with crisp fresh vegetables with salt and pepper, or with a cucumber salad, crisp bread, dessert, and coffee.

- 3 tablespoons butter
- 3 tablespoons all-purpose flour
- ½ cup liquor drained from oysters
- 1½ cups heavy cream
  Salt and pepper to taste
- 2 egg yolks
- 1 pint oysters
- 2 tablespoons dry sherry
- 4 to 6 patty shells
  Chopped parsley

Melt butter and blend in flour well; let it cook gently for a few minutes before adding oyster liquor and cream. Stir in the oyster liquor and 1 cup cream and continue stirring until the sauce is well thickened and smooth. Season with salt and pepper and then gradually stir in remaining cream mixed with the egg yolks. Continue stirring until thoroughly heated, but do not let the sauce come to the boiling point. Heat the oysters in their remaining liquor; drain. Add the sherry

to the sauce, then the heated oysters, and keep warm over hot water until ready to serve. Be sure the water does not boil under the mixture. Serve in patty shells, or in bread croustades, on toast points, or on steamed rice. Sprinkle with chopped parsley. Makes 4 to 6 servings.

OYSTER PIE

Use the recipe for Creamed Oyster Patties and fill a casserole or pie dish with the mixture. Place a small custard cup or support in the center of the dish. Top with a rich pastry which has been rolled and chilled for 30 minutes or more before topping the pie. Bake in preheated very hot oven (450°F.) for approximately 15 minutes. Reduce heat to moderate (350° F.) and continue baking for 5 minutes, or until the crust is nicely browned and baked through. Makes 6 servings.

OYSTERS EN BROCHETTE

This is a most picturesque and delicious way to serve oysters. It can be varied in many different ways.

For each brochette or skewer:

- 1 slice of bacon
- 4 mushroom caps
- 4 oysters
  Lemon juice
  Freshly ground pepper
  Butter

Run the skewer through one end of the bacon, then skewer a mushroom cap, then an oyster, then bacon, mushroom, oyster, until you have the skewer filled and the bacon laced through it. Sprinkle with lemon juice, give the whole thing a grind of pepper, and brush with butter. Broil over charcoal or in the broiler until the oysters are curled at the edges and the bacon crisp and done. It is practical to cook the bacon for a few minutes and cool it before using on the skewers. These delectable morsels are delicious served with hollandaise sauce.

■ **Variations**—Alternate small cubes of beef tenderloin and tiny mushroom caps with the oysters. Brush well with butter and sprinkle with salt and pepper before broiling.

■ Alternate small cubes of precooked ham with oysters. Broil as above and serve with Béarnaise sauce.

■ Alternate oysters, scallops, and chunks of lobster meat laced with bacon strips on skewers, and broil. Serve with lemon or with hollandaise sauce.

OYSTER PAN ROAST

These are particularly popular on the west coast. They are oysters poached in butter with high seasoning and look well when served in small copper skillets or in a large oval au gratin dish.

- ½ cup butter
- 1 pint drained oysters

Salt, pepper, cayenne, fresh lemon juice

Melt the butter in a skillet or in individual skillets; when it is hot and bubbly, add the oysters and poach them in the butter until they are plumped and curled at the edges. Add salt, pepper, cayenne, and a goodly squirt of lemon juice. Serve at once on fried toast or on crisp well-buttered toast with chopped parsley and chives. Makes 4 servings.

■ **Variations**

■ *Piquant*—Poach the oysters in butter. Season to taste and add a goodly dash of Worcestershire and a dash of ketchup or chili sauce. Serve on buttered toast.

■ *Western*—Poach the oysters in butter. Season with salt and a dash of cayenne. Add ¼ cup sherry and a little of the oyster liquor and bring to the boiling point. Serve on buttered toast points with chopped parsley.

DEVILS ON HORSEBACK
Wrap oysters in rashers of bacon and broil under a hot broiler unit until bacon is crisp. Turn once during cooking. Serve on toast.

ANGELS ON HORSEBACK
Marinate 24 oysters in enough white wine to cover. Add 1 garlic clove, chopped, and 2 tablespoons chopped parsley. Remove oysters, and wrap in thin strips of ham. Broil until ham is nicely browned and serve oysters on toast with a hollandaise sauce.

SCALLOPED OYSTERS
This is a traditional New England dish which has somehow or other worked its way into some Thanksgiving menus.

    Butter
2 cups freshly rolled cracker crumbs (they should be coarse)
1 pint oysters
    Salt, pepper, ground nutmeg to taste
½ cup heavy cream
    Buttered cracker crumbs

Butter a baking dish well and cover with a layer of cracker crumbs. Cover with a layer of oysters, seasonings, and a little of the cream; dot with butter. Cover with buttered crumbs. Add another layer of oysters and seasonings and more cream. Top with additional cracker crumbs, dot heavily with butter, and season. Add a touch more cream and bake in preheated hot oven (425°F.) for 20 to 25 minutes. Makes 4 to 6 servings.

HANGTOWN FRY I
This is a recipe which supposedly started in the west and for which there seem to be dozens of different versions.

6 to 8 fried oysters
6 eggs, well beaten
2 tablespoons water

Salt and pepper to taste
    Crisp bacon

Fry the oysters, according to the recipe for Golden-Fried Oysters, in plenty of butter. When they are golden-brown, pour the well-beaten eggs which have been mixed with water and seasonings over them and cook as you would an omelet. Pull the eggs from the sides of the pan with a spatula and when the omelet is cooked but not dry, roll it onto a hot platter and garnish with strips of crisp bacon. A perfect Sunday breakfast or dinner entrée. Makes 6 servings.

HANGTOWN FRY II
8 large oysters
    All-purpose flour
6 tablespoons butter
6 eggs
3 tablespoons cream
¼ cup grated Parmesan cheese
¼ cup chopped parsley
    Salt and pepper

Dip oysters into flour and sauté lightly in butter. Blend the eggs, cream, cheese, and parsley. Add salt and pepper to taste, pour over oysters in pan, and cook over low heat until eggs are set. Place under a broiler to brown lightly. Serve from the skillet or slip onto a hot platter. Makes 4 to 6 servings.

HANGTOWN FRY III
This version merely calls for the addition of fried oysters to scrambled eggs, allowing 2 oysters to each egg. Sprinkle with parsley and serve with crisp bacon.

HARRY HAMBLET'S GOLDEN-FRIED OYSTERS
    Butter
3 eggs
3 tablespoons heavy cream
36 to 48 oysters
    Flour
    Freshly rolled coarse cracker crumbs
    Salt and pepper

Melt plenty of butter in a heavy skillet. It should be lavishly done for this preparation. (If you wish to be safe you may add part oil to the butter so as to be certain there will be no burning of the butter.) Beat the eggs lightly and combine with the cream. Dust the oysters lightly with flour, dip into the egg mixture, and then roll in the cracker crumbs (the crumbs of soda crackers or saltines are by far the best). Let the dipped and crumbed oysters stand for a few minutes before cooking. Cook quickly, just long enough to brown the oysters nicely on both sides. Season with salt and pepper to taste when they are browned. Serve on a very hot platter with lemon wedges and coleslaw. Makes 6 servings.

■ **Variation—Oyster Pancakes:** Use individual skillets and cook the oysters close together (you will need small ones for

this), turning the oysters with a spatula so they will stay in one pancake-shape mass. Serve either in the small skillets or slip them out on a hot plate and dust with finely chopped parsley. Serve with lemon wedges.

OYSTER OMELET
Fold freshly fried oysters into individual omelets and serve with a dusting of chopped parsley and a dash of fresh lemon juice. This is a most attractive and picturesque brunch or luncheon dish which is quick and easy for a small group.

OYSTER LOAF
There are many stories connected with this dish. One such story is that they were "guilty conscience" sops in the old days of gay life in New Orleans and San Francisco. Those who lingered long and freely at the bars were often repentant and had an oyster loaf prepared for the waiting "little woman."

An oyster loaf can be most picturesque. Use a round Italian loaf or a Vienna loaf or an unsliced loaf of regular bread. Cut a slice from the top of the loaf about ¾ inch thick and scoop out the crumbs of the loaf, leaving a wall about ½ inch thick all around. Toast the loaf and the sliced-off top in preheated moderate oven (350°F.), brushing well with melted butter several times during the process. Fill the loaf with freshly fried oysters and sprinkle with chopped parsley and serve with top on or heap the oysters in a pyramid and serve with top apart; this is not quite cricket but it is effective. Serve with lemon wedges and warmed chili sauce.

OYSTERS CASINO
24 oysters on the half shell
4 pie pans filled with rock salt
1 cup butter
½ cup chopped green onion
⅓ cup chopped parsley
3 tablespoons chopped green pepper
    Fresh lemon juice
    Salt and pepper
6 to 8 bacon strips, partially cooked

Arrange the oysters, 6 to a serving, on the rock salt in pie pans. Cream the butter, and blend in the onion, parsley, and green pepper, spiked with a little lemon juice and salt and pepper to taste. Spoon the butter mixture onto the oysters and top each oyster with a small strip of partially cooked bacon. Bake in preheated very hot oven (450°F.) until the bacon is crisp and the oysters curled at the edges. Serve with additional lemon juice. Makes 4 servings.

OYSTER CLUB SANDWICH
A wonderful luncheon or midnight snack. Prepare two pieces of toast for each person. Butter the toast and top with a leaf

ENCYCLOPEDIA OF COOKERY

of lettuce, slices of tomato, crisp bacon rashers, and fried oysters.

Make it open-face with the lettuce and tomato on one slice and the oysters and bacon on another slice for a pretty service. Garnish with lemon wedges and crisp greens dressed with oil and vinegar. Serve mayonnaise with the sandwich if you wish.

MUSHROOM AND OYSTER PIE

1 pound mushrooms
8 tablespoons butter
1 small onion, grated
3 tablespoons all-purpose flour
   Salt, pepper, nutmeg, and cayenne
1½ cups heavy cream
1 pint oysters
   Rich pastry
   Beaten egg

Remove caps from mushrooms and reserve. Chop stems very fine. Melt 4 tablespoons butter in a small skillet and cook the chopped mushroom stems well, adding more butter if needed. Grate the onion into the mushroom mixture and when they are cooked through and most of the liquid is cooked down, add the flour. Blend well and season to taste. Gradually add the cream and stir until lightly thickened and smooth.

Sauté mushroom caps in 4 tablespoons butter until just lightly cooked on both sides. Combine mushrooms and oysters in a casserole or baking dish and cover with the sauce which has been tasted for seasoning. Place a support in the center and cover the top with rolled chilled pastry. Decorate with little designs of pastry if you wish and brush with beaten egg. Bake in preheated very hot oven (450° F.) for 10 to 12 minutes, or until brown. Makes 6 servings.

CHICKEN AND OYSTER SAUTÉ

1 small frying chicken, about 3 pounds
   All-purpose flour
6 tablespoons butter
   Salt and pepper
⅔ cup dry sherry
12 oysters
   Oyster liquor or chicken bouillon
¼ cup chopped parsley

Cut the chicken into serving-size pieces. Dredge lightly with flour. Melt the butter in a good-size skillet and brown the pieces of chicken on both sides over rather brisk heat. When it is nicely colored, reduce the heat, add salt and pepper to taste, and the sherry. Cover and simmer for 35 minutes, or until tender. Remove the cover.

Poach the oysters in enough oyster liquor barely to cover them. When the edges curl and they are just cooked through, combine with the chicken on a hot platter. Add the oyster liquor to the chicken pan, combine with the chopped parsley, and pour over the chicken. Makes 4 servings.

Oyster Stew

Oysters en Brochette

Hangtown Fry

Note: If you wish to thicken this sauce, use a teaspoon of arrowroot combined with a little of the liquid.

OYSTERS POULETTE

12 oysters
   Oyster liquor or chicken bouillon
2 tablespoons butter
½ cup cream
2 egg yolks
   Salt, pepper, and lemon
   juice to taste
   Chopped parsley
   Chives

Poach the oysters in ½ to ⅔ cup liquor for 1 minute. Remove to a hot dish. Add butter, cream, and the egg yolks which have been mixed with a little of the cream. Stir until mixture thickens slightly. Season with salt, pepper, and lemon juice and pour sauce over the oysters. Garnish with chopped parsley and chives. Makes 2 servings.

OYSTER SALAD

1 cup chicken bouillon or oyster liquor
   Salt and pepper
½ teaspoon tarragon
1 teaspoon chopped parsley
24 oysters
   Mayonnaise
   Greens
   Ripe olives
   Peeled quartered tomatoes and finely
   chopped chives (optional)

Combine chicken bouillon with seasonings, adding tarragon and chopped parsley. Poach the oysters for about 3 minutes. Drain and cool. Serve with a well-flavored mayonnaise on greens for a first course or a lunch dish. Garnish with ripe olives and, if you wish, quarters of peeled tomatoes and finely chopped chives. Makes 4 to 6 servings.

OYSTERS SAUTÉ

8 tablespoons butter
¼ cup finely chopped green onion
1 teaspoon dried tarragon
¼ cup dry wine
   Salt and pepper
24 oysters
   Crisp buttered toast
¼ cup finely chopped parsley

Melt the butter in a skillet, add the chopped onion, and sauté until onion is just soft. Add the tarragon, white wine, and salt and pepper to taste. Add the oysters and cook them just long enough to curl the edges, shaking the pan from side to side to bathe all the oysters with the delicious sauce. Serve on pieces of crisp buttered toast with finely chopped parsley, and be certain you drink a dry white wine with this superb dish. Makes 4 to 6 servings.

OYSTER BISQUE

⅔ cup uncooked rice
1 pint oysters
1 small onion, stuck with 2 cloves
1 cup oyster liquor or chicken bouillon
   Brandy
1 pint cream

   Salt and pepper
   Paprika (optional)
6 poached oysters (optional)

Cook the rice in boiling salted water until very soft. Chop the oysters very fine and try not to lose any of the liquor. Add the onion, the oyster liquor, and about 3 tablespoons of brandy. Bring to the boiling point and simmer gently for 10 minutes. Remove the onion and add the drained rice. Put through a fine sieve or food mill. Add the cream, and season to taste with salt and pepper. Return to the stove and heat almost to the boiling point. Or keep hot over hot water until time to serve. Serve with a dash of paprika and a poached oyster for garnish if you wish. Makes 6 servings.

Some Oyster Hints Which Are Delicious and Unusual:

■ When you make a beefsteak-and-kidney pie, combine 12 oysters with the usual ingredients you use for such a pie. Poach them in their own liquor or in a little beef or chicken bouillon before adding to the pie.

■ Oysters added to your favorite chicken pie recipe give it an entirely new twist and a really most exciting flavor and texture experience.

■ Crisp-fried oysters combined with a broiled steak is a wonderful experience in gastronomy. Or poached oysters with a steak are delicious.

■ Time was when a Pocketbook Steak meant a filet of beef cut in a thick steak with a pocket to be filled with fried oysters just before serving.

■ Of course you know that oysters added to your favorite stuffing give it something completely new and different. Try it with a stuffing of bread crumbs, butter, onions, loads of tarragon, and oysters. Superb.

■ Serve double chicken consommé boiling hot with one or two oysters poached in a little of the consommé in each cup; it is a sensational clear soup.

■ Beef consommé with an oyster or two added to each cup is another rare change from the regular diet of consommé.

■ Blanquette of veal or veal fricassee is one and the same thing. Combine a few oysters with the next one you do and see what a difference there is.

OYSTER PLANT or SALSIFY—A biennial herb, *Tragopogon porrifolius*, which is native to southern Europe, but will nevertheless thrive in cool climates. It has been cultivated in the Mediterranean and in Asia Minor for some 2,000 years, both as a food plant and for ornamental purposes. Oyster plant grows to a height of about four feet and is sometimes called "goatsbeard" because of its thin

tufted grasslike leaves. Because its purple flowers close around midday it is also known in England as John-go-to-bed-at-noon.

The root, for which it is cultivated as a vegetable, is yellowish-gray, often a foot long and two inches in diameter. Its flesh is white and contains a considerable proportion of milky juice. The flavor of the root is said to resemble that of an oyster, but many culinary experts insist that it resembles far more the flavor of a globe artichoke.

The Spanish oyster plant, or Spanish thistle, *Scolymus hispanicus,* is a larger plant, with prickly leaves and a root that is lighter in color. Its flavor is not so highly developed as the oyster plant. The black oyster plant, *Scorzonera hispanica,* is the smallest of the three, with broader leaves and a yellow flower. The skin of its root is black and it is similar in flavor to the oyster plant.

Oyster plant is a winter vegetable, although the young leaves of the plant make a delicious spring salad.

Availability and Purchasing Guide—Available from June to March in specialty food stores or vegetable stores catering to people of Spanish, Italian, and Greek extraction.

Select from well-shaped roots of medium size. Avoid large coarse roots or flabby shriveled ones.

Storage—Remove tops, if intact. Rinse, then place in plastic bag or wrap in aluminum foil and refrigerate.

☐ Refrigerator shelf or vegetable compartment: 1 to 4 weeks

Nutritive Food Values—Contains some calcium, phosphorus, iron, and vitamin C.

☐ 3½ ounces, cooked = 77 calories

Basic Preparation—Oyster plant must be scraped before cooking. As each root is scraped, it should be plunged at once into water mixed with a little fresh lemon juice or vinegar to prevent discoloration; the proportions are about 3 tablespoons lemon juice or vinegar to 1 quart water. The roots are then cut into 2- to 3-inch pieces and kept in the acidulated water until cooking time. Boil until just tender, drain, and finish in very hot butter; or fry like French-fried potatoes or fritters; or serve in a well-seasoned white sauce.

OYSTER-PLANT FRITTERS

Scrape and cook oyster plant. Mash as you would mash potatoes. Season with butter, salt and pepper, and if desired add a touch of ground nutmeg. Shape into small round flat cakes, about 1½ inches in diameter. Dip cakes into all-purpose flour. Quickly cook in hot butter until golden-brown, turning once. Serve with meats in place of potatoes, rice, or noodles.

PAELLA—A Spanish rice dish that has gained international fame. It is named for the two-handled iron frying pan in which the rice is cooked and served. *Paella* is a casserole which must always be based on rice, but in Spain its other ingredients vary according to the food available locally: *Paellas* in inland Spain generally contain meat, chicken, sausage, and vegetables; whereas the coastal regions specialize in seafood and chicken combinations. Outside of Spain it is the varieties featuring at least some seafood which have come to be most generally associated with *paella*.

It makes an excellent buffet dish and only a salad and dessert are needed with it for a complete meal.

PAELLA A LA VALENCIANA

1 lobster
½ cup olive oil
2 garlic cloves, minced

1 frying chicken (2 to 3 pounds), cut into small pieces
1 chorizo or Spanish sausage, sliced, or hot Italian sausage
3 green peppers, sliced
3 pimientos (fresh or canned), sliced
¼ cup finely diced salt pork
4 medium-size onions, sliced
6 medium-size tomatoes, peeled and cut into wedges
3 cups uncooked rice
2 teaspoons saffron threads soaked in a little chicken bouillon
  Chicken bouillon or fish stock
15 shrimps, cooked and shelled
15 mussels or clams, well scrubbed
2 cups green peas or sliced green beans
2 medium artichokes, sliced, or 1 package (9 ounces) artichoke hearts (if fresh artichokes are used, remove tough outer leaves and chokes)
  Pepper (optional)

Cook lobster until red. Remove meat, but only crack the claws and reserve them. In large skillet or kettle heat olive oil and garlic. Sauté lobster meat over medium heat for 2 or 3 minutes. Remove and reserve. Cook chicken until brown on all sides. Return lobster meat to skillet and add *chorizo* slices, green peppers, pimientos, pork, onions, and tomatoes. Cook for about 5 minutes, stirring constantly. Add rice and saffron and cook for another 5 minutes. Add bouillon to cover, plus 1 inch. Cook, covered, over medium heat for 10 minutes, stirring occasionally. Add shrimps, mussels, peas, and artichokes. Season with pepper. Cover and cook for 10 minutes more, or until rice is tender, stirring frequently. If necessary, add more bouillon, only a little at a time; the dish should be dry and the liquid all absorbed. Before serving, arrange ingredients so that some of the shrimps will show; place lobster claws on top. Decorate with additional pimiento strips, if desired. Serve hot. Makes 8 to 10 servings.

PALM—A very large family, *Palmaceae,* of highly ornamental tropical and subtropical trees and shrubs. They are generally characterized by unbranched stems which vary in size from three feet to a height of more than 100 feet. They have a terminal crown of large leaves, feathery in some varieties, fan-shape in others. Many of the palms are extremely valuable for the food products obtained from them. Chief among these are the betel palm, whose nutlike kernel and leaves yield a potent drink; the cabbage palm, whose tender central leaves are eaten as greens, and whose terminal frond (hearts of palm) is cooked, or pickled; the coconut palm; the date palm; the sago palm; the oil palm from which palm oil and palm nuts come; and the sugar palm from whose sap arrack is distilled.

PANBROIL—This is a dry-heat method of cooking meats, poultry, or fish which can often substitute satisfactorily for broiling. Tender cuts of meat one inch or less thick, frying-chicken parts, and thin pieces of fish such as fillets are particularly suitable. To panbroil, use a heavy skillet and preheat it, but do not add fat or water. Put food into the skillet and do not cover. Cook over medium heat, turning food occasionally. Drain from pan any fat that accumulates and continue cooking until meat is brown on both sides. Season to taste and serve immediately.

═══════ ✑ ═══════

PANCAKE *by Helen Evans Brown*— Pancakes, or griddle cakes, are the oldest form of bread. The first ones were made of pounded grain, mixed with water, and spread upon a hot rock to dry. The ancient Hebrews cooked their unleavened bread on a griddle and in China, the egg roll, really a pancake, has been made for untold oriental ages.

Today, every country has its own version of the pancake. They may serve as appetizers, as the Russian *blini* do; entrées, as do Italian *cannelloni;* desserts, as do French *crêpes Suzette,* but always they are welcome. All the world loves pancakes.

Nutritive Food Values—The nutrients in pancakes vary with the ingredients but they are primarily a source of carbohydrates.

☐ Homemade pancakes, 3½ ounces = 231 calories
☐ Plain or buttermilk mix, 3½ ounces, made with milk = 202 calories
☐ Plain or buttermilk mix, 3½ ounces,

made with milk and egg = 225 calories
☐ Buckwheat or other flour mix, 3½ ounces, made with milk and egg = 200 calories

Basic Preparation—Mix ingredients together lightly and quickly. Mix batter until dry ingredients are just blended and do not try to beat out all the lumps. Overbeating produces tough pancakes. Some pancake batters need to stand before batter can be cooked. Since flours are very variable, add more liquid if the batter is too thick and more flour if the batter is too thin. If you are in doubt, test the batter before using all of it. If you are using a pancake mix, follow directions on the label to prepare the batter.

The griddle you use should heat evenly. Test by dropping some water onto it. If the water sizzles and bounces, the griddle is ready.

If you are using a seasoned griddle, one of the teflon-coated griddles, or if the batter has shortening or fat in it, it is not necessary to grease the griddle. However if yours is a griddle on which the batter sticks, brush the entire surface with a small amount of fat or shortening before making the pancakes.

When the entire surface of the pancake is covered with unbroken bubbles, turn the pancake only once. The second side takes only half the amount of time needed to cook the first side. Try to serve the pancakes at once. To keep them warm for a short period of time, place them, covered with a towel, in a very slow oven (200°F.).

AMERICAN PANCAKES

SOURDOUGH PANCAKES
Anyone who has tasted a true sourdough pancake will tell you that there is no lighter or more flavorsome morsel in all the world.

Sourdough Starter
Boil some peeled potatoes, say 4, in plenty of water to cover. Do what you will with the spuds, but save the water. Mix 2 cups of it, lukewarm, with 2 cups all-purpose flour, 1 tablespoon sugar, and 1 teaspoon salt. Put in a crock and let stand in a warm spot, loosely covered, for 3 or 4 days, or until it's working merrily and has attained a peculiar and, to me, delightful sour odor. "She'll let you know when she's up," one old-timer told me, and you'll see what he means. To hasten this process, you may add a cake of yeast at the beginning, but if you have the time, let it take its natural course. When "ripe," it may be stored in

the refrigerator or freezer, or used. Makes about 3½ cups.

Sourdough Pancakes
Take 2 cups of starter from the crock; add 1 cup each of flour and water. Cover bowl and allow to stand in a warm place overnight. Next morning, stir in 1 teaspoon to 1 tablespoon sugar, ½ teaspoon baking soda, salt to taste (about ½ teaspoon), and 1 well-beaten egg. If too thick, add more water; if too thin, more flour. Stir in 2 tablespoons melted butter; allow to stand for a few minutes, then bake on both sides. Makes 6 servings.
Note: To have more starter for use at a future time, replace the 2 cups removed with an equal amount of flour and enough water to give the starter its original consistency. Then, after it begins to work again, store it in the refrigerator or freezer until you wish to use it.

BUTTERMILK PANCAKES
Combine 2 cups all-purpose flour, ½ teaspoon salt, 1½ teaspoons baking soda, 1 teaspoon sugar, 2 cups buttermilk, 2 tablespoons melted butter or margarine, and 2 beaten egg yolks. Beat the 2 egg whites and fold in. Bake on a hot griddle, making pancakes any size from that of silver dollars to dinner plates. Makes 4 to 6 servings.

SOUR-CREAM PANCAKES
Combine ¾ cup all-purpose flour, ½ teaspoon salt, 1 teaspoon sugar, 1 cup dairy sour cream, ¼ teaspoon baking soda, 1 cup cottage cheese, and 4 well-beaten eggs. Cook slowly on a hot griddle or in skillet until brown on both sides. Makes 4 servings.

YEAST PANCAKES
Scald 1¼ cups milk and cool to lukewarm. Sprinkle 1 package active dry yeast or crumble 1 cake compressed yeast into ¼ cup lukewarm water. Use very warm water (105°F. to 115°F.) for dry yeast; use lukewarm water (80°F. to 90°F.) for compressed. Let stand for a few minutes, then stir until dissolved. Add dissolved yeast to milk, 1 teaspoon salt, 1 teaspoon sugar, 2 tablespoons melted butter or margarine, 2 cups all-purpose flour, and 1 well-beaten egg. Beat for 2 minutes and set aside in a warm place to rise. When doubled in bulk, stir again and cook. Makes 4 servings.

NEW ENGLAND GRIDDLE CAKES
Combine 2 cups all-purpose flour, 4 teaspoons baking powder, 2 tablespoons sugar, 1 teaspoon salt, 1 cup milk, ¼ cup melted butter or margarine, and, at the last, 2 well-beaten eggs. Make large cakes and spread while hot with soft butter and grated maple sugar. Stack 6 high and cut like a pie. Another New

England trick is to add maple syrup to the batter, replacing the sugar and part of the milk. Makes 4 servings.

FLANNEL CAKES
They are made like the New England griddle cakes, except that the baking powder is increased to 5 teaspoons and the egg yolks and whites are beaten separately, the latter being folded in at the last. You may need a little additional milk, too. Makes 4 servings.

BUCKWHEAT CAKES
Combine 2 cups buckwheat flour with 1 cup all-purpose flour, 3 tablespoons sugar, and 2 teaspoons salt. Sprinkle 1 package active dry yeast or crumble 1 cake compressed yeast into 1 cup warm water. Use very warm water (105°F. to 115°F.) for dry yeast; use lukewarm water (80°F. to 90°F.) for compressed. Let stand for a few minutes, then stir until dissolved. Add 2 cups warm milk and ¼ cup melted butter, margarine, or sausage drippings. Stir into the dry mixture and beat smooth. Allow to rise overnight in a warm place. Next morning stir in ½ teaspoon baking soda dissolved in 1 tablespoon water; mix; cook on a griddle until a heavenly brown. Omit the soda if you wish; the pancakes will then have a pleasantly sour flavor. Serve with butter and syrup. Makes 4 to 6 servings.

JOHNNYCAKES
These, it is said, were originally called "journey cakes," as they were carried for sustenance on tedious journeys. Try them, sometime, without syrup, with broiled ham, fried chicken, or perhaps creamed tongue or turkey.

Pour 2 cups boiling water over 2 cups white cornmeal; add 1 teaspoon salt, ½ cup milk, and ¼ cup melted butter or margarine. More water may have to be added, as the batter should be soft but not thin. Bake on a griddle. Serve with butter and maple syrup. Makes 4 to 6 servings.

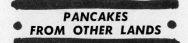

PANCAKES FROM OTHER LANDS

MEXICAN CHEESE AND CHILI PANCAKES
Make pancakes from a mix. For each cup of mix add 3 well-beaten egg yolks; then at the end fold in the 3 egg whites beaten stiff. Have ready some domino-shape pieces of Jack cheese, or sharp Cheddar. Wrap each one in a strip of canned peeled green chili, each strip about a third of a chili. Drop spoonfuls of the batter onto a hot griddle. When almost done on the bottom, put a piece of the chili-wrapped cheese on one half and fold over the other, like a turnover.

Put in preheated moderate oven (350°F.) for 5 to 10 minutes, until cheese is melted.

ENGLISH HAM AND HERB PANCAKES
These herb griddle cakes are made with any batter to which chopped chives, parsley, and thyme have been added in discreet quantities. They are cooked, then spread with cooked ham or crumbled crisp bacon, and rolled.

CRÊPES
(Basic French Pancakes)
The versatile French crêpe is a tender, rich little cake which is useful for many other dishes. When made without sugar, crêpes may be filled with meat, vegetables, fish, or cheese, rolled or folded, and served, usually sauced, for the main dish or as an accompaniment.

For about 32 crêpes, beat 4 eggs well; then add 1 cup milk, 1 cup all-purpose flour, ½ cup melted butter or margarine, 1 teaspoon salt, and if for dessert, 2 teaspoons sugar. A tablespoon of brandy may also be added to dessert crêpes for extra flavor and delicately crispy edges. Mix well; let stand in the refrigerator for 2 or 3 hours. Stir again; if thicker than a heavy cream, add a little more milk. Heat a 7- or 8-inch skillet. (My pet one, made of heavy aluminum, measures 8 inches at the rim, about 6 at the bottom, with curving sides, an omelet pan.) Brush skillet with melted butter and put in 1 generous tablespoon batter. Working quickly, tip and tilt the pan so that the batter flows evenly over the bottom. Cook quickly. As soon as the pancake browns on one side, turn quickly and brown the other. Stack and keep warm until all are made. These freeze, beautifully, I find. Pack them in stacks of 6 or 12 and wrap in foil or freezer paper. Thaw thoroughly before separating lest they tear.

CRÊPES CARLOS
Make Basic French Crêpes, see above. Cut a ripe fresh pineapple into chunks, or use canned, draining it. Cook slowly in ¼ cup butter until brown, adding more butter if needed, and ¼ cup Jamaica rum. Spread the crêpes with apricot preserves and fold each in quarters. Put in a large chafing dish, arranging them on one side. At the other side, put the cooked pineapple. Pour all the pan juices over the crêpes, and heat gently. Before serving, add 6 tablespoons more rum; flame.

GERMAN PANCAKES
Beat 6 eggs, separated; add to the yolks ¼ cup each flour, melted butter, and milk; season with ½ teaspoon salt, and fold in the beaten egg whites. This bat-

ter, ⅛ at a time, is cooked in plenty of butter in a large skillet. When the edges curl, turn and brown on the other side. The same pancakes—spread with applesauce, jam, jelly, or other fruit or rum sauce, rolled, and served with sugar and butter—make a superb dessert.

These pancakes can also be cooked until firm on one side, then placed in a preheated hot oven (400°F.) for 10 minutes or until puffed and golden. Can be cut into wedges and served.

German Apple Pancakes
Pour batter in skillet. Top with very thinly sliced apples and cook until pancake is golden-brown. Turn and brown on the other side.

ITALIAN CANNELLONI
The Basic French Crêpes (at left) are filled with any well-seasoned cooked meat or fish which has been moistened with a little gravy or with egg yolks. Some suggestions: chopped veal seasoned with a little anchovy; chopped chicken with shreds of Virginia ham or prosciutto; chopped cooked brains with hard-cooked egg, minced parsley, and pignolias. Put a generous spoonful of filling on each pancake, roll, and arrange on a buttered flat baking dish or, if preferred, on a bed of well-seasoned puréed spinach. Pour a mixture of olive oil and melted butter over all, sprinkle with grated cheese, and bake until pancakes are heated and the cheese melted.

RUSSIAN BLINI
The most famous of all appetizer pancakes are, of course, the Russian Blini. They are made exactly as Buckwheat Cakes (at left) except that only 1 teaspoon sugar is used and the batter may have to be thinned with a little water, for the cakes should be small and thin. Use melted butter for the shortening. Give each guest a plate and pass the hot pancakes as well as sour cream, melted butter, caviar, sliced smoked salmon, or any smoked or kippered fish that meets your fancy. The *Blini,* which should be about 3 inches in diameter, are buttered, dabbed with the sour cream, and topped with the fish. They are usually folded before eating.

HUNGARIAN PALACSINTA
Large light pancakes (make Basic French Crêpes, at left) are spread with a mixture of dairy sour cream and chopped cooked ham, and stacked 6 or 7 high; cut into wedges for serving. Another filling that may be used is a combination of creamed lobster and mushrooms, not too thin, with both lobster and mushrooms cut fine.

PANFRY

CHINESE EGG ROLLS

These deliciously filled rolls are sometimes made of noodle paste, but those made of a thin egg batter are far better. Beat 2 eggs slightly; add 1 cup all-purpose flour, 2 tablespoons cornstarch, 2 cups water, and ½ teaspoon salt. The batter should be very thin; if not, add more water. Make in a small frying pan like Crêpes (page 1293), being sure to tilt the pan quickly so that the batter will spread transparently thin. Use little or no butter in pan. Cook on one side only. For filling, mix ¾ cup chopped cooked shrimp, ½ cup finely diced celery; ⅓ cup each of minced cooked pork, minced water chestnuts, and minced bamboo shoots. Season with 2 teaspoons wine, 1 tablespoon soy sauce, and 2 tablespoons minced green onion. Mix with a raw egg, and form into finger-shape rolls; lay them on the cooked sides of the pancakes. Roll up, tucking in edges to seal in the filling. A little uncooked batter can be used to help seal. Chill; just before serving, brown in 2 inches of fat. Although usually served as one of the dishes at a Chinese meal, they also make a tantalizing appetizer when cut into 3 or 4 pieces and served on toothpicks.

BLINTZES

These popular Jewish pancakes are filling enough to make the main course at lunch, although they are usually served as dessert. Fill Crêpes (page 1293) with a mixture of 2 cups cottage cheese, 2 slightly beaten eggs, 2 tablespoons melted butter or margarine, ¼ teaspoon salt, and 2 tablespoons sugar. Grated lemon rind, ground cinnamon, or raisins can be added. Fold or roll filled Crêpes; then brown in butter. Serve hot with cold dairy sour cream and jam, preferably cherry, apricot, or black currant.

PANFRY—A method of cooking or frying in very little fat in an uncovered skillet or pan on top of the stove. Panfrying is synonymous with sautéing. It is a quick-cooking method used for the same types of food as is panbroiling (page 1292), but can also be used for lean meats and vegetables and fish, all of which require the addition of just a little fat to prevent sticking and achieve the desired browning.

Use a heavy skillet to panfry. Add a small amount of fat to the skillet and allow it to melt over medium heat. Add food and cook over medium heat, turning occasionally until brown on both sides. Food can be seasoned before or after cooking. Do not cover and do not add any liquid. When cooked to desired doneness, drain on absorbent paper and serve at once.

Chinese Egg Rolls

Russian Blini

Mexican Cheese and Chile Pancakes

Blintzes

Crêpes

German Apple Pancakes

PAPAW or PAWPAW—A North American fruit of the custard apple family, *Asimina triloba,* which grows naturally in rich moist soil from Lake Ontario south to the Gulf of Mexico. It is the only member of this family hardy in the northern United States. Because of the similarity in names it is often confused with the papaya, which is also called a pawpaw.

The pawpaw tree grows to a height of twenty to thirty feet, has large, long, glossy leaves and a purplish flower. The fruit varies from two to six inches in length and is shaped like a short fat banana, dark-brown to blackish in color, with a soft creamy yellow flesh in which many seeds are embedded. It is sweet, rich, custardlike, and slightly aromatic. Not available commercially, the fruit should be picked after the first frost and stored in a cool dry place until soft. They are peeled like a banana and eaten raw.

Caloric Value

☐ 3½ ounces = 85 calories

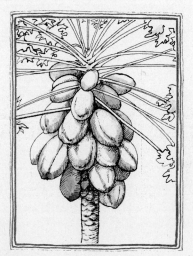

PAPAYA or PAWPAW—A small tropical tree, or more accurately, a very large herbaceous plant (*Carica Papaya*) with large, fleshy fruit which grow on stalks from the trunk, just below the leaves. The fruit, which resembles a melon, has a rind and a juicy flesh that is yellow-orange in color; one fruit can weigh up to twenty pounds. Papaya has a delicious, sweet-tart musky taste. It makes an excellent breakfast fruit and appears as a standard part of tropical breakfasts. Papayas are also used for salads, pies, and sherbets. The fruit contains an enzyme called papain which acts as a digestive ferment. Papain is also important in medicine and it is the chief ingredient in meat tenderizers.

The papaya is a true American native; the only point that is in question is whether it came from the West Indies or Mexico. The name is a corruption of the Carib word *ababai.* After Columbus discovered the New World, the plant spread quickly to other tropical countries. By 1600 it had reached the Philippines, India, and very likely Africa, too. Apart from the excellence of the fruit, the papaya tree grows very quickly, maturing in eighteen months from the time the seed is planted.

Papayas are of great importance in tropical Asia, Africa, and Hawaii, both as a staple food and commercially. In the United States, they are grown almost entirely in southern Florida and Texas since the trees are very sensitive to frost.

Availability—Papayas are chiefly available where grown, in Florida and Texas. The fruit does not ship well and cannot be sent great distances. Some papaya juice is being marketed and is sold canned or mixed with frozen juice blends.

Purchasing Guide—The flavor is best when ripe. Ripe fruit has a yellow-orange skin that yields to slight pressure. It has a fruity odor.

Storage—Let fruit ripen at room temperature. When ripe, fruit should be refrigerated.

☐ Refrigerator shelf: 1 to 2 days

Nutritive Food Values—Good source of vitamin A and an excellent source of vitamin C.

☐ Fresh, 3½ ounces, raw = 39 calories

☐ Canned juice, 3½ ounces = 48 calories

Basic Preparation—Cut papaya into wedges or quarters without removing outer skin. Remove most of the seeds. Serve with slices of lemon or lime. Or peel and cut into cubes to use in fruit cups or salads.

PAPILLOTE, EN—A French culinary term meaning "wrapped in paper." At one time parchment was used for the wrapping, but nowadays brown paper or aluminum foil is widely used. Dishes are prepared *en papillote* to hold in the juices of the meat or fish during cooking.

PAPRIKA—The Hungarian name given to a spice or condiment made by grinding the ripe dried pods of red *capsicum* or bell peppers. There are a number of paprikas, and their quality, color, flavor, and pungency depend on the variety of the bell peppers used and the way in which they are processed. Usually, paprika is made from sweet red bell peppers. The stems, stalks, and white membrane are removed before grinding because they are bitter hot, but the seeds are ground along with the pulp.

Hungarian *rose paprika* is made from the choicest *capsicum,* with a rich dark-red color and a sweet distinctive flavor and aroma. Another kind of Hungarian paprika is *King's* or *Koenigspaprika,* which has a much sharper flavor since the entire pepper is used.

Paprika is used as a seasoning and as a garnish on practically all nonsweet dishes. The best known paprika-flavored national dish is Hungarian goulash. Spanish, Mexican, Balkan, and Turkish cookery also use paprika, in varying degrees of sweetness or pungency. However, none of these paprikas achieve the excellence of the Hungarian varieties. This is not surprising, since in Hungarian cooking paprika is an essential element.

Availability—Paprika is available ground, almost always in the mild sweet variety. More pungent varieties are available in stores specializing in foreign food products.

Storage—Keep paprika in a cool dry place. Like chili powder and onion and garlic seasonings, paprika picks up moisture from the air if containers aren't tightly closed. Hot and humid storage conditions are particularly bad for paprika, changing both its color and flavor.

VEAL PAPRIKASH

1½ pounds boned veal shoulder, cut into 1½-inch pieces
2 tablespoons fat
2 medium onions, chopped
½ small garlic clove, minced
1 tablespoon paprika
1 green pepper, sliced
1 tomato, peeled and sliced
1 teaspoon salt
¾ cup water
1 tablespoon all-purpose flour
1 cup dairy sour cream
 Hot cooked noodles

Brown meat on all sides in hot fat. Add onion and garlic, and cook for 2 or 3 minutes. Add paprika, green pepper, tomato, and salt. Cover and simmer for 1 hour, or until meat is tender. Add the water when needed to prevent sticking. Just before serving, blend flour with a little cold water and stir into mixture. Cook for 2 or 3 minutes. Add sour cream and heat gently. Serve with noodles. Makes 4 servings.

PAPRIKA CHICKEN WITH SOUR-CREAM SAUCE

1 medium onion, minced
3 tablespoons shortening
1 frying chicken (3 pounds), cut up
5 tablespoons all-purpose flour
1½ teaspoons salt
1 teaspoon paprika
⅛ teaspoon pepper
¼ cup water
1 cup dairy sour cream
5 ounces broad noodles
1 tablespoon poppy seeds

Cook onion in 1 tablespoon shortening until soft. Remove from skillet. Wash chicken and dry on paper towels. Mix ¼ cup flour with ½ teaspoon salt. Dredge chicken with mixture. Brown chicken in remaining shortening. Sprinkle with onion, remaining salt, paprika, and pepper; add water. Cover and simmer for 30 minutes, or until chicken is tender. Remove chicken to a hot platter. Stir remaining flour into skillet juices. Add sour cream; heat to boiling point, stirring constantly. Pour sauce over chicken. Serve with hot cooked noodles sprinkled with poppy seeds. Makes 4 servings.

FRIED CHEESE BALLS WITH PAPRIKA

- 1½ cups (½ pound) grated mild cheese
- 3 tablespoons all-purpose flour
- ¼ teaspoon salt
  Dash of cayenne
- ¼ teaspoon powdered mustard
- ½ teaspoon paprika
- 3 egg whites
- ⅓ cup very fine cracker crumbs
  Fat for deep frying

Blend together cheese, flour, salt, cayenne, mustard, and paprika. Beat egg whites until stiff and fold into cheese mixture. Allow to stand for 5 minutes to stiffen slightly. Drop by rounded teaspoonfuls into cracker crumbs. Lift out with fork and drop into hot fat. Fry in deep hot fat (275°F. on a frying thermometer). Drain on paper towels. Sprinkle with additional paprika, if desired. Serve as an appetizer or salad accompaniment. Makes approximately 2 dozen.

PAPRIKA CHEESE SAUCE

- 3 tablespoons butter, margarine, or bacon fat
- 2 tablespoons all-purpose flour
- 1½ cups milk
- ¾ teaspoon salt
- ⅛ teaspoon pepper
- 1 cup shredded sharp American cheese
- 1 teaspoon paprika

Melt butter in a saucepan. Blend in flour. Remove from heat and stir in milk. Return to heat. Cook, stirring constantly, for 8 to 10 minutes, until mixture begins to thicken. Add salt, pepper, cheese, and paprika. Makes 6 servings.

PARAFFIN—A flammable waxy substance produced in distilling wood, shale, coal, etc., and occurring also in the earth as a constituent of petroleum or as a solid deposit. Paraffin is sold in solid form in food stores, particularly during the fall months, and is used for coating the tops of jars of jams and jellies to keep out air, thus preventing spoilage. Since it has an extremely low smoking point, it should be melted over hot water and poured over the jam or jelly to the depth of ⅛ inch. Although it is not edible, paraffin is a pure wax and it is harmless.

PARBOIL—To parboil food is to plunge it into boiling water and cook it for a short period of time. Parboiling is used for such vegetables as potatoes or green peppers to cook them partially, or to shorten cooking time. Parboiling is also used to prepare vegetables for freezing; the process shrinks the vegetables for more compact storage and retards action of the enzymes in the vegetable.

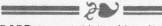

PARCH—To dry thoroughly under dry heat. Most parched foods are dried in the sun to the point where they contain very little internal moisture.

All parched foods require long cooking. Parched corn, a specialty of the American Indian, is the best example; corn on-the-cob was dried in the sun to preserve it for winter use.

PARE—To peel thinly with a sharp knife. A short-bladed paring knife is generally used for this process. Potatoes, apples, pears, and turnips are examples of foods which are pared.

PARFAIT—The word for this ice-cream dessert is the French word meaning "perfect," an opinion shared by many.

Originally, a parfait meant only a coffee cream, but in modern French usage a parfait is an ice made of a single flavor frozen in a plain mold.

An American parfait consists of ice cream served with whipped cream or fruit or other sauces, arranged in a tall narrow glass called a parfait glass. The ice cream is layered into the glass with the cream or fruit or sauce. The parfait is often topped with a generous spoonful of sweetened whipped cream and garnished with a maraschino cherry.

PARFAITS

In parfait glasses or small jelly, cheese, shrimp-cocktail, or juice glasses, alternate layers of ice cream and jam, syrup, baby or junior fruit, or marshmallow cream. The sky is the limit on combinations; just remember eye appeal as well as flavors. Here are a few suggestions:

- ■ Strawberry ice cream and strawberry jam.
- ■ Chocolate ice cream and marshmallow cream.
- ■ Vanilla ice cream and red raspberry jam.
- ■ Vanilla ice cream and sundae sauce.
- ■ Cherry ice cream and almond-flavored whipped cream.
- ■ Vanilla ice cream with apricot and apple, or pear and pineapple baby or junior fruit.

FRENCH KIRSCH PARFAIT

- 1 cup sugar
- 2¼ cups water
- 1 envelope unflavored gelatin
- ⅓ cup fresh lemon juice
- ½ cup kirsch
- 2 egg whites
- ⅛ teaspoon salt

Put sugar and 2 cups water in saucepan. Bring to boil and boil for 10 minutes. Soften gelatin in remaining water, and stir into first mixture. Add lemon juice and kirsch. Pour into refrigerator trays, and freeze until firm. Beat egg whites with salt until stiff, but not dry. Beat frozen mixture until light and fluffy. Fold in egg whites. Pour into 5-cup mold and freeze until firm. Turn mold upside down on serving plate and wrap in a cloth wrung out of hot water. Shake until mold drops onto plate. Makes 6 servings.

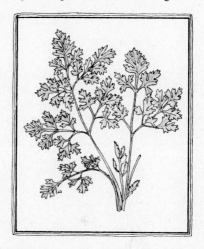

PARSLEY (*Petroselinum crispum*)—A hardy biennial herb plant, native to southern Europe and widely used for flavoring and as a garnish. The parsley family, or *Umbelliferae,* includes many herbs and spices such as anise, dill, angelica, chervil, caraway, coriander, cumin, fennel, lovage, sweet cicely, and the common vegetables celery and carrots.

Parsley is a small green plant of which there are more than thirty varieties. These are distinguished by the shape of their foliage: curled, moss-curled, double-curled, or fern-leaved, for example; and plain or common parsley, often called Neapolitan or Italian parsley, which has comparatively coarse foliage. Hamburg parsley is a sub-species, *P. crispum, var. latifolium,* grown for its fleshy carrotlike root and prepared like any root vegetable.

Bunches of parsley leaves are used whole as a garnish or in a *bouquet garni.* Chopped, either fresh or dried, parsley is used to flavor soups, meat dishes, fish stuffings, cream or cheese sauces, eggs, breads, flavored butter, marinades, and most vegetables and salads.

The word parsley is from the ancient Greek *petroselinon*, "celery growing among rocks," because it often grew there. Although not known for certain, some modern botanists believe Sardinia to have been its birthplace. At any rate, parsley did originate somewhere in the Mediterranean region, and was a widely used plant in the ancient world, often for other than culinary reasons.

The ancient Egyptians, for instance, sprinkled parsley on the graves of their dead. This association with the dead continued into Greek and Roman times, when the bodies of loved ones were strewn with parsley. This linking of parsley and death is also found in an old English proverbial expression "to be in need of parsley" which meant to be at death's door.

Another use of parsley in olden days was to ward off intoxication. No Greek or Roman would dare attempt a long banquet without a parsley wreath to protect him from too much wine. This tradition continued until the 16th century, when an English herbalist, William Turner, suggested that parsley seed taken before a drinking bout "helpeth men that have weyke [weak] braynes to bear drinke better."

Whatever the ancient history of parsley, it was one of the most popular of medieval herbs for gravies, sauces, and relishes. It could even make a quick soup, suggests a Parisian husband to his young bride in the late 14th century. He recommends: "Take parsley and fry it in butter, then pour boiling water on to it and boil it and add salt and serve your sops." Parsley was important in omelets and pickles and in fact in almost every medieval dish that called for herbs.

Since colonial days Americans have grown and used parsley widely. It was such a part of the home garden that Southerners considered it unlucky to transplant it when moving to a new house. Today, we rely on it for flavor and as an attractive garnish, and modern nutritionists support its use by recognizing its important nutritional value.

Availability and Purchasing Guide—All year round; it is grown in many home gardens and is also grown commercially. It is sold fresh in bunches. Look for clean, fresh, bright green leaves. Fresh parsley is also sold mixed with soup greens. Dried parsley flakes are available alone or in dried soup and other mixes.

Storage—Wash, shake water from leaves, and store in a tightly closed container in the refrigerator.
- [ ] Refrigerator shelf: 3 to 8 days

- [ ] Refrigerator frozen-food compartment: 2 to 3 months
- [ ] Freezer: 1 year

Nutritive Food Values—When eaten in quantity it is a good source of vitamins A and C.
- [ ] 1 tablespoon chopped = 1 calorie
- [ ] 10 small sprigs = 5 calories

Basic Preparation

- [ ] **To Chop**—Hold the stems of several sprigs together. Pinch the parsley leaves together tightly and cut across with a sharp knife or scissors until stems are reached. Discard stems.
- [ ] **To Dry**—Cut parsley clusters from heavy stems. Plunge parsley leaves into boiling water for 30 seconds. Drain. Spread the leaves on a wire screen or on a piece of heavy-duty foil that has been punched with a fork over the entire surface. Put sheet into a preheated slow oven (300°F.) until leaves are crisp and dry. Leave the door of the oven partially open. Store in an airtight container.
- [ ] **To Fry**—Wash sprigs of parsley and dry well. Fry sprigs in deep hot fat (375° F. on a frying thermometer) for a few seconds, or until they rise to the surface. Drain on absorbent paper and sprinkle with salt. Serve as a garnish.
- [ ] **To Freeze**—Choose young crisp parsley. Wash in several changes of water. Trim tough stems. Put parsley leaves or chopped parsley into freezer containers allowing ½-inch headspace. Pack parsley in small portions, enough for one preparation. Frozen parsley can only be used for cooking.

CARROT AND PARSLEY SOUP
- 2 leeks, washed and sliced
- 4 carrots, scraped and sliced
- 2 cups chicken bouillon
- ⅓ cup chopped parsley
- Salt and pepper

Combine leeks, carrots, and bouillon in a saucepan. Bring to boil, lower heat, and simmer until vegetables are tender. Put parsley into a blender. Add some of the vegetables and bouillon. Whirl until well blended. Pour mixture into a saucepan. Whirl remaining soup and pour into saucepan. Add salt and pepper to taste. If soup is too thick, add more bouillon. Serve with croutons. Makes 4 servings.

PARSLEY DUMPLINGS
- 2 cups sifted all-purpose flour
- 2 teaspoons baking powder
- ½ teaspoon salt
- 2 tablespoons butter or margarine
- ⅔ cup finely chopped parsley
- 2 eggs, well beaten
- ⅔ cup tomato juice
- Salted water or bouillon

Sift flour with baking powder and salt. Cut in butter until mixture resembles

cornmeal. Stir in parsley. Beat eggs with tomato juice. Add liquid all at once to dry ingredients. Mix well. Drop by teaspoonfuls into simmering salted water. Cover the pot and simmer for 12 minutes. Remove from liquid with a slotted spoon and serve immediately. Makes about 24 small dumplings.

PARSLEY SALAD
- 3 tomatoes, peeled and diced
- 1 cucumber, peeled and diced
- 3 scallions, sliced
- 1 bunch of parsley, washed, stems removed, and chopped (use Italian parsley if possible)
- ¼ cup fresh lemon juice
- ½ cup olive oil
- Salt and pepper
- ¼ cup chopped pitted black olives

Mix tomatoes with cucumber, scallions, and parsley. Chill until ready to serve. Beat lemon juice with olive oil. Add salt and pepper to taste. Pour dressing over salad and toss lightly. Serve sprinkled with chopped olives. Makes 4 servings.

PARSLEY-CHEESE TOASTS
- 1 loaf unsliced white, rye, or whole-wheat bread
- ½ cup softened butter or margarine
- 1 tablespoon parsley flakes
- ⅛ teaspoon garlic powder
- 13 thin slices of American cheese (about)

Cut bread into ¾-inch slices to within ¼ inch of the bottom of loaf. Leave a solid crust to hold the slices intact. Blend together butter, parsley flakes, and garlic powder. Spread on both sides of each slice of bread and insert a thin slice of cheese between each two. Spread top crust and sides with remaining butter. Put on a buttered cookie sheet. Bake in preheated moderate oven (350°F.) for 15 minutes, or until cheese has melted and bread is brown and crusty. Makes 6 to 8 servings.

PARSLEY EGG AND HAM ROLL
- 2 tablespoons butter or margarine
- 6 large eggs, beaten
- ⅓ cup milk
- 1 tablespoon parsley flakes
- ¼ teaspoon salt
- ⅛ teaspoon pepper
- 12 large slices of baked or boiled ham

Melt 1 tablespoon butter in 9- or 10-inch skillet. Combine eggs, milk, parsley flakes, salt, and pepper. Pour into buttered skillet. Stir and cook over low heat until eggs are set. Spread on large slices of boiled or baked ham. Roll up as for a jelly roll. Heat ham rolls in remaining butter only until ham is hot. Serve for breakfast, brunch, or supper. Makes 6 servings.

FRIED PARSLEY
Wash parsley. Dry extremely well on paper towel. Make sure not a drop of water remains on parsley or it will make

the fat spatter. Drop parsley by clusters into fat or oil heated to 375°F. on frying thermometer. Fry only until parsley comes to surface and has become crisp. This takes 10 to 15 seconds. Do not over-fry or color will change. Drain on absorbent paper. Serve immediately.

PARSLEY SAUCE
- ¾ cup olive or cooking oil
- 3 tablespoons plus 1 teaspoon vinegar
- Salt and pepper to taste
- 2 tablespoons finely chopped onion
- ¼ teaspoon finely minced garlic
- ¼ cup freshly chopped parsley
- ¼ teaspoon ground oregano

Combine oil, vinegar, and salt and pepper in a small saucepan. Blend well. Heat thoroughly, but do not boil. Remove sauce from heat. Cool almost to lukewarm and add remaining ingredients. Serve immediately with fish. Makes about 1¼ cups.

ITALIAN PARSLEY SAUCE
- 2 cups finely chopped fresh parsley
- 3 garlic cloves, minced
- ¼ cup chopped anchovies (1 small can) and oil
- ¼ cup finely chopped sweet basil
- Black pepper to taste
- 2 tablespoons wine vinegar
- 3 tablespoons olive oil
- ¼ cup pimientos, chopped fine
- 3 tablespoons drained capers, chopped

Mix all thoroughly; allow to marinate for at least 3 hours. The sauce will keep in refrigerator for at least 2 weeks. Serve as edible garnish with fish, steak, boiled meats, cold meats, or even as a spread for sandwiches or snack crackers. Makes about 1⅓ cups.
Note: Increase ingredients for a reserve supply.

SALSA VERDE
Combine ½ cup each of salad oil and cider vinegar. Add 1 cup chopped parsley and 3 tablespoons drained capers. Season with salt and pepper to taste. Beat well and serve with cold meats and fish. Makes 1⅔ cups.

PARSLEY CHIVE BUTTER
Add ¼ cup each of finely chopped parsley and chives and 1 teaspoon brandy to ¾ cup softened butter. Chill and then roll mixture into small balls. Serve on steak or lamb chops. Makes 12 servings.

PARSLEY CHEESE BALLS
Blend 8 ounces cream cheese with ¼ teaspoon salt and ½ teaspoon paprika. Roll mixture into small balls using hands or butter paddles. Roll cheese balls in finely minced parsley. Chill, and serve on watercress as a salad. Makes 4 servings.

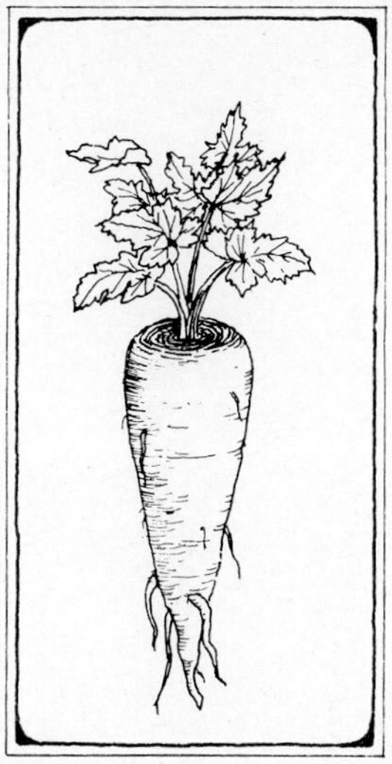

PARSNIP—The edible underground root of a biennial plant, *Pastinaca sativa,* of the carrot family. The parsnip is harder to harvest than some of the other large root vegetables because its root is entirely underneath the ground. The sweet flavor of the parsnip develops only after the first frost, as cold weather changes the starch to sugar. The roots can easily stay in the ground all winter. Parsnips were considered by the early New England colonists to be poisonous until after they were frozen.

Parsnips can be served in many ways. When properly cooked, they make a welcome change from the usual winter vegetables. They also make a good home-brewed wine, often flavored with ginger, especially popular in England.

Availability—Available fresh all year round, with peak crop during winter and spring months.

Also sold mixed with other greens in soup greens.

Purchasing Guide—Look for well-shaped firm roots of small to medium size. Woody cores are likely to be found in the very large roots. Soft shriveled roots are usually pithy or fibrous.

Storage—Refrigerate parsnips.
- ☐ Refrigerator shelf or vegetable compartment, raw: 1 to 4 weeks
- ☐ Refrigerator shelf, cooked: 1 to 2 days
- ☐ Refrigerator frozen-food compartment, prepared for freezing: 2 to 3 weeks
- ☐ Freezer, prepared for freezing: 1 year

Nutritive Food Values—Contain some iron and vitamin C.
- ☐ 3½ ounces, cooked and drained = 66 calories

Basic Preparation—Scrub, scrape, or pare. Leave whole or cut into lengthwise strips, slices, or cubes.

☐ **To Cook**—Cook in ½ to 1 inch of boiling salted water until tender, whole parsnips for 25 to 30 minutes, slices or cubes for 10 to 15 minutes. A little sugar added to cooking water improves the flavor. Drain; add melted butter or margarine.

☐ **To Bake**—Bake in covered casserole in preheated moderate oven (350°F.) for 30 to 40 minutes. Mash, and serve spiced with a dash of grated orange rind.

☐ **To Freeze**—Use young tender parsnips. Cut off tops, wash, and pare. Cut into cubes or slices. Blanch in boiling water: cubes for 1 minute; slices for 2 minutes. Chill in ice water for 5 minutes. Pack into containers allowing ½-inch headspace. Seal.

PARSNIP STEW
- 3 cups diced parsnips
- 1½ cups sliced potatoes
- ½ cup diced salt pork
- 4 cups warm milk
- 2 tablespoons all-purpose flour
- Salt and pepper

Cook parsnips and potatoes in water to cover until tender. Brown salt pork and add with its fat and the milk to undrained vegetable mixture. Bring to boil and thicken with flour mixed to a paste with small amount of cold water. Add salt and pepper to taste. Serve with toasted crackers. Makes 6 servings.

PARTRIDGE—A game bird of the Old World. The two principal species are the Gray, frequenting moors and open country and especially favoring cultivated land, and the Red-legged, or French, partridge. The Hungarian and Bohemian partridges, considered particularly suitable for propagation in the United States, are varieties of the Gray species, hardier and somewhat larger than the formerly better-known English variety.

In different parts of the United States, the title of partridge is given to various American birds. Although in strict parlance it is not applicable to any indigenous to the western hemisphere, good general usage now applies the name American partridge to the native Ruffed Grouse. In the south it is more generally applied to the Bobwhite.

The delicious plump little partridge has been hunted since the Middle Ages; one of the famous English Christmas carols "The Twelve Days of Christmas" stresses the partridge in a pear tree, showing how highly both were thought of.

Availability and Purchasing Guide—The average partridge weighs twelve to fourteen ounces, and one partridge makes one serving. Frozen fresh partridges are available in specialty food stores, as are

canned whole and canned smoked partridges.

Caloric Value
☐ 3½ ounces, raw = 168 calories

Basic Preparation—After killing, a young bird should be hung in a cool airy place for no longer than 4 days; an older one may be hung for 1 week, depending on one's taste for a high flavor. Young birds should be roasted or broiled, older birds braised or stewed and preferably tenderized by marinading before cooking. Depending on their age and plumpness, partridges may be barded before cooking, that is, wrapped in salt pork or bacon slices or coated with lard. This gives needed additional fat to their lean meat in order to keep it juicy.

☐ **To Cook**—A simple way to serve young partridges is to roast them. Season the birds with salt and pepper and roast them in preheated moderate oven (325° F.) for 1 to 1½ hours, or until partridge is tender. Serve immediately.

☐ **To Freeze**—Eviscerate partridges carefully to prevent tainting of meat from undigested food in the intestines. Since a partridge is generally roasted whole, it is frozen whole. Tie the legs and wings closely to the body. Do not stuff the birds until they are ready to be cooked. Wrap birds in moisture-proof wrapping, excluding all air, and seal tightly. Label. Freeze until firm. Storage life in a freezer is 1 year.

PARTRIDGES WITH CABBAGE AND JUNIPER BERRIES
1 medium-size green cabbage
Bacon fat
6 partridges, dressed and trussed
½ pound sliced bacon
6 carrots, scraped and sliced
6 smoked sausages
Salt and pepper to taste
6 juniper berries
2 garlic cloves, minced
2 teaspoons sugar
½ teaspoon ground nutmeg
1 teaspoon grated lemon rind

Separate cabbage into leaves and parboil for 5 or 6 minutes. Drain cabbage and cut into shreds, removing all stalks. Put half of cabbage in a roasting pan with cover. Heat bacon fat and brown partridges on all sides. Put partridges on top of cabbage. Add bacon, carrots, and sausages and sprinkle with salt and pepper. Add juniper berries, garlic, sugar, nutmeg, and lemon rind. Cover with remaining cabbage. Add enough bouillon to come halfway up the cabbage, and cover. Bake in preheated slow oven (200°F.) for about 4 hours. Makes 6 servings.

PARTRIDGES IN MARINADE
4 partridges, dressed and quartered
¼ cup cooking oil
Salt and pepper to taste
1 cup white wine
1 cup cider vinegar

2 tablespoons each of chopped fresh thyme and parsley
2 teaspoons each of chopped fresh basil and marjoram
2 garlic cloves, chopped

Brown partridges on all sides in hot oil. Sprinkle with salt and pepper. Add remaining ingredients. Bring to boil, lower heat, and simmer until partridges are tender. Serve hot or cold. Makes 4 servings.

PASSION FRUIT—The edible fruit of the passiflora or passion flower, a vine with solitary spectacular flowers which is a native of tropical Brazil. The passion flower is so named because it supposedly symbolizes the nails, wounds, and crown of thorns of Christ. The fruit is also known as granadilla. It has a sweet-acid flavor, and it is used as a table fruit, as well as for making sherbets, candy, and in very refreshing beverages.

The purple passion fruit, about three inches in length, with many seeds, is found wild in North and South America and Australia. It requires a tropical, subtropical, or warm temperate climate. In Australia, it is a crop of great economic importance. In the United States it is cultivated in Florida and other southern states; but only in California is it cultivated commercially.

Other species of passion fruit are the giant granadilla, which has greenish-yellow fruit that reach ten inches in length, and the sweet granadilla.

Availability—A highly perishable fruit, it is found only in specialty fruit markets in the fall. Some canned passion-fruit nectar is available in specialty food stores.

Caloric Value
☐ Raw, 3½ ounces, pulp and seeds = 90 calories

PASSION-FRUIT CHIFFON PIE
Crust:
2 cups finely rolled graham-cracker crumbs
½ cup sugar
½ cup melted butter or margarine
Filling:
1 envelope unflavored gelatin
Cold water
3 egg yolks, well beaten
Juice of 1 lemon
1 cup puréed passion fruit
3 egg whites
6 tablespoons sugar
Whipped cream, sweetened and flavored with vanilla extract to taste

Mix crumbs with sugar and butter. Press mixture firmly against the bottom and sides of 8-inch pie pan. Chill until ready to fill. Sprinkle gelatin into ¼ cup cold water. Let stand for 5 minutes. Beat egg yolks with ⅓ cup water and the lemon juice. Cook over low heat, stirring constantly, until smooth and thickened. Stir in gelatin and passion fruit. Chill mixture until it begins to thicken. Beat egg whites until stiff. Gradually beat in sugar, 1 tablespoon at a time, until stiff and glossy. Fold egg whites into fruit mixture. Pour mixture into crumb crust and chill until firm. Top with sweetened whipped cream. Makes 6 to 8 servings.

PASTA—The Italian word for "paste," which in culinary usage describes an alimentary paste made from semolina and water. Semolina is the purified middlings of hard wheat, the best being durum, or macaroni, wheat, grown in this country in the western north-central states, chiefly Minnesota. Durum wheat is heavy with gluten, the principal protein component of wheat and other grains.

In the manufacture of pasta, the semolina is moistened with boiling water, then worked to produce a smooth tough dough. This dough is placed in a cylinder and forced through a perforated plate called a "trafila"; then it is dried. The form of the trafila determines the nature of the pasta product. When the trafila has small holes, each with a steel pin in it, macaroni and similar hollow tubular pastas are produced. A bent steel pin turns out elbow macaroni. With smaller holes and no steel pins, the result is spaghetti. For the flat ribbonlike pastas, the trafila is perforated with slits. The short-size pastas and the small fancy shapes are sliced off by rotary knives as the pasta emerges from the trafila. Shells are made by forcing the pasta through a die.

In Italy, the country with which pasta and pasta dishes is most closely associated, there are more than 100 varieties, some large to be stuffed, like lasagna, others in small decorative shapes: stars, hearts, animals, and letters, for example. The Italian names for these varieties are wonderfully descriptive. Among them can be found *amorini,* little cupids, *capelletti d'angelo,* angels' hair, *cappelli di prete,* priests' hats, *cappelli pagliaccio,* clowns' hats, *conchigliette,* little shells, *ditalini,* little thimbles, *farfalloni,* big butterflies, *fusilli,* spindles, *lancette,* little spears, *linguine,* little tongues, *lingue di passero,* sparrows' tongues, *lumache, lumachine,* and *lumacone* or snails, little snails, and big snails, *mostaccioli,* little mugs, *occhi di lupo,* wolf's eyes, *ondulati,* wavy ones, *ricciolina,* little curls, *rigatoni,* little fluted ones, *stelline,* little stars, *stivaletti,* little boots, *vermicelli,* little worms, and *ziti,* bridegrooms.

There are also colored pastas. Spinach and beet juice are used to produce green and red pastas, eggs to make bright yellow pastas.

Availability—Pasta is available packaged in a wide variety of sizes and shapes. In Italian food stores it is occasionally available in bulk, and also packaged in a more complete selection of types. Some pastas, particularly macaroni and spaghetti, are available canned and frozen in combination with other foods.

Storage—Store in a cool dry place.
- ☐ Kitchen shelf: 3 to 6 months
- ☐ Refrigerator shelf, cooked and covered: 4 to 5 days
- ☐ Refrigerator frozen-food compartment, prepared for freezing: 3 to 4 weeks
- ☐ Freezer, prepared for freezing: 1 year

Nutritive Food Values—Enriched pastas contain some protein, thiamine, riboflavin, and niacin, and appreciable amounts of calcium, phosphorus, and potassium.
- ☐ Pasta, 3½ ounces, cooked *al dente* = 148 calories
- ☐ Pasta, 3½ ounces, cooked until tender = 111 calories

Basic Preparation—Pasta should be cooked *al dente:* to the toothsome stage when it is tender yet still resilient to the bite. To cook pasta properly, it is absolutely essential to have a very big pot with rapidly boiling salted water. Unless the pasta cooks in sufficient water, it cannot expand properly and shed its excess starch. Spaghetti, one of the most popular kinds of pasta, also presents the problem of strands sticking together. The addition of a little olive oil to the boiling water helps keep them apart, but this is not necessary when the pasta is stirred properly.

Another equally important step is to have the pasta reach the table hot, and piping hot at that, the hotter the better. The pasta must be cooked in violently boiling water, drained quickly, poured immediately onto a hot serving dish, served with a sauce that is hot, and preferably on really hot dinner plates. If these rules are observed, making good pasta dishes should present no problem.

☐ **To Cook One Pound of Pasta**—1. Use kettle large enough to hold 6 quarts of water (½ pound of pasta should be cooked in 3 quarts of water). Add 2 tablespoons salt to 6 quarts water (1 tablespoon salt to 3 quarts water).

2. Bring water to a full, rolling boil. Gradually add pasta, stirring with a long-handle, two-prong kitchen fork. The water should keep on boiling hard.

3. As the pasta begins to soften, fold it over and over in the water so that it won't stick together. Keep on stirring it frequently during the whole cooking process. Occasionally lift out a strand and taste for doneness. Different pastas have different cooking times. Thus tasting is essential to get the pasta right for one's own taste.

Pasta that is to be cooked further in a casserole should not be more than three-quarters done, or the end results will be mushy.

4. When the pasta is done, drain it immediately into a large strainer or colander. Return to pot and add seasonings. Stir to coat all strands. Serve immediately on heated platter and heated plates.

PASTEURIZE—The process of heating milk or other liquids to a certain temperature to kill harmful bacteria. Pasteurization kills all pathogenic bacteria and most of the nonpathogenic bacteria so that the milk is safe for human consumption. Pasteurization does not change the food value of milk significantly. The sale of nonpasteurized milk is illegal in the United States. The benefits of pasteurization in preventing undulant fever transmitted by raw milk are so obvious that most civilized nations of the world are following suit in making it a law that milk must be pasteurized.

Although pasteurization is most commonly associated with milk, the process was actually discovered for beer and wine. Louis Pasteur (1822-1895), the famous French scientist, experimented for years, starting in 1854, to discover the reasons for the spoilage of beer and wine and developed the process given his name. He published his final and most complete paper on fermentation in 1876. His work saved the wine and beer industries of France, and was later applied to milk.

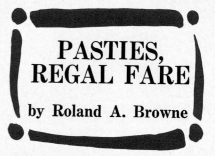

PASTIES, REGAL FARE
by Roland A. Browne

The pasty, a type of meat pie or turnover peculiar to the British Isles, is as much a part of my heritage as the English language. What chowder is to the Down-Easter, and haggis to the Scot, pasties are to the Cornish and Devon folk from whom my mother is descended. They occupy a unique place in my personal hierarchy of gustatory delights.

Pasties (the word rhymes with fast rather than with taste) are a dish of great antiquity, as integral with the English tradition as Magna Charta, the longbow, and Robin Hood. In fact, you will find references to "pastes of venysoun" in the Robin Hood ballads, and I am reasonably sure that I have run across mention of pasties in Chaucer and Shakespeare. The Cornish version of the pasty, such as my grandmother and mother made, and which I still construct, probably differs but little from those that nourished Drake's crew of Devonshiremen and so fortified them that they defeated the invincible Armada of Spain, a demonstrable fact unaccountably omitted from practically all history books.

To construct pasties (I use the verb "construct" deliberately, for they have definite architectural elements), you must assemble the necessary building materials: potatoes, onions, turnips, beef, pork, and piecrust dough. The dough should be of a sort that will make a reasonably flaky crust, not excessively rich, and moist enough to handle easily. A standard mix of about three parts flour to one of shortening, plus salt and ice water, will be fine.

Take a chunk of pastry and roll it out on a lightly floured dish towel until it makes an oval about the size of a dinner plate and about one eighth of an inch thick. If it's too thin, you'll break it for sure. If you develop any holes, patch them by wetting the broken spot with water and pressing on a moistened piece large enough to make the break watertight.

We have now to make the floor or foundation layer of the pasty. This consists of about half an inch of thinly sliced raw potatoes. This should almost cover one half of the oval of dough, leaving a clear edge of pastry about an inch wide for later use in sealing, and should not intrude on the remaining half, which will later be folded over the top as a cover. Salt the potatoes lightly. Incidentally, Maine potatoes will cook up better than Idahoes in a pasty, and will not be so granular.

Next should come a light garnish of thinly sliced onions as a sort of carpet upon which to establish a solid stratum of lean beef. For this you can use round steak cut into half-inch cubes or you can cut up a sirloin tip roast. I suppose you could use a cheaper cut of beef, but I've never had the heart to try. A respectable pasty has a lot of beef in it, a double handful or more. When this is in place, apply salt and pepper judiciously and add the next layer, which consists of enough thin slices of raw turnips (either white or yellow) to cover the layer of beef. Slice them, as well as the potatoes, as thinly as possible and put on a couple of layers, like shingles. Now should come a layer of fresh pork, reasonably lean and cubed like the beef. You can either use slices from a fresh ham or cut up a butt pork roast. Use about half as much pork as you did beef, and only a little of it can be fat. More salt and pepper are now in order. Finish off your edifice with a good layer of sliced onions. Dot the pile here and there with a slice of butter and, by way of good luck, sprinkle it lightly with marjoram or thyme.

Now, moisten the outer inch of pastry all around with a finger dipped into warm water. Wait a minute and repeat the operation. A pasty has to stick together at the seams, or it is of no account. Using the cloth to help you, ease the uncovered half of the pastry over the top of the pile and match its edges with the bottom half. You may have to roll it out a little larger. Press all around the outside with the edge of your thumb, making the indentations overlap one another to produce a tight seal. Moisten the top of the resulting seam and turn it back on itself far enough to repeat the sealing operation.

Now comes the tricky part. Gently tilt the side of the cloth next to the seam so as to rotate partly the whole pasty and bring the seam part way up over the top, instead of flat on the side.

Prick half a dozen vent holes in the crust with a kitchen fork to let steam out but keep all the juices within. Transfer the pasty gingerly to a large baking dish (I like a cookie sheet), and start making another pasty. You should allow one pasty per adult, half a pasty per child, or else make a junior-size model for the youngsters.

When your pasties are all on the pan ready to bake, slide them into a preheated moderate oven (350°F.) for the first half hour to set the crust; after which you should lower the heat to slow (300°F.), so that the pasties can bake slowly. I like to allow from 2 to 2½ hours of baking, half near the bottom and half near the top of the oven.

A pasty properly cooked is neither dry nor runny inside. Instead, the filling is uniformly moist and succulent. The flavor of the onion, delicately titillated with thyme, is carried down by the melted butter into the pork, and the pork juice impregnates and ennobles the turnips, which in turn lend a strange, poetic bouquet (half sweet, half bitter, like the memory of an old love) to the hearty, jovial whang of the beef, and the essences of all these separate ingredients finally infiltrate the potatoes, where they are combined and entrapped for the delectation of honest folk.

There is a definite ritual to the eating of pasties. I can still see the family assembled at the long dining table, my older brothers for once promptly and unbidden in their seats; my mother flushed but triumphant, with a little flour on one cheek; myself, not more than five, enveloped to the chin in a damask napkin and suitably elevated on two volumes of the *Encyclopaedia Britannica;* and my father, his gentle, scholarly countenance alight, poising a carving knife over a Blue Willow platter of gargantuan pasties, from which a scented steam arose and misted his glasses. Or were they tears of delight?

No matter. As each pasty was cut into two, my father placed one half on the recipient's plate and with a pencil wrote the person's initials on the crust of the other half for later reference. My father was a methodical man who liked to avoid family arguments.

Served smoking hot, eating them involved considerable blowing on each bite, unless you adhered to the school of thought (to which I belong) that believed in tipping up your half of pasty and pouring within a quantity of rich, thick cream to cool it. There are purists who regard this as heresy, but I suspect most of them are Scots and Welshmen.

The reason for initialing the other half of each pasty became apparent as the motion of jaws slowed down and a desultory conversation began to flicker up around the heretofore silent board. Half a pasty at one time is enough for anybody; the other half, properly identified, was set aside to be eaten later when cold, along with a tall glass of milk.

I have eaten pasties off and on since I got my first teeth and to this day I can't decide whether they taste better hot or cold.

PASTILLE—The French name for a confection which we call a "drop." Pastilles are made from sugar, water, and flavoring, and sometimes they contain medicinal ingredients, as in cough drops.

Pastilles are an old form of candy. Often they were chewed to sweeten the breath. They were made from dissolved sugar and water poured hot, drop by drop, onto a cold marble slab.

PASTRAMI—A preserved meat of eastern European origin, made from plate, brisket, or round of beef dry-cured with salt and saltpeter. The beef is then rinsed and rubbed with a paste of garlic powder, ground cuminseed, red pepper, cinnamon, cloves, and allspice, smoked and cooked. In the larger cities packaged pastrami, in slices or bigger pieces, is available in food stores. Sliced pastrami is available in delicatessens.

PASTRY—The word has two culinary meanings. First it refers to a dough made of flour, shortening, salt, and water or other liquid. Pastry doughs, shorter and flakier than bread doughs, are used for pies, tarts, small sweet foods served as desserts, and nonsweet foods served as appetizers and snacks. Commercial mixes for standard pastry dough are available.

In its second meaning, the word pastry describes a baked food. It may be one which is made with a pastry dough; or one which has the characteristic tenderness and flakiness of food made with a pastry dough, such as Danish pastry; or one which is served as pastries are, cream puffs, for example.

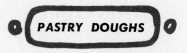

PASTRY DOUGHS

TWO-CRUST PIES
1. Prepare proper amount of Standard Pastry for pan size to be used. (See Chart, page 1303.) Divide pastry about in halves. Round up on lightly floured board or other surface.
2. Cover a rolling pin with stockinet and rub flour into it. Flatten one pastry half with hand, and roll out not quite ⅛ inch thick. Roll lightly, being careful not to add extra flour as it makes pastry tough. Keep rounding the edge of pastry. If pastry breaks, pinch broken edges together immediately. Roll pastry about 1 inch larger all around than inverted pie pan, keeping it circular as you roll.
3. Fold in half and carefully transfer to pie pan. Unfold pastry and ease loosely into pan, being careful not to stretch it. (Stretching causes pastry to shrink during baking.)

4. Prepare desired filling and put in pastry-lined pan. Trim overhanging edges with scissors.

5. Roll second half of pastry for top crust, making it large enough to extend 1 inch beyond edge of pie pan. Measure by holding pie pan over rolled round of pastry.

6. Fold pastry in quarters. Make several slits near center to allow steam to escape or top crust will puff up. Moisten edge of bottom crust with water. Put folded pastry evenly on filling and unfold. Trim with scissors ½ inch from edge of pan.

7. Fold edge of top crust under edge of lower crust on rim. Seal well by pressing with fingertips. Build up a high standing rim. Make a fluted edge by firmly placing the right index finger on the inside of the rim, left thumb and index finger on outside of pastry at that point. Pinch. Repeat all around edge. Pinch each point firmly to sharpen.

8. Bake as directed in individual recipe.

LATTICE PIES

1. Prepare proper amount of Standard Pastry for pan size to be used. (See Chart, below.) Follow Steps 1 through 3 for Two-Crust Pies. Trim, leaving 1 inch overhanging edge. Fill with desired filling.

2. Roll remaining pastry and cut into ½-inch strips. (Use a pastry wheel for a scalloped edge.)

3. Moisten edge of bottom pastry with water. Lay half of pastry strips across filling 1 inch apart. Weave first cross strip through center. Add another cross strip, first folding back every other strip going the other way. Continue weaving until lattice is complete. Fold lower pastry over strips and press firmly around edge to seal.

4. Bake as directed in individual recipe.

UNBAKED PIE SHELLS

Prepare amount of Standard Pastry for pan to be used. (See Chart, below.) Follow Steps 2 and 3 for Two-Crust Pies (page 1302). Trim, ½ inch from edge of pan. Fold pastry under, even with pan. Build up a high standing rim. Make a fluted edge by firmly placing the right index finger on outside of pastry at that point. Pinch. Repeat all around edge. Pinch each point firmly to sharpen. Fill and bake as directed in individual recipe.

BAKED PIE SHELLS

Follow directions for making Unbaked Pie Shells, above. With fork, prick shell close and deep on bottom and sides. Bake in preheated very hot oven (450°F.) for 12 to 15 minutes, or until golden-brown. Fill and complete pie as directed in individual recipe.

UNBAKED PIE TOP
(For meat pies or deep-dish pies)

Prepare proper amount of Standard Pastry for pan size to be used. (See Chart, at left.) Roll pastry about 1 inch larger around than baking pan or casserole. Make several slits in crust for steam to escape during baking. Put crust on filling, fold edge over, and flute just inside edge of pan. Bake as directed in individual recipe.

BAKED TART SHELLS

Prepare Standard Pastry. (See Chart, at left.) Divide pastry into 6 or more pieces, depending on size of tart pans. Roll each piece into a round and fit into individual pans. Trim edges. Prick with fork to prevent puffing during baking. Put pans on baking sheet and bake in preheated very hot oven (450°F.) about 10 minutes. Cool, and remove from pans.

Note: If tart pans are not available, fit pastry rounds over backs of muffin cups or custard cups, making pleats so pastry will fit closely. Prick with fork and bake as directed.

BOILING-WATER PASTRY
For one 2-crust, 8-inch or 9-inch pie or two shells:

    ⅔ cup hydrogenated shortening or lard
    ⅓ cup boiling water
    2 cups sifted all-purpose flour
    1 teaspoon salt

Put shortening in bowl and gradually add water, creaming with fork until well mixed. Add flour and salt, mixing thoroughly with fork. Follow directions for Two-Crust Pies, page 1302, for rolling, cutting, etc.

OIL PASTRY
For one 2-crust, 8-inch or 9-inch pie or two shells:

    2 cups sifted all-purpose flour
    1 teaspoon salt
    ½ cup vegetable oil
    3 tablespoons cold water

Mix flour and salt. Add oil and mix with fork or pastry blender until well blended and mixture resembles fine crumbs. Sprinkle with the water, and mix in with fork. Gather pastry together so that it cleans bowl. If too dry to form a ball, work in 1 to 2 tablespoons more oil. Press firmly into a ball. Divide dough almost in half. Using larger half for the bottom crust, put pastry between two long strips of wax paper crossed in the center, forming a 12-inch square. Wipe table with damp cloth to keep paper from slipping. Roll pastry in a circle to edges of square. Peel off top paper and put pastry in pan, paper-side up. Peel off paper and fit pastry loosely into pan. Follow Steps 4 through 8 under Two-Crust Pies (at left), for filling, etc.

CHART OF INGREDIENTS FOR STANDARD PASTRY

CRUST SIZE	SIFTED ALL-PURPOSE FLOUR*	SALT	LARD OR HYDROGENATED SHORTENING	COLD WATER
8- or 9-inch shell or 8- or 9-inch round or square top for deep-dish or meat pie	1 cup	½ teaspoon	⅓ cup plus 1 tablespoon	2 tablespoons
8- or 9-inch 2-crust pie or 8-, 9-, 10-, or 11-inch lattice pie or 10- or 11-inch shell or 13- x 9-inch top for deep-dish or meat pie or six to eight 4½- x 1¼-inch tart shells or eight to ten 3½- x 1-inch tart shells	2 cups	1 teaspoon	⅔ cup plus 2 tablespoons	¼ cup
10- or 11-inch 2-crust pie	3 cups	1½ teaspoons	1 cup plus 3 tablespoons	6 tablespoons

When using instant-type flour, follow recipe of individual manufacturer

TO MAKE PASTRY: Mix flour and salt; cut in lard. Mix in water.

For one 1-crust unbaked shell:

Prepare Oil Pastry, page 1303, using the following proportions: 1½ cups sifted all-purpose flour, ½ teaspoon salt, ⅓ cup vegetable oil, and 2 tablespoons cold water. Roll and fit into pan as in Oil Pastry recipe. Trim pastry ½ inch from edge of pan. Fold pastry under, even with pan. Follow directions for Unbaked Pie Shells, page 1303, for fluting edge. Fill and bake as directed in individual recipe.

For one 1-crust baked shell:

Prepare Oil Pastry, page 1303, using the following proportions: 1½ cups sifted all-purpose flour, ½ teaspoon salt, ⅓ cup vegetable oil, and 2 tablespoons cold water. Roll and fit into pan as in Oil Pastry recipe. Trim pastry ½ inch from edge of pan. Fold pastry under, even with pan. Follow directions for Unbaked Pie Shells, page 1303, for fluting edge. With fork, prick shell close and deep on bottom and sides. Bake in preheated very hot oven (450°F.) for 12 to 15 minutes or until golden-brown.

SPECIAL PASTRY FOR MEAT PIES
For one 8-inch round or square baking dish:

 2 cups sifted all-purpose flour
 1 teaspoon salt
 ⅔ cup lard
 1 egg, separated
 3 tablespoons water

Mix flour and salt. Cut in lard until pieces are the size of peas. Mix egg yolk and water and stir into first mixture. With hands, press together into a firm ball. Smooth edges and roll on lightly floured board to ½-inch thickness. Cut to fit top of hot meat mixture in baking dish. Fold over once and cut several slits to allow for escape of steam. Put on top of meat mixture and open to fit top of dish. Brush with slightly beaten egg white. Bake in preheated hot oven (425°F.) for 10 minutes. Reduce heat to moderate (350°F.) and bake for 20 to 25 minutes longer.

CHOCOLATE PASTRY
Good for cream pies such as banana or chocolate, or with chiffon pies.

For one 8- or 9-inch pie shell:

 1½ cups sifted all-purpose flour
 ½ teaspoon salt
 2 tablespoons cocoa
 ½ cup hydrogenated shortening
 3 tablespoons water

Mix dry ingredients thoroughly. Cut in shortening until pieces are the size of peas. Gradually add water, mixing until pastry clears the bowl. With hands, press together into a firm ball. Smooth edges. Put pastry between two long strips of wax paper crossed in the center, form-ing a 12-inch square. Wipe table with damp cloth to keep paper from slipping. Roll pastry in a circle to edges of square. Peel off top paper and put crust in pan, paper-side up. Peel off paper and fit pastry loosely into pan. Trim pastry ½ inch from edge of pan. Fold pastry under, even with pan. Flute edges. With fork, prick shell on bottom and sides. Bake in preheated very hot oven (450°F.) for 10 to 12 minutes. Cool, and complete pie as in individual recipe.

CREAM-CHEESE PASTRY
Especially good for open fruit pies such as cherry, peach, blueberry, or boysen-berry, or for citrus-flavored chiffon pies.

For one 2-crust 8- or 9-inch pie or two shells:

 2 cups sifted all-purpose flour
 ½ teaspoon salt
 ⅔ cup butter, margarine, or hydrogenated shortening
 12 ounces cream cheese

Mix flour and salt. Cut in butter and cream cheese. With hands, press together into a firm ball. Smooth edges. If pastry seems very soft, chill for 30 minutes, or until firm enough to roll.

NONSWEET FRENCH PASTRY
(Pâte Brisée)
For one 2-crust 8- or 9-inch pie, 24 tarts, or 36 turnovers:

 2 cups plus 2 tablespoons sifted all-purpose flour
 ¾ teaspoon salt
 1 cup soft butter
 2 egg yolks
 ¼ cup light cream
 2 tablespoons dry white wine

Sift flour and salt into bowl. Cut in but-ter. Add combined egg yolks, cream, and wine; mix with fork until blended and smooth. Knead lightly in bowl until bubbles begin to appear on the surface of dough. Cover and chill for 1 hour. Roll to ⅛-inch thickness on floured board. Fold twice lengthwise, then twice crosswise. Chill for 15 minutes. Roll and fold twice more. Store, wrapped in mois-ture-proof paper, in refrigerator.

SWEET FRENCH PASTRY
(Pâte Brisée Sucrée)
For one 9-inch tart, flan, or 2-crust pie, two 9-inch shells, or 12 medium-size indi-vidual pies or tarts:

 ½ cup sugar
 ¼ teaspoon salt
 ¾ cup butter, at room temperature
 2 egg yolks
 ¼ teaspoon vanilla extract
 2 cups all-purpose flour
 Grated rind of 1 lemon

Put all ingredients in bowl and blend with fingers, kneading until mixture holds together. Press firmly into a ball, smooth-ing edges. If pastry seems very soft, chill 30 minutes, or until firm enough to roll.

PUFF PASTE
Puff paste can be used for a great variety of pastries. Among them are cream horns, which are cone shapes baked on forms and filled with whipped cream; napo-leons; patty shells, both large and small; squares or circles filled with marmalade or jam, folded, sealed, and baked; fancy shapes cut out and baked for individual deep-dish pies; heart shapes baked, with a spoonful of jam put in the center of each and a fluted edge of whipped cream added; or in strips to be put together with jam or marmalade to make sandwiches.

 1 pound (2 cups) sweet butter
 4 cups all-purpose flour
 1 teaspoon salt
 1 tablespoon fresh lemon juice
 1¼ cups cold water (about)

Shape the butter into a brick about 3 x 5 x ¾ inches. Roll butter in 3 tablespoons of the flour, coating all sides. Wrap in wax paper and chill. Put remaining flour in a large bowl. Make a well in the center. Add salt and lemon juice. Grad-ually begin to add water, only enough to make a rather firm, slightly sticky dough.

Knead dough thoroughly on floured board for 20 minutes. Pound it on the table at intervals to achieve the right consistency. It should be very elastic and smooth. Form it into a ball; place on well-floured cloth. With a rolling pin, form the ball of dough into the shape of a four-leaf clover. Roll ends out, leaving the center thick. Well-rolled, the dough will have a thick cushion in the center and four thinner "petals." Put brick of butter in the center of the four-leaf clover. Fold "petals" over dough by stretching them over butter and sealing all the edges so that the butter is com-pletely enclosed. Wrap in waxed paper and chill for 20 minutes.

On a well-floured cloth, gently roll out the block of dough as evenly as possible into a rectangle slightly less than ⅓ inch thick, and about 3 times as long as it is wide. Do not roll over ends lengthwise, but when dough is long enough, roll it lightly across the width, flattening ends to same thickness as the rest of the dough. Fold down into thirds, making three layers, and chill for 20 minutes. Turn folded side toward you, roll out dough, and fold again into thirds. (Rolling, folding, and turning is called a "turn.") It is necessary to make a total of 6 turns, after which the dough is ready for use. The dough should be chilled for about 20 minutes between each turn. Wrap in moisture-proof paper and refrigerate until ready to use. Dough will keep 2 weeks.

Pastry Cook Book

A treasury of pastries
for delicious sweets:
puffs, pies, and tarts,
filled with jams,
custards, whipped cream,
or fresh fruit
and pastries for savory
fillings that make
tempting hors-d'oeuvre,
appetizers, and snacks.

NONSWEET BAKED PASTRIES

CURRIED SHRIMP DIAMONDS

2/3 cup soft butter or margarine
1½ cups sifted all-purpose flour
½ teaspoon salt
1 teaspoon instant minced onion
1 teaspoon water
1 teaspoon Worcestershire
1 cup finely chopped cooked shrimps
1 teaspoon curry powder
1 egg yolk
1 tablespoon milk

Cut butter into flour and salt. Soak onion for a few minutes in combined water and Worcestershire. Add with shrimps and curry powder to first mixture, stirring with fork until blended. Roll out on floured board to ½-inch thickness and cut into 1½-inch diamonds. Put on greased cookie sheet and brush with egg yolk beaten slightly with milk. Bake in preheated moderate oven (375°F.) for about 30 minutes. Serve hot or cold. Makes about 2 dozen.

APPETIZER CREAM PUFFS

Use recipe for Cream Puffs (page 1308). Level off 1 teaspoon dough onto greased cookie sheet. Then, using this amount as a guide for size, drop remaining dough onto cookie sheet. Bake in preheated hot oven (400°F.) for about 20 minutes. Fill with crabmeat, tuna, chicken, or lobster salad; pimiento, Cheddar, or other cheese spread. Makes about 10 dozen.

PIMIENTO PINWHEELS

Roll 2-cups-flour recipe for Standard Pastry (page 1303) into a rectangle 16 x 10 inches. Spread with 1 jar (5 ounces) pimiento-cheese spread. Sprinkle with cayenne. Roll up tightly from end, and cut into ¼-inch slices. Bake on greased cookie sheet in preheated very hot oven (450°F.) for 10 minutes. Makes 32.

Roquefort Pinwheels

Use recipe for Pimiento Pinwheels; for filling, cream 3 ounces each of cream cheese and Roquefort cheese with 1 tablespoon heavy cream. Add a dash of hot pepper sauce.

Deviled-Ham Pinwheels

Use recipe for Pimiento Pinwheels; for filling use 1 can (4 ounces) deviled ham mixed with 1 teaspoon prepared mustard.

ANCHOVY PUFFS

Roll Nonsweet French Pastry (page 1304) to ⅛-inch thickness. Cut into 1½-inch rounds. Put half on greased cookie sheet; put an anchovy in center of each.

Top with remaining rounds. Prick tops; crimp edges with fork. Brush with egg yolk beaten with 1 tablespoon milk. Bake in preheated very hot oven (450°F.) for 10 minutes. Makes 2 to 3 dozen.

Shrimp Puffs

Cut rounds of pastry as for Anchovy Puffs. Substitute canned shrimps for the anchovies. Put ½ teaspoon sandwich spread (mayonnaise-pickle type) or tartare sauce on shrimps. Proceed as directed.

CHEESE HEARTS

¼ cup soft butter or margarine
1 cup biscuit mix
¼ teaspoon each of salt and chili powder
1 cup grated sharp Cheddar cheese
Water
Paprika

Cut butter into biscuit mix; add salt and chili powder. Add cheese and just enough water to hold mixture together. Force through cookie gun onto greased cookie sheets (Y-shape disk forms hearts). Sprinkle with paprika. Bake in preheated hot oven (425°F.) for 10 minutes. Makes about 36.

SALTY PARMESAN CUBES

1 cup sifted all-purpose flour
½ teaspoon salt
Dash of cayenne
⅔ cup grated Parmesan cheese
½ cup soft butter or margarine
1 egg, slightly beaten, or undiluted evaporated milk

Mix first 4 ingredients. Cut in butter. Knead with hands until smooth. Roll out on floured board to ½-inch thickness, and cut into ½-inch cubes. Put on greased cookie sheet and brush with egg. Bake in preheated moderate oven (375°F.) for about 20 minutes. Cool. Makes about 4 dozen.

SPINACH-CHEESE STRIPS

¼ recipe Puff Paste, page 1304
1 pound spinach
2 tablespoons minced onion
1 tablespoon olive oil
½ cup grated Parmesan cheese
6 stuffed olives, sliced

Roll out Puff Paste to about 18 x 6 inches. Cut 1-inch-wide slice from both sides and ends. Put slices on main strip to form border. Wash spinach and drain very well. Tear it coarsely. Sauté onion in olive oil until golden and mix with spinach. Place on pastry strip, between borders, and top with grated Parmesan and olive slices. Bake in preheated very hot oven (450°F.) for 20 minutes, or until pastry is puffed and brown. Cut into strips to serve on plates with forks. Makes 6 servings.

SWISS PETIT PUFFS

½ recipe Cream Puffs (page 1308)
2 cups shredded Swiss cheese
½ cup butter or margarine, softened
3 tablespoons heavy cream
Dash of hot pepper sauce

Drop cream-puff mixture by half-teaspoonfuls onto ungreased cookie sheets. Bake in preheated hot oven (425°F.) for about 20 minutes. Cool. Beat remaining ingredients together until blended. Use as filling for puffs. Makes about 5 dozen.

TINY CHEESE PINWHEELS

¼ cup butter or margarine
⅛ teaspoon cayenne
1 teaspoon salt
½ teaspoon paprika
2 cups sifted all-purpose flour
2 teaspoons baking powder
½ teaspoon cream of tartar
2 teaspoons sugar
¾ cup shortening
¾ cup grated Cheddar cheese
1 tablespoon chopped parsley
⅔ cup light cream

Cream butter with the cayenne, ¼ teaspoon salt, and the paprika in small bowl. Sift together flour, baking powder, cream of tartar, sugar, and remaining salt. Cut in shortening. Add cheese and parsley. Stir in light cream with fork to form a soft dough. Divide dough into halves. Roll each half to form a 14 x 10-inch rectangle ¼ inch thick. Spread each with half of butter mixture and roll as for jelly roll, starting from the 14-inch side. Slice rolls into rounds about ¼ inch thick. Bake on ungreased baking sheet in preheated hot oven (425°F.) for 18 to 20 minutes. Makes about 5 dozen.

CHICKEN APPETIZER PASTRIES

½ cup soft shortening
1½ cups sifted all-purpose flour
¾ teaspoon salt
½ to ¾ teaspoon poultry seasoning
Chicken broth
Chicken Filling
Stuffed-olive slices

Cut shortening into sifted dry ingredients. Mixing with fork, add just enough broth to hold mixture together. Break off small pieces of dough and press into bottom and on sides of 2 dozen 1¾-inch muffin-pan sections. Fill with Chicken Filling and top each with an olive slice. Bake in pre-

heated very hot oven (450°F.) for about 15 minutes. Serve hot. Makes 2 dozen.

Chicken Filling

Cook 1 can (2 ounces) drained chopped mushrooms in 3 tablespoons butter or margarine for 2 or 3 minutes. Blend in 3 tablespoons all-purpose flour, ¼ teaspoon each of celery salt and onion powder, ¼ teaspoon pepper, and ½ teaspoon steak sauce. Stir in ½ cup each of heavy cream and chicken broth. Cook, stirring constantly, until thickened. Add 1 can (5 or 6 ounces) chicken, chopped, and salt to taste. Cool.

HA'PENNY COCKTAIL SNACKS

1 cup all-purpose flour
½ cup butter or margarine
½ pound sharp Cheddar cheese, grated
½ teaspoon salt
½ envelope onion-soup mix

Blend together the flour and butter. Add the remaining ingredients and mix well. Shape into a roll ½ inch in diameter. Wrap in foil and chill. Slice ⅜ inch thick and put on baking sheets. Bake in preheated moderate oven (350°F.) for 8 to 10 minutes. Store in an airtight container. Makes about 3 dozen.

SWEET BAKED PASTRIES

RICH BANBURY TARTS

¼ cup each of dried currants, seedless raisins, and chopped candied pineapple
½ cup chopped pitted dates
⅓ cup chopped nuts
1 cup firmly packed light brown sugar
2 eggs, slightly beaten
2 tablespoons all-purpose flour
¼ teaspoon salt
Grated rind and juice of 1 lemon
Nonsweet French Pastry (page 1304)
1 egg yolk
1 tablespoon milk

Mix well all ingredients except last 3. Roll Nonsweet French Pastry to ⅛-inch thickness and cut into 4-inch squares. Put about 1 tablespoon of filling mixture in the center of each square and fold the corners to meet in center. Put on greased cookie sheet and brush with egg yolk beaten with milk. Bake in preheated very hot oven (450°F.) for 12 to 15 minutes. Makes about 2 dozen.

HUNGARIAN CHEESE PASTRIES

½ cup plus 1 tablespoon soft butter or margarine
1⅔ cups sifted all-purpose flour
⅛ teaspoon salt
1 egg yolk, beaten
Heavy cream (about 1½ tablespoons)
Cheese Filling
Confectioners' sugar
Black-currant or other jelly

To make pastry cut butter into flour and salt. Add egg yolk, mixing with fork. Add just enough cream to hold mixture

together. Chill overnight. Roll about one third of dough to form an 8-inch square a little more than ⅛ inch thick. Put in pan (8 x 8 x 2 inches). Roll slightly more than half of remaining dough to form strips about 1 inch wide. Fit around sides of pan. Pour in Cheese Filling and spread evenly. Roll out remaining dough and cut into ¾-inch strips. Put on top of filling, lattice-fashion. Bake in preheated moderate oven (350°F.) for about 40 minutes. Cool on rack. Just before serving, sift confectioners' sugar over top. Cut into 2-inch squares and garnish each with jelly. Makes 16.

Cheese Filling

Press 1 pound dry cottage cheese through fine sieve. Add ¼ cup sugar, grated rind of ½ lemon, 2 egg yolks, and 2 tablespoons melted butter. Beat 4 egg whites stiff with ¼ teaspoon salt. Fold into mixture.

BILLETS-DOUX

¾ cup soft butter
1½ cups sifted all-purpose flour
¼ teaspoon salt
6 egg yolks
Almond Filling
¼ cup confectioners' sugar
¼ teaspoon ground cinnamon

Cut butter into flour and salt. Add egg yolks and mix well. Chill overnight. Cut dough into 21 pieces and roll each piece thin on floured board, to form a 5- to 6-inch square. Put a heaping tablespoon of filling in center, fold in thirds, and fold ends over to form a square envelope. Bake in preheated moderate oven (350°F.) for about 20 minutes. Cool; sift combined sugar and cinnamon over top. Makes 21.

Almond Filling

Beat 5 egg whites with ⅛ teaspoon salt until almost stiff. Gradually beat in ⅔ cup granulated sugar and continue beating until stiff. Beat in ½ teaspoon ground cinnamon. Fold in ¾ cup almonds, blanched and coarsely ground.

DANISH PASTRIES

¾ cup milk, scalded
Sugar
1½ teaspoons salt
1¾ cups butter or margarine
½ cup water*
2 packages active dry yeast, or 2 cakes compressed yeast
2 eggs
1½ teaspoons grated lemon rind
3½ cups all-purpose flour
2 tablespoons cornstarch
Jelly

Pour milk over ½ cup sugar, the salt, and ¼ cup butter. Mix well and cool to lukewarm. Put water in large bowl. *Use very warm water (105°F. to 115°F.) for dry yeast; use lukewarm (80°F. to 90°F.) for compressed. Sprinkle dry yeast or crumble cakes into water. Stir

until dissolved. Add lukewarm milk mixture. Beat egg yolks and 1 egg white; reserve remaining white. Add yolk mixture and lemon rind to yeast mixture. Add 1 cup flour and mix well. Mix cornstarch and remaining flour. Stir into batter until just mixed. Refrigerate. Spread remaining butter on wax paper to form a 12- x 10-inch rectangle. Chill for 1 hour. Roll chilled dough into a 16- x 12-inch rectangle. Put butter slab on three quarters of dough. Fold uncovered quarter over middle section. Fold over remaining section to enclose butter. Give dough a quarter turn; roll to a 16- x 12-inch rectangle; fold as above. Turn, roll, and fold once more; chill for 1 hour. Repeat procedure of two rollings, foldings, turnings, and chilling two more times. Then refrigerate overnight. Shape half of dough at a time, refrigerating remainder. Roll half of dough to a 12- x 9-inch rectangle. Cut into 3-inch squares. Put ½ teaspoon jelly in the center of each square. Fold to form triangles, then seal edges. Put 2 inches apart on greased baking sheets. Chill for 1 hour. Mix reserved egg white with 1 tablespoon water. Brush pastries with the mixture and sprinkle lightly with sugar. Bake in preheated moderate oven (375°F.) for 15 to 20 minutes. Makes about 2 dozen. **Note:** It is important to work the dough as little as possible when shaping the pastries. Handle quickly to keep dough cold.

CREAM PUFFS

1 cup water
½ cup butter
¼ teaspoon salt
1 cup sifted all-purpose flour
4 large eggs, beaten
Vanilla Cream Filling (page 1309)
Confectioners' sugar

In saucepan heat water, butter, and salt to full rolling boil. Reduce heat and quickly stir in flour, mixing vigorously with wooden spoon until mixture leaves the sides of the pan in a ball. Remove from heat and add eggs in 6 additions, beating after each addition until mixture is very smooth. (An electric mixer at a low speed makes this procedure easier.) Drop dough from metal mixing spoon onto greased cookie sheets, forming mounds 3 inches apart. Bake in preheated hot oven (400°F.) for 40 to 45 minutes. Remove at once to racks and cool away from drafts. Split; fill with Vanilla Cream Filling. Sprinkle with confectioners' sugar, or frost as desired. Store in refrigerator. Makes 12 large or 16 medium puffs. **Note:** Freeze puffs without filling. To recrisp, put in oven for a few minutes.

PETITS PUFFS

Use Cream Puff recipe above. Level off 1¼ teaspoons dough onto greased cookie sheet. Then, using this amount as a guide for size, drop remaining dough onto cookie sheet. Bake in preheated hot oven (400°F.) for about 20 minutes. Fill and frost. Makes 8 dozen.

ÉCLAIRS
Use recipe for Cream Puffs (page 1308), forcing mixture through pastry tube; or shape with spatula into 16 fingers, 4 inches long and 1 inch wide. Bake as for Cream Puffs. Fill with Vanilla Cream Filling (below) and spread with thin chocolate frosting. Makes 16.

VANILLA CREAM FILLING
- 3 cups milk
- ¾ cup sugar
- 6 tablespoons cornstarch
- ½ teaspoon salt
- 3 eggs, beaten
- 1 tablespoon butter
- 2 teaspoons vanilla extract

Scald milk in top part of double boiler over boiling water. Mix sugar, cornstarch, and salt. Stir into milk. Cook, stirring constantly, until thick. Cover; cook for 10 minutes longer. Add small amount of mixture to eggs; return to double boiler; cook for 5 minutes, stirring constantly. Add butter. Put in bowl and sprinkle small amount of sugar over top to prevent skin from forming. Chill; add vanilla.

Chocolate Cream Filling
Use recipe for Vanilla Cream Filling. Melt 3 ounces (3 squares) unsweetened chocolate in milk and beat until smooth. Proceed as directed.

Fluffy Cream Filling
Use either Vanilla or Chocolate Cream Filling recipes, reducing milk to 2½ cups. Just before using, fold ½ cup heavy cream, whipped, into chilled mixture.

ORANGE-PLUM TWISTS
- ¼ cup soft butter
- 2 cups biscuit mix
- 2 tablespoons granulated sugar
- 1 teaspoon grated orange rind
- 1 egg
- ⅓ cup heavy cream
- ½ cup damson-plum preserves
  Confectioners' sugar

Cut butter into biscuit mix. Stir in granulated sugar and rind. Beat egg and cream until blended; with fork, stir into first mixture. Put on floured board and knead a few times. Roll out to form a rectangle 15 x 3 inches. Spread with preserves; fold twice lengthwise to form a rectangle 1 x 15 inches. Cut crosswise into 1-inch strips. Twist each strip twice to form a spiral. Put on foil-covered cookie sheet and bake in preheated very hot oven (450°F.) for 10 to 12 minutes. Sift confectioners' sugar over tops while twists are warm. Serve warm or cold. Makes 15. Can be frozen.

RASPBERRY MAIDS OF HONOUR
- ⅓ cup butter or margarine
- 1 box pastry mix
  Raspberry jam
- ½ box white-cake mix
  Confectioners'-Sugar Frosting
  Candied violets, angelica, colored candies

Cut butter into pastry mix. Add just enough of the liquid indicated on pastry-mix label to hold dough together. Chill if necessary. Roll out to ⅛-inch thickness and cut into 24 rounds with 3½-inch cutter. Fit into 2½-inch muffin-pan sections. Put about 1 teaspoon jam into each. Prepare cake mix, and put a spoonful of cake batter on jam. Bake in preheated moderate oven (350°F.) for 20 to 25 minutes. Cool in pans and remove to racks. Spread tops with Confectioners'-Sugar Frosting. Decorate. Makes 2 dozen.

Confectioners'-Sugar Frosting
Mix 1 cup confectioners' sugar with enough milk or water to make of spreading consistency. Tint with food coloring and flavor with almond or vanilla extract.

SOUR-CREAM TWISTS
- 3½ cups sifted all-purpose flour
- 1 teaspoon salt
- 1 cup soft butter or margarine
- 1 package active dry yeast or 1 cake compressed yeast
- 2 tablespoons lukewarm water*
- 1 cup dairy sour cream
- 1 whole egg
- 2 egg yolks
- 1 teaspoon vanilla extract
- 1 cup sugar

Sift flour and salt into large bowl. Cut in butter. Sprinkle or crumble yeast into water. *Use very warm water (105°F. to 115°F.) for dry yeast; use lukewarm (80°F. to 90°F.) for compressed. Let stand for a few minutes, then stir until dissolved. Add sour cream, whole egg, egg yolks, and vanilla; mix well. Add to flour mixture; stir until blended. Cover and put in refrigerator for 1 hour. Divide dough into thirds; return two thirds to refrigerator. Roll one third on board, sprinkled with ⅓ cup sugar, to form a rectangle 18 x 6 inches. Fold over in thirds from end. Repeat rolling and folding twice more. Then roll into a rectangle 16 x 4 inches. Cut into strips 1 x 4 inches and twist in sugar to form spirals. Put on greased cookie sheets and bake in preheated hot oven (400°F.) for 15 to 20 minutes. Repeat with remaining dough. Makes 4 dozen.

CHERRY-COCONUT PASTRIES
- 1 box pastry mix
- 2 tablespoons sugar
- 3 eggs, beaten
- 1 cup firmly packed brown sugar
- ½ teaspoon baking powder
- 2 tablespoons all-purpose flour

- 1½ teaspoons vanilla extract
- ½ cup flaked coconut
- ½ cup chopped nuts
- ½ cup chopped maraschino cherries

Prepare pastry as directed on the label, adding sugar. Press into bottom and on sides of pan 9 x 9 x 2 inches. Bake in preheated hot oven (425°F.) for 10 minutes. Mix remaining ingredients; pour into pastry. Bake in preheated moderate oven (325°F.) for 35 minutes. Cool; cut into bars 3 x 1½ inches. Makes 18.

LEMON TARTS
- 2 eggs, beaten
- ¾ cup sugar
- ⅛ teaspoon salt
  Grated rind of ½ orange
  Juice of 1 large lemon
- 2 tablespoons butter
- ½ recipe Sweet French Pastry, page 1304 (6 tablespoons butter)

Mix all ingredients except Sweet French Pastry in top part of small double boiler. Cook over boiling water, stirring constantly, until thickened. Cool. Line tiny scalloped tart pans or muffin-pan sections with pastry. Bake in preheated very hot oven (450°F.) for about 12 minutes. Cool and remove from pans. Shortly before serving, fill shells. Makes 24 tiny tarts.

CHERRY TART OR FLAN
- ½ recipe for Sweet French Pastry, page 1304 (6 tablespoons butter)
- 2 cups pitted fresh red, sour cherries
- ½ cup granulated sugar
- ¼ cup firmly packed light brown sugar
- 2 tablespoons butter or margarine, melted
- ½ teaspoon cinnamon
- 2 tablespoons all-purpose flour

Put Sweet French Pastry in 9-inch round cake pan and work up the sides of the pans, pressing pastry with palms and fingers to even it. Trim edges with dull knife. Refrigerate until firm, overnight, if desired, or put in freezer for one half hour before adding filling. Mix remaining ingredients well and spoon into shell. Smooth with back of spoon. Bake in preheated very hot oven (450°F.) for 15 minutes, or until tart begins to brown. Reduce heat to moderate (350°F.), and bake 20 to 30 minutes longer, or until crust is very brown and the filling bubbles. Cool. To serve, cut in wedges. Do not attempt to remove the baked tart from the pan before cutting.

STRAWBERRY ICE CREAM TARTS
- 1 pint strawberries
  Juice of 1 lemon
- ⅔ cup sweetened condensed milk
- ⅛ teaspoon salt
- 1 cup heavy cream
  Graham-Cracker Tart Shells
  Fresh mint

Wash and hull berries. Reserve 4. Crush remainder; add lemon juice, milk, and salt. Fold in cream beaten to consistency of soft custard; blend well. Pour into refrigerator tray. Freeze for 30 minutes; then stir. Continue freezing. Fill Graham-Cracker Tart Shells with strawberry ice cream. Garnish each with 2 strawberry quarters and mint sprigs. Makes 8 servings.

Graham-Cracker Tart Shells
1¼ cups fine graham-cracker crumbs
¼ cup sugar
⅓ cup soft butter or margarine

Mix crumbs, sugar, and butter thoroughly. Using back of spoon, press firmly onto sides and bottoms of 8 greased 4-inch tart pans. Bake in preheated moderate oven (350°F.) for about 10 minutes. Cool. Remove from pans.

LANCASTER SQUARES
Standard Pastry, made with 1 cup
   flour (page 1303)
½ cup firmly packed brown sugar
2 tablespoons soft butter or margarine
⅓ cup chopped nuts

Roll pastry out on lightly floured board to form a 9-inch square. Lift pastry onto a baking sheet. Cream sugar and butter together. Spread on pastry and sprinkle with nuts. Cut into 1½-inch squares. Bake in preheated hot oven (425°F.) for 12 to 15 minutes. Makes about 3 dozen.

BRANDY NUT CAKES
4 egg yolks
⅔ cup granulated sugar
1⅓ cups nuts, chopped medium fine
⅛ teaspoon salt
⅛ teaspoon each of ground cloves
   and cinnamon
⅓ cup cracker meal
2 tablespoons brandy
¼ cup butter or margarine, melted
   Confectioners' sugar
   Candied cherries
   Angelica

Beat egg yolks until thick and lemon-colored. Gradually beat in granulated sugar. Add remaining ingredients except last 3, and mix well. Pour into greased and floured pan (9 x 9 x 2 inches). Bake in preheated moderate oven (375°F.) for about 25 minutes. Cool in pan. Turn out and cut into 1½-inch diamonds. Sprinkle with confectioners' sugar and decorate with cherries and angelica. Makes about 3 dozen.

COCONUT TEA ROUNDS
Cut ⅛ inch thick rounds of Standard Pastry (page 1303) or other pastry. Prick with fork and bake in preheated very hot oven (450°F.) for 8 minutes, or until nearly done. Brush with slightly beaten egg white and sprinkle with flaked coconut. Return to oven until coconut is lightly browned.

NAPOLEONS
For recipe see page 1206.

PÂTÉ—A meat or fish paste or a pie or patty with a filling such as meat or fish paste. Or occasionally the word is used to describe a fruit or vegetable mixture. Originally pâté referred only to the pie form since the word means "pie" in French. The most famous is the *pâté de foie gras,* or goose-liver pâté. Other noted examples are the chicken and ham pâtés from Rouen, France; those of truffled game and poultry from Périgueux, Angoulême, and Nérac; woodcock from Montreuil; duck from Amiens; game from Pithiviers, Chartres, and Nogent-le-Rotrou; and fish from Abbeville.

How To Cook Superbly: Pâtés
by Helen Evans Brown

Pâté, to most of us, means *pâté de foie gras,* a sinfully expensive concoction made of livers from specially fattened geese, and usually studded with truffles. But in France, a pâté is made of less exalted livers and of other meats, and is often known as a *pâté maison* or as a *terrine*. Originally the difference between a pâté and a *terrine* was that the former was enclosed in pastry, the latter made in a covered dish called a *terrine,* from which it is usually served. In today's restaurants you can only be sure which you are ordering if it is listed as *pâté en croûte*. At home, however, you can be sure of delighting your family and guests if you make your own, and that is not as difficult as you may have thought. It will take time, but it's wonderful fun, and it's almost as easy to produce several as one.

A pâté or *terrine* is really a glorified meat loaf because its foundation is nothing more than well-seasoned ground meat. This forcemeat, or *farce* as it's known in French culinary circles, is usually layered with diced meat or with strips *(batons)* of meat, or mixed with other ingredients so that, when sliced, the pâté will have a mosaic look. *Terrines* are sometimes baked in crust, some- times coated with aspic, and sometimes even treated both ways. As there is no particularly difficult technique involved in any of them, I'll give you several different recipes, but first a basic one.

EQUIPMENT

For a *terrine* you will need the ordinary kitchen equipment such as measuring spoons and cups, a sharp knife, a meat grinder, and loaf pans or straight-sided casseroles, with or without covers. Or, if you want to be very fancy, a French *terrine* especially made for the purpose is nice. They are usually white, with PÂTÉ straight sides and domed covers. They may be oval, round, or rectangular. (The latter, I think, is best as the slices will be uniform.) If you are making a *pâté en croûte,* you will also need a special *croûte* mold that can be opened, or else a springform mold or straight-sided pan with a removable bottom although, if you are extremely careful, a glass loaf pan can be used.

BASIC FORCEMEAT
Spice Mixture

Mix ½ teaspoon each of ground ginger, nutmeg, and cloves, and 1 teaspoon ground white pepper.

Forcemeat

1 cup minced onions
½ cup sherry
1 pound fresh pork fat, ground
1 pound lean pork, ground
1 pound veal, ground
Spice Mixture (see above)
3 eggs
1 tablespoon salt
3 garlic cloves (or more or less to taste), puréed or very finely minced

Cook the minced onions in the sherry until liquid has evaporated and the onions are soft. Watch carefully so they do not burn. (Madeira, port, or ¼ cup brandy may be used instead.) Add finely ground meats, 1 teaspoon Spice Mixture, and other ingredients, and mix well. (If you want to taste for seasoning, cook a small piece, either in the oven or in a dry skillet.) Other ground meat, up to 1 pound, may be added also. Duck is good, as is any game, particularly birds or rabbits. Ham or liver is also widely used. You now have about 6 cups forcemeat which can be used with or without garnishes.

■ **Garnishes**—The usual garnishes or decorations are *batons* or dice of various ingredients. *Batons* are strips of meat such as veal, smoked tongue, ham, or pork fat. They should be cut ¼ to ⅜ inch in width and thickness and 2 to 4 inches long. The same meats, cut into ¼- to ½-inch dice may also be used, as may whole chicken or duck livers. You can use from 1 to 1½ pounds *batons* or dice for the above amount of forcemeat. Sliced or diced truffles and whole blanched pistachio nuts, anywhere from 1 tablespoon to 1 cup, are nice additions, too. These garnishes should be marinated in a mixture of ¼ cup brandy or sherry, 1 teaspoon salt, and ½ teaspoon Spice Mixture. Drain and mix liquid with forcemeat.

■ **Pan Lining**—The *terrines* or pans used for pâtés are lined with thin slices of fresh pork fat before the mixture is added. You may be able to get this from your butcher. Ask him to give you unsalted fat back. Have it sliced about ¼ inch thick, then put it between pieces of

paper and pound it thinner. If you can't get the fresh fat, slice salt pork ⅛ inch thick, and soak it in cold water for several hours. Or use sliced bacon, 1 pound for the above amount of forcemeat.

■ **Assembling and Baking**—First measure the *terrines,* pans, or casseroles you intend to use. The above ingredients will make 8 to 9 cups, or 2 bread-size loaves. Use 1 large *terrine,* or several smaller *terrines* if you prefer. Line them with the sliced fat, allowing the slices to hang over at the top. Press about one third of the forcemeat mixture you have allotted for the *terrine* evenly over bottom. (For instance, if your *terrine* is a 3-cup one and you are using ½ pound (1 cup) garnishing, you'll need 2 cups forcemeat. (The fat lining doesn't have to be figured in.) Arrange half your *batons* or diced meats or whole livers along the top of the forcemeat layer in a symmetrical manner, alternating colors; have *batons* parallel. If truffles or pistachios are used, arrange between the meats or in a separate layer. Add another third of the forcemeat, pressing evenly as before, then the remaining garnishes. Top with the last of the forcemeat, and fold the fat over the top, covering it completely. Put a whole bay leaf and a sprig of thyme or a good big pinch of dried thyme on top. Cover with a double layer of foil and with lids, if available. Put the filled *terrines* in a larger pan and pour in enough boiling water to come halfway up the outside. Bake in preheated moderate oven (375°F.) for 1½ to 2 hours, depending upon the size; a 5-cup loaf pan takes about 1½ hours. The pâté is done when the fat runs clear when it is pierced with a sharp knife. Leave the *terrines* in the outside pan, remove covers but not the foil, and weigh down their contents. This last is important for texture and easy slicing. Use a slightly smaller vessel of the same shape, or cut cardboard to fit, cover with heavy foil, and place on top. Weigh down with canned goods or other heavy objects. Allow to cool thoroughly. Serve either directly from the *terrine,* slicing through the fat, or turn out and slice, fat and all. Serve with toast or on lettuce.

PÂTÉ IN ASPIC

If you prefer, the pâté can be encased in aspic. When planning this, don't quite fill the *terrine* before baking. Make an aspic with 2 cans (10½ ounces each) beef bouillon, ⅓ cup sherry or Madeira, and 2 envelopes unflavored gelatin softened in ⅓ cup water. Heat until dissolved, then cool until gelatin begins to set. Remove cooked pâté from the pan and scrape off fat. Wash pan, rinse in cold water, and dry. Pour about ½ inch of cooled aspic into pan and allow to

set. Place scraped pâté carefully on top, centering it. Pour more aspic on until it covers the top, preferably by ½ inch or more. Allow to set, then turn out on a platter and slice.

PÂTÉ EN CROÛTE

Pâté in a crust is made as above but it is baked in a crust. For the crust Puff Paste, regular pie pastry, or *pâte brisée* may be used, but because the pâté contains so much fat the following pastry is preferable. Using your fingertips or a pastry blender, mix ½ cup butter, or butter and shortening combined, into 4 cups all-purpose flour and 1 teaspoon of salt. Gradually add cold water, about ½ cup, until the mixture holds together. Form into a ball, wrap in wax paper, and allow to rest in a cool place for 2 to 8 hours. Roll ⅛ to ¼ inch thick and line *croûte* mold or loaf pan with it, pressing it firmly to sides first. Cut piece of dough to fit bottom and press in. Be sure corners are completely covered with dough. Make sure there are no holes in the pastry. If *croûte* mold has no bottom, place on a cookie sheet. Allow ¼ inch of pastry to hang over the top. Fill with forcemeat and garnishings as above. Moisten edge of pastry and top with another piece. Press edges firmly together, then cut off excess by passing a rolling pin over the top. If you wish, cut extra pieces into fancy shapes and decorate top. Brush with slightly beaten egg; then make a hole in the top and insert a small funnel or a tube of foil. Bake in preheated moderate oven (375°F.) for 1½ to 2 hours, or until fat in funnel runs clear. Cool. When perfectly cold, aspic may be poured in the hole at the top. As the meat shrinks this will fill up the spaces and look extra pretty when set and sliced.

COUNTRY-STYLE TERRINE

Make Basic Forcemeat according to the directions at the left. Add 2 to 3 cups finely diced meat of your choice: ham, tongue, veal, fat pork, lean pork, or game. Mix well and bake in a 2½-quart terrine for about 2 hours, as above.

QUICK AND EASY CHICKEN-LIVER TERRINE

½ cup chopped onion
1 tablespoon butter or chicken fat
½ cup sherry
1¼ pounds chicken livers
1 pound sausage meat
1½ teaspoons salt
½ teaspoon Spice Mixture (at left)
2 eggs, slightly beaten
½ pound bacon

Cook onion in butter until wilted. Add sherry and cook until almost dry. Reserve 3 whole chicken livers and grind remainder finely or whirl in the blender. Mix other ingredients except bacon. Line sides and bottom of a 5-cup ovenproof bread pan with bacon. Pour in half of mixture, arrange whole chicken livers lengthwise in the center; then add rest of mixture. Cover top with remaining bacon and with foil. Bake as above in preheated moderate oven (375°F.) for 1½ hours.

BASIC PORK PÂTÉ
1 pound pork liver
1 cup milk
1 pound pork fat
1½ pounds lean pork
2 beaten eggs
5 garlic cloves, puréed
¼ cup flour
2 teaspoons salt
2 teaspoons dried tarragon
½ teaspoon Spice Mixture (page 1312)
¼ to ½ cup blanched pistachio nuts (optional)
¼ to ½ cup diced cooked ham

Soak liver in milk for 2 hours; drain. Slice half of pork fat for lining a 4- or 5-cup *terrine* or loaf pan. Grind remainder with lean pork and liver. Add remaining ingredients and mix well. Put in fat-lined pan and bake as above in preheated moderate oven (375°F.) for 1½ hours, or until fat is clear.

KEEPING PÂTÉS AND TERRINES
Terrines will keep, refrigerated, for at least 2 weeks if they are removed from molds, wiped of any juices that have jellied on the outside, and either wrapped in foil or placed in washed pans. They can be frozen but the texture is not quite as perfect. If aspic is used, add it only a day or two before serving. *Pâté en croûte* will keep for a week or so, and can also be frozen with the same results.

Once you've mastered these basic types of pâtés, you can invent your own and call it, of course, *pâté maison* or *pâté chez nous.* You'll find it really isn't much more difficult than a meat loaf, but so much more exciting.

PATTY—A small, round, flat mass of food: dough, cereal, potato, or other vegetable, ground meat, fish, poultry, or nuts; or a combination of meat and potato and/or other vegetables. In another usage of the word, a dough shell baked to form a container for creamed dishes is referred to as a patty shell.

The word is also used to describe the small flat candies usually made of peppermint-flavored fondant.

BAKED LAMB PATTIES
1 pound ground lamb
1 cup fine fresh-bread crumbs
2 eggs, slightly beaten
¾ teaspoon salt
⅛ teaspoon crumbled thyme leaves
½ teaspoon powdered mustard
1 teaspoon Worcestershire

¼ teaspoon pepper
Hot tomato sauce

Mix all ingredients except tomato sauce lightly but thoroughly. Shape into 8 patties, and put in shallow dish. Bake in preheated moderate oven (350°F.) for about 1 hour. Serve with tomato sauce. Makes 4 servings.

FRANKFURTER AND CORNMEAL PATTIES
¾ cup yellow cornmeal
2 teaspoons salt
3 cups boiling water
½ pound frankfurters, cooked and ground or minced very fine
¼ cup fat

Gradually add meal to salted boiling water, stirring constantly. Cook until thick. Remove from heat and add frankfurters, mixing well. Drop by heaping tablespoonfuls onto platter, and let stand until cold. Cook patties slowly in hot fat until browned on both sides. Makes 4 servings.

POTATO PATTIES
Shape 3 cups cold mashed potato into 8 patties. Dredge with flour. Cook slowly in small amount of hot margarine or bacon fat in skillet until browned on both sides. Makes 4 servings.

Squash Patties
Follow recipe for Potato Patties, substituting an equal amount of mashed cooked winter squash for the potato.

PATTY SHELLS
Prepare one fourth of the recipe for Puff Paste (page 1304). Roll dough into a rectangle 18 x 6 inches. Cut out 12 rounds with a 3-inch cutter. Remove the centers from half the rounds with a smaller cutter to make rims and tops. Put both size plain rounds on a cookie sheet covered with two thicknesses of brown paper. Moisten the edges of the large rounds, and set the rings on them. Press gently. Chill for 20 minutes, or longer. Put in preheated very hot oven (500°F.). Reduce the heat 50° every 5 minutes, and bake until shells are well-risen and browned, about 25 minutes. Turn as necessary to brown evenly. Fill as desired and top with small baked rounds. Good fillings are chicken à la king; creamed mushrooms, lobster, etc.; or newburg mixtures. Makes 6 shells.

PAUCHOUSE, POCHOUSE, or POUCHOUSE—A French name for a bouillabaisse made of fresh-water fish. It is made with five kinds of fish, almost always including eel and pike. The fish is sliced, cooked with a little water and seasoning, or with court bouillon, salt pork which has been cubed and browned, white or red wine, and heavy cream.

PAUPIETTE—A meat or fish roll made from thin slices of meat or fish stuffed with forcemeat, or other dressing, browned and braised. It is more commonly called a "bird" in the United States: veal birds, beef birds, etc.

BEEF PAUPIETTES
4 cube steaks (about 1 pound)
Salt and pepper to taste
Italian herbs
Meat tenderizer
1 small carrot, cut into strips
1 green pepper, cut into strips
1 teaspoon all-purpose flour
½ teaspoon paprika
2 tablespoons fat
1 small onion, chopped
1 cup bouillon
Dash of hot pepper sauce

Sprinkle steaks with salt and pepper, herbs, and tenderizer. Put a few strips of carrot and pepper on each, roll up and tie with string. Dredge with flour mixed with paprika. Brown on all sides in fat. Add remaining ingredients, cover, and simmer for 1½ hours, or until meat is tender. Makes 4 servings.

PAVLOVA—A dessert of Australian origin which is very popular at special teas, birthday buffets, or other celebrations. It consists of a meringue topped with whipped cream and berries, or whipped cream, passion fruit, and banana slices.

STRAWBERRY PAVLOVA
6 egg whites
¼ teaspoon salt
1½ teaspoons cream of tartar
1½ cups granulated sugar
1 teaspoon vanilla extract
1 cup heavy cream, whipped
1 pint strawberries
1 teaspoon kirsch
Confectioners' sugar

Let egg whites warm to room temperature. Beat with rotary beater or electric mixer until frothy. Sprinkle salt and cream of tartar over top; beat until stiff but not dry. Gradually beat in granulated sugar, 2 tablespoons at a time. Add vanilla and continue beating until mixture is very stiff. On a 12-inch chop plate, spread about one third of meringue to within 1 inch of edge of plate. Pile remaining meringue around meringue base to height of about 2½ inches, leaving center unfilled. Bake in preheated very slow oven (250°F.) for about 1¼ hours. Turn off heat and leave in oven for 15 minutes longer. Cool. Fill center with whipped cream. Wash and hull berries and put about three fourths of them on top of cream. Press remaining berries through a sieve. Add kirsch and confectioners' sugar to taste. Pour this mixture over berries and cream. Makes 8 servings.

PEA—The seed and plant of a cool-season hardy annual, *Pisum sativum.* Chief among the many varieties are the garden, or green, pea and the field, or stock, pea, *P. Sativum var. arvense.* Garden peas are grown for their seed primarily, although one type, the sugar pea, which the French graphically call *mange-tout,* has soft thick edible pods. The seeds of garden peas can be classified as smooth-skinned or wrinkled, the former being a hardier type, but the latter being a better quality pea. Field peas, which have a small hard seed, are used chiefly for making yellow split peas and as livestock fodder.

Peas are an old vegetable; they originated in western Asia and the adjacent sections of Europe. The earlier peas were grown for dried seeds, such as we use today in split-pea soup. The Greeks and Romans used peas long before Christian times, but they were not grown in Europe very widely before the middle of the 17th century, when they became most fashionable in gourmet circles. England grew and grows excellent peas, since this vegetable thrives where the summer temperatures are cool and where there is much moisture. Dried, or split, peas, made into the "pease porridge hot, pease porridge cold" of the nursery rhyme, were for centuries a basic staple in the English diet. Peas have been known in America since the earliest days when the colonists brought the dried seeds with them.

Availability—California produces 60 per cent of the fresh green peas used in the United States; March, April, and May are the peak months. There are also shipments from August through November.

□ Canned green peas and frozen green peas are available, as are frozen peas in butter sauce, frozen peas and onions in cream sauce, and frozen carrots and peas.
□ Packaged split (dried and de-hulled) peas are available: yellow (made from field peas) and green (made from green peas).

Purchasing Guide—Fresh green peas should be fresh, tender, and sweet. Look for large, bright-green, well-filled pods with a velvety texture.
□ 1 pound in shell = 1 cup shelled

Storage—Refrigerate fresh peas, unshelled.
□ Fresh, refrigerator shelf, unshelled: 3 to 5 days
□ Fresh, cooked; and canned, opened, refrigerator shelf: 4 to 5 days
□ Fresh, prepared for freezing; and frozen, refrigerator frozen-food compartment: 2 to 3 months
□ Fresh, prepared for freezing; and frozen, freezer: 1 year
□ Canned, kitchen shelf: 1 year
□ Split peas, kitchen shelf: 6 to 8 months

Nutritive Food Values—Peas are a fair source of protein, iron, vitamin A, and also have some niacin and vitamin C.
□ Fresh, 3½ ounces, raw = 84 calories
□ Fresh, 3½ ounces, boiled and drained = 71 calories
□ Fresh, edible-pod, 3½ ounces, raw = 53 calories
□ Fresh, edible-pod, 3½ ounces, boiled and drained = 43 calories
□ Canned (early or June peas), 3½ ounces, solids and liquid = 66 calories
□ Canned (early or June peas), 3½ ounces, drained solids = 88 calories
□ Canned (early or June peas), dietary pack, 3½ ounces, solids and liquid = 55 calories
□ Canned (early or June peas), dietary pack, 3½ ounces, drained solids = 78 calories
□ Canned (sweet wrinkled peas), 3½ ounces, solids and liquid = 57 calories
□ Canned (sweet wrinkled peas), 3½ ounces, drained solids = 80 calories
□ Canned (sweet wrinkled peas), dietary pack, 3½ ounces, solids and liquid = 47 calories
□ Canned (sweet wrinkled peas), dietary pack, 3½ ounces, drained solids = 72 calories
□ Frozen, 3½ ounces, boiled and drained = 68 calories
□ Split peas, 3½ ounces, cooked = 115 calories

Basic Preparation—Shell fresh peas just before cooking. Cook, covered, in 1 inch of boiling salted water for 8 to 12 minutes.

□ **To Cook Split Peas**—When bought in packages, they have been sorted and washed, and so need only be rinsed. They may or may not need soaking according to directions on the package. Some dried peas are prepared for quick cooking. Consult package for length of cooking time. Loose peas should be sorted and washed thoroughly.

If it is necessary to soak dried peas, cook in the soaking water to save flavor and nutrients. Add salt to the pot of soaked peas (1 teaspoon for each cup of dried peas). For special flavor cook with ham, bacon, or salt pork (less salt will be needed), herbs, chopped onion, carrot, or celery. Cover pot, bring to boil, reduce heat, and cook gently until tender. If peas are to be used in soup, cook until they can be easily mashed. A pinch of ground allspice gives an excellent flavor.

□ **To Freeze**—Choose sweet tender peas. Shell peas but do not wash. Blanch in boiling water: small peas for 45 seconds; large peas for 60 seconds. Chill in cold water for 3 minutes. Drain. Pack in containers, leaving ½-inch headspace. Seal.

YELLOW PEA SOUP WITH SMOKED PORK

2 to 3 pounds smoked pork shoulder butt
3 quarts water
1 large onion, chopped
1 pound yellow split peas
1 teaspoon ground thyme
1 bay leaf
½ teaspoon coarsely ground black pepper
1 teaspoon salt

Put pork in kettle, and add water and onion. Bring to boil and simmer, covered, for 1½ to 2 hours, or until tender. Remove meat, and skim off most of fat from broth. To broth, add peas and remaining ingredients. Simmer, covered, stirring occasionally, for 1½ to 2 hours, or until soup is almost a purée. Slice meat thin and add to soup. Heat well and serve. Makes 6 servings.

SPLIT-PEA PURÉE
Cover 1¼ cups green split peas with water. Add 1 onion, 1 dried mushroom (optional, but tasty), and 1 teaspoon sugar. Bring to boil, then simmer until tender and thick, about 1½ hours. Put through blender or fine sieve. Bind with 1 tablespoon flour, season to taste with salt and pepper, and reheat gently. Makes 4 servings.
Note: Can be served topped with crisp fried onions.

HERBED CHICKEN AND PEAS
1 frying chicken, quartered
2 teaspoons salt
1 teaspoon paprika
¼ cup olive oil or cooking oil
1 teaspoon dried rosemary

½ teaspoon dried thyme leaves
1 garlic clove, cut
2½ cups water
¼ teaspoon saffron (optional)
1 cup uncooked rice
1 bay leaf
½ cup sliced pimiento-stuffed olives
1½ cups shelled fresh peas or 1 box
   (10 ounces) frozen peas

Wash and dry chicken pieces. Sprinkle with 1 teaspoon salt and the paprika. Brown on all sides in hot oil in skillet. In saucepan mix remaining salt, the herbs, garlic, and water. Bring to boil, and add chicken neck and giblets. Cover, and simmer for 25 minutes. Strain, and reserve 2 cups stock. Remove chicken from skillet and pour off all but 3 tablespoons drippings. Stir saffron and rice into drippings and brown lightly. Stir in bay leaf, 2 cups stock, and olives. Bring to boil and add chicken. Cover and cook over low heat for 30 minutes, or until chicken and rice are tender. Cook and drain peas, and add to dish just before serving. Makes 4 servings.

TUNA, PEAS, AND RICE

1 small onion, minced
¼ cup butter or margarine
3 cups hot cooked peas
3 cups hot cooked rice
1 or 2 cans (7 ounces each) tuna
   Salt and pepper to taste
   Grated Parmesan cheese

Sauté onion in the butter until golden. Toss lightly with remaining ingredients, except cheese. Serve hot, sprinkled with the cheese. Makes 6 to 8 servings.

PEA AND CHEESE SALAD IN TOMATO SHELLS

3 cups (3 pounds) cooked fresh peas
½ cup diced Cheddar cheese
3 tablespoons minced onion
½ cup French dressing
1 tablespoon prepared mustard
6 medium tomatoes, peeled and
   hollowed out
   Lettuce

Toss peas, cheese, and onion together lightly. Combine French dressing and mustard, and pour over salad mixture. Toss lightly and chill. Spoon mixture into tomato shells. Serve on lettuce. Makes 6 servings.

ALMOND, PEA, AND CHEESE SALAD

Cook 1 package (10 ounces) frozen peas. Drain and cool. Mix with ½ cup split unblanched almonds, 1 cup cubed sharp Cheddar cheese, ¼ cup chopped dill pickle, ⅓ cup mayonnaise, ½ teaspoon prepared mustard, 1 teaspoon vinegar, and salt to taste. Chill; serve on lettuce or other greens. Makes 4 servings.

HERBED CORN AND PEAS

Combine 3 cups cooked shelled fresh peas and 2 cups cooked whole-kernel corn. Add ½ cup water in which peas were cooked, a few chopped parsley sprigs, and ½ teaspoon dried majoram or oregano. Heat; season to taste with butter or margarine and salt and pepper. Makes 6 servings.

FRENCH PEAS

¼ cup butter or margarine
   Large outside lettuce leaves
2 cups shelled fresh peas
   Salt and pepper

Put 1 tablespoon butter in a large skillet with a tightly fitting cover. Wash lettuce leaves and allow a few drops of the water to cling to them. Arrange several leaves over butter. Add peas and remaining butter, and cover with more lettuce leaves. Cover tightly and cook over high heat until butter is bubbly hot. Lower heat and steam gently until peas are just tender. This takes about 15 minutes. Discard lettuce, and season peas with salt and pepper to taste. Makes 4 servings.

MUSHROOM-PIMIENTO PEAS

Cook 1½ cups shelled fresh peas or 1 package (10 ounces) frozen peas. Add 3 tablespoons butter or margarine, 1 can (4 ounces) drained sliced mushrooms, and 2 chopped canned pimientos; heat. Makes 3 servings.

CURRIED PEAS AND ONIONS

Cook 1½ cups shelled fresh peas or 1 package (10 ounces) frozen peas. Drain off all but about 1 tablespoon liquid. Add 2 cups (one 1-pound can) onions, drained, 3 tablespoons butter or margarine, and 1 teaspoon curry powder. Heat, stirring lightly once or twice. Season to taste with salt and pepper. Makes 4 to 6 servings.

PEAS WITH MUSHROOMS AND ONIONS

1½ tablespoons butter
2 tablespoons water
½ cup thinly sliced mushrooms
1½ cups shelled fresh peas or 1 package
   (10 ounces) frozen peas
1 small onion, thinly sliced
½ teaspoon salt

Melt butter in saucepan. Add remaining ingredients. Cover pan tightly, and cook until peas are tender. Shake pan occasionally. Makes 4 servings.

SAVORY PEAS

½ cup sliced green onions
2 tablespoons butter or margarine
1½ cups (1½ pounds) shelled fresh peas
½ teaspoon sugar
¼ teaspoon powdered savory
¼ teaspoon dried basil
1 tablespoon snipped parsley
½ cup water
1 teaspoon salt
⅛ teaspoon pepper

Sauté green onions in butter for 5 minutes, or until tender. Add peas, sugar, herbs, water, salt, and pepper. Cook, covered, over low heat for 10 minutes, or until peas are tender. Makes 4 servings.

CORN AND PEAS IN CREAM

1 package (10 ounces) frozen whole-
   kernel corn
1 package (10 ounces) frozen peas
1 cup light cream
1 teaspoon instant minced onion
2 tablespoons butter or margarine
   Salt and pepper
1 cup slivered cooked ham

Cook corn and peas separately as directed on labels; drain and combine. Add cream, onion, and 1 tablespoon butter; heat, and season to taste. Sauté ham lightly in 1 tablespoon butter. Pour vegetables into serving dish and top with ham slivers. Makes 6 servings.

VEGETABLE RELISH

1 can (1 pound) small peas, drained
1 can (8 ounces) French-style green
   beans, drained
1 medium green pepper, chopped
1 onion, chopped
1 cup finely diced celery
1 jar (4 ounces) pimientos, chopped
1 cup vinegar
1 cup sugar
1 tablespoon salt
1 tablespoon celery seed
½ cup cooking oil
1 teaspoon mustard seed

Combine first 6 ingredients. Mix remaining ingredients, and pour over vegetables. Toss lightly, and let stand in refrigerator overnight or longer. Serve with veal or other bland meat. Makes about 4 cups.

PEACH—The third most important fruit crop in the United States (the first is the apple, the second, orange), the peach is a cousin of the cherry, the apricot, the plum, and the almond. All are members of the *Prunus* genus. The peach is a small tree, sensitive to low temperatures. Its flowers are pink and charming, and they appear before the leaves. The peach itself is a rounded fruit, with a fuzzy velvety skin, creamy yellow when ripe. (The nectarine, a variation of the peach, has a smooth skin. The plant distinction is not absolute however because peaches may grow from nectarine seeds and vice versa, and both peaches and nectarines have been gathered from the same tree.) The flesh may be white or yellow, with a pitted or furrowed stone of the free or cling type. The yellow-fleshed freestone varieties are the most important commercially and one of the best known of these is the Elberta.

The peach tree is a native of China, where it has been grown for thousands of years, both for its fruit and its decorative flowers. It is said to have been introduced into Europe through Persia, and thus its botanical name, *Prunus persica*. Peaches once were called Persian apples.

The Spaniards brought peaches to the New World; and they were growing in Mexico in the late 1500's. The French settlers in Louisiana and the English settlers in the North planted peaches, and the Indians carried them inland.

Since time immemorial the peach has captured the imagination of poets and artists. In China, where the peach was considered the symbol of long life, porcelains were painted with a peach blossom and given as a birthday gift, to express the wish for many happy years. Both Chinese and Japanese poetry and art are lavish in their praise of the peach blossom and fruit.

Peaches are grown on a large scale on the Pacific coast, the Atlanta seaboard from Georgia to New Hampshire, and in New York, Ohio, and Michigan. The harvest amounts to about two billion pounds.

There are hundreds of ways of serving peaches fresh, canned, or dried, all delicious. Peaches are also distilled into a liqueur as well as made into nectar.

Availability and Purchasing Guide— Available fresh from May to October. Select fresh, firm peaches free from blemishes. Mature fruit has a whitish or creamy yellow undercolor. Red color is not a sign of ripeness and blush depends upon variety. Avoid green-colored fruit. These peaches were picked when immature and do not ripen well. Avoid overmature fruit; it bruises easily and must be used immediately.
- [ ] 1 pound = 2 cups sliced = 1 cup pulp

Cling and freestone peaches are available canned, halved or in slices, packed in water or sugar syrup. Some clingstone peaches are packed whole and spiced. Frozen sliced peaches are available, as are packages of dried peaches, packed by themselves or mixed with other dried fruits.

Among the other peach products available are peach nectar, butter, ice cream, jam and jelly, and baby food. Peaches are

included in mixed fruit cocktails.

Storage—Refrigerate peaches unwashed.
- [ ] Refrigerator shelf, raw: 3 to 14 days
- [ ] Fresh, cooked; or canned, opened, refrigerator shelf: 4 to 5 days
- [ ] Fresh, prepared for freezing; and frozen, refrigerator frozen-food compartment: 2 to 3 months
- [ ] Fresh, prepared for freezing; and frozen, freezer: 1 year
- [ ] Canned, kitchen shelf: 1 year
- [ ] Dried, kitchen shelf: 6 to 8 months

Nutritive Food Values—Good source of vitamin A. Fresh peaches have a small amount of vitamin C.
- [ ] Fresh, 3½ ounces, raw = 38 calories
- [ ] Canned, 3½ ounces, water pack = 31 calories
- [ ] Canned, 3½ ounces, light syrup pack = 58 calories
- [ ] Canned, 3½ ounces, heavy syrup pack = 78 calories
- [ ] Canned, 3½ ounces, extra-heavy syrup pack = 97 calories
- [ ] Frozen, 3½ ounces, sweetened = 88 calories
- [ ] Dried, 3½ ounces, uncooked = 262 calories
- [ ] Dried, 3½ ounces, cooked without added sugar, fruit and liquid = 82 calories
- [ ] Dried, 3½ ounces, cooked with added sugar, fruit and liquid = 119 calories

Basic Preparation—Sprinkle fresh peach slices with lemon juice for bright, fresh look.
- [ ] **To Stew**—For 6 servings peel 6 ripe peaches, halve; pit, if desired. Simmer ¾ cup sugar and 1 cup water for 5 minutes. Add peaches and simmer, covered, for 10 minutes, or until just tender. Cool; then chill.
- [ ] **To Freeze**—Use only firm ripe peaches. Dip peaches into boiling water for 1 minute. Remove skins. Cut peaches into halves or slices. Can be packed in a pectin syrup, sugar syrup, or unsweetened. To prevent darkening, peel and slice peaches into a container only when syrup is ready.

To make 2 quarts pectin syrup, heat 5½ cups water with 3 cups sugar until dissolved. Remove from heat and stir in one 6-ounce bottle liquid pectin and 1 teaspoon ascorbic acid.

To prepare sugar syrup, heat 4 cups water with 3 cups sugar until dissolved. Remove from heat and stir in 2 teaspoons ascorbic acid to each 4 cups water.

Pour ½ cup syrup into a freezer container and add peaches directly to syrup. Fill with peaches to within ½ inch of the top. Add more syrup to cover. Crumple water-resistant paper into top to hold peaches under syrup. Seal.

PEACH COOK BOOK

FOUR PEACH SALADS

■ Seafood—Peel and halve fresh peaches. For each serving, put 2 halves on a bed of chicory. Flatten peaches slightly, and top with a seafood salad such as tuna, shrimp, or crabmeat. Garnish with parsley.

■ Cheese and Vegetable—Arrange peach halves as in Seafood-Peach Salad. Mix 2 cups small-curd creamed cottage cheese, ¼ cup chopped green pepper, 2 tablespoons chopped chives, ¼ cup grated carrot, and 2 chopped radishes. Fill peach cavities with the cheese mixture. Makes 4 servings.

■ Chicken Salad—Arrange peach halves as in Seafood-Peach Salad. Fill with chicken salad and sprinkle with toasted slivered almonds. Garnish with a small cluster of seedless green grapes.

■ Cottage Cheese—Mix cottage cheese with chopped fresh mint. Fill peach halves, arrange on watercress, and top with maraschino cherries.

PEACHES À LA RUSSE
3 cups sliced fresh peaches
1 cup dairy sour cream
1 to 2 tablespoons sugar
¼ to ½ teaspoon grated lemon rind

Place sliced peaches in each of 5 or 6 sherbet glasses. Combine remaining ingredients, and spoon over peaches. Garnish with additional peach slices if desired. Makes 5 or 6 servings.

PEACH COMPOTE
6 large, fresh ripe peaches
¼ cup light corn syrup
½ cup fresh orange juice
⅛ teaspoon almond extract
2 tablespoons honey
2 tablespoons rum or peach brandy

Blanch peaches in boiling water, drain, peel, cut into halves, and remove pits. Bring corn syrup, orange juice, and almond extract to boil. Poach peaches, a few at a time, in this mixture, simmering gently just until peaches are barely tender. Drain peaches and put in a bowl. Boil syrup until very thick, add honey, and pour over peaches. Chill. Add rum just before serving. Makes 6 servings.

PEACH AMBROSIA
2 cups sliced fresh peaches
1 cup sliced bananas
1 tablespoon fresh lemon juice
2 tablespoons sugar
⅓ cup shredded coconut

Combine first 4 ingredients. Chill for at least 30 minutes. Just before serving add coconut and spoon into sherbet glasses. Makes 3 or 4 servings.

GINGER PEACH MOLD
2 boxes (3 ounces each) orange-flavored gelatin
2 cups hot water
2 bottles (7 ounces each) ginger ale
1 to 1½ cups thinly sliced peaches
1 cup heavy cream
1 teaspoon ground ginger

Dissolve gelatin in hot water. Add ginger ale. Chill until slightly thickened. Add peaches and put in 1½-quart mold. Chill until firm. Unmold and serve with whipped cream flavored with ginger. Makes 6 to 8 servings.

Note: This may also be served as a salad. Omit whipped cream and serve mold on lettuce with dairy sour cream flavored with ginger.

PEACH TAPIOCA
¼ cup quick-cooking tapioca
Peach juice drained from canned peaches with enough water to make 2 cups
¼ teaspoon salt
½ cup sugar
2 tablespoons fresh lemon juice
2 cups drained sliced canned peaches
⅓ cup heavy cream, whipped
Grated orange peel

Combine tapioca, peach juice, salt, and sugar in top part of double boiler. Cook, stirring frequently, until tapioca is clear. Blend in lemon juice and fold in drained peaches. Cook for 1 minute longer. Remove from heat. Serve in sherbet glasses. Top with whipped cream decorated with a sprinkling of grated orange peel. Makes 6 servings.

PEACH COBBLER
2 cups sifted all-purpose flour
2 teaspoons baking powder
½ teaspoon salt
Sugar (about ¼ cup)
½ cup shortening
¾ cup milk
3½ cups (one 1-pound, 13-ounce can) sliced peaches
1 tablespoon fresh lemon juice
½ teaspoon ground cinnamon
1 teaspoon butter
1 cup light cream, sweetened to taste and flavored with ground nutmeg

Sift flour into bowl with baking powder, salt, and 1 tablespoon sugar. With a pastry blender cut in shortening until fine. Add milk to make a soft dough. Combine peaches, lemon juice, 2 tablespoons sugar, cinnamon, and butter in casserole. Pat out shortcake dough to fit top. Bake in preheated hot oven (450°F.) for 10 minutes. Reduce heat to moderate (350°F.) and bake for 25 minutes longer, or until crust is golden-brown. Serve warm with nutmeg-flavored cream. Makes 8 servings.

PEACH DUMPLINGS
Pastry
6 large peaches, washed and peeled
Sugar
Ground cinnamon
Butter
Syrup

Roll pastry to ⅛-inch thickness and cut with pastry wheel into six 7-inch squares. Put a peach in center of each square; sprinkle with 1 tablespoon sugar and dash of cinnamon; top with 1 teaspoon butter. Moisten edges of pastry with cold water; bring points up over peaches; press edges together. Put in a large shallow baking dish. Pour Syrup around dumplings. Bake in preheated hot oven (400°F.) for 35 to 40 minutes, or until peaches are tender and crust is browned. Serve warm, with cream if desired. Makes 6 dumplings.

Syrup
Boil 1 cup water with 2 tablespoons sugar, 2 tablespoons currant jelly, and 2 tablespoons butter.

PEACH CRUMB PUDDING
18 fresh peaches, about 4 pounds
1 cup sugar
1¼ cups sifted all-purpose flour
½ cup butter or margarine

Reserve 1 peach for garnishing. Peel peaches, cut into quarters, and drop into mixture of ½ cup sugar and 3 tablespoons flour. Turn into baking dish (10 x 6 x 2 inches). Mix remaining sugar and flour; cut in butter to crumb consistency. Sprinkle crumbs over peaches. Bake in preheated moderate oven (375°F.) for 1 hour, or until peaches are tender and crumbs are brown. Garnish top as desired with sliced fresh peach. Makes 8 to 10 servings.

PEACH SOUFFLÉ
1 can (1 pound) sliced peaches
4 eggs, separated
½ cup sugar
3 tablespoons butter or margarine
3 tablespoons all-purpose flour
¼ teaspoon salt
1 cup milk
1 teaspoon vanilla extract
Grated rind of 1 lemon
Whipped cream

Drain peaches, reserving syrup. Dice peaches and put in 2-quart soufflé dish. Beat egg yolks until thick and lemon-colored. Gradually beat in ¼ cup sugar. Melt butter, and blend in flour and salt. Gradually add milk, stirring constantly. Cook, stirring, until thickened. Pour mixture over egg yolks. Mix well and cool. Beat egg whites until stiff; gradually beat in remaining sugar. Fold into egg-yolk mixture. Add vanilla and lemon rind. Pour onto peaches in soufflé dish. Bake in preheated slow oven (325°F.) for 30 to 40 minutes. Serve with reserved syrup and whipped cream. Makes 6 servings.

PEACH BETTY
½ cup sugar
1 tablespoon all-purpose flour
¼ teaspoon salt
1 cup soft bread crumbs
4 cups sliced peeled fresh peaches
2 tablespoons butter or margarine

Combine first 4 ingredients and set aside. Arrange half of peaches in 1-quart casserole. Top with half of bread-crumb mixture. Dot with 1 tablespoon butter. Repeat with remaining ingredients. Bake in preheated moderate oven (375°F.) for about 40 minutes, or until crumbs are golden and peaches are tender. Makes 5 or 6 servings.

PEACH CRISP
1 cup unsifted all-purpose flour
½ cup granulated sugar
½ cup firmly packed light brown sugar
¼ teaspoon ground nutmeg
¼ teaspoon salt
½ teaspoon ground cinnamon
½ cup butter or margarine
4 cups sliced fresh peaches
Grated rind and juice of ½ lemon
2 tablespoons water

Mix flour, sugars, nutmeg, salt, and cinnamon. Mix in butter with fork or fingers until coarse crumbs are formed. Put peaches in 9-inch shallow baking dish. Mix in lemon rind, juice, and water. Cover with crumb mixture; pat down so it sticks to fruit. Cover and bake in preheated moderate oven (350°F.) for 15 minutes. Uncover and bake for about 30 minutes longer. Serve warm with cream or ice cream, if desired. Makes 6 servings.

PEACH CRUMBLE
3½ cups (one 1-pound, 13-ounce can) homestyle peaches
½ package pastry mix
1 cup firmly packed light brown sugar
Butter or margarine
Cream

Drain peaches, and put in shallow baking dish. Crumble pastry mix and stir in brown sugar. Sprinkle on peaches. Dot with butter. Bake in preheated slow oven (325°F.) for 30 minutes, or until lightly browned and bubbly. Serve warm with cream. Makes 4 servings.

PEACH-BLUEBERRY MERINGUE
6 eggs, separated
¼ teaspoon salt
1½ teaspoons cream of tartar
Sugar (about 1⅔ cups)
¼ teaspoon vanilla extract
Almond Cream Filling
2 cups sliced peaches
Juice of 1 lemon
2 cups washed fresh blueberries

To make meringue let egg whites stand until warmed to room temperature; beat until frothy. Add salt and cream of tartar. Beat until stiff but not dry. Very gradually beat in 1½ cups sugar. Add vanilla and beat until very stiff. On 12-inch chop plate spread about one third of the meringue to within 1 inch of edge. Pile remaining meringue around edge to height of about 2½ inches, leaving center unfilled. Bake in preheated very slow oven (250°F.) for 1¼ hours. Turn off

Ginger Peach Mold

Key Lime Pie with Peaches

Peach Bowler

Peach Crème de Menthe Parfait

Peach Tapioca

Peach-Blueberry Meringue

heat and leave in oven for 15 minutes. Cool. Pour Almond Cream Filling carefully into center. Chill for several hours. Just before serving, sprinkle peaches with lemon juice and sweeten with remaining sugar. Arrange peaches and berries on pie. Makes 8 servings.

Almond Cream Filling

In top part of small double boiler mix 2 tablespoons flour, ⅓ cup sugar, and dash of salt. Stir in 1¼ cups milk. Cook, stirring, over boiling water until thickened. Gradually stir mixture into 6 beaten egg yolks. Return to double boiler and cook, stirring, until mixture coats a metal spoon. Remove from heat and add ½ teaspoon each of vanilla and almond extracts. Chill; fold in ¾ cup heavy cream, whipped.

PEACH AND APPLE PIE

Mix ¾ cup sugar, 2 tablespoons all-purpose flour, ⅛ teaspoon salt, 1 tablespoon fresh lemon juice, ½ teaspoon grated lemon rind, ¼ teaspoon ground nutmeg, and ½ teaspoon ground cinnamon. Line a 9-inch pie pan with pastry rolled ⅛ inch thick. Half fill pan with equal amounts of sliced fresh peaches and apples (about 1½ cups each). Sprinkle with half of sugar mixture. Top with 3 more cups of fruit and the remaining sugar mixture. Dot with 1 tablespoon butter. Adjust top crust, lattice if desired, and bake in preheated hot oven (425°F.) for 40 to 50 minutes. Makes 6 servings.

LATTICE-CRUST FRESH-PEACH PIE

    4 cups thinly sliced fresh peaches
    ¾ cup sugar
    3 tablespoons quick-cooking tapioca
    ¼ teaspoon salt
      Pastry for 2-crust 9-inch pie, unbaked
    2 tablespoons butter or margarine

Combine peaches, sugar, tapioca, and salt. Turn into a 9-inch pie plate lined with pastry rolled ⅛ inch thick. Dot with butter. Roll remaining pastry into a circle ⅛ inch thick. Cut into strips ½ inch wide. Arrange over pie in lattice fashion. Trim, turn under, and flute edge. Bake in preheated hot oven (425°F.) for 40 minutes or until browned over the top. Makes 6 servings.

KEY LIME PIE WITH PEACHES

To make crust, mix 1¼ cups fine graham-cracker crumbs with ¼ cup sugar and ¼ cup softened butter or margarine. Press mixture firmly onto bottom and sides of 9-inch pie pan. Bake in preheated moderate oven (375°F.) for 8 minutes. Cool. To make filling, prepare 1 package Key lime pie filling, following chiffon pie package directions. Chill. When ready to serve, top with whipped cream and sliced peaches.

PEACH KUCHEN

    1½ cups sifted all-purpose flour
    ½ teaspoon salt

    ½ cup butter or margarine
    ⅓ cup dairy sour cream
    4 cups sliced fresh peaches
    3 egg yolks, beaten
    1 cup sugar

Mix 1¼ cups of the flour and ¼ teaspoon of the salt. Cut in butter until pieces are about the size of peas. Stir in 2 tablespoons sour cream. Press mixture into a baking pan (9 x 9 inches). Bake in preheated moderate oven (375°F.) for 20 minutes. Spread peaches on baked crust. Mix remaining flour, salt, and sour cream, egg yolks, and sugar. Pour over peaches. Bake in preheated moderate oven (375°F.) for 35 to 40 minutes, or until firm. Cool; then chill and serve plain or with ice cream or whipped cream, if desired. Makes 8 servings.

PEACH SHORTCAKE

    3 cups sifted all-purpose flour
    4½ teaspoons baking powder
    1 teaspoon salt
    ⅓ cup sugar
    ¾ cup shortening
    2 eggs, beaten
    ⅔ cup light cream or milk (about)
    2 tablespoons butter or margarine, melted
    4 cups sliced fresh peaches, sweetened
      Whipped cream

Mix dry ingredients including sugar. Cut in shortening. Add eggs, and enough cream to moisten dry ingredients and to make a soft dough. Divide dough and pat half into a greased 9-inch layer-cake pan. Brush with butter. Roll out remaining dough, and put on top. Bake in preheated hot oven (425°F.) for about 25 minutes. Split and fill with half the peaches. Spoon remaining peaches on top and serve with whipped cream. Makes 6 to 8 servings.

ANGEL PEACH RASPBERRY CAKE

    1 cup heavy cream
    1 cup fresh or drained, partially thawed, frozen raspberries
    1 angel-food cake
      About 1½ cups sliced peaches

Whip cream until stiff and fold in berries. Spread on cake. Arrange peach slices around cake and on top of it. Makes 8 to 10 servings.

PEACH CRÈME DE MENTHE PARFAIT

Put a few peach slices in parfait glass. Fill with peach ice cream. Pour a little green crème de menthe over top and garnish with another peach slice.

PEACH BUTTERMILK SHERBET

    1½ cups buttermilk
    1 cup sugar
    1 teaspoon vanilla extract
    ⅛ teaspoon salt
    1½ cups crushed fresh peaches, about 1¼ pounds
    1 unbeaten egg white

Mix first 5 ingredients well. Turn into freezing tray and freeze until almost hard. Transfer to a mixing bowl. Add

egg white and beat with a rotary or electric beater until fluffy. Return to freezing tray and freeze until firm and ready to serve. Makes 1 quart.

PEACH CREAM

    8 whole fresh peaches
    1 cup sherry
    1 cup port
    2 tablespoons sugar
    1 tablespoon red-currant jelly
    1 quart vanilla ice cream

Scald peaches in hot water and peel off skins. Cut peaches into halves and remove pits. Heat sherry and port with sugar. Add 4 pits and the peach halves. Simmer slowly for about 30 minutes. Take out pits. Put peach halves in flat dish and chill. Add jelly to wine mixture and cook to thick syrup. Chill. Fill each peach half with ice cream and pour wine sauce over. Makes 8 servings.

PEACH MELBA

      Vanilla, peach, or pistachio ice cream
      Half recipe of Peach Compote (page 1316)
    1 box frozen raspberries, thawed and puréed

Put a serving of ice cream in the bottom of a wide champagne glass or serving dish. Top with a drained peach half and raspberry purée. Makes 6 servings.

PEACH RIPPLE ICE CREAM

    3 large or 4 medium fresh peaches
    1 tablespoon fresh lemon juice
    ¾ cup sugar
    1 quart vanilla ice cream
    ½ cup heavy cream
    ¼ teaspoon almond extract

Peel peaches and put through food mill, whirl in blender, or mash very fine. Mix with lemon juice and sugar, and chill for 30 minutes. Soften ice cream slightly. Whip cream until stiff and stir in flavoring. Quickly mix peaches, whipped cream, and soft ice cream, and put back in freezer until firm. Makes 1 quart.

PEACH DELIGHT

    3 or 4 medium fresh peaches
    2 cups miniature marshmallows
    ¼ cup sugar
    2 tablespoons fresh lemon juice
    ¼ teaspoon almond extract
    2 cups heavy cream
      Sweetened sliced peaches

Peel and pit peaches, and mash with masher or whirl in blender. Mix peaches, marshmallows, sugar, lemon juice, and flavoring. Cover, and chill for 2 to 3 hours. Beat with rotary beater for 3 minutes, or until marshmallows are partially broken up. Whip cream until stiff, and fold into peach mixture. Pour into shallow dish and chill for several hours, or partially freeze. Serve with sliced peaches. Makes 6 to 8 servings.

PEACH SUNDAE SAUCE

    4 medium fresh peaches
    ½ cup sugar

½ cup fresh orange juice
2 teaspoons fresh lemon juice
1 teaspoon vanilla extract

Peel and pit peaches. Crush fine with masher or whirl in blender. Mix peaches, sugar, and orange juice in saucepan. Bring to boil and simmer, uncovered, for 15 minutes, or until thickened. Remove from heat, and stir in lemon juice and vanilla. Serve warm on ice cream, with a topping of chopped nuts if desired. Makes 2 cups.

SPICED PEACH AND BLUEBERRY JAM

4 pounds fresh peaches
1 quart fresh blueberries
½ cup water
5½ cups sugar
½ teaspoon salt
2 cinnamon sticks
1 teaspoon whole cloves
½ teaspoon whole allspice

Peel and pit peaches. Force through coarse blade of food chopper. Wash and pick over berries. Combine with peaches in kettle, add water, and bring to boil. Cover, and simmer for 10 minutes, stirring occasionally. Add sugar and salt. Tie spices in a cheesecloth bag and add. Bring to boil slowly, stirring until sugar dissolves. Boil rapidly for 10 minutes, or until fruit is clear. Remove spice bag. Ladle into hot sterilized jars, and seal. Makes six 8-ounce jars.

PEACH CHUTNEY

4 pounds peaches, peeled (about 2 quarts)
1 cup seedless raisins
2 garlic cloves, minced
½ cup chopped onion
⅔ cup chopped preserved gingerroot
1 to 2 tablespoons chili powder
1 tablespoon mustard seeds
1 teaspoon curry powder
1½ teaspoons salt
4 tablespoons mixed pickling spice, tied in cheesecloth bag
4 cups cider vinegar
4½ cups (2 pounds) brown sugar

Slice peaches and combine with remaining ingredients in large bowl. Cover and let stand overnight. Turn mixture into heavy kettle. Bring to boil. Simmer, uncovered, until chutney is of desired consistency, about 30 to 45 minutes. Stir frequently to prevent scorching. Remove spice bag. Ladle chutney into hot sterilized jars. Seal. This is particularly good with curry dishes. Makes 2 quarts.

PICKLED PEACHES

3½ cups (one 1-pound, 13-ounce can) peach halves
1 cup sugar
¾ cup cider vinegar
1 tablespoon each of whole cloves and whole allspice, tied in bag
2 cinnamon sticks

Drain juice from peach halves into kettle. Add sugar, vinegar, and spices. Boil for 10 minutes; add peaches and cook for 5 minutes, or until peaches are heated

through. Remove spice bag. Pack peaches in hot sterilized jars. Fill jars with boiling hot syrup. Seal. Makes three 8-ounce jars.

PEACH CHILI

3 peaches, peeled
3 pears, peeled
3 onions, peeled
15 ripe tomatoes, peeled
1½ large green peppers
1 garlic clove, if desired
1½ cups sugar
2 cups vinegar
2¼ teaspoons ground allspice
1½ teaspoons salt

Cut peaches, pears, onions, and tomatoes into small pieces. Remove seeds from peppers, then chop. Peel and chop garlic. Combine fruits and vegetables. Add sugar, vinegar, allspice, and salt. Cook slowly (slow boil) until thick, 2½ to 3 hours. Seal in sterilized jars. Makes 6 cups.

GINGER FRESH-PEACH CHUTNEY

2 quarts sliced fresh peaches
1¼ cups cider vinegar
¼ cup chopped onion
½ cup seedless raisins
½ cup chopped red pepper
2 tablespoons whole mustard seeds
1 ounce crystallized gingerroot
1½ cups sugar

Cook peaches in boiling vinegar until tender but not mushy. Add remaining ingredients and cook, uncovered, for 1¼ to 1½ hours, or until thick and clear, stirring occasionally. Pack in hot sterilized jars. Seal at once. Makes 3 pints.

PEACH AND ORANGE CONSERVE

2 large oranges
¼ cup water
18 large peaches, about 5 pounds
Sugar
½ cup chopped blanched almonds

Wash oranges and cut into quarters. Remove seeds. Put oranges, peel and all, through medium-fine blade of meat grinder. Add water, cover, and simmer for 20 minutes. Drop peaches into boiling water for a few seconds. Peel peaches and slice very thin. Measure fruits and combine, adding an equal volume of sugar. Let stand for 4 hours at room temperature until sugar is absorbed, stirring occasionally. Then boil rapidly for 45 minutes to 1 hour, until thick and clear. Stir in almonds. Seal while hot in sterilized jars. Makes 5 pints.

GINGERED PEACH HALVES

Into a saucepan, drain syrup from 3½ cups (one 1-pound, 13-ounce can) peach halves. Add ¼ cup each of preserved-ginger liquid and chopped preserved gingerroot. Boil for 10 minutes. Pour over fruit in bowl. Chill. Serve with sour cream or with Amber Whipped Cream. Makes 4 servings.

Amber Whipped Cream

Put ½ cup heavy cream and 2 table-

spoons light brown sugar in bowl; chill for 1 hour. Then whip until stiff.

PEACH BOWLER

For each serving, pour a little chilled grenadine in bottom of shallow glass. Put in one or two peach halves. Fill with chilled ginger ale.

PEACH-PLUM MILK SHAKE

For each shake, put in electric blender ¼ cup each of sliced peaches and red plums, fresh or canned. Add 1 tablespoon corn syrup, 2 tablespoons sherry, ½ cup milk, and ½ cup finely cracked ice. Cover, turn on blender, and beat until thoroughly blended, 15 seconds to 2 minutes. Pour into tall glass.

QUICK PEACH DESSERT

About 3 cups (one 1-pound, 13-ounce can) peach halves
½ package (1 stick) piecrust mix
1 cup firmly packed dark brown sugar
Butter

Drain peaches and put in 8-inch square baking dish. Crumble piecrust mix and sugar together and blend well. Sprinkle on top of peaches and dot generously with butter. Bake in preheated slow oven (325°F.) for 30 minutes, or until brown and bubbly on top. Serve warm with cream. Makes 4 to 6 servings.

PEACOCK—The peacock, cousin of the turkey, is a beautiful bird with a brilliantly luminous tail which is marked with eyes that seem to glow.

In the days of sumptuous Roman banquets, the peacock was considered necessary for a grand feast. For centuries thereafter no banquet was complete without one. In 1470, for instance, the then Archbishop of York served 100 peacocks to his guests. It was considered superior in elegance to such medieval delights as swans.

The usual manner of preparing a peacock was carefully to remove the skin and feathers and stuff the bird with spices and herbs. It was then roasted, and the skin and feathers were put back on. Sometimes the claws and beak were gilded, or sometimes the whole bird was gilded. The brilliant tail was carefully spread. Often a piece of cotton or wool soaked in spirits was placed in the mouth. When the time for the peacock course arrived, the bird was carried, beak *en flambé*, on a gold or silver dish, into the banquet hall. It was considered a great privilege to carve the bird; the victorious knight or most illustrious guest would be offered this opportunity. King Arthur is said to have carved peacock for 500 guests, a task that must have challenged even that brave man.

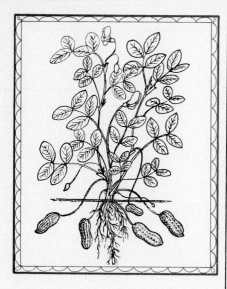

PEANUT—A spreading annual plant, *Arachis hypogaea*, related to peas and beans. The peanut plant grows to a height of about eighteen inches and bears light-green leaves and whitish flowers. At this stage of its growth its resemblance to the pea plant is great and accounts for its name. But once the flowers of the peanut plant fade, the flower stalks, which have until then been happy above ground, bend back down into the earth and develop their oblong pale brown fruit, the yellowish-brown pods containing one to three (most often two) seeds, which we call peanuts. Hence, to harvest a peanut crop the whole plant must be dug up. After this the plants are stacked for a period of weeks to cure the nuts. Peanuts are often called groundnuts, monkey nuts, ground peas, and earthnuts because of their peculiar method of growing. The popular southern name, goober, is from an African word for peanut, *nguba*.

The pods of the peanut vary. They may grow from one to two inches in length, with one, two, or three seeds. The pod shapes may also vary but usually they are contracted between the seeds and are thin, netted, and spongy. The seed has a thin papery coat which may be any color from white to purple. The most common colors are mahogany, red, rose, and salmon. The seed itself may be oblong or almost round.

Peanuts were known in South America over 2,000 years ago, and are believed to be native to Brazil. The ancient pre-Incan and Incan tribes buried their mummified dead with peanuts to give them strength on their long voyage. These ancient tribes also depicted the peanut on their pottery.

With the coming of the Spanish, the peanut left its native home for Europe, Asia, and Africa. It was cultivated in Africa as a cheap and nourishing crop. Early Virginia settlers found that their pigs, if fed on these groundnuts, were especially tasty. It is the peanut, in fact, that gives Virginia ham its distinctive flavor. Peanuts have been an important agricultural crop in the South since the post-Civil War period.

There are as many uses for peanuts as there are names for it. Peanut oil and peanut butter are two valuable by-products. Even the shells and the left-over "cakes" formed after the oil has been pressed out make extremely good cattle fodder. George Washington Carver, the famous Negro scientist, found over 300 synthetic products that could be made with peanuts, including milk, butter, cheese, coffee, flour, breakfast food, ink, wood stains, and insulating board.

Availability—Two types of peanuts are available, generally known as Virginia and Spanish. The Virginia peanut has larger and longer kernels, a lower oil content, and a more pronounced flavor than the Spanish peanut.

Peanuts are sold in the shell, or are sold shelled, roasted, and salted. When choosing peanuts in the shell, look for clean shells free from cracks; the peanuts should not rattle.

Peanuts are also sold in a great variety of glass jars, cans, and other types of packages.

☐ 1⅓ pounds unshelled peanuts = 1 pound shelled nuts = 3¼ cups

Storage—Peanuts not protected by an unopened vacuum can or jar should be stored in the refrigerator. Roasting and salting decrease somewhat the length of time peanuts will remain fresh.

☐ Vacuum-packed, kitchen shelf: indefinitely

☐ In-the-shell, refrigerator shelf: 9 months

☐ Shelled, refrigerator shelf: 3 months

Nutritive Food Values—High in fat and a concentrated source of calories. They contribute substantial amounts of protein, calcium, sodium, and potassium, and small amounts of iron, niacin, riboflavin, and thiamine.

☐ Raw, 3½ ounces = 568 calories

☐ Roasted, 3½ ounces = 582 calories

☐ Roasted and salted, 3½ ounces = 585 calories

Basic Preparation

☐ **To Roast**—Spread shelled peanuts in shallow pan; heat in preheated slow oven (300°F.) for 30 to 45 minutes. Stir several times; check on brownness by removing skins from a few nuts.

☐ **To Salt**—Cool roasted peanuts and slip off skins by pressing between thumb and forefinger. Add 1 teaspoon butter or margarine per cup peanuts and place over low heat, stirring constantly, until nuts are well coated and warm. Spread nuts on absorbent paper and sprinkle with salt while warm.

☐ **To Chop**—Use wooden board and straight knife or chopping bowl and chopper.

☐ **To Grind**—Use special nut grinder; when making peanut butter, use finest blade of meat grinder.

PEANUT SOUP, AFRICAN STYLE
1 pound raw boneless meat
  Water
1 teaspoon salt
2 onions, chopped
1 pound peanuts, roasted in shell
1 pound smoked fish
1 dried salt herring
  Cayenne
4 or 5 tomatoes, peeled and diced
6 pods okra
2 hard-cooked eggs

Cut meat into ½-inch cubes. Cover with salted water; add 1 onion. Cover, and cook over moderate heat until meat is tender. Meantime remove shells and skins from nuts. Force nuts through grinder using finest blade. Dice smoked fish and herring. Add with nuts to soup. Add tomatoes and whole okra. Cover, and continue cooking for 30 minutes. Add remaining onion and eggs forced through coarse sieve. Simmer for 20 minutes longer. Makes 6 servings.

BAKED-BEAN AND PEANUT SANDWICHES
1 cup Boston-style baked beans, drained
⅓ cup each of chopped peanuts and diced celery
1 tablespoon instant minced onion
2 tablespoons ketchup
  Salt to taste
8 slices of hot buttered toast

Mash beans and add remaining ingredients except toast. Spread between slices of toast. Makes 4 sandwiches.

PEANUT MACARONI AND CHEESE
8 ounces macaroni
  Salt
¼ cup butter or margarine
¼ cup all-purpose flour
¼ teaspoon pepper
3 cups milk
12 ounces sharp Cheddar cheese, shredded
¾ cup chopped salted peanuts

Cook macaroni in boiling salted water until tender; drain. Melt butter, and blend in flour and pepper. Gradually add milk and cook, stirring, until thickened. Stir in cheese, reserving 1 cup for top. Add ½ cup of the peanuts and salt to taste. Pour over macaroni and mix lightly. Top with remaining cheese and peanuts. Bake in preheated moderate oven (375°F.) for about 30 minutes. Makes 4 to 6 servings.

PEANUT POTATO CAKES

1½ cups chopped salted peanuts
2¼ cups mashed potato
     Few sprigs of parsley, chopped
1 egg, beaten
⅛ teaspoon pepper
     All-purpose flour
     Margarine or bacon drippings

Mix peanuts, potato, and parsley. Stir in about half the egg and the pepper. Shape into 8 flat cakes. Dip cakes into remaining egg, then into flour. Brown on both sides in hot margarine. Cakes may be dipped into fine crumbs instead of flour, if preferred. Makes 4 servings.

BANANA PEANUT SALAD

4 bananas, peeled and sliced
     Fresh lemon juice
½ cup salted peanuts, with skins removed
     Shredded salad greens
⅓ cup mayonnaise
⅓ cup dairy sour cream
     Juice of ½ lemon
2 pimientos, chopped

Brush banana slices with lemon juice. Mix with peanuts. Surround with salad greens and chill until ready to serve. Mix mayonnaise with sour cream, lemon juice, and pimiento. Serve salad with dressing. Makes 4 servings.

PEANUT STUFFING

4 cups soft bread crumbs
1 cup chopped peanuts
1 small onion, grated
¼ cup chopped parsley
¼ cup melted butter or margarine
½ cup chicken bouillon or water
     Salt and pepper to taste

Mix all ingredients together thoroughly. Use stuffing for poultry. Makes about 5 cups.

JAVANESE SATAY SAUCE

1 garlic clove
1 small onion
1 cup roasted peanuts, skins removed
2 fresh chilies
3 dried chilies
1 teaspoon sugar
1 small piece of tamarind
     Juice of ½ lemon
2 tablespoons water
2 tablespoons coconut milk*
1 tablespoon soy sauce

In a mortar or electric blender, crush together garlic, onion, peanuts, fresh and dried chilies, sugar, and tamarind. Fry this paste in a dry frying pan for a few minutes. Add lemon juice, water, coconut milk, and soy sauce and bring to a boil. Reduce heat and allow to simmer until the sauce is very thick. Satay sauce keeps in the refrigerator in a tightly closed jar for a few weeks. Makes 4 to 6 servings.
*To make coconut milk, soak shredded coconut in 1 cup cold water. Let stand, stirring occasionally, for 1 hour. Strain juice and press pulp to extract all juice.
Note: Serve this sauce with meat threaded on skewers and broiled.

PEANUT AND RAISIN CLUSTERS

6 ounces semisweet chocolate pieces
1 can (14 ounces) undiluted sweetened condensed milk
     Dash of salt
1 cup seedless raisins
1 cup shelled roasted peanuts, skins removed

Melt chocolate in top part of double boiler over boiling water. Add condensed milk and salt. Cook for 10 minutes, or until thickened, stirring constantly. Add raisins and nuts. Drop by tablespoonfuls onto wax paper. Refrigerate until firm. Makes about 20 clusters.

POPCORN PEANUT BRITTLE

1½ cups granulated sugar
½ cup dark corn syrup
½ cup water
½ teaspoon salt
1 quart unsalted popped corn
1 cup shelled and skinned peanuts
2 tablespoons butter or margarine
1 teaspoon vanilla extract

Combine sugar, corn syrup, water, and salt in heavy saucepan. Stir over low heat until sugar is dissolved. Cook over medium heat until a candy thermometer registers 300°F., or until a small amount of syrup dropped into very cold water separates into threads which are hard and brittle. Meanwhile spread popped corn and nuts in well-greased shallow pan and heat in preheated moderate oven (350°F.) for 10 minutes. Remove syrup from heat and quickly stir in butter and vanilla, stirring until butter melts. Pour over popcorn-nut mixture and stir. Spread mixture thin on a flat surface. Cool. Break into small pieces. Makes 1¼ pounds.

PEANUT CRISPS

1 cup soft butter or margarine
1½ cups firmly packed light brown sugar
2 eggs
2 teaspoons vanilla extract
3 cups sifted all-purpose flour
½ teaspoon baking soda
¼ teaspoon salt
2 cups salted peanuts
     Granulated sugar

Cream butter, brown sugar, eggs, and vanilla until light. Stir in sifted dry ingredients. Add peanuts, and mix well. Drop by rounded teaspoonfuls about 2 inches apart onto lightly greased cookie sheets. Flatten with greased bottom of drinking glass dipped in granulated sugar. Bake in preheated moderate oven (375°F.) for 8 to 10 minutes. Makes about 6 dozen.

PEANUT OATMEAL COOKIES

1 cup soft butter or margarine
1 cup granulated sugar
1 cup firmly packed dark brown sugar
2 eggs
1 teaspoon vanilla extract
1½ cups sifted all-purpose flour
½ teaspoon baking soda
3 cups quick-cooking rolled oats
½ pound salted Spanish peanuts

Cream butter until light and fluffy. Add sugars, eggs, and vanilla. Beat until light. Add remaining ingredients and mix well. Drop by teaspoonfuls onto greased cookie sheets. Bake in preheated moderate oven (375°F.) for about 10 minutes. Store in airtight container. Makes 12 dozen.

YELLOW CAKE WITH BROILED PEANUT FROSTING

1 package yellow-cake mix
¼ cup soft margarine
⅔ cup firmly packed dark brown sugar
¼ cup undiluted evaporated milk
1 cup finely chopped peanuts
¼ cup smooth peanut butter

Mix yellow-cake mix according to directions on package. Pour batter into pan (13 x 9 x 2 inches). Combine remaining ingredients and blend well. When cake is baked and cooled in the pan, spread the top with the peanut mixture. Put cake under the broiler and broil until frosting bubbles.

PEANUT BUTTER—This is a blend of peanuts which have been shelled, roasted, blanched (the skin and germ of the seed removed), and then ground. Small amounts of salt and hydrogenated vegetable oil are added. Sometimes dextrose, which absorbs oil, is added.

The inimitable taste and texture of peanut butter is indescribable. Suffice it to say that every mother in the land wonders how children were raised before peanut butter was invented in 1890 by a doctor in St. Louis who prescribed a nutritious, easily digested high-protein food for some of his patients.

The high fat content permits peanut butter's use as a partial substitute for fats in some recipes. Peanut butter is used for sandwich spreads, in muffins, cakes, cookies, candy, dessert sauces, and for an interesting flavor is added to creamy casseroles.

Availability and Purchasing Guide—Two textures, sold in glass vacuum jars, are commonly available: smooth and crunchy. The latter contains chunky bits of peanuts.

Storage

☐ Kitchen shelf, opened: 2 months
☐ Kitchen shelf, unopened: 1 year

Nutritive Food Values—Peanut butter is a concentrated source of energy because of its high fat content. It has a fair amount of protein, good niacin, and some iron.

☐ 3½ ounces, with small amounts of added fat, salt = 581 calories
☐ 3½ ounces, with moderate amounts of added fat, salt, sweetener = 589 calories

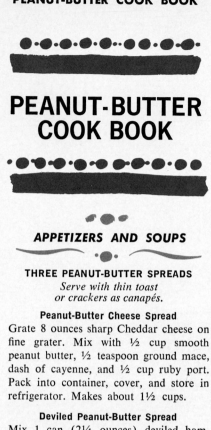

PEANUT-BUTTER COOK BOOK

APPETIZERS AND SOUPS

THREE PEANUT-BUTTER SPREADS

*Serve with thin toast
or crackers as canapés.*

Peanut-Butter Cheese Spread

Grate 8 ounces sharp Cheddar cheese on fine grater. Mix with ½ cup smooth peanut butter, ½ teaspoon ground mace, dash of cayenne, and ½ cup ruby port. Pack into container, cover, and store in refrigerator. Makes about 1½ cups.

Deviled Peanut-Butter Spread

Mix 1 can (2¼ ounces) deviled ham, ½ teaspoon celery salt, and ½ cup peanut butter. Makes about ⅔ cup.

Peanut-Butter Bacon Spread

4 slices of bacon
½ cup peanut butter
¼ cup drained pickle relish
1 tablespoon pickle liquid
Dash of hot pepper sauce

Cook bacon until crisp. Drain on paper towel, and crumble into small pieces. Mix with remaining ingredients. Makes 1 cup.

PEANUT-BUTTER HAM PUFFS

1 egg, separated
½ cup peanut butter
½ cup ground ham
1 teaspoon grated onion
¼ teaspoon salt
30 crisp round crackers

Beat egg yolk well, and mix with peanut butter, ham, onion, and salt. Beat egg white until stiff. Fold ham mixture into egg white. Put small spoons of mixture on crackers on ungreased cookie sheet. Bake in preheated moderate oven (350° F.) for about 10 minutes. Serve hot. Makes 30.

QUICK TRICKS WITH PEANUT BUTTER

■ Spread crisp crackers with peanut butter. Top with marshmallow cream. Brown lightly under broiler and dot with red jelly.

■ Season peanut butter with prepared horseradish to taste. Spread on Melba toast and heat briefly in hot oven.

■ To peanut butter add fresh lemon or orange juice to taste. Use as a stuffing for pitted dates or prunes.

■ Wash and dry celery hearts. Trim to 3- or 4-inch lengths and stuff with crunchy peanut butter.

CREOLE PEANUT-BUTTER SOUP

1 medium onion, minced
2 tablespoons butter or margarine
1 tablespoon flour
1½ teaspoons salt
½ teaspoon celery salt
½ cup peanut butter
2 cups milk
2 cups tomato juice
Chopped parsley

Cook onion in butter for 2 or 3 minutes. Stir in flour and seasonings. Blend in peanut butter. Gradually stir in milk. Cook, stirring, until thickened. Add tomato juice and bring just to the boil. Sprinkle with parsley. Makes 5 cups, or 4 servings.

PEANUT-BUTTER CELERY SOUP

1 cup diced celery
1 medium onion, chopped
2 tablespoons butter or margarine
4½ cups milk
4 chicken bouillon cubes
2 pimientos, minced
⅛ teaspoon pepper
¼ cup peanut butter
Sautéed or toasted croutons

In top part of double boiler over direct heat cook celery and onion in butter for 2 or 3 minutes. Put over boiling water and add 4¼ cups milk. Heat to scalding and add next three ingredients. Cover and cook for 15 minutes. Beat remaining milk and peanut butter until blended. Add to first mixture and blend well. Serve with croutons. Makes 1½ quarts, or 6 servings.

MEAT, POULTRY, CHEESE, AND SANDWICHES

BEEF BIRMINGHAM

1 garlic clove, sliced
1 pound beef for stew, cut into thin strips
1 cup sliced onions (3 medium)
1 cup sliced celery
2 tablespoons cooking oil
2 tablespoons peanut butter
2 tablespoons soy sauce
½ teaspoon sugar
1 cup beef bouillon
Dash of pepper
Hot cooked rice or noodles

Sauté garlic, beef, onions, and celery in hot oil until lightly browned. Add remaining ingredients except rice, bring to boil, cover, and simmer for 1 hour, or until meat is tender. Add additional liquid during cooking if needed. Serve on rice. Makes 4 servings.

NIGERIAN GROUNDNUT STEW

2 pounds boneless lamb for stew
3 large onions, sliced
1½ teaspoons salt
3½ cups water
3 large ripe tomatoes, quartered

3 chili peppers, washed and seeded
1 cup peanut butter
2 cups beef bouillon
3 to 4 cups hot cooked rice
6 hard-cooked eggs, shelled

Put first 3 ingredients and 3 cups water in large saucepan, bring to boil, and simmer, covered, for 1 hour, or until meat is almost tender. In saucepan combine tomatoes, peppers, and ½ cup water. Bring to boil and simmer, covered, for 8 to 10 minutes. Force through sieve. Mix peanut butter, tomato mixture, and bouillon; add to meat. Simmer until meat is tender. To serve, put a helping of rice in each soup plate. Put an egg in the center and cover with stew. Makes 6 servings.

Note: Dried or pickled chili peppers can be substituted for the fresh peppers.

MALAYAN PORK KABOBS

¼ cup peanut butter
1½ teaspoons ground coriander
1½ teaspoons salt
½ teaspoon cayenne
1 teaspoon ground cuminseed
4 medium onions, ground or minced
½ teaspoon pepper
1 garlic clove, minced
1½ tablespoons fresh lemon juice
1 tablespoon brown sugar
3 tablespoons soy sauce
2 pounds lean boneless pork, cut into 1½-inch cubes

Mix all ingredients except pork. Add pork and mix until meat is coated on all sides. Cover and refrigerate for several hours. Thread meat on skewers and broil under broiler unit or over charcoal coals for 20 to 25 minutes, turning to brown all sides. Makes 6 servings.

PEANUT-BUTTER HAM ROLLS

About 2 cups (one 1-pound, 2-ounce can) dry-pack sweet potatoes
3 tablespoons butter or margarine, melted
8 large thin slices of cooked ham
½ cup dark corn syrup
¼ cup smooth peanut butter
¼ cup fresh orange juice
1 teaspoon grated orange rind

Mash sweet potatoes and blend in 2 tablespoons butter. Spread about ¼ cup on each ham slice. Roll up and secure with toothpicks. Put in shallow baking dish. Mix remaining ingredients including 1 tablespoon butter and pour over ham rolls. Bake in preheated moderate oven (350°F.) for about 30 minutes, turning and basting occasionally. Makes 4 servings.

CHICKEN IN PEANUT-TOMATO SAUCE

1 large frying chicken (about 3½ pounds), quartered
¼ cup all-purpose flour
1 teaspoon salt
⅛ teaspoon pepper
¼ cup cooking oil
1 medium onion, chopped
1 garlic clove, minced
⅓ cup peanut butter

1 can (8 ounces) tomato sauce
1 tablespoon each of sugar and vinegar
1 teaspoon chili powder
1 cup water

Wash and dry chicken. Mix flour, salt, and pepper. Dredge chicken with mixture and brown on all sides in hot oil. Remove chicken and brown onion and garlic lightly in oil remaining in skillet. Blend in other ingredients and add chicken pieces. Bring to boil and simmer, covered, for 40 minutes, or until chicken is tender. Stir sauce occasionally and add more water if necessary to prevent sticking. Makes 4 servings.

CREOLE PUFF

6 slices of toast, diced
1½ cups grated Cheddar cheese
½ cup crunchy peanut butter
2 eggs
1 teaspoon salt
½ teaspoon dried oregano
¼ teaspoon pepper
1 teaspoon steak sauce
2 cups tomato juice

In shallow 1½-quart baking dish arrange alternate layers of toast and cheese. Mix peanut butter, eggs, and seasonings. Gradually add tomato juice, stirring until blended. Pour over ingredients in baking dish. Bake in preheated moderate oven (350°F.) for 30 minutes, or until firm. Makes 4 to 6 servings.

PEANUT-BUTTER SANDWICHES

■ **Peanut-Cranberry Sandwiches** — Cut canned cranberry jelly into ⅛-inch slices. Spread slices of white bread with peanut butter. Put together with cranberry jelly between.

■ **Peanut-Cheese Sandwiches** — Spread date-nut bread with peanut butter. Put together with bread spread with cream cheese.

■ **Peanut-Bacon Sandwiches**—Spread slices of seeded rye bread with peanut butter. Put together with 2 slices of crisp bacon between each 2 slices.

■ **Peanut-Honey Sandwiches**—Spread slices of orange-nut bread with a mixture of equal parts of honey and peanut butter.

VEGETABLES, SALADS, AND SAUCES

PEANUT LOAF

1 cup crunchy peanut butter
1 cup cooked rice
1 cup soft bread crumbs
2 cups milk
1 egg, beaten
2 teaspoons salt
¼ teaspoon pepper

Mix all ingredients until blended. Pack in well-greased loaf pan (9 x 5 x 3 inches). Bake in preheated moderate oven (350°F.) for 45 to 50 minutes. Turn out

on hot platter and cut into slices to serve. Makes 4 to 6 servings.
Note: A main-dish rice loaf that can be served with a celery-soup sauce.

PEANUT-BUTTER SWEET-POTATO CASSEROLE

About 2 cups (one 1-pound, 2-ounce can) dry-pack sweet potatoes, mashed
½ cup well-drained crushed pineapple
⅓ cup crunchy peanut butter
2 tablespoons butter or margarine, melted
¼ cup sugar
½ teaspoon salt
½ pound sliced bacon, partially cooked

Mix all ingredients except bacon. Spread in greased shallow baking dish. Arrange bacon on top. Bake in preheated moderate oven (350°F.) for 30 minutes. Makes 4 to 6 servings.

BRAISED CELERY WITH PEANUT-BUTTER SAUCE

3 cups sliced celery
1 medium onion, sliced
¼ cup peanut butter
2 tablespoons soy sauce

Put celery, onion, and ¼ cup water in saucepan, bring to boil, and simmer, covered, for 5 to 8 minutes. Drain, reserving liquid. Put vegetables in hot serving dish and pour liquid back into saucepan. Stir peanut butter and soy sauce into liquid. Add 3 or 4 tablespoons water to thin mixture. Heat and pour over celery. Makes 4 to 6 servings.

PEANUT-BUTTER STUFFED TOMATOES

4 ripe tomatoes
⅓ cup peanut butter
⅔ cup soft bread crumbs
¾ teaspoon salt
Dash of pepper
¼ teaspoon ground oregano
1 tablespoon minced onion
¼ cup finely diced celery
Chopped parsley

Cut a thin slice from top of each tomato. Scoop out pulp and chop. Mix with remaining ingredients except parsley. Fill tomato shells and put in shallow baking dish. Bake in preheated hot oven (400° F.) for 25 to 30 minutes. Sprinkle with parsley. Makes 4 servings.

PEANUT-BUTTER POTATO SALAD

¼ cup each of vinegar and salad oil
1 teaspoon salt
¼ teaspoon pepper
3 cups diced hot cooked potatoes (4 medium)
1 cup diced celery
¼ cup chopped green onion
1 cup diced cooked ham
½ cup mayonnaise
½ cup peanut butter

In bowl mix vinegar, oil, salt, and pepper. Add potatoes and mix lightly. Chill. When ready to serve add celery, onion, and ham. Mix mayonnaise and peanut butter. Add to mixture; toss lightly. Makes 4 to 6 servings.

PEANUT-BUTTER FRUIT SALAD

⅓ cup mayonnaise
¼ cup peanut butter
1 cup diced pineapple
½ cup chopped nuts
½ cup raisins
⅓ cup drained mandarin oranges
Lettuce cups

Gradually stir mayonnaise into peanut butter. Add remaining ingredients except lettuce and toss lightly. Chill and serve in lettuce cups. Makes 4 servings.

OLD COLONIAL SALAD DRESSING

¼ cup cider vinegar
½ teaspoon salt
Dash of pepper
¾ cup salad dressing
2 tablespoons smooth peanut butter
2 tablespoons dark rum

Put all ingredients in a covered container and shake until thoroughly blended. Good with mixed greens or grapefruit sections. Makes about 1¼ cups.

PEANUT-BUTTER PINEAPPLE SALAD DRESSING

1 cup (one 8½-ounce can) crushed pineapple, undrained
½ cup peanut butter
½ cup marshmallow cream
¼ cup fresh lemon juice
Dash of salt

Mix all ingredients thoroughly, chill, and serve. Use for fruit salads. Makes 2 cups.

PEANUT-BUTTER SAUCE

2 tablespoons cooking oil
1 small onion, minced
¼ cup minced green pepper
1 can (6 ounces) tomato paste
2½ cups water
½ teaspoon salt
¼ teaspoon ground oregano
2 bay leaves
½ cup peanut butter

Heat oil in saucepan. Add onion and green pepper and cook for 2 to 3 minutes. Add remaining ingredients except peanut butter. Bring to boil. Then stir in peanut butter. Cover and simmer for 30 minutes, or until fairly thick, stirring occasionally. Makes 3 cups, or enough for 1 pound spaghetti.
Note: Serve this on hot cooked spaghetti with a sprinkling of chopped parsley.

PEANUT-BUTTER SOUR-CREAM SAUCE

Put ¼ cup peanut butter in small bowl. Gradually stir in 1 cup dairy sour cream. Mix until blended. Fold in 1 tablespoon prepared horseradish, 1 teaspoon salt, dash of pepper, and 1 tablespoon fresh lemon juice.
Note: Serve on hot or cold cooked carrots, beets, or green vegetables.

BREADS AND PANCAKES

PEANUT-BUTTER ORANGE BREAD

2¼ cups sifted all-purpose flour
3 teaspoons baking powder
½ teaspoon salt

⅓ cup sugar
½ cup peanut butter
1 egg, well beaten
1 cup milk
1½ teaspoons grated orange rind
¼ cup chopped salted peanuts

Sift dry ingredients into bowl. Cut in peanut butter. Mix egg, milk, and orange rind and add with peanuts to first mixture, stirring to blend. Pour into well-greased loaf pan (9 x 5 x 3 inches) and bake in preheated moderate oven (350° F.) for 35 to 40 minutes. Remove from pan; cool. Store overnight.

PEANUT-BUTTER GARLIC BREAD

¼ cup peanut butter
¼ cup soft butter or margarine
1 garlic clove, crushed
⅛ teaspoon salt
1 medium loaf French or Italian bread

Mix first 4 ingredients. Slice bread into 1-inch slices not quite through to bottom of loaf. Spread peanut-butter mixture between slices. Wrap in foil and bake in preheated hot oven (400°F.) for 10 to 15 minutes.

PEANUT-BUTTER MUFFINS

1¾ cups sifted all-purpose flour
2½ teaspoons baking powder
2 tablespoons sugar
¾ teaspoon salt
2 tablespoons wheat germ
¼ cup soft shortening
¼ cup peanut butter
1 egg, well beaten
¾ cup milk
Apricot preserves

Sift first 4 ingredients into bowl. Add wheat germ. Cut in shortening and peanut butter. Mix egg and milk and add all at once to first mixture. Stir only until dry ingredients are dampened. Spoon into greased large muffin pans, filling only two thirds full. Put about ½ teaspoon preserves in center of each. Bake in preheated hot oven (400°F.) for 25 minutes, or until done. Makes 10.

PEANUT-BUTTER MARMALADE COFFEECAKE

2 cups biscuit mix
¼ cup sugar
¼ cup smooth peanut butter
1 egg
¾ cup milk
½ cup orange marmalade
Vanilla Frosting

Combine biscuit mix and sugar. Cut in peanut butter. Beat egg and milk with fork and add to first mixture. Beat for 30 seconds with spoon. Pat into greased 9-inch layer-cake pan 1½ inches deep. Spread with marmalade. Bake in preheated hot oven (400°F.) for about 25 minutes. While warm, drizzle with Vanilla Frosting. Serve warm or cold in same pan.

Vanilla Frosting

Blend ¾ cup sifted confectioners' sugar, dash of salt, ½ teaspoon vanilla extract, and 1 tablespoon milk.

Note: To serve cake out of pan: before putting in batter line pan with heavy foil, extending edges beyond edge of pan. When baked, lift cake with edges of foil. Put on plate and peel off foil.

PEANUT-BUTTER APPLE TEA STICKS

1 egg
¾ cup firmly packed light brown sugar
¼ cup milk
1 teaspoon vanilla extract
½ cup peanut butter
¾ cup sifted all-purpose flour
1 teaspoon baking powder
½ teaspoon ground cinnamon
¼ teaspoon salt
1 cup chopped peeled raw apples
Sifted confectioners' sugar

Beat egg until light. Gradually beat in brown sugar. Add milk, vanilla, and peanut butter, and mix well. Fold in sifted flour, baking powder, cinnamon, and salt. Add apple. Spread in greased pan (8 x 8 x 2 inches), and bake in preheated moderate oven (350°F.) for 30 to 35 minutes. Cool for 5 minutes. Then cut into 24 finger-shape pieces. Roll in confectioners' sugar. Makes 24 sticks.

PEANUT-BUTTER PANCAKES

Combine 1 cup pancake mix, 1 cup milk, 1 egg, and 3 tablespoons peanut butter. Beat until smooth. Bake on heated lightly greased skillet or griddle. Serve hot with syrup. Makes sixteen 3-inch cakes.

DESSERTS AND DESSERT SAUCES

PEANUT-BUTTER ICE CREAM

2 egg yolks
1 can (14½ ounces) evaporated milk
½ cup peanut butter
⅔ cup sugar
Dash of salt

Beat egg yolks well. Blend in remaining ingredients and turn into freezer tray. Freeze until frozen 1 inch from edges of tray. Turn into chilled bowl and beat until smooth. Return to tray and freeze until just firm. Makes 4 to 6 servings.
Note: This is good with hot fudge sauce and topped with salted peanuts.

PINEAPPLE CRUMB PUDDING

1 box (3¼ ounces) vanilla-pudding and pie-filling mix
2 cups milk
1 cup graham-cracker crumbs
¼ cup peanut butter
1⅔ cups (one 13½-ounce can) crushed pineapple, drained
½ cup heavy cream, whipped

Prepare pudding with milk as directed on package label. Cool. With fingers, blend crumbs and peanut butter. Stir pineapple into cooled pudding and fold in cream. Arrange alternate layers of crumbs and pudding in serving dish, ending with crumbs. Makes 6 servings.

1 — Creole Peanut Butter Soup
2 — Sandwiches: Peanut-Cranberry; Peanut-Cheese and Peanut-Bacon
3 — Peanut-Butter Ham Rolls
4 — Peanut Marmalade Coffeecake
5 — Peanut Butter Stuffed Tomatoes
6 — Chicken in Peanut-Tomato Sauce

PEANUT-BUTTER CHIFFON PIE

1 envelope unflavored gelatin
½ cup sugar
¼ teaspoon salt
1 cup milk
2 eggs, separated
⅔ cup smooth peanut butter
1 cup dairy sour cream
9-inch pie shell, baked
    Peanut-Butter Topping (at right)
    or sweetened whipped cream
1 ounce (1 square) semisweet chocolate

In top part of small double boiler mix gelatin, ¼ cup of the sugar, and the salt. Add milk and egg yolks and beat with rotary beater until blended. Put over simmering water and cook, stirring, until mixture thickens slightly and coats a spoon. Remove from heat, pour into bowl, and beat in peanut butter. Cool thoroughly. Beat egg whites until foamy. Gradually add remaining sugar and beat until stiff. Stir sour cream into peanut-butter mixture. Then fold in egg whites. Pile lightly into baked pie shell and chill until firm. Decorate with Peanut-Butter Topping and chocolate curls made from semisweet chocolate square. Makes 6 to 8 servings.

PEANUT-BUTTER CAKE

⅓ cup soft butter or margarine
2¼ cups sifted cake flour
1½ cups sugar
3 teaspoons baking powder
1 teaspoon salt
⅓ cup peanut butter, smooth or chunk-style
1 cup milk
2 eggs
1 teaspoon vanilla extract
    Chocolate Peanut-Butter Frosting

Cream butter until light and fluffy. Sift in flour, sugar, baking powder, and salt. Add peanut butter and ⅔ cup milk. Mix until all flour is dampened. Beat for 2 minutes at low speed of electric mixer, or 300 vigorous strokes by hand. Add ⅓ cup milk, eggs, and vanilla and beat for 2 minutes. Pour into two 9-inch layer pans lined on the bottom with greased wax paper. Bake in preheated moderate oven (375°F.) for about 25 minutes. Cool for 5 minutes. Turn out on rack and peel off paper. Cool and spread with Chocolate Peanut-Butter Frosting.

Chocolate Peanut-Butter Frosting

½ cup peanut butter
⅓ cup unsweetened cocoa
2⅔ cups sifted confectioners' sugar
¼ teaspoon salt
1 teaspoon vanilla extract
½ cup cream or undiluted evaporated milk (about)

Cream together peanut butter and cocoa. Add confectioners' sugar, salt, vanilla, and enough cream to give spreading consistency. Beat until smooth.

PEANUT-BUTTER APPLE CAKE

¼ cup soft butter
½ cup peanut butter
1 cup sugar
1 egg
1¼ cups sifted all-purpose flour
1 teaspoon baking soda
1 teaspoon salt
½ teaspoon ground cinnamon
¼ teaspoon each of ground nutmeg and cloves
1 cup canned applesauce

Cream butter, peanut butter, and sugar. Add egg and beat well. Sift dry ingredients and add alternately with applesauce to first mixture, stirring until smooth. Pour into pan (8 x 8 x 2 inches) lined on bottom with wax paper. Bake in preheated moderate oven (350°F.) for 40 minutes, or until done. Cool for 5 to 10 minutes. Turn out on rack; peel off paper. Cool well.

SURPRISE PEANUT COOKIES

⅔ cup shortening
⅓ cup firmly packed light brown sugar
2 eggs, separated
½ teaspoon almond extract
1 cup sifted all-purpose flour
½ teaspoon baking powder
½ cup smooth peanut butter
    About 1⅓ cups chopped salted jumbo peanuts

Cream shortening and sugar. Add egg yolks and beat until light and fluffy. Add flavoring. Stir in flour sifted with baking powder. Shape into 24 balls. Chill slightly, if necessary. Flatten balls on lightly floured board. Put about 1 teaspoon peanut butter in the center of each circle and wrap dough around. Roll each ball in slightly beaten egg whites, then in chopped peanuts. Put on lightly greased cookie sheets and bake in preheated moderate oven (350°F.) for 12 to 15 minutes. Makes 24.

PEANUT-BUTTER TOPPING

½ cup cold milk
½ teaspoon vanilla extract
2 tablespoons peanut butter
2 tablespoons sugar
1 package (2 ounces) dessert-topping mix

Blend all ingredients in small bowl of electric mixer. Then beat at high speed until topping forms soft peaks. Serve on Peanut-Butter Chiffon Pie, at left, on cakes or pudding. Makes about 1½ cups.

PEANUT-BUTTER CHOCOLATE SAUCE

Melt 2½ ounces (2½ squares) unsweetened chocolate in ½ cup milk. Add a dash of salt and ¾ cup firmly packed light brown sugar. Cook, stirring, until sugar is dissolved. Remove from heat and add ½ teaspoon vanilla extract and ¼ cup crunchy peanut butter. Makes about 1⅓ cups.

PEANUT-BUTTER CHOCOLATE FUDGE

¼ cup peanut butter
½ cup evaporated milk
1 cup marshmallow cream
1¼ cups sugar
½ teaspoon salt
1 cup (6-ounce package) semisweet chocolate pieces

In saucepan mix all ingredients except chocolate. Put over low heat and cook and stir until blended. Bring mixture to a full boil, stirring. Boil for 3 minutes, stirring constantly. Remove from heat, add chocolate, and stir until blended. Pour into buttered 8-inch square pan. Cool, and cut in 36 pieces.

APRICOT CANDY ROLL

3 cups sugar
½ cup peanut butter
1 cup ground dried apricots
1 cup milk
½ teaspoon salt
2 teaspoons vanilla extract

In saucepan mix all ingredients except vanilla. Stir over medium heat until well blended. Bring to boil and cook without stirring until a small amount of mixture forms a soft ball when dropped into cold water (238°F. on a candy thermometer). Remove from heat and cool until outside of pan feels lukewarm. Add vanilla and beat until creamy and easy to handle. Turn out on buttered platter and work with hands until very smooth and satiny. Shape into 2 long rolls and chill for at least 3 hours. Slice thin to serve. Makes about 2 pounds.

PEANUT FLOUR—Flour made from ground peanuts from which the greatest part of the oil has been extracted. The finer grades are sold to bakeries for use in the manufacture of various kinds of cakes, breads, and confections. Inferior qualities are consumed as stock food. In Europe the flour is baked into a bread which has a large sale in France and Germany. Peanut flour is available in health-food stores.

Caloric Value

☐ 3½ ounces = 371 calories

PEANUT OIL—Oil obtained by the cold pressing of peanuts. When it is well filtered, it is a sweet and delectable product, nearly colorless, and good both for table use or cooking. In France it is extensively used in packing of sardines and some other food products. The Chinese especially use it a great deal for cooking. Peanut oil is widely available in food stores.

Caloric Value

☐ 1 cup = 1945 calories
☐ 1 tablespoon = 124 calories

FRESH PEAR CHART

ANJOU
Season: October to March
Characteristics: Large, chunky, green-yellow skin, often russet; winey flavor
Uses: Eating, cooking, canning

BARTLETT
Season: July to October
Characteristics: Medium, all-purpose pear; bell-shaped, yellow with red blush
Use: Eating

BOSC
Season: October to January
Characteristics: Large, tapering neck, yellow with russet; slightly acid
Uses: Eating, cooking (bake and broil)

CLAPP FAVORITE
Season: Late August to September
Characteristics: Large, symmetrical, yellow with red blush; sweet
Uses: Eating, canning

COMICE
Season: October to January
Characteristics: Large, roundish, greenish yellow to yellow with red
Use: Eating

SECKEL
Season: September to December
Characteristics: Small, yellowish brown, buttery flesh; spicy
Uses: Eating, canning, pickling

WINTER NELIS
Season: February to May
Characteristics: Medium, russet dots on yellow-green skin; sweet
Uses: Eating, cooking, canning

PEAR—A tree and its fruit cultivated in temperate zones. The pear tree belongs to the rose family, whose varieties include a large number of such favorite fruits as apples, plums, cherries, apricots, raspberries, and strawberries. The pear is a native of the vast area stretching from central Europe to Asia. Most of the pear varieties grown in the United States are developed from the European pear, *Pyrus communis,* which originated in the area of southeastern Europe and western Asia, or they are hybrids of the European pears and the sand, or China, pear, *P. serotina.* Bartlett and Anjou pears are examples of the former, Kieffer, Le Conte, and Seckel pears, of the latter.

Pears were known to the ancient Egyptians, Romans, and Greeks. In the Middle Ages they were extensively grown in the orchards of castles and monasteries, the guardians of the civilization of their times. Pears are now grown all over the world in temperate zones; over 5,000 varieties are known in Europe. France is the leading pear-growing country. Sweet is the sight of a French pear orchard in bloom, or of espaliered pear trees, pruned to grow on wires flat against the white-washed walls of a French farmhouse.

Availability and Purchasing Guide—Pears are one of the few fruits which improve in flavor and texture when ripened off the tree. They are picked when mature but hard. Select pears that are firm but not hard. They should yield to slight pressure at the stem end.

Fruit may be roundish or bell-shape, symmetrical or uneven. It may have a long or short neck. The stem should be attached to the fruit. The skin ranges in color from green to yellow with red tinge to russet. Flesh is fine-grained and juicy. Taste may be sweet, buttery, spicy, or acid. For a description of the varieties see FRESH PEAR CHART.

☐ 1 pound = 3 to 4 pears = 2 cups, sliced

Canned pears are available whole, quartered, or sliced, packed in water, syrup, or juice. They are also available in diet packs and baby food. Pear nectar, spiced, and pickled pears are available, and pears are also found in fruit cocktail.

Dried pears are available packaged in halves and are also mixed with other dried fruits.

Storage—Keep underripe fruit in a cool, fairly humid place. Refrigerate ripe pears. Do not freeze pears.
☐ Fresh, refrigerator shelf: 3 to 14 days
☐ Canned, kitchen shelf: 1 year
☐ Canned, refrigerator shelf, opened: 4 to 5 days

Caloric Values

☐ Fresh, 3½ ounces, raw, including skin = 61 calories

☐ Canned, 3½ ounces, water pack, solids and liquid = 32 calories

☐ Canned, 3½ ounces, juice pack, solids and liquid = 46 calories

☐ Canned, 3½ ounces, light syrup pack, solids and liquid = 61 calories

☐ Canned, 3½ ounces, heavy syrup pack, solids and liquid = 76 calories

☐ Canned, 3½ ounces, extra-heavy syrup pack, solids and liquid = 92 calories

☐ Dried, 3½ ounces, uncooked = 268 calories

☐ Dried, 3½ ounces, cooked, without sugar, fruit and liquid = 126 calories

☐ Dried, 3½ ounces, cooked with sugar, fruit and liquid = 151 calories

Basic Preparation—Wash before serving. Use underripe pears for cooking.

☐ **To Stew**—To make 4 servings peel and quarter 4 winter pears. Simmer ½ cup sugar and ½ cup water for 5 minutes. (A small piece of lemon rind or 1 cinnamon stick can be added, if desired.) Add pears, cover, and simmer for 10 minutes, or until tender. Cool; then chill.

FRESH-PEAR AND SHRIMP APPETIZER
Toss diced unpeeled fresh pears, cooked shrimps, and chopped celery with lemony French dressing. Spoon into cocktail glasses lined with crisp greens.

FRESH-PEAR SNACKS
Core fresh pear halves and fill with cream cheese softened with milk or light cream and blended with chopped figs or pitted dates.

POACHED PEARS AND APPLES
Fresh pears and apples poached together in syrup made with equal parts of sugar and water and fresh lemon juice to taste make a convenient dish to have on hand for dessert, breakfast, or meat accompaniment.

FRESH PEARS AS MEAT ACCOMPANIMENT
Baked fresh pears make a delicious accompaniment for pork, ham, chicken, or veal dishes. Allow ½ unpeeled cored pear for each serving. Sprinkle with fresh lemon juice and sugar, top with ½ teaspoon butter or margarine, and bake.

CURRIED PEARS
3 large winter pears
3 tablespoons butter or margarine
3 tablespoons light or dark brown sugar
3 teaspoons curry powder, or more to taste
¼ teaspoon salt

Wash and dry pears. Do not peel, but cut into halves and core. Place pear halves in greased shallow baking pan. Combine butter, sugar, curry powder, and salt. Divide mixture into 6 parts. Place 1 part into the cavity of each pear half. Bake in preheated moderate oven (350° F.) for 30 minutes, or until tender. Makes 6 servings.

Note: Serve with pork, ham, chicken, or duck.

FRESH-PEAR AND CUCUMBER ASPIC
2 envelopes unflavored gelatin
1 cup cold water
1 cup hot water
⅔ cup sugar
⅔ cup fresh lemon juice
½ teaspoon salt
Fresh pear balls
2 cups diced fresh pears
1 cup diced cucumbers
½ cup thinly sliced cucumbers
Cottage cheese
Fresh parsley

Soften gelatin in cold water. Add hot water and stir until dissolved. Stir in sugar, lemon juice, and salt. Pour ¼ cup mixture into bottom of a 5-cup ring mold. Chill until partially set. Chill remaining mixture until thick as fresh egg whites. Press fresh pear balls into partially set gelatin in mold. Fold diced pears and diced cucumbers into remaining mixture. Pour into mold. Arrange sliced cucumbers around outside edge of mold. Chill until firm. Unmold on serving plate and fill center with cottage cheese. Garnish with fresh parsley. Makes 6 to 8 servings.

FRESH-PEAR, CHEESE, AND ANCHOVY SALAD
2 large pears
¼ cup soft process American cheese
3 tablespoons cream cheese
1 tablespoon anchovy paste
¼ teaspoon milk
½ teaspoon fresh lemon juice
Head lettuce
French dressing

Cut pears into ¼-inch lengthwise slices. Remove cores and seeds. Combine cheeses, anchovy paste, milk, and lemon juice. Spread 1 to 2 teaspoons on each pear slice. Arrange on head lettuce and serve with French dressing. Makes 4 servings.

FRESH-PEAR CACTUS SALAD
6 firm ripe Bartlett pears
1 cup sugar
2 cups water
1 tablespoon fresh lemon juice
2 cinnamon sticks

½ teaspoon whole cloves
Shelled roasted peanuts
Lettuce
Mayonnaise

Wash and pare pears. Cut into halves lengthwise and core. Mix sugar, water, and lemon juice in a saucepan. Add cinnamon and cloves. Bring to boiling point. Add pears, a layer at a time. Cover and cook for 20 minutes, or until pears are tender. Do not overcook. Remove pears from syrup, drain, cool, and chill. Stick each pear with shelled peanut halves until covered. Arrange on lettuce. Serve with mayonnaise mixed with some of the pear syrup. Makes 6 servings.

FRESH-PEAR AND CRABMEAT SALAD
2 large pears
2 cups cooked crabmeat
1 cup diced celery, white part only
⅓ cup mayonnaise
3 tablespoons fresh lemon juice
Salt and white pepper to taste
Shredded salad greens

Peel, core, and dice pears. Combine with all other ingredients except salad greens. Mix lightly but thoroughly. Serve on salad greens. Makes 4 servings.

PEAR-CHEESE SALAD
Peel and core whole ripe but firm pears. Do not cut up pears. Sprinkle with lemon juice to prevent darkening. Stuff cavities with either cottage or cream cheese, Liederkranz, Brie, Camembert, or blue cheese. Sprinkle pears with paprika, or roll in very finely chopped nuts. Chill until serving time. Slice and serve on salad greens with French dressing made with lemon juice.

PEAR DE MENTHE SALAD
About 12 (one 1-pound, 14-ounce can) pear halves
1 cup (one 8¾-ounce can) seedless grapes, cut into halves
2 envelopes unflavored gelatin
¼ cup water
Syrup from fruit
1 tablespoon honey
Dash of salt
¼ cup fresh lemon juice
¼ cup green crème de menthe
1 cup dairy sour cream
¼ cup toasted slivered almonds
Salad greens

Drain pears and grapes, reserving syrup. Set aside 6 pear halves. Dice remaining pears and mix with grapes. Soften gelatin in water. Heat syrup drained from fruits, add gelatin, and stir until dissolved. Add honey and salt. Cool. Beat in lemon juice, crème de menthe, and sour cream. Chill. When partially set, fold in grapes, diced pears, and almonds. Pour into 1½-quart mold and chill until firm. Unmold on greens; encircle with pear halves, cut side up. Makes 6 servings.

LIME-PEAR SALAD
About 6 to 10 (one 1-pound can) pear halves

1331

PEAR COOK BOOK

1 box (3 ounces) lime-flavored gelatin
1 cup boiling water
½ cup each of diced celery and
   cucumber
1 avocado, sliced
2 tablespoons fresh lime juice
½ teaspoon grated lime rind
   Salad greens
   Dairy sour cream

Drain pears, reserving syrup. Dissolve gelatin in boiling water and add syrup. Chill until slightly thickened. Fold in remaining ingredients except last two. Pour into 1½-quart mold and chill for several hours, or until firm. Turn out on greens and serve with sour cream. Makes 4 to 6 servings.

BAKED WINTER-PEAR HALVES

6 large winter pears
½ cup sugar
2 tablespoons all-purpose flour
¼ teaspoon ground nutmeg
2 tablespoons butter or margarine
½ cup hot water

Peel pears, cut into halves, and core. Place, cut side up, in a baking pan (8 x 14 x 2 inches). Combine sugar, flour, and nutmeg. Sprinkle over pears. Place 1 teaspoon butter in each pear cavity. Pour hot water into bottom of pan. Cover with foil. Bake in preheated moderate oven (375° F.) for 20 minutes. Remove cover and continue baking until pears are lightly browned and tender, about 15 minutes. Makes 6 servings.

GRATED FRESH-PEAR SNOW

3 medium pears
¼ cup fresh lemon juice
⅛ teaspoon salt
6 tablespoons sugar
2 egg whites
   Grated unsweetened chocolate
   (optional)

Grate pears (3 cups) and combine with lemon juice, salt, and 2 tablespoons of the sugar. Beat egg whites until they stand in soft peaks. Gradually beat in remaining sugar. Fold into pear mixture. Serve in sherbet glasses. If desired, sprinkle a little grated unsweetened chocolate over each serving. Makes 6 to 8 servings.

BAKED WHOLE PEARS WITH RAISIN-NUT FILLING

4 large winter pears
½ cup sugar
¼ cup each of raisins and chopped nuts
¼ teaspoon each of salt and ground
   mace
4 teaspoons strained honey
½ cup hot water

Wash pears. Cut off stem ends, and core. Place in shallow baking dish. Combine remaining ingredients except honey and water. Fill pears with sugar mixture and spoon remaining mixture around pears. Top each pear with 1 teaspoon honey. Add water to dish and cover. Bake in preheated moderate oven (375°F.) for 30 minutes. Uncover and bake for 10 minutes longer, or until pears are tender.

Serve warm or chilled, topping pears with sauce left in dish. Makes 4 servings.

FRESH PEARS WITH CHOCOLATE

6 fresh pears
½ cup plus 1 tablespoon sugar
½ cup water
¼ teaspoon salt
1 ounce (1 square) unsweetened
   chocolate
1 tablespoon butter
¼ cup light corn syrup
1 teaspoon vanilla extract

Peel, quarter, and core pears. Place in saucepan with ½ cup sugar, the water, and salt. Cover and simmer until pears are tender. Drain pears, saving syrup for later use. Melt chocolate with butter and corn syrup over hot water. Add a little of reserved pear syrup and mix well. Add remaining pear syrup and 1 tablespoon sugar and bring to boiling point. Remove from heat and add vanilla. Chill pears and sauce. Serve pears with chocolate sauce spooned over each serving. Makes 8 servings.

FRESH-PEAR CRUMB PUDDING

6 winter pears, peeled, cored, and
   thinly sliced
2 tablespoons sugar
½ teaspoon ground cinnamon
⅛ teaspoon ground allspice
2 tablespoons fresh lemon juice
½ cup firmly packed light brown sugar
½ cup sifted all-purpose flour
¼ cup butter or margarine
½ cup chopped nuts
½ cup fine dry bread crumbs

Place pears in 1½-quart casserole. Combine next 4 ingredients and toss lightly with pears. Mix brown sugar and flour. Add 2 tablespoons of the butter and cut in until mixture resembles coarse crumbs. Add nuts and sprinkle over pears. Dot with remaining butter. Top with fine bread crumbs. Bake in preheated moderate oven (350°F.) for 30 minutes, or until pears are tender and top is brown. Makes 6 to 8 servings.

FRESH-PEAR SAUCE

8 winter pears
¾ cup sugar
1 cup water
⅛ teaspoon salt
1 tablespoon fresh lemon juice
1 teaspoon grated lemon rind
½ teaspoon vanilla extract

Peel, core, and quarter pears. Place in saucepan with sugar and water and cook over low heat, covered, until pears are very tender, about 30 minutes. Mash well. Add remaining ingredients. Serve warm or chilled over your favorite gingerbread or plain cake. Makes about 8 servings.

FRESH-PEAR AMBROSIA

Wash, core, and dice fresh winter pears. Sprinkle with fresh orange juice and arrange in sherbet glasses with shredded moist coconut. For a special touch, top

each dish with a scoop of ice cream and a maraschino cherry.

PEAR DESSERT

Chill pear halves, allowing 1 per serving. Add any other frozen or fresh fruit such as grapefruit and orange sections, melon balls, or berries such as strawberries and blueberries.

PEARS POACHED IN FRESH GRAPE JUICE

5 pounds ripe juicy grapes
6 to 8 ripe but firm pears

Mash grapes well and strain through a fine sieve. Put juice in saucepan and simmer until cooked down to half of original amount. Peel and core pears. Or, if desired, cut pears into halves or quarters. Poach pears in grape juice, a few at a time. Put pears in glass serving dish. Pour remaining grape juice over pears. Chill before serving. Serve with plain heavy sweet cream or dairy sour cream sprinkled with a little ground mace. Makes 4 to 6 servings.
Note: The amount of grapes may have to be increased depending on their size and juiciness.

CARMEN PEARS

3 firm ripe Bartlett pears
1½ cups sugar
2 cups water
2 tablespoons fresh lemon juice
1 teaspoon vanilla extract
1 envelope unflavored gelatin
¼ cup cold water
2 cups fresh strawberries
1 to 2 drops of red food coloring
   Dash of salt
1 cup heavy cream, whipped
   Chopped nuts for garnish
   Rich Vanilla Custard

Wash and peel pears. Cut into halves lengthwise and core. Mix 1 cup of the sugar, the water, 1 tablespoon of the lemon juice, and the vanilla in saucepan. Bring to boiling point. Add pears, cover, and poach for 20 minutes, or until tender. Do not overcook. Cool in syrup and chill. Meanwhile, soften gelatin in cold water and dissolve over hot water. Wash strawberries, hull, mash, and sieve. Stir in remaining sugar and lemon juice, red food coloring, salt, and gelatin. Chill until mixture begins to thicken. Fold in whipped cream. Turn into glass or china bowl. Chill. Arrange drained pears over the top and sprinkle with chopped nuts. Serve with Custard. Save pear syrup to use for poaching additional pears or other fruits or for other uses as in fruit beverages. Makes 6 servings.

Rich Vanilla Custard

⅓ cup sugar
1 teaspoon flour
⅛ teaspoon salt
2 whole eggs
1 egg yolk
1½ cups milk
1 teaspoon vanilla extract

ENCYCLOPEDIA OF COOKERY

Pear-Cheese Salad ◄   Pear Cream Pie with Apricot Glaze ►

Combine sugar, flour, and salt in top part of double boiler or saucepan. Add whole eggs and egg yolk. Mix well. Stir in ¼ cup of the milk. Heat remaining milk only until hot, and add. Cook over hot, not boiling, water or over very low heat until the mixture coats a metal spoon, about 5 minutes, stirring constantly. Stir in vanilla. Cool and chill. Serve over Carmen Pears. Makes 2 cups.

PEARS DE LUXE

4 firm pears
  Juice of 4 fresh lemons
½ cup honey
½ cup rum
¼ cup chopped blanched almonds

Cut pears into halves, peel, and core. Arrange, cut side up, in baking dish. Combine lemon juice, honey, and rum; pour over pears. Bake, uncovered, in preheated moderate oven (350°F.) for 1½ hours, or until pears are tender. Baste pears every 15 minutes with syrup in bottom of pan. Remove from oven and sprinkle with almonds. Broil under low heat to toast almonds. Serve warm with sweet or dairy sour cream, or serve cold with garnish of cottage cheese. Makes 4 servings.

FRESH-PEAR COMPOTE

¾ cup water
¾ cup sugar
1-inch piece of vanilla bean or 1
  teaspoon vanilla extract
4 ripe but firm pears

Combine water, sugar, and vanilla bean. Bring to boiling point. Cook, covered, for 5 minutes. While syrup is cooking, peel and halve pears. Cut out cores. Stand prepared pears in cold water to prevent darkening. Add pear halves to syrup and cook over low heat, turning pears once during cooking. Spoon syrup occasionally over cooking pears. Cooking time depends on variety and ripeness of the pears: from 5 to 15 minutes. Pears should be just tender. Do not overcook or they will be mushy. Cool pears in syrup. Serve as is or with whipped cream, if desired. Makes 4 servings.

Note: This is the classic French way of cooking pears.

Fresh Pears Hélène

Prepare Fresh-Pear Compote. Place cooked pears in glass serving dish. Top with vanilla ice cream and hot chocolate sauce.

GINGERED PEAR COMPOTE

2 cups water
2 cups sugar
  Yellow rind of 1 fresh lemon
1 teaspoon ground ginger
6 Bartlett or Bosc pears, peeled and
  quartered
3 tablespoons chopped pistachio nuts

Combine water, sugar, lemon rind, and ginger. Bring to boil and cook for 4 minutes. Remove lemon rind. Add pears, a few at a time. Poach until pears are transparent. Do not overcook. Place pears in glass serving dish and pour hot syrup over fruit. Chill. Before serving, sprinkle with pistachio nuts. Makes 4 servings.

PEARS IN CRÈME DE CACAO

Drain 3½ cups (one 1-pound, 13-ounce can) pear halves, reserving syrup. Put pears, ¼ cup syrup, and ½ cup crème de cacao in bowl. Chill for at least 2 hours. Serve with unsweetened whipped cream with a sprinkling of instant coffee powder. Makes 4 servings.

RUBY PEARS

2 cups cranberries
1 cup water
1 cup sugar
2 tablespoons rum or applejack
Canned pear halves, chilled

Cook cranberries with water until skins pop. Strain and add sugar. Bring to a boil, stirring constantly. Stir in rum. Chill and serve over pear halves (allow 2 for each serving). Makes about 2 cups sauce, enough for 6 servings.

FRESH-PEAR CRUMBLE

3 cups sliced firm pears
Juice of 1 lemon
Grated rind of ½ lemon
½ cup sugar
¼ teaspoon ground nutmeg
½ cup soft bread crumbs
½ cup firmly packed light brown sugar
¼ cup melted butter or margarine
½ cup chopped nuts
Whipped cream or heavy cream

Combine first 4 ingredients in preheated electric skillet or baking pan of table oven. Mix the next 5 ingredients and sprinkle over top of pears. Cook at moderate temperature (350°F.) for about 40 minutes. Serve with cream. Makes 6 servings.

PEAR-ORANGE COMPOTE

½ cup sugar
1 cup water
Rind and juice of 1 orange
Juice of ½ lemon
4 large underripe pears, peeled

In saucepan combine sugar, water, shredded orange rind and juice, and lemon juice. Bring to boil and boil for 5 minutes. Add pears. Bring to boil, cover, and simmer for 20 to 25 minutes, or until pears are tender. Serve warm or cold, with sweet or sour cream, as desired. Makes 4 servings.

PEAR CREAM PIE WITH APRICOT GLAZE

1 package (3¼ ounces) vanilla pudding and pie filling
2 cups milk
Pastry for 1-crust 9-inch pie shell, baked
1 can (1 pound) pear halves, well drained
1 jar (1 pound) apricot preserves
2 tablespoons apricot or other brandy

Combine pudding and milk in saucepan. Cook according to package directions. Remove from heat. Cool for 5 minutes, stirring twice. Pour into pie shell and chill for at least 1 hour. Arrange pear halves on top of pie. Put preserves in small saucepan and bring to boil. Add brandy and simmer for 3 minutes, stirring. Force through a sieve and cool slightly. Spoon or brush over surface of pears. Chill until firm. Put a few lemon leaves in center of pie, if desired.

PEAR TART WITH CREAM

1 cup dry white wine
¼ cup sugar
⅛ teaspoon ground ginger
4 ripe but firm Comice or Anjou pears
1 cup heavy cream
1 tablespoon cornstarch
3 egg yolks, beaten
3 tablespoons sugar
2 teaspoons almond extract
9- or 10-inch pie shell, baked
½ cup apricot jam
1 tablespoon hot water

Combine wine, sugar, and ginger. Bring to boil and simmer for 3 minutes. Peel pears, cut into halves, and core them. Poach pears in wine syrup for 10 minutes, or until just tender. Drain pears and reserve syrup. Boil syrup down to measure 1 cup, or add water to bring up to 1 cup. Blend cream and cornstarch to smooth paste. Stir into syrup. Cook over low heat, stirring constantly, until mixture thickens. Beat egg yolks with sugar and almond extract. Stir syrup gradually into egg-yolk mixture. Replace over low heat and cook, stirring constantly, until thickened. Cool, and spread over pie-shell bottom. Arrange pears on top, rounded side up and pointed end to the center. Heat apricot jam and thin with water. Drizzle over pears. Makes 8 servings.

PEAR HONEY

⅓ cup water
⅓ cup sugar
Grated rind of ½ lemon
¼ teaspoon ground ginger
2 cups shredded winter pears

Put all ingredients except pears in saucepan over direct heat. Stir occasionally until sugar is dissolved. Add pears, cover, and simmer for 30 minutes. Serve as dessert or as sauce for cake. Makes 4 servings.

PEAR-PINEAPPLE CONSERVE

3 pounds (6 to 8 large) firm ripe pears
1 cup undrained canned crushed pineapple
5 cups sugar
Red and yellow food coloring

Peel, core, and slice pears; force through fine blade of food chopper. Combine with pineapple and sugar in kettle. Bring to boil and simmer, uncovered, for 20 minutes, or until thick, stirring frequently. Stir in a few drops each of red and yellow coloring. Ladle into hot sterilized jars; seal. Makes four or five ½-pint jars.

FRESH-PEAR RELISH

Bring 1 cup water, ½ cup sugar, ¼ teaspoon ground cinnamon, and ⅛ teaspoon ground allspice to a boil. Add 6 to 8 peeled and cored fresh pear halves and cook until tender. Fill pear centers with fresh cranberry sauce and arrange on a serving platter with roast chicken, turkey, duck, or goose. Makes 6 to 8 servings.

PECAN—A native American nut of the pecan tree, first found in southeastern United States and in Mexico. The trees are easy to grow and bear as early as three or four years after being set out, so that they are now grown commercially on a wide scale as far north as Virginia and Indiana, with the greatest concentration in Texas and Oklahoma. Pecans have very thin shells and the meat has a fat content of over seventy per cent, which is higher than any other vegetable product.

Pecans are associated with Southern cooking and Southern traditions. Whole pecans may be used to decorate baked products or garnish main dishes, vegetables, batters, doughs, pies, frostings, candies, ice cream, and sauces. They may also be salted, spiced, or sugared for eating out-of-hand.

Availability—Available all year round in shells, shelled, shelled and salted, and packaged mixed with other nuts. Peak crop available from September to November.

Purchasing Guide—When choosing nuts in the shell look for those which are clean, free from scars, cracks, or holes, and so well filled the kernel does not rattle. Shelled nuts should be plump and meaty, crisp and brittle, for best flavor and freshness. In-shell pecans are sold in bulk, boxed, and in packages of mixed nuts.

Shelled pecans are sold in vacuum cans; in plastic film bags; and also in vacuum jars or cans in varieties of mixed nuts. Chopped pecans are sold in plastic film bags.

☐ 2 pounds pecans in the shell = 1 pound shelled nutmeats = 4¼ cups

Storage—Store tightly covered in a cool dry place. Nuts keep longer in the shell. Shelled, they keep longer when left in large pieces. Nuts in vacuum cans keep indefinitely.

☐ Kitchen shelf, in shell: 4 months
☐ Kitchen shelf, shelled: 2 months
☐ Refrigerator shelf, in shell: 1 year
☐ Refrigerator shelf, shelled: 9 months
☐ Freezer, in shell or shelled: 2 years

Nutritive Food Values—High in fat and contain protein, iron, and B vitamins.

☐ 12 pecan halves (2 tablespoons chopped pecans) = 100 calories
☐ 3½ ounces = 687 calories

Basic Preparation

☐ **To Shell**—Carefully crack shell on all sides by gently rotating nut in nut cracker.
☐ **To Chop**—Use a long straight knife and wooden board, or a chopping bowl and chopper.
☐ **To Grind**—Use a nut grinder. For butters use a meat grinder or blender.

SOUTHERN CHICKEN WITH PECANS
1 frying chicken (about 2½ pounds), cut up
All-purpose flour
Salt and pepper to taste
¼ cup butter or margarine
¼ teaspoon marjoram
Cooked potato balls (12 to 16)
¾ cup shelled pecans

Coat chicken with flour seasoned with salt and pepper. Brown in butter. Sprinkle with marjoram. Cover; cook over low heat for 45 minutes. Add potato balls and pecans; heat. Makes 4 servings.

PECAN STUFFING
1 onion, chopped
½ cup chopped celery
½ cup butter or margarine
1 teaspoon salt
½ teaspoon paprika
5 cups diced stale bread
1½ cups chopped pecans
½ cup chopped parsley

Cook onion and celery in butter for about 5 minutes. Add salt and paprika. Mix lightly with remaining ingredients. Makes about 6 cups, or enough to stuff a 6-pound capon or other bird.

BURGUNDY PECANBURGERS
1 pound ground beef
1 teaspoon salt
¼ teaspoon pepper
½ cup coarsely chopped pecans
⅓ cup red Burgundy

Mix all ingredients except wine. Shape into 8 thin patties. Brown on both sides in skillet. Add Burgundy, cover, and simmer for 5 minutes, or until of desired doneness. Makes 4 servings.

JELLIED PECAN AND APPLE SALAD
1 envelope unflavored gelatin
⅓ cup sugar
½ teaspoon salt
1½ cups water
¼ cup fresh lemon juice
1¾ cups diced red eating apples, unpeeled
½ cup diced celery
½ cup chopped pecans
Salad greens
Mayonnaise or salad dressing

In small saucepan mix gelatin, sugar, and salt. Add ½ cup of the water. Stir over low heat until gelatin is dissolved. Stir in remaining water and lemon juice. Chill until slightly thickened. Fold in apples, celery, and pecans. Pack in 1-quart mold, and chill until firm. Unmold on greens, and serve with mayonnaise. Makes 6 servings.

PECAN-RICE LOAF
1 cup chopped pecans
1 cup dry herb-stuffing mix
⅓ cup diced celery
⅓ cup each of grated onion and carrot
1 cup cooked rice
2 eggs
⅓ cup soft butter or margarine
½ teaspoon caraway seed
1 cup tomato juice
1 cup water

Mix all ingredients, and let stand for 2 hours, stirring several times. Pack into greased loaf pan (9 x 5 x 3 inches). Bake in preheated slow oven (300°F.) for 1 hour, or until firm. Unmold, and serve hot as a main dish. Makes 6 servings.

PECAN-PIMIENTO CHEESE SPREAD
1 pound sharp Cheddar cheese
¾ cup mayonnaise (about)
½ cup chopped pecans
2 tablespoons chopped onion or chives
1 pimiento, minced

Grate cheese and bring to room temperature. Add remaining ingredients, and mix well. If too thick for spreading, add a little more mayonnaise. Makes about 3 cups.

PECAN-TUNA-CHEESE SANDWICHES
1 package (8 ounces) cream cheese
2 tablespoons fresh lemon juice
½ cup mayonnaise
½ cup chopped ripe olives
1 can (7 ounces) tuna, drained and flaked
¼ teaspoon monosodium glutamate
12 slices white bread
6 slices whole-wheat or cracked-wheat bread
Softened butter or margarine
1 cup salted pecan pieces or coarsely chopped salted pecans
Sweet-pickle sticks

Blend first 3 ingredients until smooth. Fold in olives and tuna. Add monosodium glutamate. Spread all slices of bread with butter. Spread 6 slices white bread with tuna filling; cover with whole-wheat slices. Spread with the tuna filling, and top with remaining white bread. Trim crusts and cut each in 4 triangles. Spread cut edges of triangles with filling. Then dip each edge in pecans. Garnish with sweet-pickle sticks. Makes 6 servings.

PRUNE PECAN BREAD
2 cups sifted all-purpose flour
2 teaspoons baking powder
½ teaspoon each of baking soda and salt
⅔ cup sugar
1 tablespoon grated orange rind
⅔ cup coarsely chopped pecans
1 cup coarsely chopped sweetened pitted cooked prunes
¼ cup prune juice
⅓ cup fresh orange juice
1 egg
¼ cup melted butter or margarine

Sift dry ingredients into a bowl. Add orange rind, pecans, and prunes; mix with fingers to coat. Beat prune juice, orange juice, and egg with a wire whisk or rotary beater. Pour liquid ingredients into dry, but do not overmix—just fold until well blended. Add butter or margarine and mix well. Spoon into buttered and floured loaf pan (about 9 x 5 x 3 inches), and place on a table with a thump to expel any air bubbles. Bake in preheated moderate oven (350°F.) until loaf tests done, 50 minutes to 1 hour. Remove from oven, let remain in pan for 5 minutes, loosen edges with a dull knife, and turn out onto a wire cake rack covered with wax paper. Can be frozen.

■ **Variation**—1 cup whole-wheat flour can be substituted for 1 cup all-purpose flour if desired.

PECAN COFFEECAKE
2 tablespoons granulated sugar
2 cups plus 2 tablespoons biscuit mix
1 egg
¾ cup milk
½ cup firmly packed brown sugar
2 tablespoons butter or margarine, melted
½ cup chopped pecans

Blend granulated sugar, 2 cups biscuit mix, 1 egg, and the milk. Beat vigorously for 30 seconds. Spread in greased 9-inch round layer pan or 8- or 9-inch square pan. Mix remaining biscuit mix, brown sugar, butter, and pecans. Sprinkle on batter in pan. Bake in preheated hot oven (400°F.) for 20 to 25 minutes. Serve hot.

STICKY PECAN ROLLS
1 package active dry yeast
¼ cup warm water
½ cup milk, scalded
Butter or margarine
3 tablespoons granulated sugar
1½ teaspoons salt
¼ cup water
1 egg
3 cups unsifted all-purpose flour
¾ cup firmly packed light brown sugar
2 teaspoons cinnamon
Pecan halves

Soften yeast in the warm water. Pour hot milk over 3 tablespoons butter, the granulated sugar, and the salt. Stir to dissolve butter and sugar. Stir in water and yeast. Beat in egg. Gradually add flour, and mix until well blended. Cover, and let stand for 15 minutes. Roll out dough on well-floured board to an 18- x 12-inch rectangle. Spread with butter. Mix ½ cup brown sugar and the cinnamon, and sprinkle on dough. Roll up, and cut in 1-inch slices. Arrange 4 or 5 pecan halves in bottom of each of 18 well-greased muffin cups. Sprinkle with remaining brown sugar, and dot with butter. Put rolls in pans. Cover, and let rise in warm place until double in bulk, about 1 hour. Bake in preheated moderate oven (375°F.) for about 20 minutes. Turn out of pans. Makes 18.

SPICY PECAN SQUARES

1 cup soft butter
1 cup firmly packed light brown sugar
1 teaspoon vanilla extract
1 egg, separated
2 cups sifted all-purpose flour
½ teaspoon salt
1 teaspoon ground cinnamon
1 cup ground pecans

Cream butter until light and fluffy. Add sugar, vanilla, and egg yolk. Beat until light. Add sifted dry ingredients and half of nuts. Mix well. Press into greased jelly-roll pan (15 x 10 inches) and brush top with slightly beaten egg white. Sprinkle remaining nuts on top. Bake in preheated moderate oven (350°F.) for 25 to 30 minutes. Cut into 2-inch squares. Makes about 3 dozen.

PECAN DAINTIES

1 cup soft butter
½ cup sugar
2 cups sifted all-purpose flour
1 teaspoon vanilla extract
1 tablespoon water
2 cups pecans, ground
Pecan halves

Cream butter and sugar until light and add remaining ingredients except pecan halves. Mix well and chill until firm. Shape into ¾-inch balls. Arrange on ungreased cookie sheets and top each with a pecan half. Bake in preheated slow oven (325°F.) for 20 minutes. Makes 6 to 8 dozen.

SOUTHERN PECAN DAINTIES

Mix 1 pound light brown sugar, 3 cups chopped pecans, 3 beaten egg whites, ¼ teaspoon salt, and 1 teaspoon vanilla extract. Drop by scant tablespoonfuls onto greased cookie sheets. Bake in preheated slow oven (300°F.) for about 20 minutes. Makes 6 dozen.

DATE COMFITS

1 pound pitted dates
1 cup chopped pecans
3 tablespoons chopped candied gingerroot
Confectioners' sugar

Force dates through coarse blade of food chopper. Combine dates with pecans and chopped or ground gingerroot. Dust hands with confectioners' sugar and knead mixture until blended. Roll mixture into a sausage shape (7 x 2 inches). Chill. Serve thinly sliced.

COFFEE-PECAN FANCIES

½ cup butter or margarine
½ cup granulated sugar
½ cup firmly packed light brown sugar
½ teaspoon vanilla extract
2 tablespoons instant coffee
1 egg
1 cup sifted all-purpose flour
¼ teaspoon salt
½ cup finely chopped pecans

Cream butter; gradually beat in sugars, vanilla, coffee, and egg. Sift flour and salt; stir into butter mixture along with pecans. Chill. Form into marble-size balls; put on ungreased cookie sheets. Bake in preheated moderate oven (350°F.) for 10 minutes, or until lightly browned. Makes 5 dozen.

APRICOT-PECAN STICKS

¾ cup soft butter
2 cups sugar
2 eggs
1 teaspoon vanilla extract
3 cups plus 1 tablespoon sifted all-purpose flour
Apricot preserves or jam
2 egg whites
Pinch of salt
1 cup pecan halves

Cream butter and 1 cup sugar; add eggs and beat until light. Add vanilla and 3 cups flour; mix well. Put on a greased cookie sheet, cover with a sheet of wax paper, and roll to ¼-inch thickness. Remove paper; spread dough with a thin layer of preserves. Bake in preheated moderate oven (375°F.) for 6 minutes. Beat egg whites with the salt until whites begin to hold their shape. Gradually beat in remaining 1 cup sugar and 1 tablespoon flour. Fold in pecans. Spread on top of partly baked mixture. Return to oven and bake for 15 minutes longer. Cool and cut into sticks (1 x 3 inches). Makes 4 dozen.

FROZEN BUTTERSCOTCH PECAN ROLL

1 cup heavy cream
¼ cup firmly packed dark brown sugar
½ cup chopped pecans
1 tablespoon butter
1 cup sifted cake flour
1 teaspoon baking powder
¼ teaspoon salt
3 eggs
1 cup granulated sugar
⅓ cup water
1 teaspoon vanilla extract
Confectioners' sugar
Butterscotch Sauce

Mix cream and brown sugar. Chill for 1 hour. Brown nuts lightly in butter and drain on absorbent paper. Reserve. Sift flour, baking powder, and salt. Beat eggs until very thick and lemon-colored. Gradually beat in granulated sugar. Blend in water and vanilla. Add dry ingredients and beat only until smooth. Grease a jelly-roll pan (15 x 10 inches) and line bottom with unglazed brown paper; grease. Pour in batter. Bake in preheated moderate oven (375°F.) for 12 to 15 minutes. Turn out on a towel sprinkled

with confectioners' sugar. Roll cake lengthwise in towel. Cool on a rack. Whip cream until stiff and fold in nuts. Unroll cake. Spread with cream mixture. Reroll and freeze. Cut into thick slices and serve with Butterscotch Sauce. Makes 8 servings.

Butterscotch Sauce

Combine in saucepan 2 cups firmly packed brown sugar, ½ cup undiluted evaporated milk, ¼ teaspoon salt, ⅓ cup light corn syrup, and ⅓ cup butter. Bring to boil and cook rapidly for 3 minutes (to 220°F. on a candy thermometer). Makes 2 cups.

CHOCOLATE-PECAN PIE

½ cup sugar
1 cup dark corn syrup
¼ teaspoon salt
1 tablespoon all-purpose flour
2 eggs
1 tablespoon butter or margarine
2 ounces (2 squares) unsweetened chocolate
1 teaspoon vanilla extract
1¼ cups pecan halves
Pastry for 1-crust, 9-inch pie, unbaked
Vanilla ice cream

Beat together sugar, syrup, salt, flour, and eggs. Melt butter and chocolate together; add with vanilla and pecans to first mixture. Pour into 9-inch pastry-lined pie pan. Bake in preheated slow oven (300°F.) for 50 to 60 minutes, or until filling is just set. Cool. (This pie can be baked a day ahead.) Serve with ice cream, or whipped cream if preferred.

Southern Pecan Pie

Use recipe above, omitting chocolate. Bake pie in preheated slow oven (300°F.) for 1 hour, or until set.

SUGARED PECANS

1½ cups sugar
⅓ cup water
¾ teaspoon each of ground cinnamon and nutmeg
⅛ teaspoon salt
1½ cups pecan halves

Mix sugar, water, spices, and salt in saucepan. Bring to boil and cook without stirring until 236°F. registers on candy thermometer, or until a small amount of mixture dropped into cold water forms a soft ball. Remove from heat and add pecans. Mix until a solid mass is formed. Separate individual nut halves from the sugar mixture while still hot. Let stand until cold. Makes about ¾ pound.

SALTED PECANS

½ cup cooking oil
4 cups shelled pecans
1 teaspoon salt

Heat oil in skillet until bubbles appear when a nut is added. Add nuts, 1 cup at a time; cook over very low heat until lightly browned. With a slotted spoon remove nuts to absorbent paper; sprinkle with salt. Makes 4 cups.

100 Menus
to help you plan more varied meals for your family with the recipes in this volume

*Recipes for all starred dishes found in this volume.

BREAKFAST

Mulled Grape Juice*
Crisp Sausage Links
Buttermilk Pancakes*
Honey Butter
Coffee

Grapefruit
Broiled Mullet*
Savory Corn Muffins*
Whipped Sweet Butter
Pear Honey*
Coffee

Pear-Orange Compote*
Sunday-Morning Fish Balls*
Broiled Tomato Halves
Buttered Toast
Coffee or Tea

Baked Winter-Pear Halves*
Creamed Codfish
and Baked Potatoes*
Raised Muffins*
Lemon Marmalade
Coffee

Fresh-Pear Compote*
Grilled Ham Steak
Fried Eggs
English Muffins*
Preserved Pumpkin Chips*
Tea

Tomato Juice
Fried Salt Pork
with Cream Gravy
Poached Eggs
Apple-Corn Muffins*
Margarine
Coffee

Vegetable Juice Cocktail
Broiled Mutton Chops*
Boiled Potatoes
Molasses Spiced Fruit*
Blueberry Breakfast Cake*
Coffee or Tea

Carrot Juice with Lemon
Ham Omelet*
Anadama Bread,* Toasted
Butter
Spiced Peach and
Blueberry Jam*
Coffee

LUNCH OR SUPPER

Fresh-Pear Sauce*
Molasses-Oat Waffles*
Canadian Bacon
Molasses-Honey-Butter Sauce*
Tea or Coffee

Apricot-Pineapple Juice
Cheese Omelet*
Crisp Bacon
Dumfunnies*
Warm Maple Syrup
Coffee

Mandarin Orange Segments
Harry Hamblet's
Golden-Fried Oysters*
Southern Onion Bread*
Butter
Danish Pastries
Coffee

Melon with Berries
Broiled Liver and Crisp Bacon
Custard Corn Bread*
Coffee

Yellow Pea Soup
with Smoked Pork*
Fresh Pear and Cucumber
Aspic*
Buttered Oatmeal Bread,*
Toasted
Spicy Pecan Squares*

Oxtail and Vegetable Soup*
Cheese Hearts*
Lattice-Crust
Fresh-Peach Pie*

Oyster Stew*
Garlic Black Olives*
Celery
Rice Muffins*
(split, buttered and toasted)
Jellied Cranberry Salads*

Peanut Soup, African Style*
Eggless Muffins*
Fresh Pears
with Chocolate*

Gardiners Bay
Potato Salad*
Peanut-Butter Ham Puffs*
Fresh-Pear Ambrosia*

Garlic Hamburgers
on Toasted Buns*
Insalata di Funghi Crudi
(Italian Raw-Mushroom Salad)*
Peach Bowler*

Eggs in Scallion and
Mushroom Sauce*
Indian Meal Raised Bread,*
Toasted
Peanut-Butter Bacon Spread*

Carrot and Parsley Soup*
Pecan-Tuna-Cheese
Sandwiches*
Poached Pears and Apples*

German Pancakes*
with Spinach
Tomatoes Vinaigrette*
Ruby Pears*

French Onion Soup*
Eggs Baked in Tomatoes
Parsley and Green-Onion
Stuffed Bread*
Anise Fruit Cup*

Peanut-Butter Celery Soup*
Chinese Egg Rolls*
Gingered Peach Halves*

———

Cream of Mushroom Soup*
Oyster Club Sandwich*
Jellied Mandarin Oranges*

Hungarian Palacsinta*
(with ham)
Peanut-Butter Stuffed
Tomatoes*
Snow Pudding with
Nesselrode Sauce*

———

Mushrooms with Baked
Crab in Shells*
Onion and Orange Salad*
Parsley-Cheese Toasts*
Peach Ambrosia*

Creamed Codfish
and Baked Potatoes*
Orange and Onion Salad*
Peanut Crisps*

———

Baked Fish Fillets in
Mushroom-Cheese Sauce*
Cucumber Jelly Salad*
Assorted Crisp Breads
Apple-Raisin-Nut Pie*

Beef and Onion Pie*
French Peas*
Cucumber-Pimiento Salad
Molasses-Peach Meringue*

———

Creole Peanut-Butter Soup*
French Omelet*
Hard Rolls
Almond, Pea, and Cheese
Salad*
Old-Fashioned
Apple Turnovers*

The Poor Parson's
Noodle Dish*
Lime-Pear Salad*
Sour Cream
Crisp Rye Wafers
Molasses Layer Cake*

———

Chicken Moussaka with Peas*
Cucumbers with Sour Cream*
Sesame Seed Biscuits
Butter
Steamed Apple-Prune
Pudding*

Burgundy Pecanburgers*
Pommes Mousseline*
Scallions and Beans,*
Chilled
French Kirsch Parfait*

———

Ossobuco*
Spiced Mustard Greens*
Orange and Watercress
Salad*
Hungarian Cheese Pastries*

Eggplant with Sesame*
Shish Kebab*
Pello (Iranian Pilaf)*
Baklava (Filled Pastry)*

———

Caviar*
Thin-Sliced Bread
Sweet Butter
Cherkes Tavugu
(Circassian Chicken)*
Bulgur Pilaf*
Stewed Raisins*

Arab Cheese* Olives
Kibbeh bi Sanieh
(Stuffed Meat Loaf)*
Coucou Sabzi (Iranian Spinach
and Parsley Pie)*
Maamoul (Farina Cakes)*

———

Roe Salad*
Kilich Shish (Turkish
Swordfish on Skewers)*
Mushroom-Barley Casserole*
Kadayif (Shredded-Wheat
Dessert)*

Yankee Pot Roast*
Baked Potatoes
with Coriander*
Mixed Green Salad
Peach Buttermilk Sherbet*

———

Haricot de Mouton
(Mutton Stew)*
Cabbage, Carrot, and
Spinach Salad
Vienna Bread
Whipped Butter
Pineapple Crumb Pudding*

Orange-Stuffed Veal*
Fettucine Alfredo*
Asparagus and Pimiento Salad
with Vinaigrette Dressing
Yellow Cake with
Broiled Peanut Frosting*

———

Fresh-Pear, Cheese, and
Anchovy Salad*
Hollyhock-House Mushrooms
and Chicken,
Barrister Style*
Rice with Noodles*
Angel Cake

Boiled Dinner, New England
Style* (Corned-Beef
Brisket and Vegetables)
English Mustard*
Orange-Marmalade Cake*
with Taffy Sundae Sauce*

———

Stuffed Mussels*
Baked Lamb Patties*
Peas with Mushrooms
and Onions*
Romaine and Watercress
Salad
Fresh Pears Hélène*

Mussels Marinière*
French-Fried Potatoes
Sliced Tomatoes
Hard Rolls   Butter
Strawberry and Almond
Cheesecake*

———

Mushrooms with Crabmeat*
Cold Roast Chicken*
Banana Peanut Salad*
Grape-Nuts Puff Pudding*

Beef Paupiettes*
Rumanian Noodles*
Beet and Onion Salad
Fresh-Pineapple Pie*

———

Oyster Bisque*
Salty Parmesan Cubes*
Beef-Asparagus Moussaka*
Sliced Cucumber
on Salad Greens
Orange Chiffon Tarts*

Veal Paprikash*
Hungarian Almond
Poppy-Seed Noodles*
Jellied Pecan and
Apple Salad*
Chocolate-Mint Mousse*

———

Chicken in Peanut-Tomato
Sauce*
Potato Patties*
Celery, Scallions,
and Radishes
Gingered Pear Compote*
Coconut Tea Rounds*

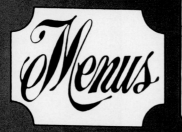

Menus

Haugesundsk Spedesild
(Haugesund Pickled Herrings)*
Reinsdyrsteik
(Saddle of Reindeer)*
Boiled Potatoes
Salat (Norwegian Lettuce)*
Kirseærsuppe
(Cold Cherry Soup)*
Krumkaker (Curled Cakes)*

◆

Mushroom Liver Pâté*
Pork Moussaka
with Brussels Sprouts*
Lettuce with Old Colonial
Salad Dressing*
Early American Pear Pie*

Meatball-Noodle Skillet*
Grated Romano Cheese
Field Greens with
Wine Vinegar and Oil
Whole-Wheat Italian Bread
Jellied Orange Ambrosia
Dessert*

◆

Ham Slice with Peanut
Butter*
Boiled White Beans*
Red and White
Cabbage Salad
Indian Pudding*

Celery and Carrot Curls
Watermelon Rind Pickle
Crusted Mushrooms and
Oysters*
Orange, Grape,
and Grapefruit Salad
Squash Pie*

◆

Fiskepudding (Fish Pudding)*
Rekesaus (Shrimp Sauce)*
Sommersalat (Summer Salad)*
Crisp Rye Wafers   Butter
Blåbærkake (Blueberry Cake)*

Florentine Cannelloni*
Vegetable Relish*
Finnochio   Ripe Olives
Italian Bread Sticks
Oranges in Red Wine*

◆

Chicken and Chorizo
Spaghetti*
Young Spinach Leaves
and Cucumber Salad
Italian Bread
Orange Delight*
Espresso

Fresh Pear and Shrimp
Appetizer*
Spanish Omelet*
Mexican Potato Chips*
Ripe Olives
Chocolate Pecan Pie*

◆

Chicken Broth with Rice
Chop-Suey Skillet*
Parsleyed Tomato Slices
Lotus Ice Cream*
Honeyed Orange Peel*

Barbecued Spareribs*
Baked Okra*
Shoestring Potatoes
Fresh-Pear Cactus Salad*
Corn Bread   Butter
Mrs. Benson's Fudge*

◆

Hot Clam Juice Cocktail*
Pork Chops with Onions*
Boiled Potatoes
Savory Peas*
Banana and Lettuce Salad
Peanut-Butter Pineapple
Salad Dressing*

Herbed Chicken and Peas*
with Rice
Tomato Aspic on Coleslaw
Hot Buttered Rolls
Cherry-Coconut Pastries*

◆

Grilled Fish with
Mushrooms and Rosemary*
Peanut Potato Cakes*
Turquoise Yogurt*
with Cucumbers

South American Onion Soup*
Paella a la Valenciana*
Ginger Peach Mold*

◆

Tomato Soup
Celery Sticks
Tuna, Peas, and Rice*
Peanut Creamed Onions*
Peach Cobbler*

Hot Fish Mousse*
Paprika Cheese Sauce*
Curried Peas and Onions*
Spinach and Carrot Salad
Peach Dumplings*

◆

Cod with Mushroom-and-
Wine Sauce*
Herbed Corn and Peas*
Tossed Green Salad*
Small Sour-Cream Pancakes*
Topped with Peach and
Orange Conserve*

Mulligatawny*   Rice
Peanut-Butter Fruit Salad*
Seeded Hard Rolls
Anthelias' Sour-Milk
Gingerbread Cupcakes*
with Vanilla Frosting*

◆

Pâté in Aspic*
Austrian Ham and Noodle
Dish*
Orange and Belgian-Endive
Salad*
Molasses Chiffon Pie*

Isbjørnøye
(Polar Bear's Eye)*
Avkokt Torsk
(Boiled Cod)*
Creamed Butter*
New Potatoes
Grated Fresh Horseradish
Telegrafkake
(Telegraph Cake)*

◆

Spinatsuppe (Spinach Soup)*
Juleskinke (Christmas Ham)*
Nedlagte Rødbeter
(Pickled Beets)*
Topped with Butter
Kong Haakonskake
(King Haakon's Cake)*

Frankfurter and Corn-Meal
Patties*
Fresh Mustard Greens
with Bacon*
Baked Pumpkin*
Vanilla Ice Cream
Peanut-Butter Apple Cake*

◆

Broiled Honeycomb Tripe
with Mustard Sauce*
Mushroom Potato Pie*
Parsley Salad*
Plum and Apple Crumble*

Cocktail Sausages with
White Wine*
Liver and Mushrooms*
Nutmeg Cheese Potatoes*
Wilted Cucumbers
Baked Apple Tapioca*

———◆———

Roast Shoulder of Veal
Green Noodles with Basil*
Pickled Beets* on Lettuce
Fresh-Pear Crumble*

Cranberry Juice Cocktail
Puss Pass (Lamb Stew
with Potatoes, Carrots,
and Cabbage)*
Pumpernickel Bread
Brazilian Orange Cake*

———◆———

Old-Fashioned New England
Fish Chowder* Crackers
Partridges with Cabbage
and Juniper Berries*
or Southern Chicken
with Pecans*
Hot Biscuits
Pickled Peaches*
Ribbon Cake*

Scallops Mornay*
Pecan-Rice Loaf*
Broccoli and Pimiento Salad
French Dressing*
Corn Sticks Butter
Pears in Crème de Cacao*

———◆———

Fried Cheese Balls
with Paprika*
Cranberry Juice Cocktail
Stuffed Green Peppers*
Parsnip Cakes*
Gourmet Relish* on
Watercress
Date-Graham Pudding*

Clam Chowder*
Orange Chicken Salad*
Orange Cream Dressing*
Sweet-Potato Muffins*
(split and toasted)
Old-Time Spiced
Bread Pudding*

———◆———

Stuffed Roast Chicken*
Fresh-Pear Relish*
Corn and Peas in Cream*
Chicory and Sliced Radish
Salad
Chocolate Mousse*

Veal with Mushrooms*
Two-Cheese Noodles*
Green Bean Salad
Bread Sticks
Cherry Deep-Dish Pies*

———◆———

Malayan Pork Kabobs*
Brown Rice
Mushrooms Stuffed with
Purée of Green Peas*
Pickled Turnips* on Greens
Baked Whole Pears
with Raisin-Nut Filling*

Karjalanpaisti
(Karelian Hot Pot)*
Split-Pea Purée*
Greek Salad*
Peach Compote*

———◆———

Roast Duck
Orange Rice for Duck*
Braised Celery with
Peanut-Butter Sauce*
Buttered Dinner Rolls
Boston Cream Pie*

Okra Stew*
Ham Mousse*
White Bean Salad
Black Olives
Pear-Cream Pie
with Apricot Glaze*

———◆———

Borscht
Onions and Eggs, Faust*
Curried Shrimp Diamonds*
Asparagus Salad
Carmen Pears*

Fårikål (Lamb and Cabbage)*
Buttered Noodles with
Cashew Nuts*
Apple and Pickled-Beet Salad
Pumpernickel Bread
Jellied Nesselrode Pudding*

———◆———

Swiss Mushroom Consommé*
Anchovy Puffs*
Kibbeh bi Laban
(Meatballs in Yogurt)*
Squash Patties*
Sesame Seed Rolls
Baked Winter-Pear Halves*

Flaked Haddock*
or Shrimps Newburg*
in Patty Shells
Brussels Sprouts
Apricot and Orange Salad
Peanut and Raisin Clusters*

———◆———

Fresh-Pear and Crabmeat
Salad*
Cheese-and-Oatmeal Snaps*
Hamburger Steak
Parsley-Chive Butter*
Garden Ragout*
Peanut-Butter Chiffon Pie*

Baked Seafood Hearthside*
Cucumber-Stuffed Tomato
Salad Garlic Olives*
Toasted Corn Bread Squares
Lemon Slump*
Salted Pecans*

———◆———

Stuffed Mushrooms,
Italian Style*
Baked Mullet*
Stewed Tomatoes and Celery
Tossed Green Salad*
Italian Orange-Rum Cake*

Hamburger Pizza Pie*
Mixed Green Salad
with Cucumbers and
Orange Segments
French Dressing*
Bread Sticks
Neapolitans*

———◆———

Angels on Horseback*
Steak-and-Olive Casserole*
Corn on the Cob*
Peach Shortcake*

Beef Birmingham*
Rice or Noodles
Sliced Tomato Salad with
Parsley Cheese Balls*
Apple Slump*

———◆———

Bean Salad
Cold Venison, Pheasant,
or other Game
with Oxford Sauce*
Bermuda Casserole*
Peanut-Butter Cake*

Olive-Avocado Appetizer*
on Greens
Roast Fresh Ham or Loin
of Pork
Fireplace Road Succotash*
Whole-Wheat Rolls
Peach Delight*
Nutmeg Logs*

———◆———

Mushroom and Oyster Pie*
Cooked Mixed Vegetable
Salad on Sliced
Celery Cabbage
Wine Vinegar and Olive Oil
Grated Fresh-Pear Snow*
with Strawberries

recipes for all starred dishes found in this volume.

GENERAL INFORMATION

The Ingredients and Measurements Used in Recipes

All recipes in this book have been tested in the Woman's Day Kitchens with standard American measuring cups (8 ounces = 16 tablespoons), measuring spoons (1 tablespoon = 3 teaspoons), and other standard kitchen equipment. All measurements are level. Liquids are measured in standard 8-ounce glass measuring cups, at eye level.

All sugar is granulated white sugar unless otherwise specified.

All flours, cake and all-purpose, are sifted before measuring unless otherwise specified. No self-rising flour is used.

All baking powder is double-acting baking powder.

All brown sugar is firmly packed when measured.

All confectioners' sugar is sifted before measuring.

All pepper is ground black pepper unless otherwise specified.

Fats and shortening are measured at room temperature, packed firmly into measuring cup and leveled with a straight knife. They are scraped out with a rubber spatula.

Salted butter or margarine, packed in ¼-pound sticks, is used unless otherwise specified. 1 stick = ½ cup = 8 tablespoons = ¼ pound.

1 tall can evaporated milk (14½ ounces) contains 1⅔ cups undiluted evaporated milk. Sweetened condensed milk is an entirely different product, and cannot be used interchangeably with evaporated milk.

⅓ to ½ teaspoon dried herbs can be substituted for each tablespoon fresh herbs. Crumble herbs before using to release flavor.

Before starting to cook or to bake, read the recipes carefully. Assemble all ingredients and equipment. Follow recipe exactly. Do not increase or decrease recipe unless you are a skilled enough cook to recognize what adjustments must be made as to ingredients, pan sizes, and/or cooking time.

Cooking Temperatures and Times

Cooking temperatures and times are approximate for meat. They depend not only on the weight and kind of meat, but also on its shape, temperature, and its bone and fat contents. A meat thermometer was used in testing.

Cooking times for meats are as recommended by the National Live Stock and Meat Board, 36 Wabash Avenue, Chicago, Illinois 60603.

Oven Temperatures

TEMPERATURES (Degree F.)	TERM
250 to 275	VERY SLOW
300 to 325	SLOW
350 to 375	MODERATE
400 to 425	HOT
450 to 475	VERY HOT
500 to 525	EXTREMELY HOT

Important—Preheat oven for 10 to 15 minutes before placing food in it. Many a cake has been spoiled by being placed in a barely heated oven. Baking times are based on the assumption that the oven is already at the stated temperature.

Check the oven temperature control frequently, especially if baking times vary from those given in recipes. (This can be done with a portable oven thermometer.) If a control is consistently off, call your public utility. They should be able to reset the oven temperature control.

Caloric Values

The caloric values, where mentioned, for each food are based on 100 grams, about 3½ ounces edible portion, as mentioned in Composition of Foods, Agriculture Handbook No. 8, Agricultural Service of the United States Department of Agriculture, Washington, D. C., revised December 1963.